'WRITING' NATION AND 'WRITING' REGION IN AMERICA

* These volumes have been produced for the European Association for American
Studies (E.A.A.S.)

'WRITING' NATION AND 'WRITING' REGION IN AMERICA

edited by

Theo D'haen
Hans Bertens

with contributions from

Ineke Bockting
Christine Bold
Doeko Bosscher
Peter Carafiol
James I. Deutsch
John Dorst
C.D. Eysberg
Richard Gray
Lothar Hönnighausen
André Kaenel
Jack Kugelmass
Anneke Leenhouts
Gene M. Moore
Raymond L. Neinstein
Duco van Oostrum
John Peacock
C. Elizabeth Raymond
Ron Robin
Esther Romeyn
Sonia Saldívar-Hull
Andrea Scheele

VU UNIVERSITY PRESS
AMSTERDAM 1996

EUROPEAN CONTRIBUTIONS TO AMERICAN STUDIES

This series is published for the Netherlands American Studies Association - N.A.S.A., and the European Association for American Studies - E.A.A.S.

General editor
Rob Kroes, Amerika Instituut, Plantage Muidergracht 12
1018 TV Amsterdam

VU University Press is an imprint of:
VU Boekhandel/Uitgeverij bv
De Boelelaan 1105
1081 HV Amsterdam
The Netherlands

isbn   90-5383-422-2
nugi   651

CONTENTS

INTRODUCTION

The present volume results from a Netherlands American Studies Association conference organised in June 1994 in the congenial surroundings of the Old Abbey in Middelburg, Zeeland.

Starting from the observation that over the last decade or so, under American New Historicism and British Cultural Studies, increasing attention has been paid to ideas of nation as discursive constructs, it was the aim of the "'Writing' Nation, 'Writing' Region" conference to look at the various regionalisms in American culture as comparable constructs, and more specifically at "'writing' region" as a subsidiary and/or counter discourse to "'writing' nation." The conference explored this theme from a variety of (inter)disciplinary angles: historical, sociological, anthropological, geographical, cinematic, and literary. For practical purposes, the essays have been arranged under three headings, dependent upon whether they take a predominantly historical, literary, or popular culture perspective of things.

The essays in the first section of the present collection look at the issues of national and regional identity from a predominantly historical perspective. Lothar Hönnighausen, in "The Old and the New Regionalism," reviews how the concept of regionalism has been used over the last few decades and in various disciplines. Though his own orientation is mainly literary, he does not hesitate to call for a resolutely interdisciplinary approach. He ends with a discussion of the "new" and "ecological" regionalism of Gary Snyder and Wendell Berry, two authors whom he finds to have surprisingly much in common on this score. Hönnighausen's more speculative piece is followed by Cees Eysberg's matter of fact survey of "Regionalism in North America." Doeko Bosscher, in "Regional Impulses for American Foreign Policy—The Middle-West and Isolationism," investigates how a specific region may influence the nation's policies, not just on the domestic but likewise on the international scene. In "From Palace to Plantation House: The Southernization of American Diplomatic Architecture in the 1920s," Ron Robin shows how the nation may avail itself of specific regional images, as embodied in symbolically significant architectural styles, to project itself abroad. However, such projection can also happen along other lines, for instance via the academic discipline officially assigned to the study of "America." This is what André Kaenel, in "After the Cold War: Region, Nation and World in American Studies," is concerned with. Specifically, he investigates how recent global political developments affect the shifting relationships between the three terms from his title —region, nation, world—when it comes to "American Studies."

The second section concentrates on matters mainly literary. In "Loaded Guns: Place and Women's Place in Nineteenth-Century New England" Raymond Neinstein looks at how regional and gender identities mutually inflect one another. He concentrates on the works of Emily Dickinson and Sarah Orne Jewett. Elizabeth Raymond traces the emergence, and development, of a specific Middle-Western regional and cultural identity in fiction, travel writing, and journalism throughout the nineteenth and early twentieth centuries in her "Middle Ground: Evolving Regional Images in the American Middle West." Cities as the site for (sub)regional identities form the subject of Duco van Oostrum's "'Dear ... I Have No Objection to Anything': Constructing Identities in Apartment Buildings in Tennessee Williams's *A Streetcar Named Desire* and Armistead Maupin's *Tales of the City*." The next four authors resolutely turn to the South for the subject of their respective contributions. Richard Gray and Gene Moore focus on the work of William Faulkner in, respectively, "'Implacable and Brooding Image': William Faulkner and Southern Landscape" and "From Regional Bears to National Myths: The Rewriting of William Faulkner." The same author's work also looms large in Ineke Bockting's "Deconstructing the 'Necessary' World: Southern Defensive Narrative and the Childhood Autobiography." Attention shifts to the South-West with Sonia Saldívar-Hull's "Political Identities in Contemporary Chicana Literature: Helena Viramontes's Visions of the U.S. Third World," in which she shows how contemporary Chicane narrative both underwrites a specific regional-ethnic identity while it at the same time overwrites this with a specific gender identity. In the closing essay of this section, Peter Carafiol, in "The Nationalist Model for American Ethnic Narrative," looks at how the latest avatar of regionalism in American literary studies takes the form of ethnic studies, yet persists in approximating its subject with methods gleaned from a nationalist paradigm.

The third section concentrates on various forms of popular culture as related to matters of nation and region. John Peacock, in "Regions of the Soul: Ethnography as Narrative," demonstrates how "ethnography," both in its most primitive forms and its more modern manifestations, has served to appropriate regional cultural beliefs as held by Native Americans to the white man's ideal of nation. In her "Mapping the Colour Line: The WPA Guidebook to North Carolina" Christine Bold reads this celebrated 1930s work as an exercise in mapping "the limits of [regional] cultural insiderism." The South, albeit a different part of it, is also the setting for the detective novels of James Lee Burke. In "Local Noir: Putting Southern Louisiana on the Map in the Crime Fiction of James Lee Burke," Anneke Leenhouts investigates how her chosen author's work relates to the social realities of the present-day South. What to non-Americans is perhaps the country's most distinctive region shifts into focus in the contributions of John Dorst, Andrea Scheele, and James Deutsch. In "Owen Wister and Emergent Discourse of the American West" Dorst relates Wister's celebrated 1902 western novel *The Virginian* to the various economies of looking that since the nineteenth century have defined our perception of this region. Scheele, in "A New West, or a New Western," follows up on Dorst's analysis by exploring how the West is looked at in a latter-day "western" such as Thomas McGuane's 1982 *Nobody's Angel*. Deutsch changes medium, and broadens the canvas to also take in what he calls the "Southern," in his "The Southern and the Western: Writing Region and Nation in Hollywood Cinema." Finally, in "Writing Alaska, Writing the Nation: *Northern Exposure* and the

Quest for a New America," Esther Romeyn and Jack Kugelmass discuss how a "region" that hitherto has received relatively little attention in cultural analysis is portrayed in a popular television series.

We gratefully acknowledge the financial assistance of the Embassy of the United States in the Netherlands, the United States Information Agency in Washington, the Royal Dutch Academy of Sciences (Koninklijke Nederlandse Academie der Wetenschappen), The British Council in the Netherlands, and the Roosevelt Study Center in Middelburg, Zeeland.

Theo D'haen and Hans Bertens
Leiden University and Utrecht University

HISTORICAL PERSPECTIVES

HISTORICAL PERSPECTIVE

THE OLD AND THE NEW REGIONALISM

L. Hönnighausen, University of Bonn

"Regions and Regionalism" is hardly a new research topic but one that grew into prominence in the thirties. This is confirmed by Nathan Glazer's foreword to Raymond D. Gastil's standard book, *Cultural Regions of the United States*, that appeared in 1975, during the lull of interest in regionalism, and thus preceded the reinvigoration of this theme in the eighties. Glazer's prefatory remarks are helpful in alerting us to the waxing and waning of the study of regions as well as in recalling for us some of characteristics of the regionalism of the thirties. As he could not anticipate the renaissance in regionalist studies we have witnessed since the eighties, it is understandable that he starts out with a complaint:

> American regionalism, it seems, is not much studied these days ... One contrasts the present situation sadly with the 1930s, when there was a remarkably urgent and rewarding concern with the variations and rich detail of American culture. Thus, one looks back with awe at the great series of WPA guidebooks which covered every state in the Union and many of the cities ... It was a time when American folksong and folklore were explored and recorded with a gusto not seen before or since, and when a National Resources Planning Board served to draw national attention to each of the major distinct areas of the country. Walker Evans and other great photographers recorded the distinctive lives of different regions and cities, and painters worked in—or maybe invented—regional modes to cover the walls of public buildings. Perhaps one must accept the judgement of current critics that American art reached greater heights when it abandoned storytelling picturesqueness in the style of Grant Wood and Thomas Hart Benton and Ben Shahn to take up abstract expressionism, "action" painting, and their varied spawn, so that American painting and sculpture from San Francisco to New York, and all the places in between, could be devoid of any regional accent, original or acquired as a sign of respect to place. Perhaps. But one doubts it.[1]

While Glazer conveys a vivid picture of the regionalism of the thirties, he does not indicate that an interest in regions and regional culture as such is a much older phenomenon. However, regionalism seems inherent in Romanticism and its new fascination with people's specific relation to their given surroundings. As one of the sociocultural consequences of the Industrial Revolution and the concomitant dislocations, migrants from rural areas into the mushrooming cities lost their assured sense of place.[2] In leaving their traditional homes and adjusting to new sociocultural surroundings, they experienced both a new sense of freedom from and nostalgia for their former environment. Apparently, the interest in regions emerges in connection with

---

[1] Raymond D. Gastil, *Cultural Regions of the United States*, foreword by Nathan Glazer, hereafter abbreviated as *CRUS* (Seattle: U of Washington P, 1975) pp. vii-viii.

[2] See several essays in *The Literature of Region and Nation*, ed. R.P. Draper, hereafter abbreviated as *LRN* (London: Macmillan, 1989).

this late 18th century sense of disorientation which was even shared by those who were not immediately involved in the migration process. Regionalism developed, as English poetry from Crabbe (*The Village*, 1783) to Wordsworth attests, as a reaction to this sociopolitical experience of dislocation and as part of the new awareness of the problematic status of place.[3]

After several manifestations of the new preoccupation with region in the nineteenth century, and particularly around the turn of the century, the sense of crisis that followed upon the bank crash of 1929 intensified an orientation towards regions and regionalism. In view of the national and international disappointments and shocks that had been suffered since World War I, the regional and local seemed to promise a more reliable basis for social and cultural values. Are there similar reasons why—after an utopian streak in the sixties and seventies and the national and international preoccupation with political and social reform—the eighties witness a re-emergence of a movement towards "Regions and Regionalism in North America?" It is, at any rate, interesting that, in spite of its affinities with older concepts of regionalism in the United States, the "new regionalism" is also breaking new ground. Clarence Mondale notes that the time when "attachment to region was a matter of relative indifference" was also the time of "futuristically oriented analysis" (Meyrowitz, *No Sense of Place*, 1985) has gone and that "as part of the post-modern complex of thought ... a reassertion of the centrality of habitat to the definition of self and culture is taking place." But he also states that the new regionalism is "quite distinct from the conventional emphasis upon the traditions of rural life."[4]

In any case, the respective tendencies towards a new regionalism are pronounced, as the conference topics of American, Canadian and German North American Studies Conferences indicate. With "Region in American Culture," the topic of its 1981 Memphis Convention, the American Studies Association turned out to be the trendsetter, and the German Studies Association duly followed in 1982 with "Regionalismus in den Vereinigten Staaten von Amerika." In 1983, William Westfall edited and introduced his *Perspectives on Regions and Regionalism in Canada*, thus heralding the particularly strong Canadian commitment to the cause.[5]

---

[3] See J.H. Alexanders's essay "Wordsworth, Regional or Provincial? The Epistolary Context," *LRN*, pp. 24-33.

[4] Clarence Mondale, "Concepts and Trends in Regional Studies," hereafter abbreviated as *CTRS, American Studies International*, 28.1 (1989): 13-37, 13. See also the book-length bibliography: Michael Steiner, Clarence Mondale, *Region and Regionalism in the United States: A Source Book for the Humanities and Social Sciences*, hereafter abbreviated as *RRUS* (NY: Garland, 1989).

[5] "Region in American Culture," American Studies Association Convention, Memphis Tennessee (1981); "Regionalism in the United States of America," Annual Conference of the German Association for American Studies, University of Eichstätt (1982). For related Canadian contributions, see *Perspectives on Regions and Regionalism in Canada*, ed. and introd. William Westfall (Ottawa: Assoc. for Canadian Studies, 1983); Don Gutteridge, "Local Culture and the National Will," *Canadian Literature* 100 (1984): 124-31; Eli Mandel, "History and Literature: Contemporary Canadian Writing," *Zeitschrift der Gesellschaft für Kanada-Studien* 3.1 (1983): 9-18; Ronald Sutherland, "Canadian Literature: The Pieces and the Whole," *Zeitschrift der Gesellschaft für Kanada-Studien* 3.1 (1983): 19-27; William J. Keith, "Centre and Periphery: Cliché or Myth," *Zeitschrift der Gesellschaft für Kanada-Studien* 13 (1988): 63-71.

Before assessing the ideological reasons for this return to the old research topic and describing some of the characteristics of the renewed scholarly interest, a backward glance seems appropriate. As always in such cases, there are programmatic books and avantgarde journals announcing the new scholarly tendencies: in 1948, Tremaine McDowell's *American Studies* appeared and, in 1949, the first issue of *American Quarterly*. The same year, the University of Wisconsin hosted a very impressive multidisciplinary symposium. The published papers, *Regionalism in America*, edited by Merrill Jensen, present an instructive overview of what since the thirties had emerged as "Regional Studies." This volume also provides a good starting point for our methodological reflections on the renewal of interest in "Regions and Regionalism."[6]

In his preface to *Regionalism in America*, Supreme Court Judge Felix Frankfurter makes the point that although the regions themselves are not the subject of the juridical process, the several aspects and phases of regionalism keep manifesting themselves in the "adjudications before the Supreme Court." He goes on offering a definition that shows his remarkable sensitivity also to the non-juridical aspects of the issues of nation and region, implying the kind of multidisciplinary approach which the volume pursues.

> There are organic developments other than the nation and its constituent states that press for expression through various forms: through national legislation recognizing regional differences, through the constitutional device of compact among different combinations of states to meet different needs, through various informal arrangements among states, through legal uniformities of one sort or another, and through all the multiform recognitions of the need for institutionalizing the harmonies and common interests and feelings within different regions .... Regionalism is a recognition of the intractable diversities among men, diversities partly shaped by nature but no less derived from the different reactions of men to nature. And since man takes increasing liberties with nature, regionalism is not a fixed concept. No region, whether natural or cultural, is stable. At bottom, the problems of American regionalism are the problems of American civilization: the continuous process of bringing to fruition the best of which American men and women are capable. (*RA* xvi)

While art historians and literary historians tended to regard the interest in regions as confined to certain periods and certain artists (nineteenth-century "local color" fiction or the regionalist murals of the thirties),[7] Judge Frankfurter regards the response to one's particular region as a general feature of all cultures. From this more comprehensive perspective, which is also the one informing the regional concepts of geographers and sociologists in *Regionalism in America*, the "local colour" stories of Sarah Orne Jewett or the paintings of Grant Wood are only specific versions of the universal artistic reaction to place. In this respect, the Nantucket of *Moby Dick* or the northern Michigan of Hemingway's "Big Two-Hearted River," as well as the turn-of-the-century New York of Henry James's "The Jolly Corner" or the Louisiana of Ernest J. Gaines's *A Gathering of Old Men,* would all come, with the same right as the works

---

[6] Merrill Jensen, *Regionalism in America*, with a foreword by Felix Frankfurter, hereafter abbreviated as *RA* (Madison: U of Wisconsin P, 1965).

[7] See *CTRS* 24: "Periodically, regionalism becomes important in the arts." See also the respective bibliographies on Wendell Berry, Flannery O'Connor, Grant Wood, Thomas Hart Benton and John Stewart Curry, 24ff.

of Sarah Orne Jewett or Willa Cather, under the heading of regionalism. According to Frankfurter, the concepts of "regions and regionalism" refer to a central and ever changing manifestation of the public will which derives from the imaginative response of human beings to their surroundings. As such, these concepts supplement those of the nation and its states. In that sense, regionalism is a main feature of American civilisation. The great diversity of human responses to regions as sociocultural constructs makes an interdisciplinary approach, combining historical and systematic inquiries, imperative.

"Regionalism and Central Culture": A Response to Philip Fisher

Since we have the pleasure of Professor Philip Fisher's company at our conference, this is a welcome occasion to respond to his use of the concept of "Regionalism"—in his introduction to *The New American Studies*—,[8] which I find very interesting and thought-provoking. There is a point of similarity in Philip Fisher's and Judge Frankfurter's reflections on the concept of "regionalism" in that Fisher, too, regards regionalism "not as a fixed concept" (Frankfurter) but rather as embodying a basic principle, as "a recognition of the intractable diversities among men." What is of methodological interest in Frankfurter, and even more expressly so in Fisher, is that both transfer the concept of "regions and regionalism" from the geographic, or more precisely, the physiographic plane to that of systematics and sociopolitical philosophy. The new context in which Fisher positions the concept of "regionalism" is the relationship between the grand unifying myths and the claim of pluralism that has obtained in the history of American culture. Accordingly, in his argument, he moves quickly beyond the original connotations of "regionalism" as a "diversity of sectional voices" and "sectional culture split along geographical lines (the New England mind, the Southern way of life, the West of the pioneer)," (*NAS*, xii) and employs the term predominantly in the social sphere. He refers to the "new ethnic regionalism that in early twentieth-century America … appeared as a result of massive immigration" (*NAS*, xiii) and affirms that "the regionalism of our own time is a regionalism of gender and race" (xiii). Furthermore, he acknowledges the respective consequences in recent institutional history and specifically mentions the regionalisation of the departments of American universities into "Afro-American studies, Jewish studies, women's studies, Native American studies, Chicano and Asian-American studies, and in some cases, gay studies" (*NAS* xiv).

To object to Fisher's widening of the reference of the term "regionalism" would be both pedantic and obtuse. Nevertheless, in attempting to follow his approach, we should anticipate the consequences of his extension of the frame of reference. As a result of the heightened sensitivity of our time to matters of metaphor, we are acutely aware of changing planes of meaning and of metaphorising effects beyond the *per se* metaphoric nature of the term regionalism. We also register a certain provocation in

---

[8] *The New American Studies: Essays from **Representations***, ed. Philip Fisher, hereafter abbreviated as *NAS* (Berkeley: U of California P, 1991).

Fisher's use of the term "regionalism" that is to intensify our perceptiveness. Further, we note the specific thematic suggestions of Fisher's metaphoric use of the term "regionalism," the abandoned hope of a unified vision and the gleeful replacement of the traditional ideology of centrality by the fashionable ideology of decentering. However, over against these thematic concerns we must not ignore the appeal of the metaphor "regionalism" to our spatial imagination and its ideological effect: by applying the term "regionalism" with its connotation of geographic units to sociopolitical phenomena such as "gender," "race," etc., we endow the latter with a peculiar solidity, a holistic, homogeneous quality, and a gestalt that make their ideological dimensions stand out even more.

Whether or not one approves of the increase in importance of the several sociopolitical regions or the phenomenon of the "regionaliziation of American studies," that Fischer discusses will depend on one's own political philosophy. However, when Fisher denies, except for a limited period in the nineteenth century, the relevance of the spatial aspect of the concepts of region and regionalism, he undoubtedly removes himself from the critical debate of specialists who continue to regard the term as primarily referring to space. While economists, geographers, sociologists and political scientists would probably endorse Fisher's understanding of region and regionalism as metaphors, they would nevertheless regard them as specific research tools for the description of spatial relations and not as general metaphors for the decentering and pluralism of ethnicity and gender.

Region and Area

Interdisciplinary or at least multidisciplinary approaches were both adopted in several of the New Deal projects, for instance those concerned with soil conservation or with native Americans in the Southwest, and in the "area training programs" for the American armed forces during World War II.[9] The goal of that wartime "area research" —the term "area" referring to "world areas"—was "to understand the nations in the foreign areas so thoroughly that we could know what to expect of them" (*ARTP* xiii), and "in most area study programs, an *interdisciplinary* rather than a *multidisciplinary* approach [was] considered necessary" (*ARTP* 8). As regards the relationship between the terms "area" and "region," it should be noted that within the compass of the study of world areas "regions" receive due attention, appearing in the system of social units between "community" and "state."

---

[9] Julian H. Steward, *Area Research: Theory and Practice*, hereafter abbreviated as *ARTP*, Social Science Research Council, Bulletin 63 (1950).

The Contemporary Context of Regionalism

In view of present-day tendencies towards regionalisation in many areas of the world, manifesting themselves for instance in the economic squabbles within the European Union and in the bloody ethnic strife in the Balkans and other former Eastern block areas, the question of the role of regions takes on particular urgency. No less important is the impact of the conflicting pull of the tendencies toward "globalisation" and "regionalisation" on the one hand and towards "multiculturalism" and "ethnic identity" on the other. Awareness of the international context will certainly reinvigorate the comparative inquiry into the history, structures and functions of regions in North America. From this perspective, the study of regionalism in North America will not confine itself to questions of regional energy resources and transport systems as prerequisites for the development of·cultural centers or concerning the evaluation of migration patterns and linguistic dualism in Texas, California or Canada. Ultimately, a study of regionalism must explore the psychological and spiritual deep-structure of regional consciousness as it emerges in the symbolism of texts and images.

In view of the violence with which regional and ethnic tensions are presently erupting in many parts of the world, it is painfully evident that a region is not just a physiographic unit but a value-charged and symbolic space. Furthermore, region as symbolic space plays a major role in the constitution of our identity, and that explains the intensity of the regionalist commitment, particularly in those cases where the regional element fuses with the ethnic. Since a region is constituted as a physical, functional and symbolic space by a conglomerate of geographic and historical, social and cultural characteristics, only a cooperative effort of experts from several disciplines can hope to do justice to it. Gastil mentions as "the most elementary reason for studying the cultural regions of the United States" that "regional analysis integrates the scattered information that is available on variations in our society" (*CRUS* 3). Such a tool for studying the U.S. or Canada is particularly recommendable to Europeans, who, looking from abroad, tend to see the national whole more in its sociopolitical and cultural stratification than in its regional diversity. Students of American and Canadian literature, in particular, who so far have viewed their field almost exclusively in terms of literary forms and historical "background," could widen their horizon considerably by making use of the regionalist orientation of cultural geographers and sociologists.

On Terminology

Before proceeding from our introductory remarks to methodological reflections some clarification and definition of the key terms seem in order. In our title "Regions and Regionalism in North America," the more neutral term "regions" refers, both in the geographical and historical sense, to the structural and functional aspect of the theme, while the term "regionalism" is more value-charged and implies the analysis of regional consciousness and its ideological component. The term "region" will be further defined in the context of "regional, federal, national, union, section, state rights," while the term "regionalism" will receive complementary specification in connection with the concepts of "sectionalism" and "nationalism" but also through its collocation with "modernism" and "primitivism," "provincial" and "local." Clarence Mondale distinguishes between "regional studies" as opposed to "studies of the concept of region (what I will call regionalism)" adding that "regional studies is taken to be the general topic, and regionalism a subtopic thereof" (*CTRS* 13-37). In view of the faddish preoccupation of our time with decentering and the marginal instead of the central, the term "regional" might lose the negative association of "provincial," acquiring the positive connotation "concrete, authentic, individual, not regulated by a central authority, genuine." Significantly, Clarence Mondale mentions Michel Foucault's criticism "that modern thought has been unduly abstract, that it has failed to acknowledge the crucial role of 'low-ranking, particular, regional knowledge.'"

The South and the West as Subjects of Regional Studies

Possible research topics might concern different concepts of regionalism and their historical changes, above all an interdisciplinary comparison and assimilation of methods and models, and, last but not least, the relation between regionalism and the conflict areas of immigration versus nativism, and the "global village" and multiculturalism versus ethnic and regional identity. Further research projects might be devoted to the socioeconomic and geographic as well as historical and aesthetic analysis of major phases in the transformation of the regional and national consciousness (for instance, Jacksonian Democracy; the Gilded Age; the "Thirties"). In this, it seems important to embrace a comparative and dynamic approach, conceiving of regionalism as an essentially international and transformational phenomenon. This hypothesis should be tested and qualified in both systematic and historical investigations of particular regions such as the American South, the old and the new West (including the contrast between California and the Pacific Northwest) and, especially, through comparative analyses of "Regions and Regionalism" in Canada and the U.S.

The American South, if we consider the all-important historical dimension, has the methodological attraction of posing beside the problem of regionalism that of sectionalism and nationalism: the antebellum South as economic and sociocultural alternative to New England, as challenger of the Union, transformed into deprived region of the losers through the "lost-cause myth"; but also the New South, the South of the New Deal era, and the present postmodernist South, symbolised by the Atlanta skyline; the South of very diverse sub-regions and enormous sociopolitical changes (slavery —segregation—rebellion of the redneck—Civil Rights—New Republicanism); finally, the South as probably the most important literary region of the U.S. in the twentieth century. How strongly developed but also how sophisticated the regional consciousness of the South has become is documented by the new *Encyclopedia of Southern Culture* (1989), co-edited by Charles Reagan Wilson and William Ferris.

In contrast to the South as a polymorphic but in its regional characteristics clearly established region, the West in the American imagination represents, above all, the "region as subject to transformation processes": "Westerners live out where the sense of place is a sense of motion" (Wallace Stegner). This is confirmed as much by the intensive discussion of Frederick Jackson Turner's concept of the "frontier" as by the new vision of the West as a bio-region emerging from the works of Gary Snyder, Wallace Stegner, Edward Abbey, Norman Maclean, and Ivan Doig.[10] We might think of the West as a series of stages in the history of American civilisation, of the Middle West changing from frontier to the heartland, or of the West that, as Pacific Rim, represents the important Asian aspect of North America so often ignored by Europeans, or of California, the now slightly shoddy anticipation of a future America, both in ethnic and socioeconomic terms. Last not least, there is the American and Canadian prairie region that, as Frederick C. Luebke's "Regionalism and the Great Plains: Problems of Concept and Method" illustrates, has proved to be such an inspiration to regional studies.[11] Both for reasons of content and method, the inclusion of the Canadian perspective in reflections on "regions and regionalism" seems seminal. In this vast country ("a mari usque ad mare"), the regions and the tensions between them and Ottawa have, in both national and international politics, always played a crucial role. Thus it comes as no surprise that, since the rediscovery of the regional topic in the eighties, Canadian contributions have been particularly numerous and inspiring.[12] The perspective of "Regions and Regionalism" opens a promising vista not only for the consideration of national Canadian features, but also for the study of economic, political and sociocultural relations between Canada and the U.S. How fruitful a comparative transnational investigation of respective regions can be has recently been shown in a German dissertation by Ludwig Deringer, who discusses the literature of both the Canadian and American Pacific Northwest against its background in the history of settlement. As it turns out, such a comparative treatment of Canadian and American regional developments also provides inspiration and categories for the comparative study of North American and European forms of regionalism.

On Concepts of Region and Regionalism in the Several Disciplines

As Fulmer Mood notes in tracing the development of the "Sectional Concept, 1750-1900," "region," as a term denoting spatial organisation, comes to replace the older term "section" only fairly late, in John W. Powell's *Physiographic Regions of the United States* (1895). But since then it has spread rapidly, appearing in several disciplines and assuming various meanings and functions (Vernon Carstensen, "The Development and Application of Regional-Sectional Concepts, 1900-1950"). However,

---

[10] See for instance Gary Snyder, "Riprap," "Milton by Firelight," "Piute Creek, August 1955"; Wallace Stegner, *Angle of Repose* (1971); Edward Abbey, *The Monkey Wrench Gang* (1975); Norman Maclean, *A River Runs Through It* (1976); Ivan Doig, *Ride With Me, Mariah Montana* (1990).

[11] *Western Historical Quarterly* 5 (1984): 19-38.

[12] For representative examples of the new tendencies in research, see the paragraph on *Suggestions for a New Regionalism* in this essay.

the relevance of the term has varied considerably both between disciplines and periods. From the time of the early Republic and Jedidiah Morse's *Geography Made Easy* (1784), "region," or its predecessor "section," has always served as a key term or rather as a leading concept in geography, where it has assumed a role of such prominence as it has rarely played in sociology. However, in the thirties, Rupert B. Vance suggested "region" as a tool for social research,[13] and in this reform-oriented time "region" gained considerable importance in the context of "regional *planning*."

In such disciplines as political science or literary history, the concept of region —depending on changes in methodological trends—has tended to play more (limited) temporary or local roles. In Hedwig Hintze's 1950 article in the *Encyclopedia of the Social Sciences*, "regionalism" is above all "a counter movement to any exaggerated or oppressive form of centralisation." In accordance with this understanding of the term, the author chooses France as a prime example and, tracing similar tendencies in several other nations, comes to the conclusion that

> in the United States regionalism has really never appeared. Such sectional manifestations as have occurred in the history of the country from time to time—the threat of New England to break away from the union in 1814, the secession of the southern states in the Civil War, the alignment of the agrarian west and south against the industrial east in 1896—were the results of economic antagonisms rather than consciously held philosophies.[14]

Since in Hintze's view "the United States has always presented the aspect of a unified grouping," she dismisses as unsubstantiated Frederick Jackson Turner's 1925 anti-cipation of regionalist developments in the U.S. (itself a very telling historical symptom that points forward to the regionalism of the thirties). Political science, dealing primarily with phenomena defined constitutionally and historically, seems to employ "region" above all as an approximative register in describing marginal and transformational processes.

Characteristically, the term occurs with frequency either in the context of evolving global regions (Nye, 1968), most recently in the case of the NAFTA concept,[15] and in connection with European regionalising tendencies whose economic and socio-cultural impact is clearer than their constitutional consequences (Burgess, 1989; Vanhove and Klaasen, 1987; Keating and Jones 1985). In recent collections of essays and handbooks as diverse as Fried Esterbauer's *Regionalism: A European Challenge* or Jochen Blaschke's *Handbook of West European Regional Movements*, "regionalism" is regarded as an important sociopolitical and sociocultural corrective to over-centralisation and regional exploitation. The metaphorics in Blaschke's preface are

---

[13] Rupert B. Vance, "The Regional Concept as a Tool for Social Research," *RA* 119-142.

[14] Hedwig Hintze, "Regionalism", in *Encyclopedia of Socal Sciences*, vol. 13 (NY: repr. 1950) 208-218.

[15] Ernst B. Haas, "Turbulent Fields and the Theory of Regional Integration," *International Organization* 30 (1976): 173-212; *International Regionalism*, ed. Joseph S. Nye (Boston: Little, Brown, 1968); Michael Burgess, *Federalism and European Union* (London: Routledge, 1989); N. Vanhove and L.H. Klaasen, *Regional Policy: A European Approach* (Avebury: Aldershot, 1987); *Regions in the European Community*, eds. Michael Keating and Barry Jones (Oxford: Clarendon, 1985).

inspired by the socialism of the seventies and those in Esterbauer by organicist traditions, with landscapes and their inhabitants appearing as "historically grown." However, both differ from Hintze's perspective in viewing regionalism more as a constituent part of political systems than as a mere alarm signal that should warn over-centralised nation states. Of particular interest is the preface to Esterbaur's volume, in which Stingl, regarding the region as an old structural principle, anticipates its new mediating role between the European member states and the European Community.

In contrast to these approaches that focus on the regional element in one particular discipline, Michael Steiner and Clarence Mondale in their book-length bibliography *Region and Regionalism in the United States*, and Mondale in his follow-up "Concepts and Trends in Regional Studies," attempt a comprehensive and interdisciplinary coverage of the theme. That Mondale starts his essay with a consideration of works on *The Psychology of Place* (Canter) and *The Ecology of the Imagination in Early Childhood* (Cobb) seems typical of the new regionalism. No less characteristic are the subtitles and their sequence in Mondale's bibliographical essay, which show the shift in the "new regionalism" from the physiographic to metaphoric uses of the concept of region: "B. Folk and Language Studies," "C. Landscape Studies," "D. Community Studies," "E. Mental Maps, Ideas and Myth," "F. Ecological and Frontier History," and "G. Regionalism and Regionalization." In linguistic geography, to which Mondale devotes his first section, "regions" are an accepted term and concept (Hans Kurath, "Linguistic Regionalism"; Carver, *American Regional Dialects: A Word Geography*, 1986; see *CTRS* 16). However, in the aftermath of structuralism, the orientation now—more than in the "old regionalism" of the thirties—is towards the sociolinguistic aspect of dialectology (Trudgill, "Linguistic Change and Diffusion: Description and Explanation in Sociolinguistic Dialect Geography," 1974).

In the study of American literature, regions and regionalism received little attention as long as English departments were under the sway of formalist New Criticism or Myth Criticism. However, the situation is different in literary history and interdisciplinary North American studies. In Spiller/Thorpe (et al.), eds., *Literary History of the United States* (1948), a representative example of traditional literary history, and in the more avantgarde *Columbia Literary History of the United States* (1988) and *Columbia History of the American Novel* (1991), the regional element is present although it is apparently confined to specific periods. In *Literary History of the United States*, regionalism occurs, for instance, in the period 1810-1865 under the heading "Forms of Regional Humor," and in the period 1865 to 1910 under the heading "local colour." In both cases, regionalism appears as a variant of realism. However, since the works identified as "regional humor" and "local colour" are abstracted from the wider political, socioeconomic and cultural context, the emergence of these examples of regionalism remains rather puzzling. Similarly, the regionalism of Sherwood Anderson, John Steinbeck, and William Faulkner would appear more plausible if discussed side by side with that of the painters Grant Wood, Thomas Hart Benton, and John Stewart Curry. With the methodological shifts in current criticism and with the closer attention paid to the interrelation between stylistic and ideological features, it will be possible to avoid such summary treatment as we find in "Nation,

Region, and Empire."[16] In the *Columbia History of the American Novel* new and illuminating perspectives evolve whenever the authors transcend the narrow confines of literary history and introduce sociological ("Race and Region," by Thadious M. Davis) or ecological considerations ("Fiction of the West," by James H. Maguire) into their critical discourse. In this regard, James M. Cox's chapter on the literature from 1910 to 1945, in the *Columbia Literary History of the United States*, is particularly interesting because the author, by adopting a subtle concept of regionalism, provides new insights into the peculiar relationship between politics and literature: "In this historical context, regions become the imaginative space created by the loss of national potentiality."[17] Still more important, Cox suggests a whole new perspective for literary studies by treating regionalism not as a matter of isolated pockets outside the literary mainstream but as a continuous though ever-changing sociocultural force, linking past and present: "To begin to glimpse the volatility at work in the making of what seem to be traditional regions is to recognize the pressures still at work on our regional vision" (Cox 763).

Suggestions for a New Regionalism

In view of the overwhelming power of recent economic developments and of the media revolution which has led to the promotion of a national and eventually international monoculture, Walker Percy has expressed doubts whether the South as a region will continue to exist. However, not only his own work but also that of Ernest Gaines and Alice Walker, Barry Hannah and Clyde Edgerton, Bobbie Ann Mason and Kaye Gibbons, provides strong evidence that the South as a literary region will continue to thrive in the postmodern era and beyond. Yet we will no longer study the South in Vance's and Odum's manner although the latter remains, particularly in its interdisciplinary orientation, exemplary.[18] The new regionalist approach of our own time, arising from a different context, asks new questions, posits new methods and demands new solutions. Above all, we have changed our ideological dispositions in returning to the old research topic "regions and regionalism."

This is even noticeable in the arrangements of survey studies that are not particularly avantgarde in their concepts and methods such as Gastil's, Draper's, Steiner's and Mondale's (see *CRUS*, *RRUS*). Naturally, this trend is still stronger in the methodological reflections accompanying the reawakened interest in the "old sub-

---

[16] See *The Columbia History of the American Novel*, gen. ed. Emory Elliott (N.Y.: Columbia UP, 1991), pp. 240-266.

[17] James M. Cox, "Regionalism: A Diminished Thing," *Columbia Literary History of the United States*, gen. ed. Emory Elliott (N.Y.: Columbia UP, 1988), pp. 761-784, 764.

[18] See Rupert B. Vance, *Human Geography of the South: A Study in Regional Resources and Human Adequacy* (Chapel Hill: U of North Carolina P, 1932),p. 44: "History, not geography made the Solid South"; Howard W. Odum, *Southern Regions of the United States* (Chapel Hill: U of North Carolina P, 1936); for new trends in research, see, for example, *Rewriting the South: History and Fiction*, eds. Lothar Hönnighausen and Valeria Gennaro Lerda (Tübingen: Francke, 1993).

ject" such as Virginia Yans-McLaughlin's "Comments on Regionalism and Ethnicity in American Literature" and Clarence Mondale's "Concepts and Trends in Regional Studies."[19] As mentioned above, the Canadian contribution to the debate on method is particularly noteworthy. However, one must not neglect parallel interests in Australia and New Zealand and discuss the phenomena involved—although by no means exclusively—as an aspect of the terminal stages of the British Empire and the Commonwealth.[20]

When Americanists of Tremaine McDowell's generation dealt with the problem of regionalism, they did so in the spirit of a holistic-organicistic and nationalistic worldview, seeking in the return to region a return to a simple, wholesome and authentic America. In retrospect, we recognize this development as the academic concomitant of a phenomenon which manifests itself as part of the modernist movement, surfacing in a great variety of ways, from William Carlos Williams's rewriting of the history of American civilisation in *In the American Grain* (1925) and Hemingway's primitivism in "Big Two-Hearted River" (1923, 1925) to the artwork, writing, and pro-native American agitation that emerged from the artists' colony in Taos after World War I (Marsden Hartley, Mary Austin, Mable Dodge, John Collier, D.H. Lawrence, Willa Cather, Georgia O'Keefe).[21]

In contrast, much in contemporary theory suggests that the return to the old topic of regionalism in the eighties is motivated by the revolt against centrism we have witnessed after the advent of Derrida and deconstructivism. By now it has become obvious that radical inversion goes hand in hand with nostalgic primitivism. What seems to go unnoticed, though, is that the ecological yearnings of the sophisticated for an unspoilt environment and the anxiety of ordinary citizens concerning the "intrusion of the foreign element" arise from the pressures of the same sociocultural situation. An appropriate response of "a truly new regionalism" to this problem might consist in comparative inquiries into the thematic complex "regionalism—nativism—racism—immigration control" in the American 1840s and present-day Europe.

What should distinguish the study of regionalism in the nineties from that of the thirties and forties, is above all the awareness that in both North America and Europe regions are no longer idyllic areas of authenticity but problem zones threatened either by the tensions between "multicultural squabbling" and "consumerist monoculture"

---

[19] Virginia Yans-McLaughlin, "Comments on Regionalism and Ethnicity in American Literature," *Prospects* 9 (1984): 463-69. See also *CTRS* 13-37.

[20] George Woodcock, *The Meeting of Time and Space: Regionalism in Canadian Literature* (Edmonton: NeWest Institute for Western Canadian Studies, 1981); Walter Pache, *Einführung in die Kanadistik* (Darmstadt: Wissenschaftliche Buchgesellschaft, 1981), pp. 82ff, 102; *Regionalism and National Identity: Multi-Disciplinary Essays on Canada, Australia and New Zealand*, eds. Reginald Berry and James Acheson (Christchurch: Association for Canadian Studies in Australia and New Zealand, 1985); Glen A. Love, "On Belonging Here: American, Australian, and Canadian Frontiers and the Opportunities for Comparative Regionalism," Paper, Annual Meeting, Western Literature Association, Texas Christian University, Tarleton State University and Sonoma State University, Fort Worth, 3-5 October 1985.

[21] See my essay "Landscape with Indians and Saints: The Modernist Discovery of Native American and Hispanic Folk-Culture," *Amerikastudien/ American Studies* 36 (1992): 299-323.

or by economic want and the aspirations of political hegemony. The positive side of this is the sense of distance that distinguishes the new regionalism from the regionalist enthusiasms of the thirties. There may be, in some representatives of the new regionalism, traces of a cautious nostalgia for regions as they are supposed to have been. However, most critics today employ the concepts of regions and regionalism as working hypotheses and "tools," welcome because they allow us to target new structural and functional aspects of literature and other forms of discourse. Under the impact of the concepts of regions and regionalism in geography, sociology and history, literary historians will no longer see the regional element as a marginal phenomenon limited to certain periods and individual artists. An interdisciplinary perspective will allow literary historians to realise more easily that the regional element as it appears in Robert Frost's *North of Boston* (1914), Flannery O'Connor's "The Regional Writer" (1960), Eudora Welty's "Place in Fiction" (1962) and Wendell Berry's "The Regional Element" (1970) is an essential feature of twentieth-century discourse, continuing the industrialist-romantic tradition of the nineteenth century. What makes the changing manifestations of the regional such an important research topic is the fact that our spatial relations play a major role in defining our identity and our values.

However, in such research we should conceive of "regions and regionalism" as an organising principle, characterised by a variety of tensions as well as by its own transformative dynamism. In studying this principle in operation, one would pay attention to its varying functions and structural changes, its degrees of homogeneity and its cohesive factors, the interplay between center and periphery and between urban and metropolitan regions, and, last but not least, the historical shifts in the role of regions. Such an approach would help us avoid the narrowness of the merely local and provincial which undoubtedly characterises some specimens of regional culture. In identifying the features mentioned above and thus in widening our perspective, the New Historicism may prove a source of inspiration.[22] Without attempting to define this dazzling term here, we should point at the specific methodological awareness associated with it as one of its main attractions. It can only prove beneficial to the "new regionalism" if in the spirit of the New Historicism we try to make reflections on our method part of our research strategy. In concrete terms, this could mean that we should establish the differences between the way "regions and regionalism" are defined in the various academic disciplines involved as starting points for individual research projects. Such an approach is possible if we take the challenge of interdisciplinary work seriously and do not misunderstand it as a mere invitation to eclectically borrow some details.

In fact, true interdisciplinary work would also entail—for instance, in the analysis of artistic forms and literary styles—an exact assessment of the ideological and socio-political implications of art. Conversely, an interdisciplinary approach to texts in geographical, sociological, and historical inquiries would demand attention to the forms of the respective discourse and to the historical contexts and the metaphoric dimension

---

[22] See, for example, Forrest G. Robinson, "The New Historicism and the Old West," *Western American Literature* 25 (1990): 103-123.

of models and terms which are ordinarily taken for granted in the various disciplines. In spite of our scepticism vis-à-vis the abstract games of some theoreticians of discourse, there is no denying the fact that the transition from the heterogeneity of the so-called factual to the homogeneity of its metaphoric communication may be regarded —while avoiding the discredited term "progress"—as a real advantage. The practical consequences of this can be illustrated if we critically reflect on the mythical aura of the term "land" in regional studies as well as regional literature of the thirties and forties and, above all, if we reflect no less self-critically on a hypothetical term such as "cultural pattern" which we might employ as a replacement. There are several advantages to discussing, under the impact of the New Historicism, the problem "regions and regionalism" on the level of discourse: such a strategy leads to an improved interdisciplinary communication and a greater flexibility in adjusting to the always shifting canon as well as to the inclusion of categories such as gender and ethnicity, which were to a large extent ignored in past regional studies.[23] For instance, a sociopolitical investigation of the attitude of African-American authors of the South towards their region, the evaluation of the change from pre-civil rights authors (e.g., Jean Toomer, Zora Neale Hurston) to their successors (Ernest J. Gaines, Alice Walker) will necessitate a total "rewriting" of the South. As a consequence first of the exclusive interest in white Southern writing and, subsequently, of the understandable pre-occupation with ethnicity, the synergetic effect of African American and white Southern writers in shaping the image of the region has hardly been studied.[24] Nevertheless, a consideration of the different responses of the ethnic groups involved, in the South or among the immigrants in California, promises a new and more adequate picture of these regions. By involving ethnologists and sociologists we will become able to assess more precisely what in the new regional consciousness of the West or Southwest derives from Native American roots and what originates from the environmentalist spirit of white writers.[25] As regards regionalism and art, we are indebted to William Westfall ("On the Concept of Region in Canadian History and Literature," 1980) for a particularly perceptive description of the situation: "Writers no longer

---

[23] Concerning "gender" in the South, see Anne Firor Scott, "Women in the South: History as Fiction, Fiction as History," *Rewriting the South*, eds. Hönnighausen and Lerda, pp. 22-34; concerning "gender" in the West, see Joanna L. Stratton, *Pioneer Women: Voices from the Kansas Frontier* (N.Y.: Simon and Schuster, 1982) and *A Harvest Yet to Reap*, researched and compiled by Linda Rasmussen, Lorna Rasmussen, Candace Savage et al. (Lincoln: U of Nebraska P, 1976); concerning "ethnicity," see Thadious M. Davis, "Race and Region," *Columbia History of the American Novel*, pp. 406-436.

[24] As an example of the new attempts to integrate "ethnicity" and "gender" into the research on regionalism, see David Mogen et al., *The Frontier Experience and the American Dream: Essays on American Literature* (College Station: Texas A&M UP, 1989).

[25] Concerning "regionalism—ethnicity," see N. Scott Momaday, *House Made of Dawn* (1968); Simon J. Ortiz, *A Good Journey* (1977) and *Fightin': New and Collected Stories* (1983); concerning method, see Dell Hymes, *"In Vain I Tried to Tell You": Essays in Native American Ethnopoetics* (Philadelphia: U of Pennsylvania P, 1981), as well as Laurie Ricou, "Crossing Borders in the Literature of the Pacific Northwest," Western Literature Association, Paper, Annual Conference, University of Oregon, Eugene, 6-8 October 1988, and "Children of a Common Mother: Of Boundary Markers and Open Gates," Paper, Annual Conference of the Association of Canadian Studies, Crainan, 15-17 February 1991.

simply reflect the region they describe; now they help to create the region itself. Art and identity are linked closely together .... The historical, economic, and social criteria might be in place, but the region achieves an identity only when it is identified in art."[26] A main object of regional studies will naturally be the reasons for the new fascination that the old research topic holds, expressed, for example, in Jules Chametzky's programmatic "New England as Region, New England as America" (1987):

> a shift in consciousness is or will be taking place: the emphasis on the local, the regional is no longer seen as an abdication from large central concerns: seeing it in all its variety and complexity, without sentimentality or tendentiousness, seeing its mosaic of race, class, gender, ethnicity and their interactions with other aspects of culture, we are looking at a dialectical embrace—we are not just either New England (the provinces) or America (the world or the center) but we are both New England and America .... Regionalism, yes, because where we stand ... is the true native ground. The perception of that home truth is an act of politics, cultural politics, a seizing of imaginative power, and the construction or reconstruction of institutions ... it is not a denial or retreat from realities and issues—it is a way through and into them.[27]

The New Ecological Regionalism: Gary Snyder's "The Bioregional Ethic" and Wendell Berry's "The Regional Motive"

The area in which the shift in regional consciousness, observed by Jules Chametzky, and the rise of a new kind of regionalism have been most notable is without doubt the ecological sphere. The poet and ecologist Gary Snyder stresses that from his childhood days "my sympathies were entirely with my place—being able to see Mount Rainer far off to the east on a clear day or to climb the bluff of the hill to the west and look out over Puget Sound and the islands and see the Olympic Mountains."[28] At the age of thirteen, he discovers, while still living on his parents' farm, the "real wilderness" (*RW*, 93) of the Cascades where he will later find work as a logger, trail-builder and fire watchman.

Gary Snyder's fellow poet and ecologist ally Wendell Berry is equally close to his native Kentucky. But what distinguishes him from Snyder is, above all, his preoccupation with history, particularly the history of a slave-owning family in the "old South." If Snyder's regionalism has an anthropological and utopian dimension, the urge to return to rediscovered archaic roots in the Western wilderness, Berry's regionalism is historically and morally oriented. Snyder's regionalism is revolutionary, Berry's is conservative. However, what both forms of regionalism have in common, and what at the same time distinguishes them from the local color-interest of the late

---

[26] William Westfall, "On the Concept of Region in Canadian History and Literature," *Journal of Canadian Culture/ Revue d'études canadiennes* 15.2 (1980): 3-15.

[27] Jules Chametzky, "New England as Region, New England as America," *The Newsletter*, published irregularly by the New England American Studies Association (Fall 1987): 6-15.

[28] Gary Snyder, *The Real Work: Interviews and Talks, 1964-1979*, ed. Scott McLean, hereafter abbreviated as *RW* (New York: New Directions, 1980), p. 93.

nineteenth century, is an insistence on ecological knowledge. As with many other representatives of the New Regionalism of our time, this knowledge of place is not only scientific but also sociocultural:

> Teaching should begin with what the local forces are. You can learn a great deal of ecology and geology from your area. But to give another dimension to that, you have to consult the Indian mythology and ritual and magic of the area .... You should really know what the complete natural world of your region is and know what all its interactions are and how you are interacting with yourself. This is just part of the work of becoming who your are, where you are. (*RW* 16)

In addition, this regional knowledge, including what amounts to sociocultural geography[29] is characterised by a new political awareness which has emerged as one of the principles of the new Cultural Studies and, in Germany, as *Ideologiekritik* in the context of the German political left of the seventies. Interestingly, this political dimension of the new ecological regionalism is as evident in the conservative Berry[30] as it is in the utopian Snyder, but then radically conservative and revolutionary sociocultural critics have often been very close, as the examples of John Ruskin and his disciple William Morris demonstrate. With regard to the political aspect, it is of interest that Snyder should emphasize the contrast "between political [and economic] and ecological boundaries," offering out of his knowledge of his native Nevada County the example of the difference between the white way with settlement and boundary (exclusively determined by mining property) and "the ecological Indian boundaries or settlements" (*RW* 24). In Snyder's view, "one of the key problems in American society now ... [is] people's lack of commitment to any given place ...." (*RW* 117). He himself can no longer identify with American society as a whole, but he still feels close to his own region:

> I no longer feel the necessity to identify myself as a member of the whole society. *Chowka*: North American society? *Snyder*: Yes. It's too large and too populous to have any reasonable hope of keeping your fingers on it ... What I realistically aspire to do is to keep up with and stimulate what I think is really strong and creative in my own viable region, my actual nation: northern California/southern Oregon, which we might call Kuksu county, subdivision of Turtle Island continent. (*RW* 125)

In the interview with Michael Helm, published under the title "The Bioregional Ethic" (*RW* 138ff.), Snyder has pursued this line of thought further, spelling out in detail the "*economic, ecological,* and *spiritual benefits* ... of a sense of place." Helm's opening question, besides underlining the role of regionalism within the wider context of environmental concerns, points again at the ecological basis which Snyder shares with Wendell Berry: "Gary, in recent years you, along with people like Wendell Berry, Raymond Dasmann and Peter Berg, have been in the forefront of urging people to

---

[29] Snyder has defined it further in "On Earth Geography" (*RW* 23ff.).

[30] Wendell Berry, *The Unsettling of America: Culture and Agriculture,* hereafter abbreviated as *UA* (1977; San Francisco: Sierra Club, 1986), 4ff., on the exploitation of the Indians as well as of the colonists; p. 6ff., on "the similarity between this foreign and the domestic colonialism that, by policy, converts productive farm, forest and grazing lands into strip mines."

rediscover a sense of place" (*RW* 138). Wendell Berry frequently expresses his regionalist sympathies[31] but the companion piece in his work to Snyder's "The Bioregional Ethic" is the essay "The Regional Motive" in *A Continuous Harmony* (1972). What makes his statements particularly relevant is the fact that he, as someone whose life and work were indeed strongly influenced by his native Kentucky, has been often identified with a kind of "regionalism" of which he is in fact highly critical. Berry's probing of the "Regional Motive" displays the same intense sociopolitical awareness as Snyder's "The Bioregional Ethic." The Cultural Studies approach or *Ideologiekritik*, practiced by both Berry and Snyder, is characteristic of the new ecological regionalism and constitutes its chief difference from former variants of regionalism such as the Local Color School of the late nineteenth century or the Agrarianism of the thirties:

> In thinking about myself as a writer whose work and whose life have been largely formed in relation to one place, I am often in the neighborhood of the word "regional." And almost as often as I get into its neighborhood I find that the term very quickly becomes either an embarrassment or an obstruction. For I do not know any word that is more sloppily defined in its usage, or more casually understood. There is, for instance, a "regionalism" based upon pride, which behaves like nationalism. And there is a "regionalism" based upon condescension, which specializes in the quaint and the eccentric and the picturesque, and which behaves in general like an exploitive industry. These varieties, and their kindred, have in common a dependence on false mythology that tends to generalize and stereotype the life of a region. That is to say it tends to impose false literary or cultural generalizations upon false geographical generalizations. The evils of such generalizations are abundantly exemplified by the cult of "the South."[32]

Reacting strongly against specific examples of "the moral distortion of exploitive or sentimental regionalism" (*CH* 65), Berry castigates the "tendency to love the land, not for its life, but for its historical associations" (*CH* 66) and identifies the "regional motive" as false in a way characteristic of the critical modern Southern heirs to this spurious Southern heritage. "The regional motive is false when the myths and abstractions of a place are valued apart from the place itself; that is regionalism as nationalism" (*CH* 67).

While wholly accepting Berry's critical stance, we must not overlook the fact that, his moral disapproval notwithstanding, precisely this kind of regionalist stereotype or false myth continues to have a powerful effect on the popular imagination and hence on political, socioeconomic and cultural processes. Therefore, the study of the many forms of this "false regionalism," be it the Hollywood trivialisation of the South or the politically even more fatal manifestations of narrow and bigotted provincialism, must go on because these kinds of distortions are endemic of many phases of cultural history. Meanwhile, one has no difficulty in subscribing to Berry's definition of the

---

[31] Wendell Berry, "The Ecological Crisis as a Crisis of Character," *UA* 22: "... our culture must be our response to our place, our culture and our place are images of each other and inseparable from each other."

[32] Wendell Berry, "The Regional Motive," *A Continuous Harmony: Essays Cultural and Agricultural*, hereafter abbreviated as *CH* (NY: Harcourt, 1972), p. 63.

"right" kind of regionalism. As with Snyder, it is a regionalism not fired by sentimental cliché but informed by local ecological knowledge:[33]

> The regionalism that I adhere to could be defined simply as *local life aware of itself*. It would tend to substitute for the myths and stereotypes of a region a particular knowledge of the life of the *place one lives in and intends to* continue to live in. (*CH* 67; emphasis added)

---

[33] For a characteristic and very convincing example of a relevant publication see Gary Paul Nabhan, *Gathering the Desert* (Tucson: Arizona, 1985).

REGIONALISM IN NORTH AMERICA

C.D. Eysberg, Utrecht University

Regional politico-economic and cultural-political differences or contrasts, and even out-spoken regional antagonisms are not unknown in the USA and Canada. Why did we not really expect this? Other than old, divided Europe, with its legacy of pluriformity, this part of the New World would seem to be characterised by a large measure of uniformity, with the possible exception of Quebec. The huge integrated domestic market, with its sophisticated transportation and communication technologies and the high mobility of its inhabitants, would even seem to generate cultural convergence.

My first encounter with a manifest symptom of American regionalism took place on the border of Oregon and California. An improvised billboard demanded, "Californians go home." The animosity was directed against tourists and second-home owners. The deeper roots of this antagonism, as I was told, must be sought in the remarkable differences in cultural identity between the populations of Oregon and California. Oregon was the earliest colonisation area in the West. The state was originally populated by Yankees from New England and the Upper Midwest and by Scandinavians. Moreover, it has not attracted many recent immigrants. Consequently, Oregonian society is relatively old and homogeneous. The populace is for a large part white and Protestant. Oregon belongs to that northern belt of states with a moralistic political culture, moderate views, and consensus-based characteristics (Elazar). In contrast, California had a totally different population development. Settlement picked up momentum with the goldrush. Since then, the state has continuously exerted an almost magnetic attraction on immigrants from inside and outside the USA. As a result, California is more cosmopolitan and has a fairly individualistic political culture.

Regionalism: a general explanation

Regionalism is a more or less explicit form of regional opposition to a dominant central bureaucracy or to another region.

The threat of cultural standardisation within a nation-state can be a sufficient reason for parts of the population to strive for more cultural autonomy. A sense of neglect or exploitation may also be responsible for the growth of regionalism. Regionalism is stimulated in depressed regions, where the national government fails to restructure the economy. Typically, a dominance-dependence relationship exists between the core and the periphery. The core is the locus of financial and political decision-making while the periphery is known for its disinvestments, outmigration of young educated people, and outflow of capital. The tension is heightened when

economically strong regions object to central government using their money to sub-
sidise inefficient and poor parts of the country. Especially when this economic discord
coincides with strong feelings of cultural identity and a peripheral location, the stage
is set for the development of a regional movement. Its goal will be more autonomy.

Regional culture: reassessment of a concept

Regional antagonism is only likely to arise when there are differences with regard to
regional identity or regional culture. Some time ago, "the communications revolution
promised to make the world a global village—the abolition of geography itself—with
American its common language" (Clarke 56) Yet we are confronted more than ever
with that concept of regional identity that is so difficult to grasp. It refers to culture
and feelings of being different, often with a strong emotional component. Abstract
social theories are inadequate if we want to explain the phenomenon. They have to be
complemented with region-specific explanations. And that requires research in a
realistic time-space context (Pieper).

Until recently, many social scientists looked upon this approach with a certain
distain. Equipped with quantitative methods and general theories they were only
concerned with unifying processes of social change at a global scale. A regionally
specific form of culture was only seen as a deviation, "as a place that refused to
become placeless." The humanistic belief in the forward march of civilisation prevailed
after the Second World War in a period of decolonisation, international cooperation,
rebuilding, and reconciliation. This was the ideological soil for an approach that
accentuated the characteristics common to all of mankind. Which man or woman
belonging to the post-war generation in North America and Western Europe does not
remember turning page after page of stunning photographs collected in *The Family of
Man*? That coffee-table book was a popular icon of an inclusive attitude that may be
seen as a reaction to the social-darwinism embraced by the Nazis. It was an implicit
debunking of genetically and physical-geographically determined "Volkscharakter."
Instead, it promoted a view of cultural behaviour as a product of social structure and
outside influence.

Unlike the inclusive humanist and social-darwinist ideologies, the marxist
paradigm considered only political power relations and economic exploitation to be
relevant to an explanation of regional conflict. Accordingly, regional identities and
affinities were said to only obscure the view of the class struggle, which is the only
relevant conflict from a marxist perspective. Still, the most recent elections in Canada,
those of October 1993, demonstrated that regional political ambitions and socio-
economic aims form the warp and woof of that country's political fabric.

The recent destruction of the marxist "brave new world" marked the definitive
disappearance of this modern paradigm. Simultaneously, a postmodern, and more
realistic outlook on human behaviour and society has won ground on all fronts where
the course of society, politics, and science is under discussion. This seems to lend
credence to my point of view that human geography is the terminus of the social

sciences, where the different disciplines come together in the real-world context of a region. Consequently, I will focus on regionalism in North America at a low level of abstraction. But first I will briefly introduce the phenomenon in more general terms.

Roots of regional cultures

Apparently there exists a group instinct, a social-psychological desire to be unique, positively different from other groups, based on territorial, ethnical or other criteria. In case of need a regional identity can be artificially created just "to be different."

Paradoxically, this need to be different might increase rather than decrease, as people sense a loss of identity in a mass society that becomes ever more uniform. Rising levels of prosperity, mobility, general education, and the dissemination of information have eroded regional dialects and languages, as well as other expressions of regional culture. But the same developments have aroused people's interest in their own regional culture and history. Fairly often this is accompanied by cultural inversion. Especially older people who have a low level of education and work in traditional occupations have been the exponents of regional culture. Recently, this role has been taken over by the younger generation, who are better educated. In Brittany, for instance, the regional language of the traditional fishing communities, Celtic, is losing ground to French, the national language. This shift is largely due to the democratisation of education. But a more insidious inroad is through children's television. Popular foreign programmes are invariably in French. Yet students at Rennes University are studying Breton. And other young people with higher education levels are enthusiastic about conserving the region's cultural legacy.

Nationalistic and regionalistic movements may base their cultural identities on manipulated and subjective perceptions of their own political and cultural role in history. Each group usually defines its own role in contrast to the roles ascribed to others. Still, even an artificial self-image can become a reality, a signpost that guides human behaviour.

However, most of the time, the central values of a regional culture can be traced back to the particular demographic and social development of a regional society. Indeed these core values may be regarded as the ideological reflection of the region's history. In many parts of North America, we can identify the original blueprint of the first colonisation or formal political organisation in the area. This is wholly in line with Zelinsky's doctrine of first effective settlement (first formulated in 1973). How this historical continuity can be explained is not quite clear, however. Could it be that the institutional organisation of a regional society plays a decisive role?

The next section of this article will present the outcome of a comparative analysis of the USA versus Canada. It reveals a remarkable difference in the relevance of geographical and political preconditions of formal regionalism in these neighbouring countries.

Preconditions of regionalism in the USA versus Canada

There are striking differences between the USA and Canada in the way regional contrasts and conflicts have developed. In the USA, the development of the formal political system and the way it works in practice bear witness to a high degree of centralisation and nationbuilding within the federal system. These tendencies are so strong that the very thought of a territorial separationist movement seems ridiculous. In Canada, we see just the opposite. There, federal power has been shared increasingly with the provinces. Meanwhile, regional conflicts are becoming more threatening. How can we explain this difference between the two countries? The geographical conditions and the federal system peculiar to each country would seem to be responsible.

The Canadian population is concentrated in a number of areas, separated by almost uninhabited land. The settlements are islands in a huge continental space between the Atlantic and the Pacific. This settlement pattern creates the preconditions for drifting apart, developing other orientations, and entrenching core-periphery contrasts. Western Canada was for the most part populated directly from Europe. In this respect, Canada differs from the USA, where the West was settled by people from the eastern regions of the country. The Canadian population is still less mobile than their neighbours to the south. Consequently, the melting-pot process was less strong in Canada. Also because of the great distances, the low level of mobility helped conserve regional differences in ethnic background and culture. Moreover, the cultural and economic boundaries of regional societies coincide with political borders. In fact, the cultural and economic divides reinforce the provincial boundaries in Canada. Whereas the USA has 50 states, many of which are relatively small, Canada has only 10 provinces. Of these, Ontario, Quebec, Alberta and British Columbia are disproportionately large. By this fact alone, they can be mighty opponents of the central government.

After the Second World War, the developing welfare state coincided with a general tendency towards increased central power. In the USA, the federal system grew stronger. But in Canada, where the welfare state was more advanced, the opposite development of "province building" took place. Since the 1960s, the provincial governments have played an increasing role in national affairs. Moreover, the exercise of property rights with regard to natural resources is a mainstay of provincial power.

Another difference between the two countries is that territorial representation is very effective within the federal system of the USA. Paradoxically, this has only increased federal power (Gibbins). Canada, on the other hand, has very few opportunities for territorial representation, which has contributed to a rising regional frustration. In the very pragmatic, flexible, and individualistic American system, governors have to compete with senators, congressmen, and representatives of lower-tier governments. Senators, as territorial representatives, are independent of the state governments and can vote as individuals. Party discipline is weak, so that regional or local interests can often be given priority. Because the federal government serves a fixed term, Congress can launch an offensive without suffering the consequences of a governmental crisis. In Canada, on the contrary, a government can be dismissed. Because of this and the strong party discipline in Parliament, only the opposition will attack the government. The way to exert influence in the USA is through lobbying. States, counties, and cities act like interest groups. They have offices with professional staff in Washington, D.C. In Canada, formal diplomacy is conducted on the highest level between provinces and the federal administration. The governors have a provincial monopoly, which is given a lot of publicity. The Canadian Senate, intended to be the body for regional representation, has little power.

The Cabinet is the true federal body in Canada. It is composed of ministers with different regional backgrounds. But here, consensus and national party discipline count while the opposition is not represented. Furthermore, the basis of the US constitution is carved in stone, so to speak. In Canada, however, the constitutional debate among the provincial authorities is a continuing story. Obviously, the political system of Canada, more than that of the USA, creates the preconditions for the development of regionalistic movements.

Cases of regionalism in Canada

Central Canada has long been the undisputed urban industrial core area. Situated in the southern parts of Ontario and Quebec, it runs through the lowlands between the Great Lakes and along the St. Lawrence River. This integrated urban system, extending from Windsor up to Quebec City, includes the two largest cities of Canada, Toronto and Montreal, as well as the federal capital, Ottawa. The provinces of Quebec and Ontario account for 65 percent of the country's GNP and 62 percent of its population. It is here that decision-making takes place. The big concerns, financial institutions, and the federal administration have their headquarters here. And this is where the majority of the electorate lives.

Atlantic Canada. The way these unimportant, thinly populated Atlantic provinces are related to the economic heartland is generally described in terms of a dependent periphery versus a dominant core. The resource-based, export-dependent regional economy is characterised by low incomes, high unemployment, and a high volume of transfer payments. It leans heavily on the federal treasury. Due to this dependence, there is a centralistic attitude in federal affairs. Nevertheless, because federal economic policies in the past were focused on the interests of Central Canada, those policies are blamed for the regional economic decay (Bickerton). Some define the relationship of the Atlantic provinces with Central Canada in terms of feudal federalism or regional ghettoisation, which illustrate the regional sense of frustration and alienation.

Western Canada. The alienation of the western provinces is not rooted in economic deprivation. It is on the contrary, a side effect of the economic dynamism of the region. Over the last 40 years, various factors have generated an economic upswing here: the internationalisation of the economy; the simultaneous spatial restructuring of the economy of the USA in a western and southern direction; the rise of the Pacific Rim; and the autonomous economic development of Alberta, based on the oil industry. Together, these factors have stimulated the development of a second economic core area, stretching from Vancouver via Calgary up to Edmonton (see Fig.1). Vancouver is by far the most important sea port of Canada. Wheat from the prairies, coal, wood products and paper from British Columbia, and oil from Alberta are shipped from there to Pacific Rim countries. Calgary and Edmonton have grown through the enormous expansion of the oil industry. Now they have a diversified and autonomous economic base. Western Canada wants to have more control over its recently generated wealth. The authorities resent having to fill Ottawa's purse without getting a proportional amount of political power in return.

The first big political controversy between the new West and Central Canada was the National Energy Programme (NEP) established by Trudeau and his Liberal Party in 1980. This was seen as "the most comprehensive and sophisticated orchestration of policy in the name of centralized federalism that Canadians had ever seen" (Milne 71). The aims of the NEP were to keep domestic energy prices low and to raise import tariffs for industrial products. These aims were perceived as benefiting only the old industrialised provinces of Central Canada and as actually detrimental to the energy-rich West.

The West has a successful young economy. With its self-assured neo-capitalistic optimism and its entrepreneurial spirit, it is a far cry from the old industrial urban core of the East. Eastern Canada is now confronted with economic and social problems, and it is struggling with the interests of labor unions and the welfare ideology. Not surprisingly, Mulroney and the progressive conservatives, who instigated a Free Trade Agreement with the USA, received support from the West.

The economic stagnation and a constitutional debate that drags on around the central issue of Quebec's demand for autonomy have given momentum to the mainly western Reform Party. This has resulted in a spectacular success in the national elections of October 1993. The party won 52 percent of the votes in Alberta and 36 percent in British Columbia. It opposes official bilingualism, scorns the civil servants in far-away Ottawa, and dares stand up to Quebec.

Quebec, "la révolution tranquille." The "pièce de résistance" of Canada's regional contrasts and conflicts is Quebec. Here we have not a case of economic-political provincialism, as in the regions described above. Rather, the issue is cultural-political nationalism.

Till the 1960s, the French community was an "inward-looking society" (Robinson). It was predominantly rural and conservative Roman Catholic. The urban economy was the domain of the English, Protestant outer world, where only the labor force was francophone.

As in other parts of the Western World, the 1960s brought Quebec its fair share of social change. The emancipation of the Québecois, "la révolution tranquille," was primarily a liberation from the social grip of the Catholic Church. This institution dominated all aspects of daily life. The Church was in charge of education, the public health service, labor unions, and politics. The intention, of course, was to protect the flock from the Protestant English outer world. The dramatic drop in the birthrate, from the highest to the lowest level in Canada, demonstrates the success of this quiet revolution. Another result was the increasing participation of Québecois in higher education, especially in business schools.

The political radicalisation of the Front for the Liberation of Quebec (known as the FLQ, yet one more liberation movement of those days) led to the murder of Minister Pierre Laporte in 1970. At first, people feared the worst was yet to come. With hindsight, however, this murder may be interpreted in the context of the times as a "fashionable" act. More in line with the rules of a parliamentary democracy, the administration of the nationalistic Parti Québecois, 1976-1985, called for the implementation of a very aggressive frenchification programme by way of language laws. At the same time, positive discrimination was introduced to elevate the profile of the French-speaking population. Due to the prevailing leftist and nationalistic francophone climate, especially as established by the language laws, many firms decided to leave Montreal and go to Toronto. That reinforced an already established trend of a western shift in the economic center of gravity. Montreal lost its prime position as business center and first city to Toronto. However, the intended secession of Quebec proposed by the Parti Québecois was rejected in a provincial referendum by 60 percent of the inhabitants. Was this rejection due to a lack of economic self-confidence? We know for a fact that Quebec's economy not only lost ground to Ontario but also had an outdated infrastructure.

The Parti Québecois government diagnosed these economic problems. It wanted to attack these problems by opening up the economy for the play of market mechanisms and for private entrepreneurship. This route was proposed in the programmatic publications "Bâtir le Québec" of 1979 and, especially, "Le virage technologique" of 1982. Thus the Parti Québecois abandoned the path of social-democratic governmental intervention in accordance with the spirit of the times.

Trudeau hoped to accommodate Quebec's wishes by giving French, alongside English, the status of official language in all of Canada. But in Quebec it was considered more important that the province should be recognised as a "distinct society" in the new constitution. However, the negotiations that took place at Meech Lake in 1988 and Charlottetown in 1992 failed to produce a new constitution. Opinion polls held in November 1990 showed that 62 percent of the population of Quebec and 73 percent of the francophones in this province are in favour of sovereignty (Wood 13). In 1980, political-economic insecurity prevented Quebec from seeking its destiny outside the federation. This insecurity is less relevant at present. After a period in which the cultural-nationalistic aspirations had hurt the provincial economy, the economic trend shifted at the end of the 1980s. Montreal's CBD showed a revival. The electronics giant Ericsson, for instance, moved from high-priced Toronto to Montreal (Van Bemmel). The case of Ericsson moreover illustrates the qualitative upgrading of the labour market by better education. In addition, the management vacuum that was caused by the exodus of the anglophones has been filled by a new francophone business elite.

A growing trade and investment relationship with the northeastern United States opens up alternatives to intra-Canadian commercial relations. Furthermore, due to the language barrier, Québecois feel less threatened in their cultural identity by the USA than do anglophones in other parts of Canada. In fact Quebec is pro-NAFTA, according to Bouchard, the leader of the Bloc (Bouchard).

The francophones are concerned about their decreasing share in the Canadian population. Since the Second World War, that share has declined from one-third to less than one-fourth of the population. And it will probably continue to shrink, due to a relatively low birthrate and because the French language forms an impediment to most immigrants. The Bloc is currently in charge in Quebec. According to its plans, the population of Quebec should in 1995 be consulted by way of a referendum about a possible sovereignty for the province. The Bloc wants to retain close economic ties with the rest of the country, including the use of Canadian currency and the responsibility for part of the national debt (Bouchard).

Secession seems to be a logical and inevitable consequence of a number of developments in western society during the post-war period. Old political ties have been fading away. The economy is internationalising. Economic relationships are expanding with increases of scale and with intensifying communication. And the welfare state has come into full flower. All these developments have helped generate a consciousness of Canadian identity and nationalism. Previously, the regional anglophone communities had few relations which each other and none at all with the francophone one. Indeed, the whole macro-economic system had been in the hands of the anglophones. This was also the case in Quebec, where the French-speaking population lived in a sort of social quarantine. It is evident that a growing consciousness of a Canadian identity leaves no room for the Quebecois attitude of "Je me souviens" (the provincial slogan on license plates).

Cases of regionalism in the USA

As I have already noted, the preconditions for regional movements are much weaker in the USA than in Canada. On the national scale, only two recent cases seem to warrant the use of the term regionalism. However, at a less encompassing level, we know about the contrasts between, for instance, Northern and Southern California. These have been responsible for many proposals to split up the state. And the writer Ernest Callenbach attracted attention in 1975 with his bestseller *Ecotopia*. That book describes the secession in 1999 of the magnificently wooded and environmentalist-oriented Northern California, Oregon, and Washington from "the nuclear-and-foreign-oil-addicted, materialistic, wasteful, polluting, military-industrial-oriented, racist, sexist, soul-mangling" USA. As the author's choice of a title clearly suggests, the environmentally motivated secession is essentially like any other utopian vision: a figment of the imagination.

The Northeast-Midwest versus the South.
An acute regional-political controversy grew out of the Snowbelt-Sunbelt shift in the economy. It showed up in the 1970s as a conflict between the Northeast-Midwest on one side and the South on the other. It came to light in the 1970 statistics that the

economy of the old industrial heartland, the urban core, had lost ground to the Sunbelt. For the first time in history, the metropolises of the Northeast reported an absolute decrease in population. This rather unexpected effect of the spatial restructuring of the economy and of migration patterns made headlines. A lot of publications soon dealt with its economic, demographic, and political consequences. For the Northeast, traditionally the dominant part of the federation, it was hard to accept that it could be surpassed by the once-dependent periphery. It was especially painful to be overtaken by the South, which was perceived as inferior. It was easy to find a scapegoat, the so-called federal spending gap. This is the gap that it was supposed existed between the considerable federal tax revenues and the less generous federal spending in the Northeast. Supposedly, Northern wealth was being used to finance a federal budgetary and non-budgetary favouritism toward the South. The regional frustration of the Northeast, focused on the South, was vented in articles such as "The Second War between the States" in *Business Week*, May 1976, and "The North's Loss is the Sunbelt's Gain" in *The New York Times*, also May 1976. The accusations of federal favouritism were not always backed up by fact. Moreover, for convenience's sake, the publicists ignored that just as much capital from the Northeast—including, rather cynically, labour-union funds—was used to finance the economic growth of the Sunbelt (Weinstein and Firestein). The Northeast-Midwest Congressional Coalition (Fig.2) was established to tackle the assumed regional favouritism in Congress. The Southern Growth Policies Board, originally established to tackle the joint problems of growth management, decided to take up the challenge. Meanwhile, the southwestern Sunbelt kept out of the fray. Obviously, it was especially the South of the Stars and Bars that felt under attack by its old enemy. The founding document of the Board claims that: "The independence of each state and the special needs of subregions are recognized and are to be safeguarded" (Markusen 174). This standpoint unambiguously defends the traditional political culture of the region, which stood for a Southern commitment to the federalised state. With the arrival of Reagan, the federal pie diminished. The only piece of the federal pie worth fighting over was the military budget. But defence dollars are allocated by the Pentagon and existing military bases.

So the political clash of the 1970s between the North and the South was in part a legacy of the Civil War. The deep sense of cultural distinctiveness in the South "proved to be a tenacious source of regional identity and an ongoing context within which new regional antagonisms could flare up" (Markusen 184).

The Intermountain West versus The Northeast.
Western regionalism in the 1970s was sparked by the federal reaction to the energy crisis, Project Independence. The energy boom rekindled the idea that this region should function as a resource colony. In 1976, the Western Governors' Regional Energy Policy Office was established. In the beginning, WGREPO was openly environmentalist and strove to preserve the Western way of life. The fragile natural environment was being threatened by strip mining, power plants, power lines, explosive boomtown growth, etcetera. Concern over the environment had already blocked the proposed 1976 Winter Olympics in Colorado and the Kaiparowitz power plant in

southeastern Utah. In 1977, a merger of WGREPO and the old public-private Federation of Rocky Mountain States resulted in the Western Governors' Policy Office, the WESTPRO. By taking a balanced growth standpoint, this office gradually changed into an economic development agency (Markusen 204). In the 1980s, not economic development but environmentalism came under attack. Obviously, the Northwesterners who took the initiative needed some time to organise their region's corporate interests and to induce them to participate.

Another issue that has been a latent source of Western regionalism is the pattern of extensive federal land ownership in the West (Fig.3). The ideologies of both individualism and federalism are undermined by this. Private property rights and states rights are in jeopardy. Dependending on which regional political coalition one belongs to, one may criticise the negative impact on regional economic growth, property tax revenues foregone by local government, or poor management and misuse. Some say that federal decisions on land use do not satisfy local interests and preferences, while making it impossible for local authorities to control their own region's future. In 1970, the state governments of Nevada and Arizona requested, without success, that the federal government donate 2.4 million hectares (6 million acres) of federal land to each state (Birdsall 352). The Wilderness Act of 1964, the Forest and Rangeland Renewable Resource and Planning Act of 1974, and the Federal Land Policy and Management Act of 1976 were effective in eliminating and/or restricting economic uses such as grazing or in raising the fees charged to ranchers for such use. This stimulated anti-federal feelings that reached a peak in 1978. In that year, Nevada passed a law claiming that all land falling under the Bureau of Land Management and all National Forest lands within its borders belonged to the state (Birdsall 352). This state-rights movement, called the Sagebrush Rebellion, did not achieve its aim and died out in the late 1980s.

This regionalism, in the form of political action, had become manifest for the first time in 1948. That was when the Governor of Colorado invited five other states in the region to collectively oppose the discriminatory freight rates imposed by the East. Earlier, in 1943, the West had apparently not yet been ready to agree to a proposal of the South to band together to fight this unfair policy (Garnsey 257).

Of course, feelings of regional identity in this young region, with its highly diverse population, are not comparable with the deep-seated resentment one finds in the South. Nevertheless, they did play a role, even though they may be largely based on nostalgia for a bygone lifestyle and a romanticised myth of the West.

Conclusions

Although there are more informal types of regionalism in the USA, the North-South and East-West controversies are the more explicit and most persistent examples of regional tensions. But a more complex and deconcentrated spatial economic structure is developing. It has a less dominant urban core and a more complex set of inter-relationships. In that light, it is probable that the economic basis for regionalism in the USA will decrease in the future. But the unity of the Canadian federation is vulnerable.

The secession of Quebec seems to be inevitable. If Quebec does break away, the breach will be a consequence of post-war anglophone Canadian nationalism. In particular it will be due to the growing inability of English-speaking Canadians to accommodate the new self-confident francophone cultural nationalism. But even an anglophone Canada would need to revise its political system in order to prevent unnecessary regional tensions from flaring up.

WORKS CITED

Bemmel, N. van. *Nieuws uit Canada*. The Hague: Canadian Embassy/Embassade du Canada, September 1988.

Bickerton, J. "Atlantic Canada: The Dynamics of Dependence in a Federal System." M. Burges, ed. *Canadian Federalism: Past, Present and Future*. Leicester: Leicester University Press.

Birdsall, S.S. and J.W. Florin. *Regional Landscapes of the United States and Canada*. New York: Wiley, 1992.

Bouchard, L. "Different visions." *The Gazette* (Montreal) 21 September 1993.

Bradshaw, M.J. *Regions and Regionalism in the United States*. London: Macmillan, 1988.

Clarke, J. "'There's no place like ...': cultures of difference." Doreen Massey and John Allen, eds. *Geography Matters*. Cambridge: Cambridge University Press, 1984. 54-67.

Elazar, D.J. *American Federalism: A View from the States*. New York: Crowell, 1972.

Eysberg, C.D. "Canada's identiteit en territoriale integriteitstaan op het spel." *Geo grafisch Tijdschrift* 4 (1991): 345-353.

Eysberg, C.D. "Regionale cultuurverschillen in de Verenigde Staten, ideologisch cement." Geografie 5 (1992):

Garnsey, M.E. *America's New Frontier: The Mountain West*. New York: Knopf, 1950.

Gibbins, R. *Regionalism: Territorial Politics in Canada and the United States*. Toronto: Butterworths, 1982.

Markusen, A. *Regions, the Economics and Politics of Territory*. Totowa, New Jersey: Rowman and Littlefield, 1987.

Pieper, R. "Region und regionalismus, zur wiederentdeckung einer räumlichen Kate gorie in der soziologischen Theorie." *Geographischen Rundschau* 39 (1987) H.10.

Robinson, J.L. *Concepts and Themes in the Regional Geography ofCanada*. Van couver: Talonbooks, 1983.

Weinstein, B.L. and R.E. Firestein. *Regional Growth and Decline in the United States*. New York: Praeger, 1978.

Wood, N. "Quebec seeks its own way." *Maclean's*, December 1990, 12-14.

Zelinsky, W. *The Cultural Geography of the United States*. Englewood Cliff, NJ: Prentice-Hall, 1992.

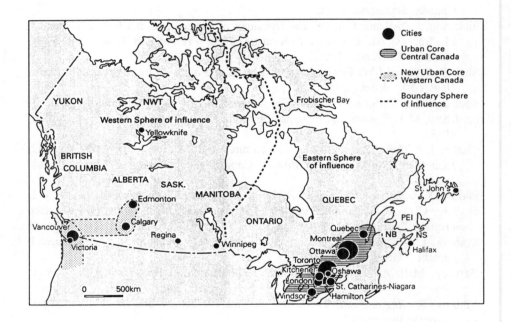

1. Urban Core Areas, Canada.

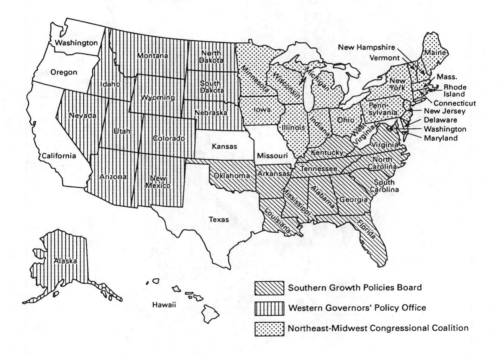

2. Regional Organisations in the USA, 1980.

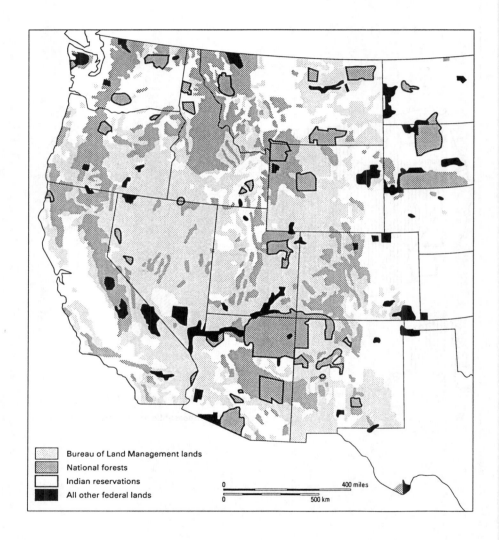

Bureau of Land Management lands
National forests
Indian reservations
All other federal lands

0   400 miles
0   500 km

3. Federal Lands in the Western USA.

REGIONAL IMPULSES FOR AMERICAN FOREIGN POLICY THE MIDDLE-WEST AND ISOLATIONISM[1]

Doeko Bosscher, University of Groningen

American foreign policy has never been exempt from popular pressure. In a democracy politicians standing for frequent reelection cannot avoid public opinion. As Dexter Perkins put it in one of his 1952 Gottesman Lectures at the University of Uppsala:

> Politicians seek to strengthen their position with the voters. They will not leave these problems to the professionals. They insist upon having a hand in them. And the American people wish them to do just this.[2]

The pressures from the voters described by Perkins have traditionally derived from a wide variety of origins. Although they intertwined more often than not in the course of more than two centuries of American history, the following components, among others, may be distinguished in the shaping of electoral influence on foreign policy: people's party affiliation, their economic interests, ethnoracial loyalties, and regional biases.

The question as to how far the voters' influence goes will not be discussed in this paper. Of course it is debatable to what extent the foreign policy establishment, which consists of both the politicians mentioned by Perkins and the professionals in the State Department supposedly controlled by them, actually listens and orients itself towards the people. And perhaps Perkins' description of the making of foreign policy is too optimistic. Some of those involved in it surely are more responsive to well-organised special interests than to the preferences of the public. Some legislators might simply respond to what they read on the op-ed page of the newspapers in their districts, assuming that it is an expression of public sentiment (but what editors write is clearly not the same as public opinion). Presidents lead public opinion as well as follow it. It is both their weapon and their guide. We heard much about a "bully-pulpet" in the latest election. As Theodore Roosevelt once described his own attitude toward public preferences: "I simply made up my mind what they ought to think and then did my best to get them to think it."[3] The assumption underlying this paper is, however, that the public at large exercises a substantial influence on the people who formulate and shape foreign policy.

---

[1] I wish to thank Professor Dennis Thavenet of Central Michigan University for his knowledgeable advice.

[2] Dexter Perkins, *The American Approach to Foreign Policy* (Cambridge, 1952), p. 169.

[3] C.W. Kegley, Jr. and E.R. Wittkopf, *American Foreign Policy: Pattern and Process* (New York, 1987), pp. 305-306.

I

The partisan approach to foreign policy originated shortly after the Republic was established. Many examples of partisanship in these matters can easily be drawn from the early decades of the United States' existence. Federalists and Anti-Federalist opposed each other on a considerable number of issues in foreign affairs (e.g. the Jay Treaty and the purchase of Louisiana), and so did Whigs and Democrats in later days. Before the Civil War the Republicans were generally less expansionist than the Democrats, but not necessarily more isolationist. Until Americans had settled the continent from the Atlantic to the Pacific, expansionism and isolationism could go hand in hand. After the war the Democrats changed their position. They were surpassed in expansionist fervor by the Republicans. By the end of the 19th century expansionism axiomatically implied internationalism, even war. The continent was settled, and beyond its borders hardly any territory was left that was not settled by others. So in the 1890s, Republicans and Democrats fought over the implications and consequences of American involvement in the Cuban war of liberation and the acquisition of the Philippines. McKinley's and Theodore Roosevelt's policies triggered strong criticism from at least some Democrats. Admittedly the romantic drive to liberate Cuba was as widespread in Democratic circles as in Republican ones, or maybe even stronger. But concerning the conquest of the Philippines, many influential Democrats eventually came down on the side of moderation, arguing that the United States government should not cave in any further to jingoistic notions. A few Republicans vocally opposed any departure from their isolationist tradition, but on average they were more agressive and supported "their" presidents' activism more enthusiastically (senator Albert Beveridge from Indiana is a good example in this respect).[4]

If one looks for partisanship in foreign affairs in the 20th century, an obvious example is the struggle in the United States Senate surrounding the Versailles Treaty in the years following World War I. The Republicans, led by Henry Cabot Lodge, were on one side; the Democrats, acting on behalf of president Wilson, on the other. In the end, the Democrats voted with the "irreconcilable" Republicans to defeat the "amended" treaty. That, however, occurred only because Wilson gave up the idea of having the original version of "Versailles" ratified in order to avoid the embarrassment of adopting a treaty that was Lodge's brainchild more than his own.

In the twenties and thirties Republicans remained on average somewhat more "isolationist" than Democrats, with some notable exceptions. Gradually, however, the Republican Party in general reached the conclusion that the very freedom of America would be put in jeopardy if isolationism were maintained. Their candidate of 1940, Wendell Willkie, supported FDR's opposition to Hitler and the president's sympathy

---

[4] William Jennings Bryan, then the leader of the Democratic Party, voted for the Treaty of Paris that resulted from the Spanish-American war (December 19, 1898), but he did so primarily to help end the fighting. If the Democrats would win the elections of 1900 they would grant independence to the Philippines, he said. Alexander DeConde, *A History of American Foreign Policy* (New York, 1971), pp. 353-354.

towards Great Britain's war effort including the destroyers-bases swap and lend-lease. While the isolationist Robert Taft wing of the Republican Party kept singing their familiar tunes, men like Senator Arthur Vandenberg laid the foundations for the bi-partisanship that would characterise American post-war foreign policy. At a crucial meeting on Mackinac Island (Michigan) in the summer of 1943, Vandenberg charted a new course for his party, receiving endorsements from its leading members for participation of the US in a future United Nations Organization.[5] Later, Vandenberg was instrumental in convincing the Republican Party of the merits of the "Truman doctrine" and American participation in NATO.

As for the way in which economic interests make themselves felt as a significant ingredient in the shaping of foreign policy, asserting generalisations is easier than providing evidence in specific cases. Various kinds of "determinist" historians have claimed (and notwithstanding the demise of Marxism still claim) that economics is the prime mover of history. Their theory also applies to the field of international relations: "capitalism guides the course of American foreign policy." Whether it holds true is not at issue here. Much research has been done, a lot more has to be undertaken.

In the 1950s, but especially from the 1960s onwards, a new wave of historical theorising linking economics and foreign policy emerged, deriving from concerns about the Cold War and in particular about the war America was fighting in Southeast Asia. Some of it was Marxist and determinist, and in that sense biased, partial, and con-fused; some of it was excellent scholarship. Its basic premise, the idea that the rela-tionship between economics and international issues has traditionally received far less attention from historians than it deserved, steadily gained ground.

Suffice it to mention William Appleman Williams, standard-bearer of the "revi-sionist" school, which has put continuous emphasis on the significance of economic considerations in determining American foreign policy. In Williams' view, the question when the United States stopped being isolationist was a "pseudo-question," inasmuch as America had never been isolationist. Its economic activity, which defined its approach to international affairs, had never allowed it to. Therefore, Williams con-tended, the historian's main focus should be on the undramatic but highly important areas of international trade, foreign loans, and investments.[6] According to Williams, and the various authors who substantiated his thesis with their research, the Cuban crisis at the turn of the century derived primarily from an American "crusade for a free world marketplace."[7] America's entry into the First World War he explains in terms of its material (economic) interest in an Allied victory and the way "militarism" was intertwined with "industrialism."[8] Those Americans who defeated the League of

---

[5] Henk Meijer, "Hunting for the Middle Ground: Arthur Vandenberg and the Mackinac Charter, 1943," *The Michigan Historical Review* 19.2 (1993): 1-21.

[6] W.A. Williams, ed., *The Shaping of American Diplomacy: Readings and Documents in American Foreign Relations*, vol. 1 (Chicago, 1970), p. xvi.

[7] Williams, pp. 336-339.

[8] Willaims, vol. 2, pp. 2-3.

Nations after the war supported, as he sees it, "the idea of a community of interest among the industrialised powers of the world led by an American-British entente as against the colonial areas and the Soviet Union."[9]

At first glance the ethnic factor seems to be somewhat less complicated and less difficult to analyse. One has to keep in mind, however, that the ethnic origins of groups within the electorate do not always work in one direction only. Depending on the number of generations standing between these groups and the immigrants they descend from, their commitment to the mother country's cause may become ambivalent or disappear altogether. In individual cases repulsion can be stronger than attraction.[10] At any rate, there have been various easily identifiable instances in which ethnic groups have put pressure on the American government to influence foreign policy. During the First World War, to mention just one case, the combatant nations and nationalities in Europe found support among their former compatriots in the United States, the so-called "hyphenated Americans." Some hyphenates did what they could to let America come to the rescue of their homelands or stay out of the war, depending on whether they or their immediate ancestors came from countries belonging to the Entente or from parts of the Central powers. Their "dual allegiance" understandably angered if not scared many Americans who argued that their own loyalty was to the United States alone and that everyone's should be. A resurgence of radical "nativism" was the result.[11]

But who exactly were those hyphenated Americans with dual loyalty? Some Americans are more hyphenated than others, Bernard Fensterwald says, comparing Italians with Canadians.[12] Alexander DeConde also warns us in his *Ethnicity, Race, and American Foreign Policy* that there is more to the complex of issues concerning the relationship between ethnicity and foreign policy than meets the eye. When studying the ethnic component in the electorate's preferences in foreign affairs, one should not focus too much on ethnic "minorities," a term that leaves the Anglo-British ethnic group out of the picture. As much as DeConde avowedly avoids WASP-bashing, he nonetheless does treat Americans with British ancestry as a distinct ethnoracial group with distinct political predilections, particularly where foreign affairs are concerned. The fact that this group traditionally forms the backbone of the elites that determine the course of the State Department enhances, in his view, the need to scrutinise its outlook on foreign policy.[13] According to DeConde Anglo-Americans tend to define American national character in terms of their own ethnic heritage and to

---

[9] Williams, vol. 2, p. 104. The quote is from Williams' famous article "The Legend of Isolationism in the 1920's," *Science & Society* 58 (1954): 1-20, which appears as a reprint in various "problems" readers on American foreign policy and diplomacy.

[10] Bernard Fensterwald, Jr., "The Anatomy of American 'Isolationism' I," *Journal of Conflict Resolution* 2 (1958): 111-139; 135.

[11] Louis L. Gerson, "The Influence of Hyphenated Americans on U.S. Diplomacy" in: Abdul Aziz Said, ed., *Ethnicity and U.S. Foreign Policy* (New York, 1981), pp. 19-31; 22.

[12] Gerson.

[13] A. LeConde, *Ethnicity, Race, and American Foreign Policy: A History* (Boston, 1992).

couple loyalty to the United States with an affection for their mother country.[14] In this they differ little from other hyphenates.

In their study *Ethnicity* (published in 1975), Nathan Glazer and Daniel Moynihan predicted that American foreign policy would be affected profoundly by future changes in the ethnic composition of the American electorate. Because foreign policy responds "probably *first of all* to the primal facts of ethnicity," they said, the immigration process is "without too much exaggeration [its] single most important determinant."[15] Incidentally Glazer's and Moynihan's apparent dismay derived less from the prospect of increasing strife among ethnic groups than from what they perceived as an odd refusal of the State Department to acknowledge it. Although ethnic self-assertion has become ever stronger in America in recent years (a development contrasting sharply with the immediate pre- and postwar years in which it declined due to the reduced flow of immigration) it seems that the dire predictions of Glazer and Moynihan have so far not fully come true. But that does not mean they never will.

II

Let us now turn to the main theme of this paper, the regional pressures on foreign policy in the years before the United States came of age as the enforcer of the Western World's *Pax Americana*. As was stated above, the partisan, economic, ethnic, and regional factors cannot be neatly separated. Particularly the latter two factors are clearly interwoven. Ethnic groups are not dispersed equally across the United States. African-Americans used to live primarily in the South and in the East, and great numbers of them still live there. After the "Great Black Migration" they also composed the largest ancestry group in a fair number of urban congressional districts in the West and in the North. As immigrants tended to seek, along with shelter and jobs, the security of belonging to a group that could serve as a kind of extended family ("host colony"), they settled in distinctive regional constellations.[16] British immigrants went in relatively great numbers to the Northeast and the West, Scandinavians to the North and Northwest, Germans to the Midwest, Russians to the North, Italians to the Northeast and the West. Canadians and Mexicans on average did not stray far from the borders of their native countries. Depending on the definition of the Midwest one chooses, it was affected less or more by the 1862 free-farm Homestead Act, which encouraged settlement not only of Europeans coming from the East, but also of Americans coming from everywhere, including the South. By that time large portions of the Northern and Eastern Midwest had already been occupied by earlier settlers.

---

[14] LeConde 69. DeConde is using the past tense here, speaking about the first decades of the twentieth century. Later in the book he makes clear that he feels the Anglo-American attitude has not changed significantly over the years.

[15] Nathan Glazer and Daniel P. Moynihan, eds., *Ethnicity: Theory and Experience* (Cambridge, 1975), p. 23.

[16] R. Ueda, *Postwar Immigrant America: A Social History* (Boston and New York, 1994), p. 74.

A new wave of immigration starting in the 1960s, primarily from Asia, Latin America, the Caribbean, and the Middle East, did not end the traditional ethnic configuration of the United States but overlaid it with new colonies in gateway metropolitan areas.[17] At this point the ethnic makeup of America's geographical regions needs no further elaboration. What is important here is to note that in so far as ethnicity was and is an ingredient in electoral pressures on foreign policy, it contributed in one way or another to political sectionalism in this field. We shall return to this theme below.

Political sectionalism is as old as the Republic. Americans tend to vote in accordance with a distinct regional pattern, more than on a state-by-state basis. The two big parties are relatively strong in one region, relatively weak in another. With presidential elections it rarely happens that the outcome creates the picture of a chessboard. Normally it looks like a painting where the artist has applied the colours in broad brush strokes. Unfortunately little research has been done on political divergence and convergence among different regions or sections of the United States. There are various theories concerning cultural diversification and homogenisation in general, but they pay only slight attention to the regional patterns of political preferences and voting behaviour (in short: political geography).

American cultural geographers seem to be in agreement that during the first two hundred years after the first European settlement in the US, cultural diversification was dominant, and that around the 1850s several processes which stimulated cultural unity and uniformity began to prevail.[18] It is unclear if and how this very general conclusion holds true for the political realm as well. But we do know that whatever processes fostering political homogeneity across the nation may have taken place, diversity has persisted and perhaps even increased.

In his widely acclaimed book *The Cultural Geography of the United States* (first published in 1973) Wilbur Zelinsky identifies five to ten (he prefers five) "subnational regions, each comprising parts or all of several states."[19] These culture areas, "naïvely perceived segments of the time-space continuum distinguished from others on the basis if genuine differences in cultural systems,"[20] are "the result of importing European colonists and ways of life and the subsequent interactions among and within social groups and with a novel set of habitats."[21] Calling interstate boundaries "curiously irrelevant," Zelinsky postulates as the two main characteristics of a distinct culture area: 1) "the extraordinary number of ways in which it is manifested physically and behaviorally," and 2) "the condition of self-awareness on the part of participants."[22] The five most important regions, divided by "first-order cultural boundaries," are (see appendix): New England, the Midland, the Middle West, the West, and the South.

---

[17] Ueda, p. 78.

[18] See for instance W. Zelinsky, *The Cultural Geography of the United States* (rev. ed.: Englewood Cliffs, 1992), p. 85.

[19] Zelinsky, p. 113.

[20] Zelinsky, p. 112.

[21] Zelinsky, p. 117.

[22] Zelinsky, p. 112.

Besides, Zelinsky perceives some 25 subregions and sub-subregions, divided by second- or third-order cultural boundaries.

Drawing the borders of the five main culture areas Zelinsky, in line with his definition of the phenomenon as initially and still basically the product of European settlement, focuses primarily on their origins in terms of their settlers' ethnic make-up. His description of the culture areas' mentality remains shallow and vague. Regarding their political attitude he offers no characterisations, let alone explanations or analyses, other than very general, casual references to e.g. a sense of individuality, awareness of identity, or "strong political and literary traditions" in this or that region. The prevalent outlook on foreign policy in specific areas is not dealt with at all in the book. And inasmuch as no major survey studies the characteristics of all culture areas in the United States, those who want to know more must resort to works concerned with one region in particular.[23]

III

From here on the focus of this article will be on the Middle West, a region often characterised as having relatively strong isolationist feelings as far as foreign policy goes. Reading what general works such as textbooks have to say about policy preferences in America's culture areas one almost inevitably comes across casual allusions to the Midwest's "isolationist" perceptions. But what exactly do they imply (if they are real, which still has to be determined)? How strongly are they held and against which historical backdrop should they be explained?

The preliminary issue to be dealt with in this context are the boundaries of the Midwest. According to Zelinsky's definition it encompasses all of Minnesota, Iowa, Wisconsin, and Michigan. Furthermore large portions of North and South Dakota, Nebraska, Kansas, Missouri, Illinois, Indiana, and Ohio. Tiny sections of Oklahoma, West Virginia, Pennsylvania, and New York also belong to it in his view. Ray Allen Billington in the article discussed below (1945) counts as the Midwest the twelve states figuring most prominently in Zelinsky's definition, but he has his doubts concerning Missouri, "which has remained predominantly southern in its social attitudes."[24] Most other authors harbour far more limited conceptions of the Midwest. Kleppner in his analysis of Midwestern politics in the second half of the 19th century focuses on Illinois, Indiana, Michigan, Ohio, and Wisconsin, a region called "East North Central States" in census reports. More specifically his interest concerns Michigan, Ohio, and Wisconsin. He adds the proviso, however, that "I do not suggest that these states were

---

[23] See also M. Jensen, ed., *Regionalism in America* (Madison, 1951). The number of possible regional combinations greatly varies by author and in one extreme case reaches more than a hundred. See Ralph H. Smuckler, "The Region of Isolationism," *The American Political Science Review* 47. 2 (1953): 386-401; 387.

[24] R.A. Billington, "The Origins of Middle Western Isolationism", *Political Science Quarterly* 60. 1 (1945): 44-64; 44.

microcosms of the nation, or even of the Midwest," leaving it unclear what exactly he understands by the term.[25] Russell B. Nye describes (1951) the Midwest as a region "too fluid, too subdivided and disunified, to be defined as more than a state of mind, a regional self-consciousness that knows no clear demarcation lines."[26]

The matter of the Midwest's borders can never be settled satisfactorily until the criteria on which the definition is based are made explicit. As Smuckler rightly observes in an article published in 1953, "our question should not be 'Is the Midwest the outstanding area of isolationist strength?,' but rather 'Is there any region of outstanding isolationist strength?' Then, if such an isolationist region is found, it can be compared to a consensus Midwest region derived from the definition of those who use the phrase 'midwestern isolationism.'"[27] To follow this recommendation through to its completion would require too large an inquiry for this article. For its limited purpose the definitions mentioned above (Zelinsky, Kleppner, Nye) are probably enough to go by.

The next problem to be addressed are the political particularities of the region. In what sense was (is) it politically distinct from other parts of America? In Kleppner's Midwest there was a Republican majority in all presidential elections from the Civil War through 1880 (with the exception of Indiana voting for Tilden in 1876). In the two following elections the Republicans still received a plurality of the vote (Indiana voted for Cleveland in 1884), only to be beaten by the Democrats in 1892 (Michigan and Ohio remained Republican). In the four succeeding elections (1896-1908) the Midwest was solidly Republican again, but Wilson won in 1912 (Michigan voted for Theodore Roosevelt). In 1916 the Midwest was back in Republican hands, except for Indiana. There it remained until 1932 (Wisconsin chose LaFollette in 1924). Franklin Roosevelt carried the Midwest both in 1932 and 1936. Then the Republicans began making inroads in Democratic strength. Willkie had Michigan and Indiana behind him in 1940; Roosevelt lost many votes everywhere across the Midwest, but not that many states. Dewey took Wisconsin, Indiana, and Ohio in 1944 and Michigan and Indiana in 1948. Thereafter Eisenhower carried all of the Midwest twice in a row. Of course the outcome of presidential elections tells only part of the story, but it does provide some idea of the relative strength of the major parties in the region.

Within the scope of this article it is impossible to determine all of the issues around which the political battles in the Midwest were fought. What is sure, however, is that it did become a distinct area in political terms in the second half of the 19th century, notwithstanding the great diversity of its population, or perhaps thanks to this great diversity. In no other American region such a varied pattern of ancestries existed, due to the unique settlement patterns it had experienced. Its political culture was at least to a degree the reflection of that. As characteristic traits of Midwestern politics Nye lists among others the clear and direct desire of the people to protect their

---

[25] P. Kleppner, *The Cross of Culture: A Social Analysis of Midwestern Politics 1850-1900* (New York, 1970), p. 4.

[26] Russell B. Nye, *Midwestern Progressive Politics: A Historical Study of Its Origins and Development 1870-1950* (East Lansing, 1951), p. 2.

[27] Smuckler, pp. 387-388.

interests; their inclination toward socialisation in the sense that faced with strong monopolies of private interests, they resorted to giving the state positive control over the economy and social life as a means to secure their needs; the "colonial complex" or "provincial feeling" that was discernable everywhere, resulting from the dependence of the Midwest on the East; its spirit of protest.[28]

This last crucial element in Midwestern political culture derived from the predicament of farmers and workers who were confronted with what Nye calls "the paradox of poverty amidst progress."[29] While entrepreneurs acquired enormous fortunes, the life of many workers was one of suffering and hardship. A large number of farmers in the Midwest fought a "triple alliance" of railroads, banks, and industry. This prevented them, businessmen—but smaller—in their own right, from reaching their markets at decent freight rates, from getting credit at bearable interest rates, and from selling their products for a good price. This is why the Midwest became an area of revolt, where radicalism or "progressivism" thrived.

Particularly in the wake of recurrent crop failures, price drops, or other kinds of economic crises the voices of discontent were raised on a wide scale. Workers and farmers rallied around leaders advocating strong practical, rather than revolutionary measures. Fringe political parties came and went, of "reformers" or "independents" who challenged and sought to force concessions from the two larger parties. Of these the Republican Party was the dominant one, as shown above. "Vote the way you shot," was the Republicans' slogan. For a long period after the Civil War the Democrats were compromised and disqualified from playing a leading role in the region's politics. Their leaders offered no clear alternative to Republicanism to those with grievances. They were "Bourbons in the sense of being wealthy, self-esteemed, self-appointed guardians of an already fixed pattern for living and making a living."[30] Inasmuch as the Democratic Party failed to play the part of the champion of the disenchanted, these people could do nothing but "kick over the old party fences and build their own."[31]

In the 1870s and 1880s "third parties" emerged in the Middle West, backed by the farmers alliances that emerged at the same time. They became awesome competitors for the Republicans as they took up all the issues the GOP preferred to ignore (or did too little about). In some states the Republican Party managed to hold its ground by making concessions and enacting "progressive" laws. In others, like Kansas and Nebraska, it took a heavy beating. In the 1892 presidential elections the Populist Party (founded in St. Louis in that same year, to voice the West's grievances) went national as a "third party." Its candidate (James Baird Weaver) carried four states, of which only Kansas belonged to the Midwest. He also got one elector behind him in both Oregon and North Dakota. In some state elections his party joined forces with the Democrats. When the Democratic Party nominated free silver advocate W.J. Bryan,

---

[28] Smuckler, pp. 1-10.
[29] Smuckler, p. 19.
[30] H.S. Merrill, *Bourbon Democracy of the Middle West 1865-1896* (Baton Rouge, 1953), p. vii.
[31] Merrill, p. 77.

a "Westerner" from Nebraska, as its candidate for 1896 and let down incumbent president Cleveland, the Populists endorsed him, knowing he was their best bet to further their cause. Notwithstanding the widespread support for Bryan's themes in the region, South Dakota, Nebraska, Kansas, and Missouri were the only Midwestern states (in the broadest definition of the Midwest) to vote for him in the national elections, which he lost to McKinley. Four years later Bryan suffered an even worse defeat. This time only Missouri stayed with him.

When Roosevelt succeeded McKinley after the president had been assassinated, a new era of "Progressivism" began. Roosevelt's action scheme was oriented towards urban areas and the problems connected with the industrial revolution (however strongly he and a majority of his fellow-reformers disliked the city).[32] The Populists of the Midwest no longer felt much need, however, to forcefully push their own agenda and to oppose the Republicans with a Populist ticket. They regarded the new president as a warrior for their cause as well as for the urban workers. With the frontier fading from the region the emphasis on individualism gradually weakened, and so did whatever was left of the Midwest's rebelliousness.[33] Midwestern Progressivism incorporated some elements of Populism. It took the middle road between socialism and extreme individualism and viewed local, state, and national government as guarantors of the public welfare. The state where it showed its character most clearly and uncompromisingly was Wisconsin; hence its denomination as "the Wisconsin idea." There Robert M. La Follette was elected (Republican) governor in 1900 against the opposition of his party's stalwarts. Under his intellectual leadership Midwestern Progressivism took its definitive form.

When Roosevelt declined to run for the presidency in 1909, with Taft succeeding him, progressive discontent was already on the rise. Many people thought that TR's achievements as a proponent of Progressivism had not matched his promises. Paradoxically it was Roosevelt's disenchantment with the Republican ("progressive") record four years later that forced a break with Taft over the Republican nomination. When the GOP chose Taft over both TR and La Follette, he started his "Bull Moose" campaign as a third party (the Progressive Party) candidate. Of the Midwestern states he took South Dakota, Minnesota, and Michigan, beating Taft nationwide, but losing against the Democratic candidate, Woodrow Wilson, who took all other Midwestern states. In 1916 Roosevelt did not run. His fellow-Progressives split between Wilson (the majority) and the Republican Party's candidate, Charles Evans Hughes. Both presidential contenders of 1916 tried to outdo the other in their zeal to keep the United States out of the war that had been raging in Europe since 1914, but in 1917 the whole nation stood behind Wilson when he decided that the time had come to declare war on Germany. Shortly after the war, however, big differences concerning the League of Nations emerged along party lines. Later, in the middle of the interwar period a great variety of persuasions could be discerned in both parties. The dichotomy international-

---

[32] George E. Mowry, *The Age of Theodore Roosevelt and the Birth of Modern America 1900-1912* (New York, 1986), pp. 90-91.

[33] R.B. Nye, pp. 198-199.

ist/Democratic versus isolationist/Republican had all but disappeared, or better, was no longer applicable. America was for "peace." The dividing issue was how to maintain it. One might try to accomplish peace both by relying on oneself—the "conservative" option—and by joining the League of Nations—the "progressive" option. In either party propagandists for either course could be found, but the Democrats generally favoured the latter. Public opinion in the Midwest was no exception to this rule.

IV

So much for a general description of the Midwest's political character. In what way and to what degree, if any, did the region hold distinct views of its own concerning foreign policy? In March 1945 Ray Allen Billington published an article, "The Origins of Middle Western Isolationism," in the *Public Opinion Quarterly*, in which he identified and tried to explain a swing to isolationism in the Midwest coinciding with "the free silver excitement, which solidified political divisions and intensified sectional jealousies."[34] This new attitude took hold of the region for a long time to come. The Midwest did not waver and remained loyal to its isolationist inclinations, Billington contended, until the last moment before the Japanese bombed Pearl Harbor.

What follows is a resumé of Billington's argument. In the nineteenth century the Midwest vigorously supported liberal uprisings in Europe (Greece in the 1820s, France in 1830 and 1848, Hungary in the 1840s), reflecting its self-image as the cradle of democracy, which was enhanced by "the influence of the frontier." In the first two decades of the twentieth century this attitude changed. The shrinking of the Atlantic made the Midwest realise that meddling might bring about involvement. The region decided that Europe was beyond redemption and Midwesterners contented themselves with protecting "their own interests on their own soil."[35] The election of McKinley in 1896 marked the first shift from aggressive humanitarianism to greater caution. Until then the Republican press was very outspoken in its support for Cuban independence, more so than the Democratic papers. After the Republican president had captured the White House the reverse held true: the majority of Republican newspapers in the Midwest became less belligerent toward Spain, whereas the Democratic editors pressed harder for American intervention on Cuba's behalf. After the war had been won and the issue of permanently taking over the Philippines was at stake, business interests were expansionist, as they hoped to benefit from the opening of the Asian market. But now that the humanitarian misson had been fulfilled, the farmer and the labourer had second thoughts about overseas adventures, fearing that they would suffer under a flood of cheap, tariff-free goods and higher taxes to pay for the development of colonial possessions. In so far as the Midwest remained on the whole "imperialist,"

---

[34] Ray Allen Billington, "The Origins of Middle Western Isolationism," *Public Opinion Quarterly* 60.1 (1945): 44-64.

[35] Billington, p. 45.

only Republican domination of the West accounted for this. The Democratic press now saw expansionism as a ploy to "steal" colonies under the pretext of humanitarianism, and as a prelude to world war.

The struggle for free silver moved its protagonists further toward isolationism. The farmers blamed Eastern and British capitalists for their plight. They despised anything sanctioned by these adversaries, including intervention in world affairs. In the Progressive Era, when urban and agrarian discontent merged, "thousands of westerners came to believe that intervention was only another tool of the trusts in their battle against the people."[36] Meanwhile, the Midwest experienced a threefold increase in its industrial production. The degree of economic self-sufficiency the region accomplished was unmatched by any other section of the United States: all products could be sold in the surrounding rural regions. The manufacturers' interest in overseas markets declined accordingly. Another factor contributing to increasing Midwestern isolationism was the influx of immigrants from Germany and Scandinavia, nearly three-fourths of the total number of immigrants. The great mass of these were isolationist, as intervention came to denote intervention against the Central Powers. As a result, until 1917 most people in the Midwest were either indifferent to the outcome of the war in Europe or pro-German. Only unrestricted submarine warfare against American ships and the Zimmerman note could tilt the balance. But even then a group of diehards remained opposed to war. The majority of votes cast in the Senate and in the House against American participation came from the Midwest.

Midwestern isolationism was back in full swing during the debate on American membership of the League of Nations. In Billington's version of the events leading to Wilson's defeat, the greatest emphasis was on partisan politics, as in his account of the reversal of alliances around the turn of the century. Bryan's campaign of 1896 made Republicans out of people who until then had not considered themselves solid Republicans, everywhere in the United States but most clearly in the Midwest. After World War I the same polarisation occurred. Republicans did not want to have anything to do with a "Democratic" cause, and vice-versa. Only one Republican from the Midwest challenged party discipline and voted for the League; only one Democrat against it. Harding's landslide of 1920 was most clearly visible in the Midwest, where the Republican Senators on his coattails outnumbered the Democrats 21 to 3. Of the 143 Midwestern seats in the US House, only five were left to the Democrats. Isolationism remained dominant afterwards. In the 1935 vote on the World Court, a majority of the Senators from the Midwest were opposed, while every other region of the United States favoured the Court with a two-thirds majority of their Senators. This means that it was the Midwest which defeated American membership all by itself.

Billington's reasoning is to a large degree convincing, all the more so because he used as evidence every available opinion poll, but his article lacks the nuances to clearly distinguish between economic, geographic, and ethnic factors in the shaping of an isolationist Midwest. Particularly confusing—or just too summarily explained—

---

[36] Billington, p. 51.

are his observations on the changes in the political climate occurring around 1900. At the very moment people in the Midwest flocked to the Republican Party to defeat Bryan and free silver, they helped elect an internationalist president (and vice-president). Bryan himself, a hero of the Democrats in the Midwest, whether isolationist or not, was at first a "humanitarian" internationalist, who enlisted in the First Nebraska Volunteers at the beginning of the Spanish war, and who only belatedly turned against "imperialism."[37] Billington provides few clues as to how and why political developments in the Midwest in the 1895-1905 period must or can be interpreted as formative in terms of a shift towards isolationism. After him other authors have tried to fill the gaps and solve the paradoxes.

Before considering some of these other observers' premises and theories, a brief review of the factual data should be undertaken. For this article none of the opinion polls Billington used to corroborate his findings were reexamined, as it can be assumed that he read the figures with enough care. Other than those, few raw data that would allow a researcher to assess public opinion in the Midwest before Pearl Harbor are available. In 1935 *The Literary Digest* launched a "College Peace Poll" at 118 American colleges and universities in cooperation with the Association of College Editors. The following questions were asked, the answer to which could be either "yes" or "no":

1. Do you believe that the United States could stay out of another great war?
1. (a) If the borders of the United States were invaded, would you bear arms in defense of your country?
1. (b) Would you bear arms for the United States in the invasion of the borders of another country?
2. Do you believe that a national policy of *an American navy and air force second to none* is a sound method of insuring us against being drawn into another great war?
3. Do you advocate government control of armament and munition industries?
4. In alinement [sic] with our historic procedure in drafting man-power in time of war, would you advocate the principle of universal conscription of all resources of capital and labour in order to control all profits in time of war?
5. Should the United States enter the League of Nations?[38]

Some of these are clearly leading questions. The *Digest* was very explicit in its pacifism, stating as its goal "to wipe out war." For this purpose it advocated American membership of the World Court (the League of Nation's International Court). The attitude of those who opposed America's joining the Court it denounced as "jingoism" and "arrogant nationalism." In that sense the *Digest* was anti-isolationist (anti-conservative), but it does not make sense to call a journal which shunned all wars internationalist, let alone interventionist. The effort to poll the opinions of American students was made right before the Senate voted on the World Court. It may be assumed that the journal aimed at influencing the outcome and preventing a rejection

---

[37] Richard Hofstadter, *The American Political Tradition And the Men Who Made It* (New York, 1951), p. 196.
[38] *The Literary Digest* 12 January 1935: 38.

of the League's Court. The first results of the Peace Poll, indicating that a slim majority of the colleges polled favoured entry into the League and that all of them had answered the other questions the way they were expected to, were made public under a caption that read "Thirty Colleges Point Way to Wipe Out War."[39] Unfortunately for the *Digest* the first ballots coming back were not representative for the final results. A month after the poll was launched, the journal admitted that the League's advocates had lost. Fifty-five colleges were for the World Court; sixty-three were opposed. Of 112,607 ballots which were returned (more than one-third of the ballots mailed to students) 50.53 per cent had turned down the Court.[40] Support for the League was strongest in the East, but to say that the West and the Midwest were a solid block of opposition is putting it too strongly. While Michigan State University opposed, the University of Michigan favoured it. Chicago (where a particularly large majority supported the Court, 941-429) and Illinois also cancelled each other out. Kansas and Kansas State both voted for the Court, as did De Pauw (Indiana), Iowa, Oberlin (Ohio), Washington (St. Louis), Wisconsin, and Western Reserve in Ohio.[41]

By this time the Senate had already taken action. Only fifty-two Senators had voted for the Court, seven fewer than the required two-thirds majority. A majority of those who had joined forces to defeat president Roosevelt were Democrats, but of all Democratic Senators a majority had voted "yes." Of the opponents (Democrats and Republicans) a relatively great number represented Western states, but not particularly *Mid*western states. All Senators from Michigan, Indiana, and Missouri supported the Court. The Senators from Wisconsin, Illinois, and Ohio split. Straight "no's" came from Minnesota, Iowa, North and South Dakota, Montana, Washington, and California. Not only in this case were the Senators from the states West of "the Midwest proper" more isolationist than those from "the Midwest" as a whole. In his detailed analysis of Congressional voting behaviour with regard to foreign policy issues in the inter-war years, *Sectional Biases in Congress on Foreign Policy*, George Grassmuck concluded that the Great Plains states (Wisconsin, Minnesota, Iowa, North and South Dakota, Nebraska, and Kansas) were far more isolationist than the Lake States (Illinois, Indiana, Michigan, and Ohio), which he calls "the zone of transition and contradiction between East and West, and between metropolitanism and non-metropolitanism."[42] Under the Republican presidents the legislators from the Great Lakes region supported administration measures in the field of foreign policy more than did their parties. After 1932 the reverse happened. Both Republicans and Democrats tended to check the administration's inclination to increase international involvement (with one exception: Democratic Senators from the Great Lake states favoured foreign loans more than all Democrats in the Senate taken together).[43] The Great Plains

---

[39] *The Literary Digest* 26 January 1935: 6.

[40] *The Literary Digest* 16 February 1935: 7.

[41] *The Literary Digest* 2 February 1935: 6. *The New York Times* 2 February 1935.

[42] G.L. Grassmuck, *Sectional Biases in Congress on Foreign Policy* (Baltimore: Johns Hopkins UP, 1951), p. 157.

[43] Grassmuck, pp. 157-159.

states stood out much more as opposed to a big army and a big navy, the repeal of neutrality restrictions, and in their defiance of party discipline.

Strangely enough this difference in legislators' attitudes between the Great Lakes and the Great Plains was not, or not always, parallelled by public opinion as shown in the polls. Opinion polls held in the second half of 1939 indicated that while all of the greater Midwest was indeed more opposed to changing the neutrality laws (so as to make it possible to help Britain and France) than the rest of the nation, people in the Great Lakes states (called the East Central States by the *Public Opinion Quarterly*) were slightly more negative than people in the states West of Michigan and Illinois.[44] Whatever the discrepancy between roll call votes in the US Senate and the US House and public opinion polls may indicate, it constitutes an effective warning against the assumption that members of Congress automatically vote the opinion of their constituents as they perceive it. Private opinions and party discipline sometimes outweigh other considerations. Furthermore it should be kept in mind that opinion polls register not only the opinions of the truly informed and interested, but also of those who have only a vague notion of foreign policy issues. Members of Congress for obvious reasons attune their ear to constituents who they suppose to entertain strong feelings on the subject.

What about public opinion in the final stage of the war? For the Spring 1945 issue of *Public Opinion Quarterly* Frederick Williams, a public opinion researcher at Princeton, evaluated the poll-based data he had at his disposal. His study, which he called "an extensive investigation of pertinent public opinion polls" (apropos differences in opinion about international affairs among the regions of the United States), offered, as he said, "a fresh line of approach for those concerned with making the United States more international-minded."[45] From what he had seen, he inferred that "the differences in attitudes between any two regions are not large" and that there was "a solid majority" in each region favouring cooperative international action. Not the regions diverged as far as opinions on foreign policy was concerned, but educational groups (high versus low level of education) and socio-economic groups (wealth versus relative poverty). The discrepancies between the views held by those groups explained the (small) differences between regions: in terms of education and income level each region had its own character. In general, the lower the economic and educational levels of a region, the less internationalist it was. As in the 1939 opinion polls mentioned above, and again surprisingly, the East Central States (the Great Lakes states) ranked below the West Central states (the Dakotas, Nebraska, Kansas, Minnesota, Iowa, and Missouri) in international-mindedness. On the whole however, the greater Midwest had caught up with the rest of the United States in internationalism. Possibly the volte-face of well-respected Senator Arthur Vandenberg of Michigan, who drew a lot of positive as well as negative attention when he swung from isolationism to internationalism—the Republican *Chicago Tribune* reprimanded him time and again, but his constituents did

---

[44] *Public Opinion Quarterly* 4.1 (1940): 103-105.
[45] Frederick W. Williams, "Regional Attitudes on International Cooperation," *Public Opinion Quarterly*, vol 9, Spring 1945, 38-50; 38.

not turn him down—offers an explanation. The turnaround of a Senator who was known to wield great influence in international affairs on Capitol Hill may have contributed to a gradual conversion of the electorate in all of the Midwest.

V

It is time now to put this in perspective. What exactly did Midwestern isolationism imply and what did it derive from? As it turns out there is little agreement on the subject among scholars.

Graham Hutton, an English observer who was travelling the Midwest when the Second World War broke out and made him stay there for a number of years, in his *Midwest at Noon* submits that "insularity of outlook on the world was natural to midwesterners for most of their short history."

> "From their very beginnings ... Midwest attitudes to American foreign policy, to foreign affairs, and to foreigners were highly colored by their sympathy and generosity, their own local and sectional concerns, and their own folk myths. More than any other regions of America, the Midwest and Great Plains had taken the discontented and the rebels, the enterprising, the young and the "non-conformists" of many nations and of the older America, and had performed miracles with them. ... It was natural for [Midwesterners] from the outset to side with the discontented, the individuals who rebelled against authority, and to identify them all over the world, indiscriminately, as the underdogs, the apostles of liberty and freedom—provided, of course they seemed to offer no threat to the American or the Midwest way of life. ... The sympathy of midwesterners was always expressed in material generosity, at home or in Congress; but midwesterners remained chary of entanglements in foreign policy and particularly of war. They were not imperialistic. ... More than anything else, they wanted perpetual peace for their country, for peace was the best foundation of prosperity and material progress.[46]

As Hutton saw it, immigrants naturally look down patronisingly upon the country from which they come. They have reached a higher standard of living than they could have achieved in Europe; this is a source of resentment against the former fatherland. In the Midwest this loathing went deeper and further than elsewhere, Hutton suggested, as the populating of the Midwest with so many different European peoples who got along fine in their new environment strengthened the idea that there was something terribly wrong with Europe (if the Europeans could get along well in the US, why couldn't they in that other continent?) and enhanced the region's desire to have nothing to do with Europe politically. In addition, the fact that the Midwest is "a melting-pot that has not yet melted its contents" gives the area many reasons to fear and dislike Europe: conflicts in Europe led to conflicts in the Midwest. Hutton makes a clear distinction between the Midwest's insulation and an isolationist mentality which, as he sees it, has been wrongly attributed to this part of the United States. A lack of interest in, and lack of knowledge of, the world outside America does as such not make for isolationism. Neither does an obvious dislike of Europe. The Midwest, Hutton asserts, has suffered from publicity given to isolationist organisations which happened to have their

---

[46] Graham Hutton, *Midwest at Noon* (Chicago, 1946), pp. 308-310.

headquarters in the region.[47] The polls he claims to have studied, taken between 1939 and 1942 in a number of big American cities, show little difference between this and other parts of the nation on the big isolationist-internationalist issues.[48] His conclusion is that the Midwest proper at the end of the 1930s was less isolationist than the Great Plains region. Up to 1941 the Far West was even more isolationist than the Plains. After Pearl Harbor things changed. As the Japanese danger loomed larger, the Far West turnèd internationalist, Hutton said.[49] This underscores his impression—or so he thinks—that *insulation* from a particular conflict or theater may cause isolationism. The more visible the conflict and its consequences become, the less appeal isolationism will have.[50] Hutton's insulation theory is just an example of the widely held belief, holding sway in many textbooks, that the core of isolationism was geographical, at least to a degree.

In his classic study *The Future of American Politics*, which is referred to in practically every book on American foreign policy, Samuel Lubell takes exception to the geographical approach. His emphasis is on ethnic and emotional factors.[51] Lubell found that of twenty counties throughout the United States where Roosevelt lost more than 35 percent of his vote in 1940 (compared to 1936), nineteen were predominantly German in background. In another thirty-five counties where his electionary loss was less but still large (in the 25 to 34 range), with the exception of only four German was the first or second nationality of origin. German predominance held also true for 83 of the 101 counties in a third group, those where Roosevelt lost between 20 and 24 percent of his vote. While FDR lost votes in the country as a whole and in these counties in particular, he won votes in the area of the original English settlement. Support for aid to Britain was also strong in the South, especially in those areas where the issue of isolationism versus internationalism could not be exploited by a relatively strong Republican Party. In the South, a region where few European immigrants had settled, a German tradition was absent (with the exception of Texas). The German-American swing was not geographical, nor was it rural and agricultural. In predominantly German city precincts the pattern was the same.

Lubell proceeded to claim that, clear as the influence of the ethnic factor was at the end of the thirties, it had diminished considerably since the early 1920s, inasmuch as the ethnic base of isolationism had shrunk from including Swedes and Norwegians besides Germans to just Germans.[52] He also pointed at changes in its economic background. While the early isolationism had been part of a poor people's revolt

---

[47] Hutton, p. 314.

[48] I have not been able to check Hutton's interpretation of these polls as some are not clearly identified by the author and others were not available for my research.

[49] The dissertation of K.G. Feig, *The Northwest and America's International Relations, 1919-1941: A Regional Study of the Domestic Formulation of Foreign Policy* (University of Washington, 1970) only partly confirms this opinion.

[50] Feig, p. 315.

[51] Samuel Lubell, *The Future of American Politics* (New York, 1951), pp. 129-157.

[52] Lubell's assertions concerning the attitude of Swedish-Americans are by and large confirmed in F.H. Capps, *From Isolationism to Involvement: The Swedish Immigrant Press in America 1914-1945* (Chicago, 1966).

against vested interests, the later variety was used by conservative Republicans as a weapon against the New Deal. The Progressives who were against American entry into the First World War, out of concern for unsolved problems at home, had been brought over to the Democratic Party by Roosevelt in 1932. Except for the German segment most of them stayed there, the president's internationalism notwithstanding. With regard to Truman's victory of 1948 Lubell saw a reason to speak of "one-time isolationists" with respect to those who belonged in the post-1932 Democratic Party in terms of ideology, but had not been able to bring themselves to vote for Roosevelt in 1940 because of the impending war against Germany.

In his 1953 article mentioned earlier, Smuckler reviewed the assumptions of such authors as Lubell and examined "non-regional factors ... for their possible relationship to geographical centers of isolationist strength" in the past.[53] After analysing 73 roll-call votes in the US House and 88 in the US Senate having to do with international affairs, Smuckler identified a "percentage of isolationism" for each state of the United States in the 1933-1950 period. His conclusion is that measured by the *House* votes North Dakota, Idaho, Kansas, Nebraska, Wisconsin, and Minnesota were the most isolationist states (in that order). If one's aim is to identify a *region* of isolationist strength in this same period (again measured by the *House* votes) it centers in a North Dakota to Kansas belt and reaches from Idaho in the West to Kansas in the South and Ohio in the East. Votes cast in the Senate suggest only a minor change of this picture: Ohio and Nevada are in this case among the six most isolationist states, replacing Minnesota and Wisconsin, but the *region* of isolationism remains roughly the same. It is important to note that the North Dakota-Kansas-Ohio region never monopolised isolationist thinking. Pockets of isolationist strength existed all across the nation. In the first third of the 1933-1950 period (1933-1938) Northern New England was as isolationist as the "isolationist triangle," or even more so. This leads to the conclusion that measured over the whole period isolationism gradually shifted from the East to the West.

On the basis of his roll-call votes analysis Smuckler suggested that the typical region of isolationism extended further West than does the Midwest.[54] Its core (the Dakotas, Nebraska, Kansas) was located on the Midwest fringe. Using methods of comparison too complicated to summarise here, Smuckler also concluded that rural areas were more isolationist than metropolitan areas. More surprisingly he submits that in contrast to opinion poll findings, isolationist strength correlated positively with a higher educational level in the congressional districts represented by those whose voting pattern he studied (at any rate more so than with higher living standards). This part of his analysis does not go to great lengths in explaining the research methods he applied, so it is not possible to verify his findings. Neither does he try to explain the positive correlation. As regards the link between isolationism and the dominant presence of certain ethnic groups, he, in so many words, takes exception to Lubell's

---

[53] R.H. Smuckler, "The Region of Isolationism," *The American Political Science Review* 47.2 (1953): 386-401; 386.
[54] Smuckler, p. 396.

conclusions: "Though the relationship [between isolationism and national origins found in Samuel Lubell's works] exists, it is but one of several such correlations, and does not seem to be the strongest."[55]

VI

Given the abundance of evidence that it is based on a misperception, it is surprising that the Midwest continues to be defined in textbooks as *the* region of isolationism in the period when isolationism was at its peak. The misperception concerns either the definition of the Midwest as a region or the degree of isolationism in the "consensus" Midwest (the core of states that belong to the Midwest by any definition). Isolationism seems to have been stronger—although this is not confirmed in all public opinion polls—in the states West of "the Midwest proper." But even so, when challenging the myth of Midwestern isolationism one should be careful not to trade one myth for another. Isolationism may have been more prominent in the Central time zone than in the Midwestern part of the Eastern time zone, but it was never so strong as to completely dominate political thinking even in that most isolationist region and its geographical basis within that region was scattered and diffuse.

As to what caused isolationism, it is asking too much to take sides with one author in particular, if only because their disagreements do not amount to very much. None of the observers mentioned above puts everything on one card. They all tend to acknowledge the doubts surrounding the definition of an isolationist region. Besides, they all agree that regional and non-regional factors (such as partisan affiliation, the metropolitan-rural antithesis, educational level, standard of living, and ethnicity) should be taken into account to explain a high or a low degree of isolationist sentiment.

Concerning the ethnic factor in regional pressures on foreign policy this writer sollicited the comment of subscribers to the H-DIPLO list (an H-net list on e-mail). Numerous reactions came in. Richard Jensen (University of Illinois-Chicago) wrote that Midwestern Germans insofar as their attitude was different than the attitude of other groups did not thereby demonstrate any special concern about Germany itself. Their political behaviour should rather be explained as "a reflection primarily of severe psychological pressures on a once-proud ethnic group in the process of destruction." At the end of the 1930s they would do their utmost to avoid "the very real threat of 1917 all over again." So when the Republicans nominated "a German" (Willkie) in 1940, they rallied to his cause, as they would do again in 1952, when they voted for Eisenhower.[56] Jensen also reported that a study undertaken by the National Opinion Research Center (University of Chicago) during World War II on "the effect of German and Italian origin on certain war attitudes" found that "Germans" were only slightly more hostile to Britain than "non-Germans." "People with [only] one parent born in Germany were almost exactly like the national average."

---

[55] Smuckler, p. 401.
[56] Richard Jensen to H-POL, March 26, 1994.

After the Second World War the United States assumed leadership of the Western Alliance and committed itself to the defense of Europe. Although the small Herbert Hoover/Robert Taft wing of the Republican Party remained vigorously opposed to foreign entanglements (Taft would rather speak of a policy of "the free hand" than of isolationism[57]), America's overseas obligations were no longer a highly controversial issue. Journalistic interest in isolationism as a phenomenon (measured by the attention paid to it) all but disappeared. Scholarly interest remained, but with time the political scientists' and historians' preoccupations and frames of reference changed. Concern about the implications of isolationism gradually made way for detached analysis. A 1980 conference in Iowa City organised by the Center for the Study of the Recent History of the United States (a joint venture of the University of Iowa, the Hoover Library, and the Iowa State Historical Society) on Midwestern isolationism was probably the most recent comprehensive effort to shed new light on some aspects of this region's presumed opposition to an activist foreign policy. There Frederick Adams, commenting on preceding lectures on the politics of the three distinct isolationists Gerald Nye, Robert Wood, and John Lewis, concluded that "Midwestern isolationists have bequeathed a puzzling legacy to Americans."[58] Adams and the other speakers may have clarified some distinctions between tendencies and strains in Middle Western isolationism (liberal-labour [Nye and Lewis], business [Wood], and ethnic), but to solve the mystery created by those who invented the Midwest as the region standing out in isolationist thinking once again proved to be an impossible task.

What was left of isolationism in America after the beginning of the Cold War went under a great variety of names and epithets. W.M. Carleton distinguishes unilateralism (which included the crypto-imperialism of people like Joseph McCarthy and Barry Goldwater), pacifism, and nationalism.[59] Although the reputation of the Midwest as a region of isolationism lingered on, it seems to have had less and less of a basis in fact, if it ever had any to begin with. As far as opinion polls and roll-call votes in Congress were concerned the Midwest did not stray far from the national average. In the 1940s and 1950s about 70 per cent of all Americans felt that the United States should take an active part in world affairs. Since then this percentage has steadily decreased to a low of 54 in 1982.[60] Afterwards it increased to 64 in 1986, at which level it remained for some time. The election of president Clinton in 1992, whose main theme was that it should be the United States' priority to get her own house in order, seemed to point at a shift in the general mood and a downward trend in the rating of an activist foreign policy. There are no indications that the Midwest has taken any lead in this respect. Reading *The Detroit Free Press* during his stay as an exchange scholar

---

[57] William G. Carleton, *The Revolution in American Foreign Policy: Its Global Range* (New York, 1963), p. 124.

[58] Frederick Adams, "Three Faces of Midwestern Isolationism: Comments," John N. Schacht, ed., *Three Faces of Midwestern Isolationism: Gerald P. Nye, Robert E. Wood, John L. Lewis* (Iowa City, 1981), pp. 35-44; 35.

[59] Schacht, pp. 124-125.

[60] John E. Rielly, ed., *American Public Opinion and U.S. Foreign Policy 1991* (Chicago: The Chicago Council on Foreign Relations, 1991), p. 12.

at Central Michigan University, this writer frequently did come across articles, columns, and editorials that showed ambivalence with regard to problems in the European "back yard" or unequivocally stated that the United States has no business in the Balkans as long as there are so many hot spots in America, and "we can't keep the peace within our own borders." But then, Detroit is indeed a city where one easily comes to such a conclusion.

FROM PALACE TO PLANTATION HOUSE
THE SOUTHERNISATION OF AMERICAN DIPLOMATIC
ARCHITECTURE IN THE 1920S

Ron Robin, University of Haifa, Israel

Beginning in the early 1920s, and as part of an ambitious plan to expand American diplomatic representations throughout the world, the U.S. Department of State began experimenting with a variety of symbolic, politically laden architectural styles for a new generation of diplomatic representations abroad. This seemingly simple objective soon became a complex mission, as diplomats, politicians, and architects laboured to develop a uniquely American image for export as well as a pertinent form of federal symbolism for a nation that still claimed multiple sectional and cultural identities.

Prior to the Great War, the purchase or construction of embassy buildings had been practically non-existent. In the early 1920s, in response to the demands of the business community for greater governmental representation in the many new potential markets for American goods, the State Department requested and received a large congressional allocation for a diplomatic construction program. By 1932, the United States owned property in forty different overseas locations, and the administration had requested an additional multi-year funding program to construct almost one hundred new diplomatic outposts.[1]

Defining a respectable American image in foreign lands was not an easy process. To begin with there were no pertinent role models. Monumental government architecture in the United States had not adapted to the changing times, and well into the Roosevelt years an unimaginative emulation of classicism characterised federal architecture.

A further complication arose from the unclear contours of America's ambitions abroad; there was no single pattern to the enterprise. Economically, the United States sought a variety of goals, ranging from stark colonial exploitation and protectionism in its own hemisphere, to the grand ideals of free trade in other parts of the world. Political goals were equally diffuse, moving intermittently from aggressive intervention in Latin America to altruistic and somewhat vague support for freedom and democracy in the world at large. These fluid concepts of empire hindered the search for a pertinent archetype of national symbolism abroad.

---

[1] United States Congress. House of Representatives. Committee on Foreign Affairs. Seventy-First Congress, *Hearings on H.R. 15774* (Washington, D.C., 1931); Letter from Frederick Larkin to Miss O.L. Nelson (4 April 1932), in State Department Records, Record Group 59, Decimal Files 124.01, National Archives, Washington D.C. (Hereafter: R.G. 59).

The Palace as Embassy

The first steps towards establishing a symbolic international presence in the immediate postwar period were predictably hesitant and devoid of a uniquely American context. Unused to their new status of world leader, and lacking internal guidelines, Americans tended to measure themselves according to the imperial practices of other powers; their place under the sun acquired meaning only by comparison with the British, French, and German examples, as well as less ambitious models too. The federal government set out to acquire and build diplomatic abodes that merely claimed a place for the United States as a power among powers; the architecture did not focus on anything that was specifically American.

This vague sense that national greatness was best expressed through architectural extravagance led to the construction of a series of opulent, yet unimaginative structures. The mimesis of well-worn tastes of grandeur, according to this strategy, would convince skeptical foreigners of the existence of a mature and powerful American nation.[2] In such divergent corners of the globe as Spain and Chile, Mexico and Germany, the United States either acquired or constructed an array of palaces. When purchasing a palace, the government would often highlight the fact that these new acquisitions had housed the potentates of present or defunct regimes.[3]

The newly-constructed palatial embassies were built in accordance with prevailing regional imperial styles. The role model was architect Frank Packard's embassy building in Rio De Janeiro (1923) which was designed in the "Portuguese Colonial style" (Figure 1). One year after the Brazilian project the United States erected a new palatial legation in Mexico City. This edifice was the work of an American architect, J.E. Campbell, who had twenty-five years of practice in Mexico City and was considered an expert on the "Mexican Beaux Arts" This school of architecture espoused the use of neo-classical design together with Hispanic ornamentation, a conciliatory marriage between two cardinal contributors to the contemporary Mexican heritage.[4]

The palatial approach to the diplomatic outposts of the early 1920s aroused much criticism at home. Opponents lashed out at the pretensions embodied in the philosophy of opulent political architecture. "I am simple-minded enough to think that a good case, simply stated, cutting out the fog and mystery of diplomacy and the elegance of surroundings, is more likely to be carried out to a successful conclusion," observed Martin B. Madden, chairman of the powerful House Appropriations Committee. Like other luxuries, grand governmental architecture appeared superfluous, if not pernicious, for it served no real need. Ornamental structures, usually the products of a

---

[2] On the obsession with the architectural opulence of both great and second-rate powers see: U.S. House of Representatives. 64th Congress, *Report No. 1332 Purchase of Embassy, Legation and Consular Buildings* (Washington, D.C., 1917), pp. 4-7.

[3] See various reports in the *New York Times* on the acquisition of palaces for American diplomatic posts: 22 March 1922: 16; 8 March 1923: 9; 1 January 1926: 11; 28 May 1926: 21; 16 July 1926: 4.

[4] "New Embassy Building at Mexico City," *American Foreign Service Journal* 2 (1925): 336-337; "United States Embassy at Mexico City," *Bulletin of the Pan American Union* 59 (December 1925): 1247-1249.

Figure 1
Palatial Embassy in Rio de Janeiro, Brazil, Ca. 1923
Frank Packard, architect
(Courtesy, U. S. National Archives)

decadent leisure class, had no place in a society which placed dynamic individualism and egalitarianism at a premium. These palaces also had obvious divisive social connotations. Old world aristocracies had been their patrons, and to cultivate their tastes implied an acceptance of foreign class divisions. Moreover, rich architecture, like other luxuries, was the product of aging societies; it foreboded imminent decay. Indeed, the traumatic events of the Great War suggested that extravagant opulence preceded national decline. Luxuriant edifices aroused associations of corruption, tyranny and dissolution, not greatness, democracy, and progress.

An alternative strategy, the transfer of commissions for the design of embassies from ambitious private architects to the pedestrian office of the Supervising Architect of the Treasury Department, proved equally displeasing. The repertoire of the Treasury Department was limited to the run-of-the-mill federal buildings of the period. Thus, when commissioned to construct an embassy in Beijing, and lacking any clear guidelines from the State Department, the Treasury architects constructed an embassy compound of four buildings, all built in the style of a typical "Middle West Post Office," which according to the understated criticism of the *New York Times* looked "a bit odd in China"[5] (Figure 2). Lacking guidelines for monumental government architecture abroad, the architects of the Treasury fell back on the only type of physical building they knew how to do.

Indeed, the buildings in the Chinese embassy compound bore a striking resemblance to the new post office headquarters in Newport, Kentucky, it too the work of the Supervising Architect of the Treasury (Figure 3). Like the Newport post office, the Chinese representation of the American way had an inordinately high ceiling and cavernous wasted space on the ground floor. "Oppressively low" ceilings on the second level forced much of the embassy's functions into crowded quarters which were more suitable for the sorting of mail than the provision of regular office space. The ordinary post office as embassy was, indeed, a stark reminder of the absence of clear expectations in American foreign policy in the immediate postwar years. Precise aims and intentions had yet to be articulated beyond the urge to cut an impressive figure.

The Foreign Service Building Commission (FSBC)

Greater clarification of ambitions and objectives abroad appeared by the mid-1920s. If official attitudes towards embassy buildings are to be seen as a reflection of policy, then 1926, the year in which the Foreign Service Building Commission (FSBC) was established, represented a turning point. The FSBC consisted of the secretaries of State, Treasury, and Commerce, and ranking members of the Foreign Relations Committees of Congress. Their task was to select sites, decide on priorities, and devise an architectural policy for diplomatic edifices.[6] Stephen G. Porter, a Democrat from Pennsylvania and chairman of the House Committee on Foreign Affairs was the most

---

[5] "Uncle Sam's Homeless Diplomats," *New York Times Magazine* 10 February 1924: 4.
[6] *New York Times* 18 February 1926: 27; 8 May 1926: 6.

Figure 2
Post Office Style Embassy, Beijing, China, Ca. 1920
Supervising Architect of the Treasury Department
(Courtesy, U.S. National Archives)

Figure 3
U.S. Post Office, Newport, Kentucky, 1898
Supervising Architect of the Treasury Department

active committee member. He handled much of the committee's routine work and
devised its philosophical framework. Porter achieved bi-partisan support for his plans
by cooperating with J. Charles Linthicum, the Republican representative from nearby
Maryland. Both congressmen were active advocates of increased government involvement in world affairs. Almost by default Porter and Linthicum were given free
rein in deciding where and how to build American legations. Within the scope of four
years they criss-crossed the globe, presenting both Congress and the executive branch
with well-defined plans which were routinely approved well into the early Roosevelt
years.

Foremost among the tasks undertaken by the FSBC was the rationalisation of
haphazard architectural procedures for America's diplomatic edifices. A "standardisation of appearances" was intended to deflect criticism from palatial embassies and
remove the stigma of aristocratic airs. Standardised procedures were the epitome of
a "democratic doctrine"; they restricted extravagance and produced a dignified, sober,
and creditable image of the nation.[7] Standardisation also served a didactic purpose. A
modular political architecture with simple, decipherable motifs and recognisable
symbols hammered home a clear, unambiguous political message.[8] "A uniform style
... of legation buildings in all capitals," a seasoned diplomat observed, "would be
distinctive of our country and at once recognized."[9]

Guided by these thoughts on repetition and simplicity, the Commission never considered the ponderous classicism of federal architecture in the United States. Instead
they sought the implementation of a simple, yet uniquely American style. The commission's choice was quite predictable; the FSBC opted for a historical style as an
American embassy prototype. The identification of a robust nation with historic roots
was very much in accordance with international conventions. Greatness in the international arena was evoked through the use of retrospective architecture. Historical
continuity—the transferal of an imperious style from a nation's golden age to the
present—implied endurance, stability, and strength, all the qualities in demand during
an age of confusing social change and volatile international relations.

The commission's first attempt to articulate a historical diplomatic style called for
the planting of "little White Houses all around the world."[10] On a purely practical
level, the White House was an ideal model for a functional embassy. This multi-pur-
pose structure included an office wing, living quarters and a ceremonial section, too.
Its architecture was considered "a splendid example of that colonial type which is

---

[7] *American Embassies, Legations, and Consulates Mean Better Foreign Business* (New York,
American Embassy Association, 1910), p. 7.

[8] See the introduction to Helmut Lehman-Haupt, *Art Under a Dictatorship; Using Architecture as
a Triumphant Symbol of Conquest* (New York: Doubleday, 1973) for an interesting discussion of the
use of political architecture in the twentieth century.

[9] RG 59, Decimal File 124.01: Letter from Horace G. Knowles, Minister to La Paz, Bolivia, to
the Secretary of State (15 September 1911).

[10] *New York Times Magazine*, 10 February 1924: 15. The article attributes the idea of White
House embassies to Senator Robert La Follette. This is a mistake, as all other material suggests that the
idea was presented by Senator Porter. See for example "White House For Tokio," *American Architect*,
118 (1920): 484.

distinctively American."[11] The White House was simple, easily copied, and uniquely American.

Aside from the very pertinent nationalistic overtones inherent in this outstanding example of early American architecture, the White House plan for foreign legations addressed anxieties about the apparent affinities between luxury and decadence, opulence and corruption, which had been raised during the era of palatial embassy procurement, prior to the establishment of the FSBC. The neo-classical design of the White House had monumental yet terse proportions; it avoided the visual richness and elaborate ornamentation that supposedly characterised the monumental structures of decadent societies. At the same time, the neo-classicism of the White House was not bound too rigidly to a levelling, indiscriminate democratic ideology. Indeed, its first great occupants had been patricians, even slaveholders.

And yet, despite initially enthusiastic support for the White House as embassy, the FSBC abruptly shelved, in fact, abandoned plans for White House embassies as symbols of American political virtues. Nothing in the surviving records indicates why the executive mansion lost favour. One can only speculate that perhaps the committee's most dominant figures—Congressmen Porter and Linthicum—became wary of the political implications involved in adopting an archetype which hailed the virtues of the rival executive branch of government.

Still, applying the same philosophical reasoning of seeking a historical, uniquely American style, the Commission remained loyal to its quest for a uniform, historical, and uniquely American embassy prototype. Instead of the White House the FSBC chose the Southern plantation mansion.[12]

The Plantation House as Embassy

The adaptation of the plantation house made a certain amount of sense because, practically speaking, the commission sought first and foremost a residential structure; the need for office space was of secondary concern. Politically, one could argue in favour of the plantation house because the essence of America's unique brand of democracy had been formulated by country gentlemen from the South. Nevertheless, the choice of a Southern model rather than a New England manor or a far western domicile requires an explanation. Southern architecture also represented the spirit of secession and conjured up memories of internal divisions which had brought the nation to the brink of self-destruction.

The surviving FSBC minutes are somewhat laconic, and do not elaborate on the arguments in favour of the plantation manor. But upon examining the prevailing myths of contemporary American society, the attractiveness of the plantation house appears quite compelling. To begin with, a Southern representation of the American spirit seemed all the more appealing given the fact that in foreign lands the stereotypical

---

[11] *Ibid.*
[12] "Our Buildings in Foreign Countries," *American Foreign Service Journal* 8 (1931): 51-53.

assessment of Americans was often that of the predatory Yankee, or the violent, irresponsible, cowboy. One of the few positive stereotypes of American history in the early twentieth century was the resurrected Southern gentleman.

The new century witnessed a massive sentimentalisation of the Old South; modern mainstream American society selectively remembered plantation society as the epitome of a noble way of life, not a vile setting for human exploitation. The sentimentalisation of the plantation milieu, according to historian William Taylor, was an expression of widespread reservations concerning the restless mobility and aggressive materialism of contemporary society. Modern Americans developed pronounced longings for the antithesis of their self image. "They longed for a class of men immune to acquisitiveness, indifferent to social ambition, and hostile to commercial life, cities, and secular progress."[13] Alarmed by the impact of immigrants on American life, and disturbed by new and seemingly "foreign" aspects of modern America, the country's wielders of power embarked on a nostalgic journey to a golden age, the main port of which was the mythic, innocent South of the ante-bellum years. After all, the essence of American democracy had emerged from the soil of this region.

From the very beginning of the new century, American culture showed numerous signs of being enraptured with a sentimental version of the South. In literature this tendency was eloquently expressed in the works of Thomas Dixon. In his best-selling novels *The Leopard's Spots* (1902) and *The Clansman* (1905) the Southern domicile symbolised fundamental values of the American way which had supposedly originated in the South: order, permanence, and a stability derived from close contact with the soil.

Dixon was followed in the waning years of the twenties by a cast of "Agrarian" writers, who discovered redeeming qualities for the entire nation in the innocent and noble agrarian South. The epitome of a healthy American society, according to this school of literature, lay in the deep South with its "fair balance of aristocratic and democratic elements." Donald Davidson, literary critic and articulate spokesman of the Agrarian movement in literature, stated that nowhere were the redeeming qualities of Southerners more evident than in their architecture which "was in excellent harmony with their milieu." The old plantation houses, "with their pillared porches, their simplicity of design, their sheltered groves, their walks bordered with boxwood shrubs," spelt order, grace, and unity and counterpoised contemporary complexity, philistinism, and fragmentation.[14] This love affair with the plantation house was by no means restricted to literary circles. During this same period, suave New York moguls were building summer houses in the style of Southern plantations, and employing for these purposes America's premier architects.

---

[13] William Taylor, *Cavalier and Yankee; The Old South and American National Character* (New York: Doubleday, 1957), pp. 201, 334, 341.

[14] Davidson as cited in F. Garvin Davenport, *The Myth of Southern History; Historical Consciousness in Twentieth-Century Southern Literature* (Nashville: Vanderbilt University Press, 1967), p. 61.

The Political Significance of the Plantation Embassy

By 1928, the FSBC had approved the construction of ten new legations. Three projects were designated for Japan, Canada, and France; in these three countries the Commission chose not to build plantation embassies. Plantation manors were planned for all of the other sites. Four buildings were slated for Latin America: Lima, Peru; Managua, Nicaragua; Matanzas, Cuba; Panama City, Panama. The remaining three buildings were planned for Aden, China, and India. Considering the locations that were targeted for immediate construction, the plantation house broadcast a distinctly imperial tone. The plantation house was always domineering and often architecturally incongruous in these foreign surroundings.

The ostensible reason for focusing on Central America and the "Orient" was that in these parts of the world "health conditions were bad and European amenities non existent."[15] Yet this explanation appears spurious; it disguised intentions more than it explained. Irrespective of the differences in weather and sanitary conditions at the Asian and Latin American sites, they were all stigmatised as wilderness areas with vaguely tropical climates, for which plantation architecture was both politically and environmentally appropriate. Using oppressive weather as a metaphor rather than an objective assessment of prevailing climatic conditions, the State Department in effect divided the world into two blocs. In the empires and "civilised" countries of the world the United States did not use the Southern-colonial style; in the "uncivilised" corners of the globe a stereotypical tropical climate was invented in order to rationalise condescending representations of the American body politic. Regardless of climatic, topographical, and cultural differences, the American government planned for diplomatic replicas of the Old South in Asia and in the capital cities of central and south American client states.[16]

Inadvertently or otherwise, the plantation architecture was a revealing reflection of American objectives in Latin America. The region often appeared to be an extension of the American South in the sense that its economic structure was dominated by an American planter class. As for the unexploited regions of Asia, these were part of America's new frontier designs; they figured prominently in the economic and cultural expansionism of the period.

Lima, Peru, the Chinese cities of Amoy and Mukden, Managua, Nicaragua, and Aden, the gateway to the Persian gulf, were considered the most urgent sites for variations of the plantation embassy, although by the early 1930s only the Amoy building was actually completed (Figure 4). Here, on the banks of a river, a "Georgia colonial" mansion did little to dispel the notion that the United States was less concerned with the freedom of the Chinese than with the freedom to exploit the great China market.

---

[15] *New York Times* 23 May 1927: 10.

[16] Foreign Service Buildings Commission, *Report of the Progress on the Purchase of Sites and Construction of Buildings For the Foreign Service of the United States* (Washington, D.C.: Government Printing Office 1929), p. 19.

Figure 4
American Consulate, Amoy, China, 1931
Elliot Hazzard, architect
(Courtesy, *Foreign Service Journal*)

Due to the Great Depression, the construction of other plantation sites was never completed. Such grandiose plans as the construction of a plantation-legation in Managua remained at the stage of a plaster model (Figure 5). Nevertheless, their architectural sketches and plans reveal much about their salient qualities as political artifacts, as well as the speciousness of the argument for the climatic appropriateness of these structures. The sketch of the Lima embassy, for example, was, according to State Department officials, a faithful variation of Mississippi plantation architecture (Figure 6). However, the cool, arid, perpetually cloudy weather in Lima had nothing in common with the climatic conditions of the American South.

The selective implementation of these southern-colonial prototypes illustrated the manner in which the State Department had sorted the world into two distinct diplomatic territories: countries where the United States merely intended to show the flag in a dignified fashion; and unexploited regions of the world in which the United States had economic and/or territorial designs.

In those countries where the United States limited its objectives to a dignified display of the flag, the State Department continued its policy of either purchasing or building palaces. The plantation embassy, by contrast, never displayed such sensitivity. The use of Southern-colonial architecture in other parts of the world suggests that rather than being approached as individual countries, the New World was considered virgin territory of insignificant cultural and political divisions upon which enterprising Americans could still make their mark without fear of arousing the wrath of any meaningful political entity.

The Demise of the Plantation Embassy

By the 1930s, the embassy as plantation house appeared to be losing favour. Once again, the changing mood and growing disillusionment with the plantation manor as symbol of the national self was registered quite vividly in the literature of the times. Margaret Mitchell's epic saga of the South, *Gone With The Wind* (1936), ended dramatically with Scarlett O'Hara gazing at the charred ruins of Tara. The novels of William Faulkner, for instance *The Sound and the Fury* (1929) and *Sanctuary* (1931), were scattered with descriptions of rotting, almost fetid Southern mansions.

The cheerless representation of the plantation house in literature coincided with the disenchantment with Southern virtues in political circles. If the South represented anything, according to the new President, Franklin D. Roosevelt, it was the epitome of the infirmities of the nation. The South was the most economically backward and socially reactionary section of the country. There was, according to the newly elected President, a Southern problem plaguing the United States.[17]

The plantation house as embassy lost favour for more practical reasons, too. Dissenting voices claimed that these and other attempts at self-aggrandisement were

---

[17] Roosevelt quoted in Davenport, p. 92.

Figure 5
Model for American Legation, Managua, Nicaragua, 1927
Aldrich and Chase, architects

Figure 6
Artist's Impression of American Embassy, Lima, Peru, 1931
Architect, unknown
(Courtesy, *Foreign Service Journal*)

counter-productive. America's international relations were being jeopardised by the country's "attitude of the superior helping the inferior," warned James McDonald, the executive director of the Foreign Policy Association. "As long as Americans continue to boast that they are different from and better than other nations," he added, "they are sowing the seed of much ill feeling among other nations."[18]

With the changing of the presidential guard in the early 1930s, and within the context of a new socio-economic age, plans for a series of "little White Houses" replaced the plantation manor as prototype for new embassies. Despite the specter of global conflict and economic turmoil, three little White Houses were constructed in Yokohama, Japan (1932) (Figure 7), Baghdad (1932), and Chungking (1942). The economic and political events of the 1930s and 1940s halted any further proliferation of embassies, many of which were planned to be White Houses.

The Significance of the Embassy Construction Programme of the 1920s

The embassy construction programme reveals certain important aspects of American foreign policy in the post World War I period. To begin with, these activities took place during the reign of Republican presidents often remembered for their inactivity, and incorrectly categorised as presidents who were disinclined to think about their country as an international player. Presidents Harding, Coolidge, and Hoover laid the foundations for using architecture as a tool of foreign policy. In the years following the Second World War, the federal government would initiate an unprecedented expansion of its political architecture abroad, the fundamental rationale of which was derived from the experiences of the 1920s.

Building on the precedent of plantation embassies, but employing a different style, embassy architecture in the 1950s and 1960s would be used as a tool for both defining and controlling a uniquely defined Pax Americana. The elements of this process had been elaborated during the 1920s. The necessary infrastructure of a political advisory board and a supervising bureaucracy were already firmly in place in the 1920s and formed the basis for expanding the role of the State Department some thirty years later. The unassuming Republican administrations of the 1920s had quietly developed an important diplomatic mechanism for years to come.

The embassy construction programme furnishes, as well, a fascinating reflection of internal cultural trends within the United States on the making of the country's foreign policy. The iconography chosen to represent the United States abroad, was the continuation of a domestic cultural discourse on federalism and sectionalism, the nature of American culture, and the contribution of the South to the cultural framework of early twentieth century America. Under the facade of a single-minded pursuit of pure foreign policy objectives lay a continuously shifting battle between competing cultural interests in the United States between North and South, between nostalgic isolationism

---

[18] *New York Times* 23 May 1929: 24.

Figure 7
White House Style Consulate, Yokohama, Japan, 1932
Jay Morgan, architect
(Courtesy, Foreign Service Journal)

and aggressive *Realpolitik*. Inner tensions between change and continuity, regionalism and federalism, accounted for much of the country's diplomatic symbolism during the years separating the two world wars.

AFTER THE COLD WAR
REGION, NATION AND WORLD IN AMERICAN STUDIES

A. Kaenel, University of Nancy II

In the late 1940s, when it emerged as a full-fledged movement within American higher education and was simultaneously exported to Europe, American Studies rested on a three-tiered model of the relations between region, nation and world. This model has persisted, although among the three levels the nation has remained the unquestioned priority (the discipline is after all called American Studies). Both within and without American Studies, however, the relations between region, nation, and world, let alone the meaning of these terms, and, above all, the role of the nation as an imagined political community, in Benedict Anderson's apt phrase, have undergone profound changes. Americanists, in the United States in particular, have been engaged since the 1960s in important questionings of the putative coherence and singularity of their discipline's object, the national culture of the United States. There has also been much talk of late, within the American Studies Association, of the need to acknowledge more fully the international dimension of the discipline. Not surprisingly, given the (discursive) proximity of international Americanists to their American colleagues, the various terms of the debate have for long percolated abroad but the time is ripe, with the end of the Cold War geopolitical order, for international practitioners of American Studies to engage directly the question of the place of America (and hence of the discipline that professes America) in the fast evolving world of the 1990s.

In the early years of the Cold War, when it started being exported, American Studies had an openly double mission, at once *nationtial* (the study by Americans of their culture, history, political tradition, etc.) and *international* (the study of America abroad). American civilization, as it was then called, was offered to elites in the United States and in Europe as a channel for the propagation of the liberal democratic values of the would-be leading nation of the "free world." In the words of Linda Kerber's Presidential address at the 1988 ASA Convention, "a cold war agenda ... underlay much of the American Civilization curriculum [in the 1950s], and it involved the strident validation of American exceptionalism" (419). In its exported variant, American Studies was implicitly aligned, ideologically speaking, with such rescue operations as the Marshall Plan or the Berlin Airlift.

The double nationalist and internationalist agenda which informed the rapid academic dissemination of the discipline at home and abroad was stressed by the movement's forefathers themselves. In the first part of this essay, I shall focus on one such acknowledgment, an important programmatic book by Tremaine McDowell simply entitled *American Studies* (1948), and in particular on his discussion of the links between region, nation and world (the book's final chapter is called "Region, Nation,

World"). I shall then turn to the redefinitions of these links in the context of the post-Cold War geopolitical remappings and examine the possible consequences of those recent changes on the theory and practice of American Studies in Europe. To adapt the title of a Raymond Carver story, "What do European Americanists today talk about when they talk about 'America'?"

McDowell's primary aim is pragmatic. He wants to offer practical recommendations for the establishment of interdisciplinary American Studies programmes and courses in American higher education. American Studies, as he and his fellow founders (e.g. Robert Spiller, Henry Nash Smith) understand it then, is a movement rather than a discipline. It is an academic experiment whose aim is to provide a meeting ground for various disciplines within the humanities (above all history and literature, but also art, philosophy or sociology) dealing with American subjects but most often separated by academic cloisterings. To be sure, a handful of American Studies programmes had existed in the United States since the 1930s but the aim of McDowell and others is far more ambitious: to participate in the "contemporary movement in education [which] is a trend away from extreme academic specialization toward a synthesis of knowl-edge" (v). This trend, McDowell adds, was accelerated by "the actualities of World War II" and the "equally bitter actualities of the postwar years" (24). Creating a new discipline for a new (American) age is also an unequivocally civic imperative: "no other curriculum offers fuller opportunity for balancing education in facts with edu-cation in values" (28). (McDowell names the values of "individualism," "democracy" and "the pursuit of happiness)."

In his final chapter entitled "Region, Nation, World," McDowell returns to the important civic function of American Studies as he recapitulates the imbrications of the three levels:

> McDowell's educational model, open, integrated and integrative, simultaneously aims at con-ceptualizing the political and cultural relations between the nation and its regions on the one hand, and between the nation and the world on the other. A system of checks and balances, which McDowell's sentence itself underlines ("on the one hand... on the other"), is mobilized in the service of American Studies' main object, "the study of national culture." McDowell's ambitious educational plan, his triple "reconciliation" in and through American Studies of the region, the nation and the world, is accompanied by a parallel call for reconciliation in the spheres of politics and culture, hence his avoidance of the potentially divisive issues of class, "caste" and race. In his words, such a recon-ciliation appears all the more urgent in "this epoch of uncertainty." (82)

McDowell's educational model, open, integrated and integrative, simultaneously aims at conceptualising the political and cultural relations between the nation and its regions on the one hand, and between the nation and the world on the other. A system of checks and balances, which McDowell's sentence itself underlines ("on the one hand ... on the other"), is mobilised in the service of American Studies' main object, "the study of national culture." McDowell's ambitious educational plan, his triple "reconciliation" in and through American Studies of the region, the nation and the world, is accompanied by a parallel call for reconciliation in the spheres of politics and culture, hence his avoidance of the potentially divisive issues of class, "caste" and race. In his words, such a reconciliation appears all the more urgent in "this epoch of uncertainty."

Pursuing the idea of reconciliation, McDowell proceeds to laud regionalism. Unlike "sectionalism," which is "based on the assumption that each area is or may become a unity within itself, the concept of regionalism is based on the belief that unity exists only in the nation of which the regions are subareas" (84). Regionalism is thus today "an inclusive movement" that necessarily moves beyond itself to address broader (and higher) levels of meaning, be they national or international. Regional art, he writes, is not "merely local. It employs unmistakably regional language to express the universal—otherwise it is not art" (85). The region represents a valuable political and cultural entity because it bridges the "tangible loyalty" to a local community and the "elusive" loyalty to a "vast continental nation": "Out of regional loyalties ... Americans can and frequently do build national patriotism" (86). The region's importance thus lies in its capacity to foster and nurture valuable attachments to the nation.

McDowell's rejection of sectionalism in favour of the more inclusive regionalism is paralleled by his rejection of nationalism in favour of what he calls "cultural nationality." "Cultural nationality" is the animating principle of the nation understood as an imagined community, a community cemented by two essential features, a common language and a common culture. Four other features may intervene, McDowell adds: territorial, political, racial and religious unity, all of them indispensable for nationalism but not for nationality (to illustrate the crucial difference between nationality and nationalism, he cites in passing the Germans and the Japanese who "have prostituted their cultural nationality to promote the aims of inflamed nationalism" [87]. Remember: this is 1948). In the United States, McDowell goes on, nationality and nationalism have often been at odds. American history itself teaches us that "nationality becomes dangerous when it is the tool of diseased nationalism and that the latter becomes diseased when economic or political pressures are too powerful" (89, his examples of clear nationalistic ventures are the War with Mexico and the Spanish American War). That is why one of the "functions" of American Studies in the interdependent post-World War II world is "to guide students in American courses to a repudiation of political and economic nationalism and to an acceptance of cultural nationality" (90).

Cultural nationality provides the glue that binds together the region, the nation and the world. This bond rests on a logic that fuses national politics and culture into a utopian vision of new possibilities for a new world order, as evidenced in the following incantatory passage, which I quote in full:

> Continuing with this assessment of our strengths and our weaknesses, any student of American culture will admit that our sectionalism may have been and perhaps still is stronger than our regionalism, and likewise that our politico-economicnationalism may still be stronger than cultural nationality. But we all know that the American ideal is a family of regions united in one nation and a family of nations united on the planet. Despite all unhappy discrepancies between aspiration and accomplishment, America's achieved realities and partly achieved ideals for region, nation, and world offer as sound a precedent for a community of man as has yet emerged anywhere in the world. At two points, then, American Studies can contribute largely to the creation of world order: first, through exploration and exposition of this unique American pattern of region, nation, world and, second,through the education of America for critical self-knowledge.Since a federation of the world can be formed neither out of zeros nor out of intransigent sovereign states, an enlightened American nationality is one of the

essentials to an effective league of mankind. Self-knowledge is therefore aprerequisite to citizenship
both in the United States and in a world community (93).

McDowell's fascinating global imaginary here maps out "region," "nation," and
"world" in relation to one another *within and through* American Studies. By collapsing
the regional and the international onto the national, the region thus becomes a sub-
category (a "subarea," as McDowell puts it) of the nation and the nation itself a
stepladder for international projection. In brief, while the nation should operate as a
relay or bridge between the region and the world, it actually relegates the region to a
secondary status at one end and envisions the world as a terrain for national expansion
and regulation at the other. The discipline itself gets construed in the same breath as
the repository of valuable cultural and political principles ("the American ideal") *and*
as an instrument or channel for their planetary projection (the contribution of American
Studies to "world order"). But the nation remains the unquestioned core of a discipline
called *American*, not "regional" or "world," studies. America's international ascend-
ancy begins at home, McDowell affirms, and American Studies must play an instrumental role in telling the nation's story to the world.

What American Studies recommends, beyond its immediate educational and
academic concerns, is a rededication and strengthening of the nation and its values via
the coordinated study of America envisaged a totality sui generis. At a time of manifest
sectionalism on a world scale (what came to be known as "the Cold War"),
McDowell's inclusive, synthetically Whitmanian programme is offered as a precious
instrument for the repair of a national and international space damaged by factionalism
and War. It is therefore no coincidence if the poet of Leaves of Grass, a "persistent
reconciler of opposites" in McDowell's words, is consistently invoked in his book as
a seminal example for articulating the conciliatory, inclusive mission of the new
discipline. Whitman operates in his text as an authoritative guide for grounding American Studies as an educational project and as a civic mission.[1]

There is even a sense in which the reconciliatory hopes invested in American
Studies served, in the nascent Cold War order, a function comparable to that of
Whitman's poetry in the antebellum years: that of containing, that is of warding off
through an act of incorporation, threats to the national security in an "epoch of
uncertainty." To rephrase the close ideological fit between American Studies and the
Cold War: the cultural politics deployed by American Studies in the late 1940s were
analogous, despite obvious differences in scope and implementation, to the "policy of
containment" of the Soviet Union which became the official Cold War policy of the
U.S. as of 1947.[2]

---

[1] The Whitman connection is explored further in my "Les Études américaines, Whitman et le
nationalisme américain."

[2] This analogy needs further thought but a possible place to start might be the "Epilogue" of R.W.B.
Lewis's *The American Adam* (1955), in particular its jeremiad about American belatedness: "Ours is an
age of containment; we huddle together and shore up our defenses; both our literature and our public
conduct suggest that exposure to experience is certain to be fatal.... Instead of looking forward to new
possibilities, we direct our tired attention to the burden of history, observing, repeatedly, that it is later than

Tremaine McDowell's *American Studies* is a key text for understanding the formation of an American Studies discourse with far-reaching national and international implications, a discourse of which American and international Americanists today are, willy- nilly, the heirs.[3] It also places the new discipline firmly (though sometimes obliquely) in the context of the emerging Cold War bipolarity. (Its defense of the region as the locus for developing "national loyalty," for example, echoes the security checks introduced in 1947 by the Truman administration's "Loyalty Review Board" to keep subversives away from governmental posts.) The reigning paradigm of American Studies from the late 1940s, in other words, was characterised on the one hand by an organic linkage between region, nation and world, with the nation as the dominating principle *and*, on the other, by the discipline's tacit mission of countering and containing Communism at home and abroad via the democratic principles lodged within the texts of American culture.

In making these broad claims I am not proposing a deterministic or mechanistic interpretation of international American Studies as an instrument of American foreign policy or as a tool of American cultural diplomacy (though there were of course, and continue to exist, important convergences between American Studies and American cultural diplomacy).[4] I am not ignoring either the radical critiques of America that have been part of the discipline itself. Nor am I denying the liberatory and even subversive role that studying America played for some European scholars after World War II.[5] American Civilisation presented early Americanists with a body of texts and strategies for reconstructing or, as the case might be, for opposing national identity formation in Europe. In many instances, choosing to profess things American was an act of daring, contestation, or resistance (it could even become a form of resistance to America itself). In any event, for either teachers or students, an involvement in American Studies never implied pledging allegiance to the American flag or signing loyalty oaths. But it did, and I shall argue, still by and large does mean operating within the parameters of the discipline, that is within a discourse that defines and validates specifically *national* forms of scholarly attention.

For if the so-called "consensus" scholars of the forties and fifties implicitly subscribed to a "cold war agenda" that "involved the strident validation of American exceptionalism" (Kerber), recent adepts of the "dissensus" approach to American cultural studies have been taken to task for what their critics view as an endorsement of "America." In her introduction to a recent collection of essays she coedited with Donald Pease, *Cultures of United States Imperialism*, Amy Kaplan takes exception to the "new pluralistic model of diversity" which, she fears, runs the risk of reproducing a compromised model of national and cultural unity and thereby "revoic[ing] the

---

[3] Clearly, Tremaine McDowell did not single-handedly fashion American Studies into existence. I have chosen to focus on his book because it is the most useful for understanding the cultural politics of the discipline at a crucial moment in its history and in the history of the American nation.

[4] See for example the essays by Richard T. Arndt and Richard P. Horwitz in Horwitz, ed., *Exporting America*, and Michael Vlahos's "Culture and Foreign Policy."

[5] For a sample, see the articles collected in the special issue of the *Journal of American History* on the internationalisation of American history.

rhetoric of cold war exceptionalism." "By defining American culture as determined precisely by its diversity and multivocality," Kaplan goes on, "'America' as a discrete entity can cohere independently of international confrontations with other national, local and global cultural identities within and outside its borders. The critical force of multiculturalism thus may lay itself open to recuperation by a renewed version of 'consensus' (15)."[6]

Kaplan's critique of the cooptative power of American Studies, of the discipline's silencing of its imperial(ist) underpinnings, a critique aimed principally at the Americanist establishment in the United States, should resonate equally with international Americanists, albeit with different institutional and intellectual accents.[7] Their "America," because it is a projection, the construct of a necessarily bifocal vision, has been less liable to cohere as a discrete national entity, although their institutional, linguistic or cultural distance from "America" has rarely been addressed or theorised.[8] Kaplan is right, in any case, to insist on the problematic coherence of "America," a coherence which McDowell seeks to reinforce (no quotation marks around "America" for him) but which today is shrouded in suspicion.

America coheres in difference, McDowell insists. It is a blend of the many cultures of Europe, all of them "contributors to that fresh and new yet not always fortunate synthesis of civilisations which is American civilisation (92)." America, in short, resembles a Whitmanian "nation of nationalities unified by the new American culture" (91). "But while that culture was taking shape," McDowell adds, "the world has shrunk beyond our comprehension. The countries from which our ancestors voyaged by sail and by steam have moved westward across the Atlantic. Today England rises in the fog just off the coast of Maine; France lies not far beyond the tip of Long Island; Spain replaces Cuba off the Florida shore; behind them all looms Russia" (91). The fate of the synthetic, unified culture melted in America's pot is in jeopardy. This culture of immigrants, of many nationalities, is today, in the late 1940s, confronting a world whose legibility is uncertain: new means of travel have brought the rest of the world closer to America but they have also brought a looming Russia closer as well. This is the precise geopolitics of the Cold War that informs McDowell's book: the world has become a smaller, more menacing place for the "new American culture."

---

[6] See also the two special issues of *boundary 2* on "New Americanists" edited by Donald Pease and by Paul Bové. The first "New Americanists" collection contains a critique of Sacvan Bercovitch's politics of dissent (see esp. pp. 19-29) which is further developed in Bové.

[7] One quibble, though: by focusing her critique on its *American* practitioners, notably Perry Miller, Kaplan herself allows *American Studies* a modicum of national coherence. Her American Studies is a specifically American field with a specific American genealogy. Thus Perry Miller's epiphanic vision of America, his realisation of his Americanist calling while working on an oil tanker in the Congo in the 1930s (later recounted in the Preface to his *Errand into the Wilderness*), which Kaplan rightly identifies as a key moment in the formation of American Studies, remains a fully American affair. Once returned to America with Miller, American Studies, in Kaplan's scenario, gets domesticated and nationalised.

[8] On the European historian's "double loyalties" see Vaudagna.

Today, in the 1990s, Russia (let alone the Soviet Union) is no longer menacing, it no longer "looms." Yet the end of the Cold War, the dismantling of the Soviet empire and the sudden termination of nearly fifty years of large-scale bipolar confrontations have ushered in another "epoch of uncertainty" for the United States (as well as for Europe and other parts of the world). With the patent fiasco of the Gorbachev/Bush vision of a "new world order," U.S. uncertainty about its role in world affairs has extended to all levels of international relations (strategic, military, political, diplomatic, ideological). Lacking an identifiable enemy, deprived of recognisable moorings, the United States is currently undergoing a major crisis on a national and global scale.

What happens to a nation historically identified as an emblem of multiplicity and difference (*e pluribus unum*) in a world that blurs the profiles of national cultures? By what means can such a nation cohere in a post-Cold War, multipolar world? By what means, for that matter, can any nation-state cohere in the increasingly globalised world of the 1990s, a world about which it could be said with McDowell that it has "shrunk beyond our comprehension"? What happens, specifically, to the relations between region, nation and world formalised by American Studies? Such questions unavoidably pose themselves to a discipline which is characterised by a close meshing of subject matter, critical discourse, and ideology, and whose animating principle, the "national culture" or "civilisation" of the United States, appears increasingly porous and moot. As Gertrude Stein might have put it had she asked the question about the American nation today: is there a "there" there?[9]

From two directions, acute pressure is being exercised on the discipline of American Studies: the first is the dwindling economic and cultural relevance of the nation-state; the second is the corresponding erosion of categories such as "national literature," "national history," or "national culture." Exit the national, enter the transnational, the global, whether in the guise of units like NAFTA and the European Union or via the reshaping of literary and cultural studies into broader linguistic or geographical ensembles (e.g. "world literature in English," "Hispanic literature," "literature of the Pacific Rim") or via interdisciplinaty and transnational formations like the recent CAAR (Collegium for African American Research).[10]

These regroupings should give Americanists food for thought. American Studies in particular still relies on a model of the links between region, nation and world inherited from the Cold War. In the United States, for example, there are thirteen regional chapters (Rocky Mountain, New England, Pacific Northwest, Mid-Atlantic etc.) federated within one national organisation, the ASA (American Studies Association). In Europe, we have national and joint national associations of American Studies federated within EAAS (European Association of American Studies). Similar

---

[9] For a skeptical view of the question, see Reich and Laïdi. On the other side of the spectrum, Nye and Valladao, among others, have no doubt that the U.S. will not only be there but everywhere in years to come.

[10] The declared aim of CAAR, as stated in its first Newsletter (Spring 1993), is to establish a field of study that is "distinguished by being international, interdisciplinary, inter- racial, comparative, and collegial." One particularly promising feature of CAAR, which distinguishes it from American Studies affiliations abroad, is that CAAR membership is on "an individual basis and not by national bodies."

ensembles exist in other parts of the world. American Studies thus comes in different incarnations, whether regional, national or bi- national, all differently imbricated, with different accents and priorities yet unified by a common object, a fuzzy entity called "America" or "American culture."

But Europe is itself a fuzzy entity (there may not be a "there" here—yet). And its fuzziness impinges directly on the discipline's future prospects. For European Americanists are today faced with a double fuzziness, on the one hand that of a United States seeking a new global ascendency (Bill Clinton's "partnership for peace" notwithstanding) *and*, on the other, with that of a Europe slowly and unevenly fashioning itself into a transnational or supranational union. Insofar as Europe's self- definition as a geopolitical unit depended for over forty years on its being a crucial terrain for the confrontation between East and West, the kinds of disciplinary and institutional questions I am raising become pressing also for European Americanists, by virtue of their double affiliation as Europeans and as Americanists. The larger question can be put as follows: what does it mean to be an Americanist in a Europe whose boundaries are being extended to the East, to that "Other" whose ideological leverage was instrumental in the exportation of American Studies to Europe that began in 1947, the year of the Salzburg Seminar in American Civilisation, but also the year of the Truman Doctrine and the Marshall Plan?

There is no single or right answer to the question. All answers can only be local and tentative, but one certainty emerges: the United States and the rest of the world underwent major changes between 1947 and 1989, and so did American Studies. Unfortunately, the latter, in the United States and abroad, has not fully registered the globalised realities of the 1990s. Among the many disciplines in the humanities, American Studies still hangs on to its national core, even as other disciplines are calling it into question.[11] It has not reached what Paul Bové calls, in a powerful critique of the politics of American criticism, "the point of 'exile' in relation to itself and its nationalist projects" (63). Bové means "exile" mainly as ascesis, as a "demanding discipline of critical self-making" (63). "One must be in exile," Bové writes, "in relation not only to the national but to the regional, local and international effects of culture as well" (62). (To which one could add, bearing in mind Bové's own academic background in critical theory and philosophy, the importance of institutional exile or displacement.[12] This is a tall order but it is one which European Americanists, preciously "exiled" from America, should start pondering as they embark on the necessary task of rethinking their professional anchoring in the transregional, transnational world after the Cold War.

---

[11] This is for instance the case of American history. See Higham.

[12] Indeed, it is telling that some of the most innovative and challenging work within American Studies in the United States should have been produced by the so-called "New Americanists," most of whom are either not Americanists by training (e.g. Jonathan Arac) or by intellectual sensibility (e.g. Donald Pease, who has been molesting American Studies by smuggling in continental theory and philosophy).

WORKS CITED

Bové, Paul, "Notes Toward a Politics of 'American' Criticism." Rprt. In *The Wake of Theory*, Hanover: Wesleyan University Press, 1992.

Higha, Joh, "The Future of American History," *The Journal of American History* (March 1994): 1289-1309.

Horwitz, Richard P., ed., *Exporting America: Essays on American Studies Abroad*, New York: Garland, 1993.

The Journal of American History 79 (September 1992), "Toward the Internation alization of American History: A Roundtable."

Kaenel, André, "Les Études américaines, Whitman et le nationalisme américain," *Idéologies dans le monde anglo-saxon* 6, Grnoble: Université Stendhal, 1993: 45-57.

Kaplan, Amy and Donald E. Pease, eds., *Cultures of United States Imperialism*, Durham: Duke University Press, 1993.

Kerber, Linda K., "Diversity and the Transformation of American Studies," *American Quarterly* 41 (1989): 415-31.

Laïdi, Zaki, ed., *L'Ordre mondial relâché: Sens et puissance aprè la guerre froide*, Paris: Presses de la Fondation nationale des sciences politiques, 1993.

Lewis, R.W.B., *The American Adam: Innocence. Tragedy, and Tradition in the Nine teenth Century*, Chicago: University of Chicago Press, 1955.

McDowell, Tremaine, *American Studies*, Minneapolis: University of Minnesota Press, 1948.

Nye, Joseph S., Jr., *Bound to Lead: The Changing Nature of American Power*, New York: Basic Books, 1991.

Pease, Donald E., ed., "New Americanists: Revisionist Interventions into the Canon," *boundary 2* 17 (Spring 1990).

——, "New Americanists 2: National Identities and Postnational Narratives," *boundary 2* 19 (Spring 1992).

Reich, Robert, *The Work of Nations: Preparing Ourselves for 21st-Century Capitalism*, London: Simon & Schuster, 1991.

Valladao, Alfredo G.A., *Le XXIe siècle sera américain*, Paris: La Découverte, 1993.

Vaudagna, Maurizio, "The American Historian in Continental Europe: An Italian Perspective," *The Journal of American History* 79 (September 1992): 532-42.

Vlahos, Michael, "Culture and Foreign Policy," *Foreign Policy* (Spring 1991): 59-78.

LITERARY PERSPECTIVES

LOADED GUNS: PLACE AND WOMEN'S PLACE IN NINETEENTH-CENTURY NEW ENGLAND

Raymond L. Neinstein, Eötvös Loránd University[*]

> "These external regions, what do we fill
> them with / Except reflections...?"
> Wallace Stevens, "Notes
> Toward a Supreme Fiction"

> "When is it that women began to photo-
> graph men?"
> Don DeLillo, *Mao Two*

In April 1994, the brother and sister-in-law of an American friend of mine came to Budapest to visit him. My friend is in his early fifties, and his brother seemed close to him in age. His wife (they were newly-weds) also appeared to be in her middle years. They live in Wyoming, near a town I'd never heard of, in the north-east corner of the state, near South Dakota. I asked my friend's sister-in-law, Elsie, what she and her husband did in Wyoming. "My husband's a photographer," she said,"and I'm a rancher." "A rancher!" I thought. "What exactly do you do?" I asked. "I breed bulls and cows and raise the calves and sell them off to feed-lots. I also raise, and race, thoroughbred race-horses. And I hunt." I don't think Elsie would have defined herself as a feminist. Rather, she was a modern woman of the American West, with long hair and blue eyes to match her blue jeans, and lots of Indian turquoise jewelry. A few moments later, she pulled out an album of photographs, mostly of her recent wedding to my friend's brother. But the last few photos weren't wedding pictures. "I said I hunted. Here's me and an elk I got. That there's an elk," she said, pointing to a huge animal which looked like it was sleeping peacefully. In the photo, she was squatting down beside it, one hand on its enormous rack of antlers, in her other hand a high-powered rifle with a telescopic sight. I thought of photographs of Ernest Hemingway, grinning beside a "bagged" rhino. But that photo wasn't all. Elsie had snapped the next one, which showed her husband posing, rifle in hand, atop an eagle's nest, wearing nothing but his Stetson hat and cowboy boots. Here was the male hunter as Playboy of the Month, not boasting of his prowess as a killer, but the object of a woman's amused and erotic gaze.

I now thought of the lines LeRoi Jones/Amiri Baraka gives to Clay, the enraged

---

[*] I am grateful to Michael Neff of Philadelphia for his insights into the Narcissus myth.

and doomed middle-class Black man in his play *Dutchman*: "Bird [Charlie Parker] would've played not a note of music if he just walked up to East Sixty-seventh Street and killed the first ten white people he saw."[1] What I thought was, "Emily Dickinson wouldn't have had to write a line of poetry if she could have ranched, raised thoroughbred race horses, hunted for elk with a high-powered rifle with a telescopic sight, and then photographed a man atop an eagle's nest, naked except for a cowboy hat and a pair of cowboy boots."

I also thought once again of Hemingway and the sex role reversals he was imagining in *The Garden of Eden*. I didn't know whether to wish he could have seen those photos, or to be thankful he was over 30 years in his grave, safe from these real-life embodiments of his most secret fears and fantasies.

Two pictures—the woman with the rifle, posing beside the fallen game: Woman as Hunter; and then, Woman as Photographer, taking a photo of a naked man, the photo itself a parody of both the cult of the Hemingway he-man and of that cult's standard photo of the big-game hunter with his gun as phallic substitute. (The camera, like the gun, is, of course, something we also load, point, and shoot.) But as I thought of guns as phallic symbols, I remembered a question a woman I know had once posed: a gun may be a symbol of a penis, but what is a penis the symbol of? That is, what is it that we're *really* talking about when, to paraphrase Raymond Carver, we talk about love, or sex, or symbols? What do phallic symbols really *stand for*?

This paper will be an attempt to show how two women writers of 19th-century New England appropriated traditional male imagery—hunting, guns, the woods, etc.—and especially the hunter's rifle, items familiar to us from classic tales of the American forest like "Rip Van Winkle" or the *Leatherstocking Novels*—how these two women appropriated these symbols and used them for purposes of their own.

I

My Life had stood—a Loaded Gun—
In Corners—till a Day
The Owner passed—identified—
And carried Me away—

And now We roam in Sovereign Woods—
And now We hunt the Doe—
And every time I speak for Him—
The Mountains straight reply—

And do I smile, such cordial light
Upon the Valley glow—
It is as a Vesuvian face
Had let its pleasure through—

---

[1] George McMichael, ed., *Anthology of American Literature*, 4th Edition (New York: Macmillan, 1989) II, 1994. *Dutchman* was originally published in 1964.

And when at Night—Our good Day done—
I guard My Master's Head—
'Tis better than the Eider-Duck's
Deep Pillow—to have shared—

To foe of his—I'm deadly foe—
None stir the second time—
On whom I lay a Yellow Eye—
Or an emphatic thumb—

Though I than He—may longer live
He longer must—than I—
For I have but the power to kill,
Without the power to die—[2]

The final stanza seems paradoxical. The first couplet asserts that "He" (the "Owner" of the "Loaded Gun") *must* live longer than the gun itself, or longer than the speaker of the poem, who is imagining herself *as* the gun. The second couplet then *seems* to say that the gun has only the power to kill without the power to die. A gun, that is, can't die; it can only kill. In that case, how can the "Owner" live longer than the gun?

There is a second grammatically possible reading of the closing couplet which makes more sense logically in terms of what the first couplet says. That is, "Without X, I have only Y," or "if I lacked this, I'd have only that." Think of statements such as "Without love, you have nothing," or "Without the power to buy, you're nobody." If you turn the latter statement around, you have, "You're nobody without the power to buy." When the speaker of Dickinson's poem says, "I have but the power to kill without the power to die," she may be understood as saying, "if I lacked mortality, my power, my gift would simply be deadly."

Of course, the real question is, who am "I" and who is "He," the "Owner"? In whose service, on whose behalf does the "I" of the poem speak, to protect whom from what "foe"? "Foe" is one of the few words in the poem that rhymes fully with another word, and that word is "doe"—"and now We hunt the Doe—": Doe, a female deer.

I and He—He "identified and carried Me away." "I speak for Him," "I guard his Head," "I'm deadly foe" to "foe of his," "He" must live longer than "I." We have gender and we have place—the Woods, the Mountains, the Valley, and the bed (the pillow). We hunt together; "I" speak for "Him"; and "the Mountains straight reply." Literally, this is the echo of the gun. Less literally, the speech of the place is an echo of "my" sound. There is a connection—a relationship of Speech and Echo—between my sound, my speech, my art, and the speech of the place. This is not the relationship Wallace Stevens posits when he says, "A mythology reflects its region."[3] In Dickinson's poem, the place, the region, in echoing the report of the loaded gun, echoes the speech of the poet. Here, in a sense, region reflects mythology.

---

[2] Poem #754, in Thomas H. Johnson, ed., *The Complete Poems of Emily Dickinson* (Boston: Little, Brown, 1960), pp. 369-70.

[3] "A Mythology Reflects Its Region," in Holly Stevens, ed., *The Palm at the End of the Mind: Selected Poems and a Play by Wallace Stevens* (Hamden, Ct.: Archon Books, 1984), p. 398.

Image, echo, and reflection suggest not only mythology, but a particular myth, that of Echo and Narcissus. Let me get to that myth by way of the second couplet of the first stanza of Dickinson's poem: "The Owner passed—identified—/And carried me away." I'd like to linger for a moment on the word "identified." What, exactly, does this word mean? What is "identity"? From a Greek root meaning "the same," our words *identity*, *identical*, and *identify* come. What is *identity*? It is two completely different, completely opposite things. "Let's see proof of your identity"; "Have you got any means of identification?"; "I'm looking for my identity"; "He's having an identity crisis." Here, *identity* means who you specifically are, in contrast to all others. My *Webster's* says, "the distinct personality of an individual regarded as a continuing entity—individuality. The set of personal characteristics by which an individual is recognizable." But *identity* also means the exact opposite of individuality: "the quality or condition of being the same as something else," as in "identical twins" or in the mathematical meaning of the word: complete and absolute equality. This equals that in each and every respect; this is identical to that. So, we use the same word to mean two completely different things, and we use a word that means *both* "same" and "different." Thus, we understand our identity by understanding how we are both the same as and different from others.

Narcissus, falling in love with his reflected image, confused sameness and difference, saw Self and thought it Other. "A mythology reflects its region," according to Stevens. In Dickinson, the region reflects, or echoes, its mythology. Echo loved Narcissus, who mistook Self for Other, same for different. Echo's fate was to pine away (no etymological similarity, alas, between pining away and Sarah Orne Jewett's beloved pine tree) to nothing but a sound, that sound simply a repetition of the last thing said in her presence. Thus an echo is the auditory twin of the reflection in the Narcissus myth, the visual reflection Narcissus loved (instead of the nymph) repeated as sound. We see ourselves; we hear ourselves.

Dickinson's poem of Self and Other, of "My Life" and "The Owner," of "I" and "He," is a monodrama, an examination of oneself *as if* there were two, as if there were an Other. As such, and aware of itself as such, it contains references to reflection and echo, and in the word *identify*, it poses the basic problem of sameness and difference.

II

Sarah Orne Jewett is most often considered in terms of late 19th-century "local colour," that is, as a writer for whom *place*, region (in her case, Maine), was the primary consideration. Lately, in light of feminist studies, she has been re-examined as an early feminist, even as a "lesbian" writer. Here the focus is on gender, not place.

I would like to find a way to look at *both* in Jewett's writing, and I would like to suggest that in Jewett's work, place and gender are used as metaphors for each other. Willa Cather recalls Jewett saying that when an old house and an old woman came together in her brain with a click, she knew that a story was under way.[4] An old house—a place—and an old woman—gender—and the click in the brain, the recognition that the two together form the basis of her particular kind of art, an art that sees both place and gender metaphorically. Place and gender are Jewett's subjects, or *place and gender* is Jewett's subject. And both place and gender are problematised. As a regional writer, Jewett gives us "her place," but at the same time, she withholds it from us, does not really give us anything, on second reading, except an image of our own desire, as Outsiders, to know about her place, a place she protects, conceals, from the destructive, prying, inquisitive gaze of the outsider. Looking in at Jewett's "place," what we see, like what Narcissus saw, is the reflection of ourselves looking. Jewett's clever craft is in convincing us that what we're looking at is the "real thing," the "place itself."

At the same time, Jewett's picture of gender is a complex and problematical one. As perhaps a lesbian writer—we know that after her father's death, the great relationship in her life was a nearly 30-year-long "Boston marriage" with Annie Fields, the widow of the editor-in-chief of *The Atlantic*, James T. Fields—Jewett was aware of the dangers, in fact the impossibility, in the last two decades of the 19th century, of representing clearly the nature of her desire. In a letter to her friend Sarah Whitman, to whom she had sent a copy of her story, "Martha's Lady," Jewett writes:

> You bring something to the reading of a story that the story would go very lame without; but it is those unwritable things that the story holds in its heart, if it has any, that make the true soul of it, and these must be understood, and yet how many a story goes lame for lack of that understanding. In France there is such a code, such recognitions, such richness of allusions, but here we confuse our scaffoldings with our buildings, and—and so![5]

Representations of gender and of sex roles are often confusing and confused in Jewett's work, and we are often led to a consideration of the arbitrariness, indeed the reversability, of sex roles. In Jewett's story "An Autumn Holiday" (1880) we are told about an old senile captain who believed himself, in the afternoons, to be his own sister (who had died a few years earlier). Emily Dickinson writes, "I started Early—Took my Dog—/And visited the Sea." Here the sea is presented as a man, and the encounter between the poem's speaker and that man is decidedly sexual. The language of the poem is so specifically erotic that it hardly needs commentary:

> But no Man moved Me—till the Tide
> Went past my simple Shoe—
> And past my Apron—and my Belt
> And past my Bodice—too—

---

[4] Quoted in Richard Cary, "The Literary Rubrics of Sarah Orne Jewett," in Gwen Nagel, ed., *Critical Essays on Sarah Orne Jewett* (Boston: G.K. Hall, 1984), p. 203. Cather's remark was first published in her introduction to her edition of *The Best Short Stories of Sarah Orne Jewett* (Boston: Houghton Mifflin, 1925), p. xvi.

[5] Quoted in Glenda Hobbs, "Pure and Passionate: Female Friendship in Sarah Orne Jewett's 'Martha's Lady,'" in Gwen Nagel, *op. cit.*, p. 103. The letter was first published in Annie Fields, ed., *Letters of Sarah Orne Jewett* (Boston: Houghton Mifflin, 1911), pp. 112-3.

And made as He would eat me up
...

...
And then—I started—too—

And He—He followed—close behind—
I felt His Silver Heel
Upon my Anklè—Then my Shoes
Would overflow with Pearl

...

...
... bowing—with a Mighty look
At me—the Sea withdrew—[6]

In this poem, place (the sea) and sexuality are each metaphors for a kind of experience, an initiation into experience. In Jewett's story, the unmarried narrator starts early, takes her dog, and goes for a long walk in the hills near the sea. "I am very fond of walking between the roads," she says. "One grows so familiar with the highways."[7] So, she leaves the familiar highway and goes off, cross-country. Where she ends up is the home of an old lady, Miss Polly Marsh, who is also being visited by her sister, Mrs. Snow. Polly Marsh tells the narrator the story of the old senile captain, named, interestingly enough, Captain *Gunn*. Captain Gunn is said to have suffered a bout of sun-stroke, following which he believed himself to be his own sister, Patience. In the mornings, Captain Gunn was "himself." But when he'd awaken from his after-dinner nap, "he was in a dreadful frame o'mind, and had the trousers and coat off in no time, and said he was Patience. ... Folks used to call him Miss Dan'el Gunn" (*Best Short Stories of Sarah Orne Jewett*, 62). Captain Gunn, in the afternoons and evenings, wears his dead sister's dresses. Soon, "the neighbors got used to his ways ... and I never thought nothing of it after the first week or two" (63).

This tale within a tale, told by old Miss Polly Marsh to our story's narrator, of gender confusion and cross-dressing—of confusion between Self and Other, between sameness and difference: Captain Gunn even goes dressed as a woman to a meeting of the Female Missionary Society, where he eats a great supper and upon leaving, "kissed 'em all round and asked 'em to meet at his house"—this tale is framed by the narrator's approach to and departure from Miss Polly Marsh's house. As she approaches, "I went down through the pasture land and just then I saw my father drive away up the road, just too far for me to make him hear when I called. That seemed too bad at first, until I remembered that he would come back again over the same road after a while" (58).

Miss Polly's long tale is abruptly ended in mid-sentence—"There was one day, though—" by her sister's announcement to the narrator, "here comes your father." The narrator "reached home when it was growing dark and chilly. ... It was a much longer

---

[6] Poem #520, in Johnson, *op. cit.*, pp. 254-55.
[7] "An Autumn Holiday" in Charles G. Waugh, Martin H. Greenberg and Josephine Donovan, eds., *Best Short Stories of Sarah Orne Jewett* (Augusta, Maine: Lance Tapley, 1988), p. 56.

way home around the road than by the way I had come across the fields" (66).

This is all like a dream. The narrator has been walking not on the highways, but "*between* the roads" (my emphasis). When she sees her father driving away, "too far for me to make him hear when I called," she thinks it's "too bad *at first*" (again my emphasis). In his absence, she hears this strange tale of a man who lived, in a way, "between the roads," a man in the mornings and his own sister in the afternoons, a tale of the transgression of the boundaries of self and other, of gender, of difference. The narrator's father's magical, or again dream-like, re-appearance means the end of this strange, funny, delightful, and sun-filled ramble off the socially marked highways. Father drives her home *on* the road. "It was growing dark and chilly," and it's a much longer way home than by the way she had come, *across* the fields. A ramble through the woods, or a ramble through the confusing thickets of gender? Or both, each a metaphorical representation of the other?

Jewett's father had died shortly before the composition of this tale. The father's departure in the story seems to allow the narrator, to give her permission, to hear this story of "*Miss* Dan'el Gunn," to entertain this "between the roads" wish-fulfillment dream of being a man in the morning and a woman in the afternoon. Father's re-appearance marks the return of a level of consciousness, a kind of Super-Ego, which abruptly ends the idyll of sex-role-confusion. Father takes her back *on* the highway. The bright, sunny day is over. "It was growing dark and chilly."

Considering that James T. Fields had just stepped down after a long career as editor-in-chief of *The Atlantic* at the time Jewett started publishing there, and that Jewett was soon to spend the rest of her life in a kind of marriage with Fields's widow Annie (Fields died in 1881, a year after "An Autumn Holiday" was published), is it too much to hear in the phrase, "I had come across the fields," something more than simple topographical description?

Next to her book-length novel-like narrative, *The Country of the Pointed Firs* (1896), Jewett's most famous and most widely written-about story is "A White Heron" (1886). This story of a nine-year-old girl who loves the woods and her meeting with an ornithologist who kills the things he loves, is a story with both regionalist and feminist implications. All the details of Dickinson's "My Life had stood—a Loaded Gun" and "I started early—took my Dog" are here (except the dog): the gun, the mountains, the woods, the sea. In addition, we have a heron (the object of the ornithologist's quest) and a giant pine tree, both clearly presented as either male (the heron) or as a symbol of the male. (One writer on this story calls this tree the largest phallic symbol in all American literature.)

The story is easily summed up: Sylvia, an urban transplant to her grandmother's place in Maine, has become, as her name indicates, a woods-girl. Squirrels and birds feed out of her hands. Her grandmother says, "There ain't a foot o' ground she don't know her way over, and the wild creatures counts her one o' themselves" (*Best Short Stories*, 84). One day, while bringing the cow home, Sylvy, as she is called, hears a whistle in the woods —"not a bird's whistle, but a boy's whistle, determined, and somewhat aggressive" (83). Sylvy tries to hide in the bushes, but "she was just too late. The enemy had discovered her." The "enemy" is a handsome young man, an

ornithologist. He has been hunting birds and has lost his way. "Speak up," he says to
Sylvy, "and tell me what your name is and whether you think I can spend the night at
your house." Sylvy finds it hard to speak up. In fact, aside from telling her name,
which she just barely whispers, she is silent throughout the story, a silence that will
become all-important in the end.

Sylvy leads the young man home to her grandmother's house, where he "stood his
gun beside the door, and dropped a lumpy game-bag beside it" (83). He asks for, and
receives, a night's lodgings. During the evening, Mrs. Tilly, Sylvy's grandmother,
brags about Sylvy's knowledge of the woods. The hunter then asks Sylvy whether she
knows the nesting place of the white heron he's been unable to find so far. Sylvy
knows the bird he means:

> She knew that strange white bird, and had once stolen softly near where it stood in some bright green
> swamp grass, away over at the other side of the woods. There was an open place where the sunshine
> always seemed strangely yellow and hot, where tall, nodding rushes grew, and her grandmother had
> warned her that she might sink in the soft black mud underneath and never be heard of more. Not far
> beyond were the salt marshes just this side of the sea itself, which Sylvia wondered and dreamed
> about, but had never seen (85).

"I can't think of anything I'd like so much as to find that heron's nest," the young
hunter says, and he offers Sylvia ten dollars as a reward if she leads him to it.

Sylvy spends the next day in the woods with the ornithologist. He tells her all
about the birds he studies, and gives her a jack-knife as a present. "All day long he did
not once make her troubled or afraid except when he brought down some unsuspecting
singing creature from its bough. Sylvia would have liked him vastly better without his
gun; she could not understand why he killed the very birds he seemed to like so much"
(86).

That evening, they return to her grandmother's house, where the stranger will
spend another night. This is the end of Part One. The problem is posed for us, and for
Sylvy: the heron, or the hunter? She has already developed a "crush" on the young
man: "the woman's heart, asleep in the child, was vaguely thrilled by a dream of love"
(86). Besides, he has offered her ten dollars. Will she betray the nesting place of the
white heron to the handsome young hunter, the male, the scientist, the Outsider, the
one with money in his pockets, the one who seeks to know, but whose form of
knowing necessitates the death of the object of his knowledge?

In Part Two, Sylvy sets out before dawn the next morning to find the heron's
nesting place. She is, at this point, eager to satisfy the hunter and "make known the
secret." To find the nest, Sylvy has to make, like Dickinson's visitor to the sea, what
is clearly a mythic or symbolic journey into Experience. And just as in Dickinson's
poem, this journey is presented in terms of a sexual experience. Sylvy must go "to the
farther edge of the woods," where, on the *highest* point of land, stands a great pine
tree, not only the tallest in the vicinity, but "the last of its generation," the only
survivor of the virgin forest that has long ago been chopped down. Towering over its
second-growth neighbours, this landmark pine can be seen from miles away. Sylvia
now thinks of this tree: "for why, if one climbed it at break of day, could not one see

all the world, and easily discover from whence the white heron flew, and mark the place, and find the hidden nest?" (87)

Sylvy climbs this gigantic tree, climbs to Experience in a passage whose language is clearly erotic—"The tree seemed to lengthen itself out as she went up, and to reach farther and farther upward" (88). She is scratched by sharp, dry twigs; she is smeared with pine-pitch; her frock is torn and tattered. But she reaches the tree-top, and is rewarded with the transcendent vision she has earned: "There was the sea with the dawning sun making a golden dazzle over it, and toward that glorious east two hawks with slow-moving pinions. ... Westward, the woodlands and farms reached miles and miles into the distance. ... truly it was a vast and awesome world!" (88-9).

Sylvy finally sees the heron—"a white spot of him like a single floating feather comes up and grows larger, and rises, and comes close at last, and goes by the landmark pine with steady sweep of wing and outstretched slender neck and crested head." Sylvia sees where the heron's nest is, "she knows his secret now, the wild, light, slender bird that floats and wavers and goes back like an arrow to his home in the green world beneath" (89).

Back at Sylvia's grandmother's house, the ornithologist wakes up from a dream, sure that today the little girl must really be *made to tell*. And here she comes, her dress torn, smeared with pine pitch. "The splendid moment has come to speak." But Sylvia keeps silent: "The murmer of the pine's green branches is in her ears, she remembers how the white heron came flying through the golden air and how they watched the sea and the morning together, and Sylvia cannot speak; she cannot tell the heron's secret and give its life away" (90). Instead of becoming an adjunct to the hunter's loaded gun, her voice giving it aim, her silence opposes and defeats the ornithologist's desire to know and to kill.

The story has mythic resonance, and can be read from many productive angles, among them regionalism and feminism.[8] Jewett, who in her letters identified herself with "the last wild thing left in the woods" and also spoke of feeling, on her thirtieth birthday, like a nine-year-old girl, was able to separate and represent her conflicting feelings in the form of Sylvy, the heron, and the hunter.[9] The bird is, interestingly, a migrant to Maine, or "has perhaps been chased out of its own region by some bird of prey." Sylvy, the woods girl, is herself a recent transplant from "a crowded manufacturing town," where a "great red-faced boy used to chase and frighten her." The parallels between Sylvia and the bird are clear. What is interesting is that no one, except the grandmother, is really a *native* of this place.

Since the story is told from Sylvy's point of view, we share her privileged initiation into experience, seeing the sun rise out of the ocean, seeing the wide world—ocean, farmland, villages and forest—and finally seeing the flight of the heron. Her refusal to betray the heron to the hunter is the choice we are led to hope she will

---

[8] See, for example, Louis A. Renza, *"A White Heron" and the Question of Minor Literature* (Madison: University of Wisconsin Press, 1984), especially chapters 1 and 2.

[9] Judith Roman, "A Closer Look at the Jewett-Fields Relationship," in Nagel, *op. cit.*, p. 125. See Fields, *op. cit.*, p. 125.

make, since because of the way the story is structured the hunter—and everything he comes to stand for—is the foil, the enemy: the Male; the cold, Hawthornian scientist who kills what he studies; the representative of the outside world which wants to pry into and learn—and *kill*—the secrets, the specifics of the region.

But if we switch our point of view for a moment to that of the frustrated ornithologist, who wants to know, and whose efforts are met with kindness and hospitality, but also finally and most importantly with baffling silence, we have the situation of *The Country of the Pointed Firs*. There too, the narrator is an outsider, a woman writer who has come to a small town on the coast of Maine for the summer to complete a piece of writing. She is what Mainers call someone "from away," and whom they don't completely trust, no matter how kind and hospitable they may seem.

Jewett's strategy of writing "regional" or "local colour" literature for an urban, sophisticated audience (many of her stories were published in *The Atlantic*, and Henry James was an admirer of her work) was determined in part by the need not to "betray" her place, not to give up its secrets too easily. Her narrator, in *Pointed Firs*, is similarly met with kindness and hospitality—and *silence*—by the natives of Dunnet Landing. Jewett gives us what seems to look like a glimpse of her region, but what we really see is a reflection of our own gaze, our own desire to know.

From Emily Dickinson's metaphor of her own sense of herself as a loaded gun serving the interests of "the Owner"—variously identified as her sense of her own poetic power, or an actual person, or perhaps God—to Sarah Orne Jewett's gentle parody, in the person of "*Miss* Dan'el Gunn," of another famous American hunter named Daniel, turning the mythic mighty hunter into a "lady" who is, in fact, a slightly crazed cross-dresser, to the silence of a little girl frustrating or deflecting the loaded gun of a male quester after scientific knowledge, we have seen imagery of guns, hunting, woods and mountains used by two American women writers as metaphors both of place and of gender. Sylvy's ascent of the landmark pine is as sexually charged as is the narrative in Dickinson's poem about visiting the sea. But in both cases, sexuality itself is a metaphor for a kind of initiation into Experience, an experience that dwarfs mere genital sexuality as the landmark pine dwarfs the hunter's gun. Sylvy sees the ocean for the first time, as does, presumably, the speaker in Dickinson's poem. And the "oceanic experience" puts into perspective specific social constructs and definitions. Having shared the golden dawn with the white heron from atop the highest tree in the region, Sylvy has no need to betray her new-found knowledge for ten dollars, a jack-knife, and the approval of the young hunter.

"Place" and "gender" are metaphors Dickinson and Jewett use in an art which undermines and never satisfies our expectations. Our inquisitive gaze is met with a Narcissus-like reflection. The loaded gun introduced in Act One, Chekhov said, must go off in Act Three. In 19th-century New England, in the hands of Emily Dickinson and Sarah Orne Jewett, as in the photo taken by Elsie from Wyoming, the gun is re-appropriated as a metaphor and pointed back at us, who thought we knew what phallic symbols stood for.

MIDDLE GROUND
EVOLVING REGIONAL IMAGES IN THE AMERICAN MIDDLE WEST

C. Elizabeth Raymond, University of Nevada, Reno

In a 1976 article entitled "How the Middle West Became America's Heartland," historian Martin Ridge points to what now seems an eternal verity of the U.S. landscape. Ridge observes in passing that "the visual image of the American farm is neither the cotton field nor the vineyard, but the corn and wheat fields of the Middle West" (19). To a people taught from childhood to celebrate their nation's natural beauty in terms of spacious skies and amber waves of grain, there is perhaps nothing remarkable in the statement. Yet neither is there any inherent reason why it should be so. The emergence of Midwestern rural landscapes as somehow normative was by no means inevitable or "natural." The landscapes themselves were physically constructed—both before and after Euroamerican settlement—and imbued with successive meanings, in a complicated historical process of interaction between people and place.

In popular parlance, the interior agricultural reaches of the United States are the country's "corn belt," its "bread basket." It is a place where flat land spreads out in seemingly endless vistas, and roads following the lines of Thomas Jefferson's rectangular survey meet at precise right angles in predictable one-mile intervals. Despite the fact that most of its population lives in cities, the region remains symbolically rural, marked in the popular mind by the looming verticals of silos and grain elevators rather than skyscrapers. Although the Middle West's varied immigrant ethnicity is celebrated in numerous churches and festivals, racial diversity is implicitly erased from its public image. The resulting reputation as the nation's heartland is one of the more enduring U.S. regional stereotypes.

Widely understood, it is infrequently analysed. When reporter David Foster Wallace was commissioned by *Harper's Magazine* to write an article about the Illinois State Fair, for example, he envisioned himself doing "pith-helmeted anthropological reporting on something rural and heartlandish" for Eastern editors who had suddenly "remember[ed] that about 90 percent of the United States lies between the coasts" (35). Folk singer Joel Mabus gently satirises the phenomenon in his song, "Hopelessly Midwestern":

> Now if you live life in the middle and not on the edge,
> You're hopelessly midwestern.
> And if a big Saturday means clipping the hedge,
> You're hopelessly midwestern.
> If you shop at Sears, drink a lot of ice tea,
> You like to dance the polka and watch TV,
> The jury is in and the critics agree,

You're hopelessly midwestern.
(Lyrics quoted by permission.)

Middle Western landscape, however, was not always America's symbolic repository of identity; and the heartland was not always so conventional and bland. The region emerged in its contemporary role only after passing through several distinct historical stages of development. In each phase, actual physical landscapes and perceptions of their meaning by both residents and observers intersected to create distinctive images of the area now known as the Middle West.[1]

Physical definitions of this region are notoriously various, and debates about its eastern and western boundaries, in particular, are heated. I define the region topographically, as a subset of the 12-state North Central census district that extends from Ohio west through the Dakotas, Kansas, and Nebraska. Within that broad area of the Middle West, I concentrate on the region initially covered by tall-grass prairie, where native grasses were plentiful and well-watered, and grew to a height of 6 to 8 feet. This area is characterised by flat, open, relatively featureless terrain, and devoted today primarily to agricultural uses, especially the cultivation of corn, soybeans, and wheat. On the basis of native vegetation, and the rainfall that its presence suggests, the region can be distinguished both from the forested terrain to the east and north, and from the more arid, short-grass prairie areas to the west, now commonly known as the Great Plains. This Prairie Midwest does not coincide neatly with state boundaries, but includes Iowa and Illinois; northern Missouri; eastern Kansas, Nebraska, and the Dakotas; southern and western Minnesota; southern Wisconsin and Michigan; and portions of western Indiana (see Figure 1).

The soil here is fertile and black, and extends toward the sky in every direction to create a full 360-degree horizon. Although cities and industry contain the population and dominate the economy, farms are central to popular perception of "the Corn Belt." Space is somehow of its essence, and isolated family farmsteads surrounded by flat fields are its icon. Virtually every observer of this peculiar landscape has recorded its effect in terms similar to those employed by essayist Paul Gruchow to describe the Cayler Prairie in northwestern Iowa: "There is no place to hide on the Cayler. This was the feature of the prairie landscape that overwhelmed so many pioneers, the realisation that it was so exposed, so naked. There was something relentless about the

---

[1] Aspects of this subject have received attention from numerous other scholars. In addition to Ridge, these include: Andrew R.L. Cayton and Peter S. Onuf, *The Midwest and the Nation: Rethinking the History of an American Region* (Bloomington: University of Indiana Press, 1990); Joanne Jacobsen, "The Idea of the Midwest," *Revue Française D'Etudes Américaines* 48-49 (April-June 1991): 235-245; James R. Shortridge, *The Middle West: Its Meaning in American Culture* (Lawrence: University Press of Kansas, 1989); Michael C. Steiner, "Frederick Jackson Turner and the Meaning of the Midwest," Unpublished paper delivered to the Nordic American Studies Association, August 1993; Robert Thacker, *The Great Prairie in Fact and Literary Imagination* (Albuquerque: University of New Mexico Press, 1989). In this essay I sketch the successive stages of a development that I hope to treat more carefully in a book-length study of the historical evolution of the Prairie Midwestern landscape. An earlier, partial version of this essay appeared in "Alternative Narratives of Nature: Middle Western Sense of Place," *Cañon* 2 (Fall 1994): 26-43.

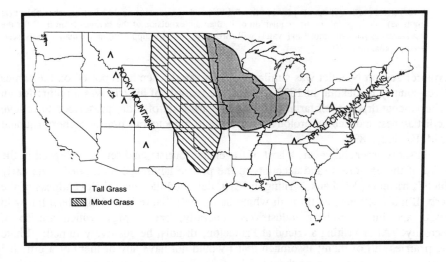

Figure 1. The Prairie Midwest is the area formerly occupied by tallgrass prairie, shaded more darkly on this map

scale of it" (*Journal*, 21-22). In the midst of such oceanic openness, both observers and inhabitants were challenged to construct a place more human in scale. They did so in discrete phases, each marked not only by physical transformations of the landscape but also by depictions in documents including explorers' journals, settlers' diaries, maps and atlases, fiction, poetry, and art. The region now thoroughly familiar as the Midwest has, in fact, been written into the nation in several distinct versions.

Initially, the prairie landscape was a curiosity to Euroamericans, an apparently empty, unknown place that failed to correspond to familiar systems of land assessment. Reports from early French and British explorers presented two competing images of the region, as garden or desert, but neither was well established when 19th century Americans first encountered the region. Stephen Kearney, for instance, crossing Iowa from Omaha to Minneapolis in 1820, evinced no high hopes for the landscape he encountered:

> A very great portion of the country in the neighborhood of our route could be of no other object (at any time) to our govn't in the acquisition of it, than the expulsion of the savages from it ... for the disadvantages [lack of timber and water] will forever prevent its supporting more than a thinly scattered population (357).

Explorer Joseph Nicollet was similarly unimpressed when he reported on the James River country in Dakota, in 1839. Among the records of his trip was a recipe for an "effervescent draught" of tartaric acid and bicarbonate of soda, prescribed to relieve the listlessness induced by prolonged exposure to monotonous prairie scenery (quoted in McFarling, 183).[2]

In short order, however, a host of travellers, tourists, and settlers followed in the wake of the explorers; and accounts of the prairie landscape multiplied. One early English traveller, W. Faux, writing in 1819, deplored the general slovenliness of the early Illinois settlements through which he passed: "Here is nothing clean but wild beasts and birds, nothing industrious generally, except pigs, which are so of necessity." After visiting a friend at Princeton, Illinois, he positively fumed: "I hate the prairies, all of them; insomuch that I would not have any of them of a gift, if I must be compelled to live on them" (221-222). Faux was responding in this work to the particularly optimistic claims of English speculator Morris Birkbeck, whose 1818 *Notes on a Journey in America* was written to promote his Illinois prairie settlement. The skeptic found himself part of a minority perspective, however, amidst a growing body of romantic prairie paeans. The next few decades brought further enthusiastic descriptions that downplayed the presence of people and concentrated instead on the new landscape's features: its grandeur and extent, the mysteries of its origins, the beauty of its flowers, and—and a particularly common theme—its uncanny resemblance to settled English countryside.

---

[2] For prevailing images prior to American exploration, see John Logan Allen, *Passage Through the Garden: Lewis and Clark and the Image of the American Northwest* (Urbana: University of Illinois Press, 1975) and Thacker, *The Great Prairie in Fact and Literary Imagination*.

Figure 2. Map of Liberty Township, Iowa from *Atlas of Warren County* (1874).
Illustration courtesy of Newberry Library.

American journalist Edmund Flagg, for example, waxed lyrical in 1838 about the prairie sunset:

> There is not a more magnificent spectacle in nature than summer sunset on the Western prairie. ... One moment, and the whole vast landscape lay veiled in shadowy dimness; the next, and every grass blade, and spray, and floweret, and nodding wild-weed seemed suffused in a flood of liquid effulgence; while far along, the uniform ridges of the heaving plain gleamed in the rich light like waves of a moonlit sea, seeping away, roll upon roll, till lost in the distance to the eye. (vol. 1, 234-5)

In 1855, Scottish adventurer Laurence Oliphant acclaimed the "wonderful combination of civilisation and barbarism" he found in the newly settled prairies of Minnesota (257); while American John van Tramp concluded authoritatively that the Illinois prairies were fully the equal of the country's most acclaimed and venerable scenic wonder, Niagara Falls:

> Her expanded prairies, decked in their holiday array that outvies "Solomon in all his glory," besides their landscape beauty, inspire a feeling of sublimity, from their vastness, like unto that experienced by a first view of old ocean; and perhaps no natural object in our country—not even excepting the classic Niagara—would more fix the admiration of a visitor from the Old World, than a view of the Grand Prairie in its summer attire. (471-2)

Collectively these early accounts stimulated a "prairie craze," a popular convention of prairie viewing that prevailed well into the century and made the Midwest into a significant tourist attraction as well as a settlement destination. Land agents and foreign travellers alike conspired to render the new landscape enticing to the reading public. Their settlement guides and travel accounts referred to the region as the "Great West," and taught at least two generations of readers to regard it as a both instructive and unique landscape, worthy of extended contemplation, not to mention purchase.

Devotees of this tradition of scenic veneration displayed their own taste and sophistication through their aesthetic appreciation of prairie landscape. Fictional depictions were downright hyperbolic, exemplified by a descriptive passage in a popular 1849 novel by Emerson Bennett, *The Prairie Flower*. This work purports to be a factual narrative. The author's description of his first sight of the prairie landscape, however, contrasts markedly with Stephen Kearney's:

> The prairie! the mighty, rolling, and seemingly boundless prairie! With what singular emotions I beheld it for the first time! ... Thousands upon thousands of acres lay spread before me like a map, bounded by nothing but the deep blue sky. What a magnificent sight! A sight that made my soul expand with lofty thought, and its frail tenement sink into utter nothingness before it. (24)

In time, as transportation improved and settlers domesticated the tallgrass prairies, the focus of romantic tourism moved still further west, to the more dramatic expanses of California and the Rocky Mountains, a process Anne Hyde traces in her book, *An American Vision*. In the area of the Prairie Midwest, by contrast, fences, drainage tile, and section line roads replaced waving grasses by the 1870s, to create a geometric, agricultural landscape that gradually took on a new identity as just one among many distinct western districts. No longer *the* west, and certainly not the Great West of early nineteenth-century fame, the region slowly emerged in a more mundane form as the nation's middle West (see Figure 2).[3]

Tourists whose expectations had been shaped by earlier accounts were confounded by the change. By mid-century, the conventions of prairie viewing were well established, so that English parson Harry James, travelling in 1874, could report, "The prairie is much like what I expected to see" (35). Similarly, the Scottish minister John Kirkwood recorded his disappointment, in 1887, at not seeing the promised features of the prairie landscape: "We did not, indeed, see much, if anything, [on the way to Chicago] of primeval grass, so famous for its flowers and fires. Yet that grass abounded only a few years ago" (192).

Indeed, the conventions of prairie scenery were so well understood by then that writers could manipulate them for literary effect. Beginning in the 1860s, the purple prose began to fade and a strain of parody emerged in prairie descriptions. Sometimes it was relatively mild, as when Englishman George Borrett admitted that the settled Illinois prairie he encountered in 1864 was not the same scene described by earlier travellers: "But people have 'gushed' and poetised [sic] enough upon the rolling prairies of the West, and I, who have not seen them in their primitive glory, have no right to follow suit. For myself, I must confess that I like variety of outline in preference to solemnity of repetition ..." (115-6). Such a passage made sense only if one had confidence that one's readers were already familiar with more highly embellished passages like Bennett's.

Others used the very conventionality of prairie descriptions as an excuse not to pursue the matter themselves, as did George Sala in 1883: "But what good could I have done by descriptively going over the ground which has been so often and so exhaustively gone over by those guide-book writers whose name is legion?" (vol. 1, 190). The prairie had become its own trope, rendering characterisation redundant. Englishwoman Emily Pfeiffer, travelling during the 1870s, was less generous to the guidebook writers, and took them to task for their misleading rhetoric:

> It is amusing to contrast the inflated descriptions which are issued to travellers gratis, with the reality of what we have seen on ... our way from Chicago. A less interesting tract of country, from the point of view of the picturesque, than that which the [railroad] line traverses through the States of Illinois and Iowa, it has never happened to me to behold (116).

Her countryman, humorist George Rose, was not so amused:

---

[3] The term Middle West was apparently first used by Frederick Jackson Turner in an 1896 article for *Atlantic Monthly*, though commentators had been searching for an appropriate regional label for some time previous (see Shortridge, *The Middle West*). Michael Steiner makes the important point that absence of the defining label does not necessarily imply lack of a coherent regional self-consciousness ("Turner and the Meaning of the Midwest"). It is intriguing to speculate about when (and whether) such self-consciousness emerged. A study of U.S. atlases from the Rand McNally Collection at the Newberry Library reveals that states were not arranged in the present alphabetical sequence until the late 1920s. Prior to that time, states of the Ohio River Valley tended to be grouped sequentially, but Midwestern states west of the Mississippi River followed no predictable pattern of arrangement.

Having a great desire to see the Prairies, I took my departure from St. Louis, so as to have an opportunity of passing through them on my way to Chicago. I would strongly advise my readers not to put themselves to any inconvenience in following my example, for however the Prairie may be in the far west, the hunting-ground of the Redskin, the home of the bison and the antelope, where stampedes excite, and Indians scalp the traveller, that portion of it traversed between St. Louis and Chicago only resembles a bad crop of coarse hay (217).

By the middle of the nineteenth century, then, the romantic prairie was so well established as a landscape convention that subversions of various sorts were possible. Like Niagara Falls and other icons of the nineteenth-century American landscape, the prairie was a culturally sanctified "sight," a tourist destination that at least two generations of cultivated middle and upper-class travellers had been taught to regard as worthy of contemplation. Devotees of this tradition of scenic veneration displayed their own taste and sophistication through their aesthetic appreciation of the prairie landscape. Without the slightest hint of irony, tourists like William Ferguson, in 1856, could dutifully exclaim: "A western prairie! a dream realized!" (335). And Grace Greenwood, almost twenty years later, was similarly moved. In an image that confounds the modern scenic aesthetic, she inquired: "If a cornfield of several thousand acres is not 'a symbol of the infinite,' I should like to know what is" (12).[4]

It was the corn field that caused trouble in the erstwhile prairie paradise, of course. By the 1880s, open tallgrass prairies were relatively scarce. Except in areas requiring significant drainage, the grasslands had been cleared, fenced, and planted. As the prairies gave way to farms, the tourist literature waned and new chronicles appeared. In this second phase of its historical identity, from approximately 1860 to 1890 (later in more western areas), the emerging region was enthusiastically hailed as the quintessential embodiment of America's agrarian destiny.

The Prairie Middle West's new image was created while the physical landscape was transformed by its inhabitants. It was recorded and celebrated first in the maps, county atlases, and local histories of the mid-19th century, and later in numerous memoirs, diaries, and journals of what came to be known as the pioneer period. Eventually it found its way into the popular press. In these multiplying texts a regional mythology of environmental triumph and transformation—progenitor of the modern breadbasket myth— was first produced.

Here, the perspective was internal, rather than external, as residents recorded their pride in having physically recast the prairies to make them into extremely productive farms. When Norwegian immigrant, later judge, Andreas Ueland summarised the process retrospectively, in his 1929 autobiography, his sense of personal achievement was palpable:

I see farms to the right and left with comfortable dwellings and big, red barns, sheltered in groves of planted trees. I see herds of cattle, horses, hogs and sheep burrowing for food or shelter into huge straw piles left from the fall threshing. ... I pass through towns with fine buildings for dwellings and business. I reflect that when there wasn't yet a wagon road where I now ride in a Pullman, Norwegian

---

[4] For the nineteenth-century U.S. landscape aesthetic, including a discussion of Niagara Falls, see John Sears, *Sacred Places* (New York: Oxford, 1989).

and Swedish immigrants came here in canvas-covered wagons pulled by oxen, and where they found no human trace on the ground they unhitched, built log or sod houses for shelter, and out of the wilderness made what I now see. (261)

The judge interpreted the productive Minnesota landscape as a valuable human creation, not as an element of nature to be contemplated. An environmental intimate, he knew the emotional and physical cost of those farms and roads, and was accordingly proud of what he and his countrymen had made.

Writer Hamlin Garland summarised the process of change, which he clearly saw as improvement, in *A Son of the Middle Border*: "Day by day the settlement thickened. Section by section the prairie was blackened by the plow," culminating in "land [that] needed only to be tickled with a hoe to laugh into harvest" (144). But the story belonged as well to less articulate recorders, to the anonymous Illinois farmer who in 1848 enthusiastically compared his new situation to his previous home: "In Ohio a feller has to fight hard for every inch o' ground he gets, and when the ground is once cleared off, it can't begin to compare with this soil, all clear and slick to your hand" (quoted in Regan, 44).

The new landscape was documented for middle-class consumption in the pages of *Harper's*, complete with elaborate engravings of the new machinery that made large-scale prairie cultivation possible. There the Midwestern bonanza wheat farms were extolled as agrarian counterparts to the technological wonders of the steam engine. Even small scale nineteenth-century prairie farmers, however, men who did not own steam-powered threshers or large acreages, left proud records of their accomplishments. Untold hundreds of them (and a few women as well) paid to record their accomplishments for their peers and posterity in the farmstead engravings that illustrated the ubiquitous county atlases of the period. Here homely pride in the bounteous new environment they have composed fairly leaped from the pages, in a visual counterpart to Andreas Ueland's reminiscences (see Figure 3).[5]

The lessons of these farmstead engravings are not complicated. Here is no infinite prairie expanse, reaching off to the sunset. Instead the atlas illustrations lovingly depict domesticated spaces, neatly fenced and plowed, furnished with an impressive assortment of outbuildings, animals, and equipment. Abijah Powers's 1872 example is typical, including a view of his impressive farmhouse and outbuildings, and an assortment of fat and healthy looking animals. The cattle in the foreground, presumably accompanied by their owner at the right, are clearly the featured product of the farm. Some atlas illustrations were more candid than others, and the degree of detail varied

---

[5] For the atlases, published from the 1860s throughout the century, see Michael P. Conzen, "The County Landownership Map in America, Its Commercial Development and Social Transformation 1814-1939," *Imago Mundi* 36 (1984): 9-31; and "Maps for the Masses: Alfred T. Andreas and the Midwestern County Atlas Trade," in Conzen, ed., *Chicago Mapmakers: Essays on the Rise of the City's Map Trade* (Chicago: Chicago Historical Society, 1984), pp. 46-63. For agricultural abundance as the basis of Prairie Midwestern sense of place see C. Elizabeth Raymond, "Learning the Land: Sense of Place in Prairie Midwestern Writing," *MidAmerica* 14 (1987): 28-41.

Figure 3. Residence of Abijah Powers from *Standard Atlas of Lee County Illinois* (1872).
Illustration courtesy of Newberry Library.

Figure 4. Residence of Svend Nelson, Olmsted County, from *Illustrated Historical Atlas of the State of Minnesota* (1874). Illustration courtesy of Newberry Library.

Figure 5. View on the Farm of J. Hammond, Esq., from *Illustrated Atlas of Knox County Illinois* (1870). Illustration courtesy of Newberry Library.

with the particular illustrator. Viewers would have understood how to interpret their nuances, however.

In Figure 4, Svend Nelson's Minnesota house and barn were rather stark and plain in 1874. Compared to Abijah Powers's Illinois stock farm, the scale here is quite modest. Nonetheless, there are clear tokens of progress. Centrally featured are the decaying log house where the Nelson family presumably began its prairie sojourn, and the modern convenience of a pump to water the stock. The furrowed field in the foreground, with its sprouting corn, is still being fenced. Nelson was obviously in the early stages of what was forecast as a prosperous future.

In Figure 5, J. Hammond's more established Illinois farm is represented in 1872, in all its glory. Although the residence is centrally featured, separate outbuildings also merit individual cameos, including his weighing scales, carriage house, and barns. In addition there are two overall views of the farmstead, one from the road and another, in the top center panel, next to a portrait of its owner. The whole is framed with depictions of the fruits of Hammond's husbandry, as wheat sheaves and twining grapevines burst exuberantly from the margins of the illustration and fill up the interstices between panels. The prairie spaces occasionally open out behind the buildings, but the fruits of Hammond's labor dominate this view.

To the people who effected and who witnessed such changes in the Midwestern landscape, it was by no means a simple matter of profit and progress. The prairie was widely admired for its beauty before it was cultivated. John van Tramp's 1867 impressions are not at all unusual:

> The gayety [*sic*] of the prairie, its embellishments, and the absence of the gloom and savage wildness of the forest, all contribute to dispell [*sic*] the feeling of lonesomeness, which usually creeps over the mind of the solitary traveler in the wilderness. Though he may not see a house nor a human being, and is conscious that he is far from the habitations of men, he can scarcely divest himself of the idea that he is traveling through scenes embellished by the hand of art. The flowers, so fragile, so delicate, and so ornamental, seem to have been tastefully disposed to adorn the scene. The groves and clumps of trees appear to have been scattered over the lawn to beautify the landscape, and it is not easy to avoid that decision of the fancy which persuades the beholder, that such scenery has been created to satisfy the refined taste of civilized man. (117)

Van Tramp's use of the term "created" is significant. Like other nineteenth-century prairie observers, he assumed that the prairies were a human artifact, created and maintained by virtue of frequent firing by the native Indian peoples. Other writers commented on the fact that a section of prairie outside St. Louis that had been protected from fire was covered by trees after only a few years. Early white settlers conscientiously continued the practice of fall firing to maintain prairie meadows after they had displaced the native peoples.[6]

---

[6] This conclusion is based on an extensive survey of travel accounts, local histories, and other nineteenth-century narratives of the prairie. See for example [Elizabeth] Ellet, *Summer Rambles in the West* (New York: J. C. Riker, 1853), p. 64, where she makes virtually the same observation as Van Tramp. For Indians maintaining the prairies by burning, see Ellet, pp. 36-9, and James Caird, *Prairie Farming in America* (London: Longman, Brown, Green, Longmans & Roberts, 1859), p. 76. The story

Thus imagined by settlers as a place that had been deliberately shaped by its previous occupants, the prairies were assessed instrumentally, in terms of their susceptibility to further "improvement." As James Morgan observed of Iowa in 1839:

> It would seem to have been an order of Providence. ... There is just enough of prairie for the timber, and just enough of the timber for the prairie—and go in any direction you may, over this vast region, you will find, on all sides, beautiful and rich farms, measured by the hand of nature, and calculated, in every respect, for all the wants, conveniences and wishes of the farmer. (quoted in Plumbe, 45)

Compared to "the life-long drudgery of woodland pioneering," the prairie struck many settlers as a heaven on earth, a place where making a cultivatable 40-acre field did not take the better part of a decade (Parker, 36). Its ease of cultivation was an important part of its appeal.[7]

Caught in the narrative imperative of their own stories, settlers construed change as the proper and inevitable destiny of the Prairie Midwest. Such modification involved not only uprooting the indigenous peoples, but also plowing the native grasses. More than a few prairie settlers echoed Minnesota farmer Mitchell Y. Jackson, who in 1854 noted in his diary that "this great Prairie flower garden as arranged by the hand of the Creator is now exposed to the plow ... and it is plain that the native beauty must give way to the artificial" (quoted in Loehr, 126). Iowa novelist Herbert Quick echoed the sentiment in *Vandemark's Folly*: "Breaking prairie was the most beautiful, the most epochal, and the most hopeful, as I look back at it, in one way the most pathetic thing man ever did, for in it, one of the loveliest things ever created began to come to its predestined end" (28).

Similarly, at least some prairie residents clearly sympathised with those native peoples who were displaced from the prairies with the arrival of Euroamerican settlers. Despite its condescending rhetoric, for example, the 1896 Peoria, Illinois, atlas clearly pitied the Fox Indians who had been forced to depart from their homeland for reservations in the Louisiana Purchase: "The lamentations and cries of men, women and children were enough to soften a stone; they could not see why they should leave the land of their fathers, they had no understanding of the high goddess of 'civilisation' to whom they were to be sacrificed ..." (82). Indeed, in this particular case, the disconsolate Fox leader was allowed to return with his family, and a plot of land was

---

about the St. Louis prairie is from Jacob Ferris, *The States and Territories of the Great West* (New York and Auburn: Miller, Orton, and Mulligan, 1856), p. 209. Modern scholars concur in the notion that frequent Indian burning at least maintained, if it did not create, the prairie grassland. See John Madson, *Where the Sky Began: Land of the Tallgrass Prairie* (San Francisco: Sierra Club Books, 1982), pp. 47-50.

[7] In regard to favourable impressions of the prairie, including its ease of cultivation, geographer Douglas R. McManis concludes that the traditional story of settlers avoiding prairies in the belief that they were barren is not true. Making an argument remarkably like Walter Prescott Webb's in *The Great Plains*, McManis suggests that absence of appropriate technology (John Deere's 1837 steel plow) and justifiable fears about the unhealthiness of wet prairies slowed settlement of those areas, but that settlers moved rapidly onto dry prairies (*The Initial Evaluation and Utilization of the Illinois Prairies, 1815-1840* [Dept. of Geography Research Paper #94, Chicago: University of Chicago, 1964]).

purchased specifically for their use (although it goes without saying that such relatively benign treatment was the exception rather than the rule).

The new generation of prairie chroniclers were settlers rather than tourists, natives rather than newcomers. As such they incorporated an element of change over time into their understanding of the prairie landscape. They constructed not only a new landscape of fences and fields, but also a new regional image, one that acknowledged environmental losses but justified the sacrifices in terms of what had been substituted for the wild prairie of earlier years. As "spatial historian" Paul Carter observes of Australia, the process of settling and comprehending a new environment is never a simple, linear one to those who experience it: "Nothing could be less appropriate to the evocation of historical space than the one-way logic of positivist chronology. Pioneers did not yield to citizens. Men went bush and they came back. They passed on to other countries and began new lives. ... Imagination was constantly on the move" (293). Carter suggests that people use familiar images for new places at least in part "to neutralize the reality of a space that [is] turbulent, unpredictable, rebellious" (305).

For prairie settlers, this turbulence was allowed full expression only in retrospective accounts produced by those who succeeded. People like Andreas Ueland and Hamlin Garland, who had witnessed the process of settlement and had benefitted from it, could afford to record the genuine hardships of prairie life. They magnified their own heroism through a detailed enumeration of the various trials through which they and their neighbours had passed to make the prairie into fields. Glorification of the struggles of those Euroamerican pioneers is a ritual aspect of Midwestern novels like Ole Rølvaag's *Giants in the Earth* or Willa Cather's *O Pioneers!*; it appears first, however, in a more mundane setting, in the hundreds of county atlases and histories issued in the Midwest in the last third of the nineteenth century. There the prairie was often rendered as an obstacle, and its residents as brave pioneers. The object of their endeavors was farmland: "The villages have sprung up as it were in a day. ... The stately thickets have grown to luxuriant forests, from which the deer have fled, and what was then a paradise to the eye has become the fruitful garden of the world" (Lee County Atlas, 5).[8]

But such fruitful farmland was not an automatism. Midwestern residents understood that it had to be produced and maintained, just as the prairie before it was produced and maintained through the efforts of the Indian tribes. And there was no proven formula for doing so. Paul Gruchow captured the contingent nature of the process in a 1992 essay:

> To each day, and to each season, was dedicated a suitable labor, but no labor was ever exactly repeated. No year was ever the same as another, and each field had its own character, so farming the land was always new work; it was in the nature not of a repetition but of an experiment, always unfolding, destined never to be completed. ... Farmers cannot afford the luxury of Cartesian thinking;

---

[8] Henry Nash Smith's discussion of this agrarian triumphalism in *Virgin Land* (Cambridge: Harvard University Press, 1950) is still worthwhile. See also John R. Stilgoe, *The Common Landscape of America, 1580 to 1845* (New Haven: Yale University Press, 1982).

they are obliged to work in the real world, the whole world, where one thing is indivisibly connected to another. (79)

Writers and readers of the county histories were painfully aware of that fact, and stressed it in their accounts. Published volumes—of which the 1867 *Map of Bureau County, Illinois, With Sketches of Its Early Settlement* is emblematic—assured their readers that "few can form a correct idea of the hardship and inconvenience of settling a new country," while lovingly recounting the numerous sacrifices that prairie settlers made to produce their seemingly mundane, rectilinear landscape (10).

In the process of this labor, the settlers developed a profound and personal connection with the landscape they made. In their accounts, the Prairie Midwest gained a new identity as home rather than tourist attraction. Diaries and journals detailed the work required to establish the glorious new breadbasket of the nation. One Frisian immigrant gave dramatic new meaning to the notion of "his land" when he recounted to an interviewer the travails of installing the drainage system on his swampy Illinois land. Here the farmer literally created his own fields:

> We took teams and put scoops on behind and scooped that land off toward the middle there. Then we widened and deepened that ditch by using shovels and hoisting the dirt up out of there and hauling it out into the road. We packed it down there and that is how the roads got higher than the land on the sides. Then we dug more ditches in the same way along each side of the road and all around our farms. ... Then you see we had to build bridges across the ditches (quoted in Corner, 73-4).

Here was no natural bounty, but instead a remarkable human creation, a place where, as *Harper's Magazine* explained of Kansas in 1888, "the defects of climate and the disasters of husbandry are indulgently explained and excused as the foibles of a friend from whom better things may be anticipated thereafter" (162). And where, one might add, the power of technology was routinely evoked to supply what nature had neglected to provide.

The "grasshopper years" of the 1870s, when annual plagues of locusts destroyed standing crops in the field, were an occasion of particular poignancy. Lyon County, Iowa, for example, was dreadfully afflicted in 1873, as its 1905 history made clear:

> Fields of ripening wheat and oats that at sunrise gave promise of a beautiful crop, before sundown were cut to the ground, as if beaten by a threshing flail. Corn fields one day waving in their green and growing glory—the pride of their owners and to be their debt paying, family supporting crop, in a week's time —sometimes a day—were cut down and picked to shreds (134).

The setback was so great that many people sold or abandoned their claims and left the county altogether. Lyon County stagnated for a full decade thereafter; but those who remained told their story triumphantly to the twentieth-century interviewer. Other, similar accounts chronicled tremendous blizzards, early years of isolation, the death of children, the absence of schools, roads, markets, and churches. Such narratives enhanced the significance of the resulting farmland, by accentuating the human costs of creating "the fruitful garden of the world."[9]

This second version of Midwestern regional identity was internally produced but nationally disseminated. By the end of the century, drought and depression notwithstanding, the agricultural Prairie Midwest had become the normative American environmental symbol. As celebrations of prairie agriculture multiplied, and harvests steadily increased, landscapes farther west were subjected to similar expectations. In *Virgin Land*, Henry Nash Smith has recounted the environmental disaster that resulted when rainfall regrettably failed to "follow the plow" out onto the Great Plains. A generation later, however, during the Progressive Era of the early 20th century, environmental optimism still ran high.

When the country's first federal reclamation project was dedicated, in Nevada, in 1905, commentators once again confidently predicted that the newly opened land would follow the now familiar pattern set by Iowa. Journal editor Mrs. M.M. Garwood predicted that future Nevadans would commemorate the event as Irrigation Day, when, as a result of the federal project, "the lands through which we are now passing, white hot and bare, should be green with whispering trees and broad waving fields, healthy happy homes for future generations" (*Progressive West*, 35). Unfortunately, even the prototype region eventually betrayed its image. In the early twentieth century, changing national developments combined with a series of Midwestern environmental misfortunes to produce a striking counterpoint to the prevalent image of prairie abundance.

This third phase in the evolution of Prairie Midwestern regional identity began in the late nineteenth century, as rural and urban distinctions gained new significance and visibility in U.S. society, and regional literature emerged as a distinct genre. Nineteenth-century scenic tastes had not distinguished significantly between natural and industrial wonders, and tourists were instructed by guidebooks to seek out and appreciate both. America's fin-de-siècle intellectuals, however, began to develop a wilderness aesthetic that relied heavily on the value of undisturbed "nature" as a social and psychological restorative. In this context, the relentlessly agrarian landscape of the corn belt abruptly became mundane, neither wild enough to suit newly fashionable scenic tastes nor sufficiently efficient and technological to inspire progressive engineers. Abundance was no longer remarkable, simply assumed.[10]

---

[9] This retrospective magnifying of hardships may be a factor in the determinedly negative tone that Liahna Babener observes in her essay on memoirs of Midwestern childhood, "Bitter Nostalgia," in Elliott West and Paula Petrik, eds., *Small Worlds: Childhood and Adolescence in America, 1850-1950* (Lawrence: University of Kansas, 1992).

[10] In an interesting argument, Richard Brodhead suggests that late 19th-century regional literature was a form of mental tourism for acquisitive, educated elites in perpetual search of the "unmodernized picturesque." (*Cultures of Letters: Scenes of Reading and Writing in Nineteenth-Century America* [Chicago: University of Chicago, 1993], p. 133). His examples are from New England and the South, however, and the Middle West seems less well suited to his model. For the wilderness aesthetic, see Peter Schmitt, *Back to Nature: The Arcadian Myth in Urban America* (New York: Oxford University Press, 1969) and Roderick N. Nash, *Wilderness and the American Mind* (New Haven: Yale University Press, 3rd ed., 1982). For technological tourism, see David Nye, *American Sublime* (Cambridge: MIT Press, 1994) and C. Elizabeth Raymond, "'A Place One Never Tires Of': Changing Landscape and

In this third incarnation, "middle" became a pejorative term. The emergence of consumer culture and the significant impact of industrialisation and immigration in U.S. cities gave rise to a contemptuous dismissal of rural culture as smug, socially backward, and intellectually confining. The literary manifestation of this development was the early 20th century "revolt from the village" identified most prominently with Sinclair Lewis's 1920 novel, *Main Street*, but incorporating as well other Midwestern writers including Floyd Dell and Sherwood Anderson, Susan Glaspell, and George Cram Cook. For them, and in the national press as well, the Prairie Midwest no longer signified either national fulfillment or individual achievement. Carrying on the economic critique of writers like Hamlin Garland and Joseph Howe, later writers bitterly criticised the region's failed promise by exposing the blighted lives of its residents.[11]

Other texts echoed the change. Early 20th-century atlases were no longer exuberant visual records of expansive farmsteads and prize-winning livestock. Now they were merely sober records of property ownership, sometimes excluding even the names of those who merely rented land. Novels of the dust bowl years of the 1930s, like Josephine Johnson's *Now in November* or Frederick Manfred's *This Is the Year*, no longer blithely assumed that the culture of the Midwest was germane to the rest of the country. Instead they portrayed the region once again from an external perspective, plaintively explaining its particular concerns to a disinterested and possibly contemptuous readership.[12]

Twentieth-century works recorded the tremendous personal and social price of environmental failures as farms and hopes were lost to erosion and foreclosure. In Manfred's novel, for example, protagonist Pier Frixen's efforts to make sense of the loss of his farm during the Great Depression of the 1930s are both heroic and tragic:

Ae, he had tried to catch his anchor into the soils, had tried to get his roots down so deep that neither the wind nor flood, heat nor cold, could ever tear him out again ... and had failed.

Image at Lake Tahoe," in Peter Goin, *Stopping Time: A Rephotographic Survey of Lake Tahoe* (Albuquerque: University of New Mexico Press, 1992), pp. 11-23.

[11] For the emergence and political significance of opposition between rural and urban value systems, see Sarah Burns, *Pastoral Inventions* (Philadelphia: Temple University Press, 1990), and Don S. Kirschner, *City and Country: Rural Responses to Urbanization in the 1920s* (Westport, CT: Greenwood Press, 1978). Sally McMurry documents systematic attempts to improve rural housing in order, among other things, to make rural living conditions competitive with middle-class city life in *Families and Farmhouses in Nineteenth-Century America: Vernacular Design and Social Change* (New York: Oxford University Press, 1988). For the revolt from the village, see Barry Gross, "In Another Country: The Revolt From the Village" *MidAmerica* 4 (1977). The art of Midwestern regionalist painters of the 1930s, including John Stuart Curry, Thomas Hart Benton, and Grant Wood, can be seen at least in part as a response to this third-phase critique.

[12] For the successive phases of the atlases, see Michael P. Conzen, "The County Landownership Map in America." Critic Robert C. Bray makes the observation that Illinois literature of this period (roughly 1870-1920 in his division) is based on a conviction among regional writers "that the farms and towns of rural Illinois were centers of cultural value, and this important fact they wished to dramatize to a skeptical country at large" (*Rediscoveries: Literature and Place in Illinois* [Urbana: University of Illinois Press, 1982], p. 6). For an argument about the ultimate irrelevance of the Midwest to national culture, see Jacobsen, "The Idea of the Midwest."

Did a man have to die before he became a part of the old lady earth? Did a man's land work easier after it had been sweetened with the dust of his blood and brains? (611)

In a significant variation upon the previous regional narrative of triumph, Frixen's failure to adequately learn the land produces disaster. Manfred's message is clear: manipulating the land is not always improvement. Mistreated prairie soil will not produce. The third Midwest has betrayed its optimistic creators, whose heirs have produced instead of the heralded nineteenth-century agricultural utopia an isolated twentieth-century social backwater and exhausted cropland. In the words of contemporary essayist, Howard Kohn, "The land mocks the farmer by outlasting him and outlasting his family, no matter the number of successive generations" (269).[13]

Yet, even as agricultural production in the Prairie Midwest has become increasingly irrelevant to the national economy and family farms have decreased in number, in recent decades the region once again impinges more positively on the national consciousness. In recent decades, the Prairie Midwest has been portrayed as the symbolic "heart of America," seen in movies and television programs as the most American of American regions, a visible incarnation of Jeffersonian agrarianism. Not only is the Midwestern landscape the quintessence of American farmland, but, in the view of critic Barry Gross, the Midwest has become as well the symbolic heartland, the psychological standard by which the rest of the country is measured:

The suspicion persists that what goes on at either coast is the extreme, the perverse and bizarre, the grotesque and the Gothic, unreal and worse, unAmerican. The belief persists that the middle represents the heart and the center, the norm against which the extreme East and the extreme West are measured as abnormal, aberrational. (108)

Iowa native son Ronald Weber, a journalism professor, echoes this comforting notion of the Prairie Midwest as the physical embodiment of pastoral idealism: "Iowa is like that for me, an attractive idea, an imaginative center crowded with memories, a landscape of unstartling beauty. There more than most places, a gentle balance seems to have been struck between God's bounty and man's hand." His description could serve as a compendium of modern Midwestern characteristics: gentleness, comfort, balance, nostalgia. Significantly, however, Weber ends his description with a rejection: "Yet, returning, I'm never tempted to stay" (29). Like most contemporary Americans, he understands the Midwest as a good place to be from, but not necessarily a good place to be.

Once this region was enthusiastically depicted as the successful culmination of a national effort, a landscape of created abundance, produced through the heroic labor of human agents over successive generations. Now, however, the image of the Prairie

---

[13] Impressive numbers of depression-era Midwestern novels were published from the 1930s through the 1950s. For a representative summary of their concerns, see C. Elizabeth Raymond, "Down to Earth: Sense of Place in Prairie Midwestern Literature," Unpublished Ph.D. dissertation, University of Pennsylvania, 1979. Environmental disaster marked the final repudiation of the second-stage triumphalism in a way that national social scorn never could, and apparently triggered another fruitful period of exploring the implications of the regional image.

Midwest has shifted once more, acquiring the nostalgic cast of a Grant Wood painting. In the postindustrial U.S., landscape architect Robert L. Thayer, Jr. observes, "looking at rural landscapes is therapeutic compensation for the pressures of a technological world." In this context, people visit the prairie again as tourists, seeking psychic renewal and the assumed simplicity of a past landscape, but not the complications of the modern U.S. farm crisis. Both landscape and culture are sentimentalised. Ironically, the region once proudly extolled as a kind of technological marvel is now construed once again as "natural," removed from history and frozen in time, to serve as a place of psychic refuge for beleaguered citizens of a consumer-oriented, postmodern American society.[14]

WORKS CITED

Bennett, Emerson, *The Prairie Flower; or, Adventures in the Far West*. Cincinnati: J.A. and U.P. James, 1849, rev. ed., 1850.

Borrett, George Tuthill, *Letters from Canada and the United States*. London: J.E. Adlard, printed for private circulation, 1865.

Carter, Paul, *The Road to Botany Bay: An Exploration of Landscape and History*. Chicago: University of Chicago Press, 1987.

Combination Atlas Map of Lee County [Illinois]. Chicago: Everts, Baskin & Stewart, 1872.

Compendium of History Reminiscence and Biography of Lyon County, Iowa. Chicago: George A. Ogle, 1904-5.

Corner, Faye Emma, "Culture Change in a Low-German Rural Community in Champaign County, Illinois," Unpublished M.A. thesis, University of Illinois, 1930.

Faux, W., *Memorable Days in America: Being a Journal of a Tour to the United States, Principally Undertaken to Ascertain, by positive evidence, the condition and prospects of British Emigrants; including accounts of Mr. Birkbeck's Settlement in the Illinois*. London: W. Simpkin & R. Marshall, 1823.

Ferguson, William, *America by River and Rail; or, Notes by the Way on the New World and Its People*. London: James Nisbet, 1856.

[Flagg, Edmund], *The Far West: or, A Tour Beyond the Mountains*. New York: Harper, 1838.

Garland, Hamlin, *A Son of the Middle Border*. Boston: Grosset & Dunlap, 1917.

---

[14] The conservative overtones of this heartland image are inescapable. Representation of the Midwest as the symbolic family farm that every American symbolically comes from denies the urban, multicultural reality in which most Americans live (including the majority of the Midwestern population). This vision implicitly excludes people of color just as the environmental mythology of shaping "empty" prairie ignores the displacement of the indigenous peoples from their native locales. Regional imagery that allows attention to focus on rural landscape and culture to the exclusion of more populous Midwestern cities allows this symbolic "whitening" to occur.

Greenwood, Grace, *New Life in New Lands: Notes of Travel*. New York: J. B. Ford, 1873.

Gross, Barry, "In Another Country: The Revolt From the Village," *MidAmerica* 4 (1977): 101-19.

Gruchow, Paul, *Journal of a Prairie Year*. Minneapolis: University of Minnesota Press, 1985.

——, "Rosewood Township," *Townships*. Ed. Michael Martone, Iowa City: University of Iowa Press, 1992, pp. 67-83.

Hyde, Anne Farrar, *An American Vision: Far Western Landscape and National Culture, 1820-1920*. New York: New York University Press, 1990.

A London Parson [James, Harry], *To San Francisco and Back*. London: Society for Promoting Christian Knowledge [1875].

"Kansas," *Harper's Magazine* LCCVI (1888) reprinted in *The Midwest, A Collection from Harper's Magazine*. New York: Gallery Books, 1991, pp. 146-162.

Kearney, Stephen, "An Expedition Across Iowa in 1820," *Annals of Iowa*, 3rd ser., 10 (January, April 1912).

Kirkwood, Rev. John, *An Autumn Holiday in the United States and Canada*. Edinburgh: Andrew Elliot, 1887.

Kohn, Howard, *The Last Farmer: An American Memoir*. New York: Harper and Row, 1988.

Loehr, Rodney C., ed., *Minnesota Farmers' Diaries*. St Paul: Minnesota Historical Society, 1939.

Manfred, Frederick [Feike Feikema], *This Is the Year*. Garden City, NY: Doubleday, 1947.

Map of Bureau County, Illinois, With Sketches of Its Early Settlement. Chicago: N. Matson, 2nd ed., 1867.

Mcfarling, Lloyd, ed., *Exploring the Northern Plains, 1804-1876*. Caldwell, Idaho: Caxton Printers, 1955.

Oliphant, Laurence, *Minnesota and the Far West*. Edinburgh: William Blackwood & Sons, 1855.

Parker, N. Howe, *Iowa as It Is in 1856*. Chicago: Keen and Lee, 1856.

Pfeiffer, Emily, *Flying Leaves from East and West*. London: Field & Tuer, 2nd ed.

Plumbe, John, Jr., *Sketches of Iowa and Wisconsin, Taken during a Residence of Three Years in those Territories*. St. Louis: Chambers, Harris & Knapp, 1839.

Progressive West 1, 2 (July 1905): 35-36.

Quick, Herbert, *Vandemark's Folly* Indianapolis: Bobbs-Merrill, 1922.

Regan, John, *The Emigrant's Guide to the Western States of America*. Edinburgh: Oliver & Boyd, 2nd. ed., [c. 1848].

Ridge, Martin, "How the Middle West Became America's Heartland," *Inland* 2 (1976): 9-20.

Rose, George [Arthur Sketchley], *The Great Country; or, Impressions of America*. London: Tinsley Brothers, 1868.

Sala, George Augustus, *America Revisited*. London: Vizetelly, 1883, 2 vols.

Standard Atlas of Peoria City and County [IL]. Chicago: Ogle, 1896.

Thayer, Robert L., Jr., "Pragmatism in Paradise: Technology and the American Land-
    scape," *Landscape* 30 (1990): 1-11.
Ueland, Andreas, *Recollections of an Immigrant*. New York: Minton, Balch, 1929.
van Tramp, John, *Prairie and Rocky Mountain Adventures, or Life in the West*.
    Columbus, OH: Segner & Condit, 1867.
Wallace, David Foster, "Ticket to the Fair," *Harper's Magazine* 289 (July 1994): 35-
    54.
Weber, Ronald, "My Middle West," *Notre Dame* 14 (1985): 28-36.

"DEAR ... I HAVE NO OBJECTION TO ANYTHING" CONSTRUCTING IDENTITIES IN APARTMENT BUILDINGS IN NEW ORLEANS AND SAN FRANCISCO IN TENNESSEE WILLIAMS'S *A STREETCAR NAMED DESIRE* AND ARMISTEAD MAUPIN'S *TALES OF THE CITY*

Duco van Oostrum, University of Groningen

When Mary-Ann Singleton in Armistead Maupin's *Tales of the City* (1978) moves into her apartment on 28 Barbary Lane in San Francisco, she asks her landlady, Mrs. Madrigal, "Do you have any objections to pets?" Mrs. Madrigal answers, "Dear ... I have no objection to anything" (Maupin 16). Indeed, the next morning Mary-Ann finds a joint, named Beatrice and grown in Mrs. Madrigal's mysterious garden, attached to her door as a welcoming present from her landlady. Contrary to the fixed family values, rootedness, and lawfulness of her parental home in Cleveland, the apartment complex in San Francisco appears to offer Mary-Ann room to create an entirely new individuality, based on surprises, lawlessness, and pleasure.

When Blanche DuBois in Tennessee Williams's play, *A Streetcar Named Desire* (1947) arrives at her sister's apartment in Elysian Fields in New Orleans, she's stunned by the claustrophobic flat in the two-story apartment building. Blanche exclaims to her sister Stella, "why didn't you let me know ... that you had to live in these conditions!" Stella responds, "Aren't you being a little intense about it? It's not that bad at all! New Orleans isn't like other cities" (Williams 1. 121). Moving from the spacious plantation Belle Reve, with a stopover in Laurel, into the apartment complex in New Orleans, Blanche feels displaced and deprived of her traditional living quarters, forced to wriggle her identity into an oppressively small apartment with no room of her own.

Armistead Maupin's first collection of columns from *The San Francisco Chronicle* and Tennessee Williams's classic American play illustrate and complicate the inter-relations between discourses of regionalism, American national identity, and archi-tecture. On the one hand, the authors situate their respective texts in arguably the most regional cities of the United States, San Francisco and New Orleans. San Francisco stands tall as capital of liberalism and as the gay heaven on earth, whereas New Orleans harbours, as Kenneth Holditch phrases it, the "literary mystique" of the entire South (Holditch 63). On the other hand, both authors almost fetishise national mythol-ogies about individual self-realisation in an American landscape. Characters appear free to roam around and to choose their own, self-willed identity, ultimately realised in material success. But while the regional city may hold one set of identities—in San Francisco closely associated with sex and gender, in New Orleans with sex and mystery—and a national mythology another set, the local living space also shapes identity. The rules of the house and the literal space demarcated by walls add a significant component to writing identity.

For both authors, the structure of apartment buildings in the cities of New Orleans and San Francisco represents a region in which an alternative nation is written. Contrary to, for example, Saul Bellow's use of the city as a metaphor of fragmentation, displacement and alienation, both Williams and Maupin celebrate the (multipli)city of "alternative" New Orleans and San Francisco.[1] In this essay, I will argue that the discourse of the apartment buildings in these atypical cities offers an alternative to traditional structures within a national architectonics of America. Specifically, the individuals who occupy the apartments find other constructions of identity, such as "other" gender constructs, different structures of family, and alternative measures of success. In particular, I will examine the apartments in the city as "functional sites" for the formation of identity, as formulated in another context by Michel Foucault in *Discipline and Punish* (143). As Foucault suggests, architectural space plays an integral part in the configurations, the possibilities and limitations, of identity. The "functional sites," in Foucault's words, "code a space that architecture generally left at the disposal of several uses" (143). The "site" and "use" of the apartment building thus form a crucial locale for the formulation of identity on a local level.

In *Streetcar* and *Tales*, the "functional site" of the apartment building in combination with the regional characteristics of New Orleans and San Francisco lays the foundations for a new design of a local America. Williams chronicles the change from a Southern mythic construct of America to a vital, virile and violent America via the multi-racial, multi-nuclear family inhabitants of the apartment building on the edge of the French quarter in New Orleans. In other words, the apartment building in the city is "used" to dispose of an old regional identity and to shape it into a new stable identity. Maupin seeks the space for a self-created family, gender, and social structure in the apartment building of Mrs. Madrigal, "the Mother of us all" (26). San Francisco and the space it gives to the singles in the apartment complex functions to allow new structures within a national construct that do not appear to stabilise into one dominant typology. Both Williams and Maupin use the apartment in the city as a literary base to narrate a changed national identity, but with different results. To Williams, the apartments come to stand for classification and restriction, whereas for Maupin the apartments open new areas for self-definition.

The choice of literary texts for this analysis of structures of living in America, more specifically in regional cities and in apartment complexes, in relation to the writing of an increasingly localised identity, was made on the grounds of the interrelations between discourses of national, regional, and individual identity in these texts. Coincidentally, both New Orleans and San Francisco have their particular mode of transportation in the streetcar and the cable car, marking the cities with a further regional identity. In his presentation at the "Writing Nation, Writing Region" confer-

---

[1] Cf. Saul Bellow's *The Victim* (1947) and *Seize the Day* (1956) as examples of novels that present male protagonists wandering through the incomprehensible jungle of the modern city.

ence, Philip Fisher argued that notions about regionalism and national identity become more and more meaningless because of the particular make-up of American society. Facilitated by all sorts of modern transportation, Americans move around to such an extent that no one should feel confined to one place because they cannot get out of their home town. The ability to go from one place to another, according to Fisher, severely hampers parental control because children are much more able to determine their own lives, and a traditional family structure no longer governs the individual's formation. In addition, the relatively uncomplicated moving of entire families from one area of the country to another for professional or other reasons makes Americans so mobile that it becomes almost senseless to speak of determined regional identities. Fisher's argument relocates writing about regional identity to the familiar setting of the American mythology about self-reliance and self-determination. In a climate of increased attention to the determining effects of class, gender, and race on the formation and possibilities of identity (and above all on its limitations), Fisher provocatively resituates the individual as the agent of her/his cultural identity.

Both *A Streetcar named Desire* and *Tales of the City* are crucially engaged with identity formation in an American landscape of mobility and loss of family structure. The protagonists migrate to other American settings in the latest means of transportation. Blanche DuBois arrives in Elysian Fields on a streetcar, and when Stanley uncovers the "truth" about her identity, he offers her a bus ride back to Laurel. The bus becomes in this play of the 1940s the condition of possibility for moving from the country to the city for both Blanche and Stella (who must have taken the ride earlier). The bus and streetcar contrast with the plane and the cablecars in *Tales of the City*. As an indication of the modernisation of travel and the increasing possibilities of escaping one's region, Mary-Ann in 1976 travels across the U.S. from Cleveland to San Francisco. Whereas Blanche remains within the South, Mary-Ann escapes the provincialism of Cleveland.

Blanche's relative mobility in terms of changing from one place to another metaphorically illustrates the restrictions of her self-determination. Her arrival at the apartment complex displays only too brightly her previous regional identity. By taking a "streetcar named Desire," Blanche DuBois arrives at her sister's flat in New Orleans. In a fairly typical way, Blanche represents a stereotype of a mythic South.[2] Trying to impersonate the ideal of the Southern Belle, Blanche lives as the last of an aristocratic DuBois family, having desperately tried and failed to hold on to their plantation "Belle Reve" ("beautiful dream"), the "great big place with white columns" (1. 119; 8. 198-9). The beautiful dream of Southern life had been built on the reality of slavery and oppression. The story Blanche tells about the loss of Belle Reve dates back hundreds of years and the plantation disintegrated because, as Blanche tells Stanley, "our improvident grandfathers and father and uncles and brothers exchanged the land for their epic fornifications" (2. 140). The males of the family lost their moral values, succumbed to desire, and after a procession of funerals, only Stella and

---

[2] See, for example, Lionel Kelly, "The White Goddess" 125.

Blanche remained. With Stella's marriage to Stanley Kowalsky, and Blanche a widow, the French Huguenot family name will cease. The disintegration of the family, represented by the termination of their family name, the play implies, also signals the end of a traditional representation of American Southern culture.

What better place to show the difference between of an old mythic South of huge plantations and a new realistic South than a small, two-room apartment, the kitchen and bedroom only divided by transparent drapes? Blanche's insistence on Southern values becomes ludicrous and reveals that she is out of place. In an almost comic attempt to recapture her mythic role of Southern Belle, she needs to stay out of the light, otherwise her age, thirty, will become too apparent. Also, her sexual desires (critics have frequently labelled her as a nymphomaniac)[3] do not fit her virginal role, and increasingly Blanche seems to live entirely in her fantasies. She proves unable to live according to her image, based on a traditional role for white upper class women (ladies) in New Orleans. Her past comes back to haunt her and reveals her "true" identity.

In "New" Orleans, the Old South is uncovered as a lie. Stanley Kowalski, Stella's husband, traces Blanche's stories and discovers that Blanche had multiple affairs in a seedy hotel (the Flamingo) and that she lost her teaching position in Laurel because of her intimacies with a seventeen-year old student. In the apartment building on Elysian Street, there is no room for such a history, and Stanley buys her a bus ticket back to Laurel. The old architectonics expressed in the reverberating romantic names of Blanche DuBois ("white woods," she explains to the sweaty hulk Mitch), the beautiful dream of Belle Reve, and the Streetcar named Desire that leads to the playground of the blessed in Elysian Fields are subsumed in and bluntly rejected by Stanley Kowalski's apartment.

What is possible in New Orleans and what is different from Belle Reve especially becomes visible in the "new" American, Stanley Kowalski. In contrast to Blanche's Huguenot ancestry, Stanley declares his second generation American identity: "I am not a Polack. People from Poland are Poles, not Polacks. But what I am is one-hundred-per-cent American, born and raised in the greatest country on earth and proud as hell of it, so don't ever call me a Polack" (8. 197). The entire block in Elysian Fields is inhabited by people of multi-ethnic backgrounds: negro, Mexican, middle-class American. As Williams puts it rather romantically: "for New Orleans is a cosmo-politan city where there is a relatively warm and easy intermingling of races in the old part of town" (1.1821).[4] All in their mid-twenties to early thirties, the occupants share an interest in making money and dealing with hard facts. Stanley searches for ways to claim what's left of Belle Reve and wants to know the facts about Blanche. Coarse, brutal, associated with physical strength and compared to an animal, Stanley embodies a new American, only concerned with real material conditions. The gender divisions

---

[3] As William Kleb tells us in his summary of the reviews of the play, "for many she was simply a prostitute, a nymphomaniac, or both." William Kleb, "Marginalia" 30.

[4] Interestingly, Williams's play and its image of New Orleans in the play created, as Kenneth Holditch has argued, "a national image for the city." Kenneth Holditch, "South Toward Freedom" 64.

within the flats are clear; the men take care of business, play poker, go bowling or drink; the women stay at home. The extended family of the plantation makes place for a small nuclear family in a two-room flat.

Both Steve and Eunice Hubble in the upstairs apartment and Stanley and Stella in the downstairs apartment reflect such a new American family. In the play, Stella is pregnant and in scene 10 (in the hospital, off stage, of course) gives birth (the sex of the child is never given). The play ends with Stella holding her child, suggesting that Stanley and Stella carry the future for a new America. Even though the structure of a young couple and their child in their own small apartment in New Orleans might seem an idyllic portrait, the actual closing scene and the earlier descriptions of the marriages in the play produce far more disturbing effects. This new American family is locked into classifications and cannot accommodate both desire and individuality.

The apartment complex in Elysian Fields serves as a functional site in the transformation from the old Southern identity to a new all-American identity. The similarity between the two couples in the apartment building is striking and, as I will argue, functional in teaching new roles in the city. Apparently the couples duplicate the structure of each others' domestic relations. While Steve and Eunice and Stanley and Stella are much in love and actually brag about their great sex life, in both cases their heterosexual desire is coupled to domestic violence. During poker night, in scene 3, Stanley's violence is the most visible as he first smashes the radio and then hits his pregnant wife. In scene 5, the audience hears the noise from the Hubbles upstairs, culminating in Steve hitting Eunice. Blanche cannot fathom that the marriages in fact continue, yet Stella confesses to her that on their wedding night Stanley smashed all the light bulbs with his slippers and that she was "sort of thrilled by it" (4. 157). The violence in the marriages becomes normalised because the walls between upstairs and downstairs neighbour in the apartment complex transmit rather than shut out the noise of fights between husbands and wives. This makes, as Stella explains, domestic violence the norm in their building. In *Streetcar*, violence is inherent in heterosexual relations and standard behaviour within the apartment building.

The close relationships and the flimsy walls within the complex set up a norm. Identity in the apartment is based on the dominance of the husband and the subservience of the wife, and the sexual relationships in the complex both reflect and continue the norm.

Blanche clearly resists the normalised relationships and roles of individuals within the apartment, precisely by locating her difference in sexual experience. In the fringes of the play, Blanche searches for non-violent sexual relations only to discover that such relations lie outside of normalised relationships. Her marriage to the young poet Allan Grey ended when he committed suicide. She had found her husband in bed with an older man, after which she exposed him cruelly during a dance, screaming "I saw! I know! You disgust me" (6. 184).[5] When she seduces other men in the play, they do not fit this pattern of violent heterosexuality. Both the paperboy she kisses in New

---

[5] Gilbert and Gubar have argued that Blanche's rape by Stanley can be viewed as punishment for her cruel exposure of Allan Grey's homosexuality. See Sandra Gilbert and Susan Gubar, *No Man's Land* 51.

Orleans and the seventeen-year old high school student in Laurel are under her control. Furthermore, when she seduces Mitch during poker night (stripping in the lamplight), she chooses the least threatening of the men. In fact, Mitch still lives with his sick mother and explicitly tells Blanche that he seeks someone to replace her. The possibility of an alternative sexual relationship, however, cannot be accommodated and is thus not recognised in the apartment building. Stanley only reveals the "truth" about Blanche's many affairs, but, as Stella points out, says nothing about Blanche's earlier marriage to, as she phrases it, "a degenerate" (7. 190); her experience of sexuality falls outside the norm of the nuclear family.

The apartment is also a functional site to deal with the problem of the "abnormal" Blanche. Not only does the building facilitate surveillance through hearing, but the lack of walls and the claustrophobic space within Stanley's apartment also enables a surveillance through seeing.[6] In one of the earliest stage directions concerning Stanley, he is described as sizing "women up at a glance, with sexual classifications, crude images flashing into his mind and determining the way he smiles at them" (1. 128). As soon as the men discover the "truth" about Blanche's affairs, they move her from the category of Southern Belle to the category of whore. Just as the myth of the aristocratic South is debunked by its evil history of slavery and oppression, so is Blanche's myth exposed by the revelation of her true "evil" history. When Mitch shows up late for his date with Blanche, he confronts her with her past. He now "sees" her as she really is. Amazingly, he informs her that he doesn't want to marry her because she's "not clean enough to bring in the house with [his] mother" (9. 207) but at the same time he is moving in on her in an attempt to rape her. In this case, she is able to resist by screaming fire, the traditional recourse of the lady in distress rather than the powerful female role she's been playing up to this moment.

When Stella is in labour at the hospital, Stanley enforces the norm through violence. Claiming that "We've had this date from the beginning" (10. 215), he rapes Blanche and thus uses power and sex to move her into the category of the subservient woman.[7] The classification of the roles of men and women in the structure of the nuclear family does not have room for a non-violent relationship. The closing scene of the play shows Stella watching Blanche being carried off to an insane asylum because Stella will not believe that Stanley has raped her sister. Sobbing "with inhuman abandon," Stella, holding her new born child, is comforted by Stanley's "now, love. Now, now, love," while his fingers "find the opening of her blouse" and while the men sit down for yet another game of poker (11. 226).[8]

---

[6] Cf. Foucault's analysis of "Panopticism," based on Jeremy Bentham's architectural design for a new prison (also called "the seeing machine"), governed by principles of surveillance. The apartment structure in *Streetcar* also becomes a place with little privacy in which all actions might be observed (Michel Foucault, *Discipline and Punish*, esp. ch. 3).

[7] Kathleen Lant even argues that after the rape, Blanche "ceases" to be human and becomes "merely a figure." Kathleen Margaret Lant, *A Streetcar* 226.

[8] Ronald Hayman suggests that "Stella represents the young America, torn between its loyalty to antiquated idealism and the brutal realism of the present, while Blanche incarnates the pretensions of the old South." Ronald Hayman, *Tennessee Williams*, p. 112. This reading too easily conflates the possibilities

The transition from Belle Reve to the two-story apartment building thus proves to be the transition from one type of classificatory system to another. While the new American nuclear family seems to cast off its historical restrictions, in fact they appear now within the tiny, two-room flat. Especially at the end of the play, the celebratory mood and atmosphere with music and multi-racial friendships that was so evident at the beginning has changed into a stifling atmosphere of enclosure. The entire stage breathes an atmosphere of confinement. When Blanche remarks on one occasion that "there is no privacy here. There's just these portieres between the two rooms at night" (6. 181), she also describes Stella's final predicament. Trapped in an apartment which has a built-in surveillance system as part of its architectural design, Stella watches the "abnormal" Blanche being carried off to an insane asylum.[9] Under pressure of the nuclear family, Stella refuses to believe Blanche's truth about Stanley and thus must agree with Blanche's "abnormal" status.[10] Stella's role seems to reside entirely within that two-room flat, raising her child, dependent on and subservient to Stanley.

In relation to constructing an American identity, it is particularly significant that Stella has now been type-cast into the role of submissive wife and mother. Stella is the one who, as it were, tried to escape the past of Belle Reve and make it all by herself in the big city. Fleeing the constrictions of a mythic South, where she as younger sister was dependent on Blanche (in the play, she's also constantly waiting on Blanche, which, she says, "makes it seem like home" [5. 170]), Stella tries to become independent. As Blanche makes only too clear to her, Stella abandoned Belle Reve and left Blanche to cope with maintaining the plantation: "you left! I stayed and struggled! You came to New Orleans and looked out for yourself" (1. 125-6). Stella answers with her tentative declaration of independence: "The best I could do was make my own living, Blanche" (1. 126). Improved means of transportation, increased mobility and loss of parental control and family structure have not resulted in a self-determined individual American identity, as Fisher suggested. Stella's gender, a new family structure and the confined quarters of the apartment have in fact moved her from one determining setting to another.

In *Tales of the City*, Mary-Ann Singleton flees from her parental home and secretarial job at Lassiter Fertilisers in Cleveland to her new apartment on Barbary Lane in San Francisco. Mary-Ann's flight, her ability to find a new job, and her impulsive decision to break with her parents exemplify problems with current discussions about American regionalism in the terms expressed by Fisher: transportation, mobility, loss of parental control and lack of family structure. The American individual is free to choose her

---

of women in the South with "idealism" and "realism" and specifically ignores any structural gender inequalities.

[9] In *Madness and Civilization*, Michel Foucault traces the process by which "madness" became a medical condition which was best treated by institutionalisation. The way in which madness increasingly served to uphold a norm applies well to Blanche's institutionalisation. By removing the abnormal from Stanley's environment, his norm remains unchallenged.

[10] Cf Foucault, "the family [becomes] the privileged locus of emergence for the disciplinary question of the normal and the abnormal" (Michel Foucault, *Discipline and Punish*, p. 216).

identity. While the genre and tone of *Tales of the City* and *Streetcar* differ considerably, the preoccupation with new definitions of identity links the two works, reinforced by the intertextual reference to *Streetcar* in *Tales of the City* which immediately points to overlapping concerns with desire and identity in the two works. When Michael Tolliver, Mary-Ann's downstairs neighbor, seduces his lover gynecologist Jon Fielding, he quotes Blanche DuBois: "I want to deceive him just long enough to make him want me" (Maupin 119; Williams 5. 187). Powerful female sexuality, which is a transgression of the norm in *Streetcar*, becomes the norm in Maupin's work. In *Tales of the City*, the equivalent of Blanche's wish for non-violent heterosexual relations is homosexual desire. Rather than imposing limitations on identity through gender and sex, the world of *Tales* opens up new realms of desire and gender. As in *Streetcar*, most of the protagonists in the apartment building are between twenty-five and thirty, searching to fulfil their American dream of independence and self-determination. Yet in contrast to Blanche and Stella's move to their city of possibilities, New Orleans, which is ultimately a city of impossibilities, the main characters in *Tales of the City* are able to construct new identities, independent of their past limitations. Mary-Ann's declaration of independence seems to invoke typical narratives of American identity. In her version of "going West," Mary-Ann decides to leave the stability of Cleveland and to lead her own life. On her first visit to San Francisco during an eight-day vacation, she calls her stunned mother: "I'm not coming home, Mom ... I just want to start making my own life ... have my own apartment and all" (8). Mary-Ann's decision opens a book (or, series of column articles) in which the reader is introduced to various San Francisco characters, who in some odd Dickensian way are all connected to one another. As in *Streetcar*, the unit of the apartment building in San Francisco plays a formative role in shaping the regional American identity outlined in Maupin's book.

What seems to be typical of San Francisco is the way in which the characters create and stylise their own lives. In an interview with Paul Rabinow, Foucault asks: "But couldn't everyone's life become a work of art? Why should the lamp or the house be an art object, but not our life?" To which Rabinow answers: "Of course, that kind of project is very common in places like Berkeley where people think that everything from the way they eat breakfast, to the way they have sex, to the way they spend their day, should itself be perfected" (350). Indeed, *Tales of the City* thrives on the hilarious stories of characters trying to perfect their lives: the Bohemian DéDé Day, who lost 18 pounds in two weeks at The Golden Door (a fat farm for the wealthy) for a mere $3,000; the black model D'Orothea, who only became black through taking pills and having ultraviolet treatments; Michael Tolliver, who tries to pick up dates wearing a huge Pan outfit; or Vincent, at the Bay Area Crisis Switchboard, who perfects his own "organic" suicide (178). All of these wild tales which illustrate a supreme American individuality could be called examples of what Foucault called "arts of existence." In his analysis of ultra-privileged groups of free males in ancient Greece, Foucault tries to uncover modes of being which fall outside a disciplinary structure. What attracts him to ancient Greece are the so-called "arts of existence":

> What I mean by the phrase are those intentional and voluntary actions by which men not only set themselves rules of conduct, but also seek to transform themselves, to change themselves in their singular being, and to make their life into an *oeuvre* that carries certain aesthetic values and meets certain stylistic criteria. (*Use of Pleasure* 10-11)

San Francisco and the Bay area appear to be the territory of the new Greeks, free from the restrictions of society and the body, at least for the privileged. *Tales* disregards the ubiquitous problems of race and poverty and focuses solely on those who are not hindered by cultural disadvantages in their search for individual perfection. Yet what *Tales* demonstrates is that the individual stylisation of life according to an aesthetic code may lead to a condition of weightlessness, in which all stability and structure is lost. In all these fantastic stories of creating oneself, it is the apartment building that is offered as a stable foundation against a fragmentary life-style.

What *Tales* shows over and over again is that self-stylisation and complete independence results in a loss of self. Mary-Ann's temporary stay at the apartment of her high school friend Connie Bradshaw shows her the nightmare of living alone. Living from one one-night stand to another, Connie endures a life of utter loneliness. Mrs. Madrigal's apartment building offers respite from such a destitute sense of self. Contingent upon creating a new identity, the novel seems to suggest, the characters also need to create new families. What's interesting in this collection of wild tales is the continual search for a structure of belonging. The independence or the "stylisation of self" that is possible in San Francisco is not in itself enough to shape one's life. Mrs. Madrigal's apartment building provides a family organisation offering room for individualism that can hardly be classified in traditional terms.

The entire simulated family structure replaces the tenants' real family. Mrs. Madrigal, landlady and "mother" of the three-story house, nurtures her "children" in unusual ways. Contrary to Mary-Ann's real mother whose life-experience seems made up of popular television shows, for example, Mrs. Madrigal is literary and helps all her tenants in unseen ways. Her identity seems entirely self-willed; having grown up in a whorehouse called Blue Moon Lodge in Nevada, she renamed herself twelve years ago and now, as she phrases it, runs "a house of my own" (55). Mona Ramsey, thirty-one years old, copy-writer for Halcyon Communications, resides in the apartment on the first floor, rooming off and on with the pronounced homosexual Michael Tolliver. Mary-Ann Singleton lives on the second floor, with across from her the pronounced heterosexual Brian Hawkins, ex-lawyer for causes. Norman Neal Williams, p.i., middle-aged, determined to reveal the true identity of Mrs. Madrigal and thus bring her down, occupies the small apartment on the third-floor. In a metaphorical sense Williams embodies the principle of surveillance, so dominant in the apartment building in Elysian Fields in *Streetcar*. From the roof, Williams can oversee Barbary Lane and within the apartment, he, in a manner similar to Stanley Kowalski's enquiries in *Streetcar*, tries to uncover Mrs. Madrigal's sexual history.

These characters' multiple stories unfold in such a way that they come to recognise their mutual relations as resembling those of a family. Mona moves out to live with her ex-lover D'Orothea, only to discover D'Orothea's assumed African-American identity. When Michael Tolliver's real parents come to visit from Orlando, he is immediately straight-jacketed into a heterosexual identity, which becomes rather problematic when, on their way to dinner on Halloween, Michael and his parents run into a few of his transvestite friends on roller-skates. Within the apartment, new relations and communications between very different people become possible. Brian and Michael even go cruising together at the end of the novel. The difficulties with the freedom and instability of San Francisco are somehow countered by the structure of the apartment building and the self-created family. When Mary-Ann announces to Michael her return to Cleveland, she declares that she longs back to the stability of Cleveland:

> Michael, there's no stability here. Everything's too easy. Nobody sticks with anybody or anything, because there's always something just a little bit better waiting around the corner. ... I can't handle all this Michael. I want to live somewhere where you don't have to apologize for serving instant coffee. Do you know what I like about Cleveland? People in Cleveland aren't "into" anything! (112)

In the end the self-created family offers the stability Mary-Ann seeks, by sticking together. When Mrs. Madrigal's position as landlady is threatened by Williams's investigations, Williams himself, who appeared to be the only stable person in the house, is exposed as deeply involved in child pornography. Mary-Ann confronts a very drunk Williams with her discovery while they are walking along a cliff. When Williams slips, Mary-Ann tries to save him by grabbing his tie; however, "He left behind his clip-on tie, dangling limply from her hand" (262). Even his tie was not real or reliable. Mary-Ann burns Williams's incriminating files about Mrs. Madrigal, and the entire family unites in a traditional Christmas party at their home on 28 Barbary Lane. Williams's death shows that there is no room for an oppressive surveillance system in Mrs. Madrigal's apartment building.

In conclusion, the move from one type of traditional American identity, a mythic Southern identity or a middle-class Midwestern one, to identities developed in apartments in New Orleans or San Francisco, proves dramatic. Stella's and Blanche's settlement in the flat in New Orleans results in constrictions that rule out possibilities outside a recognised classificatory system of gender and class. In the apartment building in San Francisco, however, there is room for creating identities of all sorts, with at its solid base the foundation of the imaginary family.

This brief and limited analysis of moving from one place to another in America and in particular of the regional characteristics of residing in apartment buildings serves to problematise notions of national identity. New Orleans, according to Stella a city unlike other cities, forms the location of a Southern culture that is moving from a world of illusions to hard facts. But what are we to make of San Francisco? "Nobody's *from* here" (46), Brian tells Mary-Ann and perhaps it's better to believe in Mrs. Madrigal's theory, which seems to echo Foucault, that the inhabitants of San Francisco are in fact reincarnations of ancient Greece: "There's a theory ... that we are all Atlanteans" (175).

WORKS CITED

Bellow, Saul, *Seize the Day*. New York: Viking, 1956.

——, *The Victim*. New York: Penguin, 1971.

Fisher, Philip, "Reparable and Irreparable Regionalisms in America." Unpublished paper delivered at the NASA-Conference "Writing Nation, Writing Region," Middelburg 1994.

Foucault, Michel, *Discipline and Punish: The Birth of the Prison*. Trans. Alan Sheridan. New York: Vintage, 1979.

——, *Madness and Civilization: A History of Insanity in the Age of Reason*. Trans. Richard Howard. New York: Vintage, 1988.

——, "On the Genealogy of Ethics." Interview with Paul Rabinow. *The Foucault Reader*. Ed. P. Rabinow. New York: Pantheon, 1984. 340-380.

——, *The Use of Pleasure: The History of Sexuality*. Vol. 2. Trans. Robert Hurley. New York: Vintage, 1985.

Gilbert, Sandra and Susan Gubar, *No Man's Land: The Place of the Woman Writer in the Twentieth Century*. Vol. 1. New Haven: Yale UP, 1988.

Hayman, Ronald, *Tennessee Williams: Everyone Else is an Audience*. New Haven: Yale UP, 1993.

Holditch, Kenneth, "South Toward Freedom: Tennessee Williams." *Literary New Orleans: Essays and Meditations*. Baton Rouge: Louisiana State UP, 1992, pp. 61-75.

Kelly, Lionel, "The White Goddess, Ethnicity, and the Politics of Desire." *Confronting Streetcar*, Ed. Philip C. Kolin, pp. 121-132.

Kleb, William, "Marginalia: *Streetcar*, Williams, Foucault. *Confronting Streetcar*, Ed. Philip C. Kolin, pp. 27-43.

Kolin, Philip C., *Confronting Tennessee Williams's A Streetcar Named Desire: Essays in Critical Pluralism*. London: Greenwood Press, 1993.

 "Reflections on/of *A Streetcar Named Desire*." *Confronting Streetcar*, Ed. Philip C. Kolin, pp. 1-17.

Lant, Kathleen Margaret. "A Streetcar named Misogyny." *Violence in Drama*. Ed. James Redmond. Cambridge: Cambridge UP, 1991, pp. 225-238.

Maupin, Armistead. *Tales of the City*. London: Black Swan, 1992.

Williams, Tennessee. *A Streetcar Names Desire and Other Plays*. London: Penguin, 1959.

"IMPLACABLE AND BROODING IMAGE"
WILLIAM FAULKNER AND SOUTHERN LANDSCAPE

Richard Gray, Essex

Geography matters in Southern writing. As one fairly minor Southern writer has put it, "More than any other people of the world, the Southerners have that where-do-you-come-from-sense." W.J. Cash, famously, went further than this in *The Mind of the South*: by insisting on a general relation between Southern climate and character. Extravagant colours, lush fertility, perpetual heat-haze, and a prevailing mood of what he called "drunken reverie" disrupted by violent thunderstorms: all of these, Cash argued, contributed to a "physical world" that was, as he put it, "a sort of cosmic conspiracy against reality," and helped predispose the regional character towards dreamlike animation and emotional excess. As a climatic generalisation, let alone a cultural one, this seems highly arguable: not even the single state of Mississippi has a uniform landscape and weather, let alone the South as a whole. Nevertheless, a peculiar pattern of indolence punctuated by violence *is* noticeable in Southern narratives at least as far back as *The Adventures of Huckleberry Finn* and, before that (if we are willing to accept Poe as a Southern author), *The Narrative of Arthur Gordon Pym*. And, as for William Faulkner, there does seem to be a peculiar and peculiarly close connection between the weather and the physical world that were Faulkner's familiars and his habits of mind, the landscape of his imagination. As one critic of Faulkner has put it, nature often seems to "generate ... mood" in the Yoknapatawpha novels and stories. In the short story "Dry September," for instance, a lynching seems to issue from the "sixty-two rainless days" that precede it—from a claustrophobic, combustible physical environment that only requires one spark, one small occasion, to set it alight. "That's the trouble with this country," a character declares in *As I Lay Dying*:

> everything, weather, all, hangs on too long. Like our rivers, our land's opaque, slow, violent: shaping and creating the life of man in its implacable and brooding image.[1]

Feelings like this are, of course, partly a matter of attribution. Faulkner was well aware that we make a landscape in the process of perceiving it: that we attempt to give

---

[1] William Faulkner, *As I Lay Dying* (1930; London: Penguin, 1963 edition), p. 38. See also, "Dry September," *Collected Stories of William Faulkner* (1959; New York: Random House, 1977 edition), p. 169; Eugene Walter, *Untidy Pilgrim* (New York: Alfred A. Knopf, 1954), p. 21; Wilbur J. Cash, *The Mind of the South* (New York: Alfred A. Knopf, 1941), pp. 46-8; Cleanth Brooks, William Faulkner: *The Yoknapatawpha Country* (New Haven, Conn.: Yale U.P., 1963), p. 30.

our lives a geographical location, a local habitation and a name and then, having done this, are inclined to confuse effect with cause. But Faulkner was no more a solipsist than he was a positivist. His characters may be keen to leave some "fragile and indelible" evidence of themselves on the surface of the earth—like the girl in *Requiem for a Nun* who scratches her name on a window-pane in the Jefferson town jail— something (we are told) that says, *"Listen, stranger; this was myself: this was I."*[2] The activity is not, however—at least, as Faulkner sees it—a matter of simple imposition. For all that Shreve, in *Absalom, Absalom!*, may describe the South as "a kind of vacuum," it has its own idelible contours, its own harsh weather patterns and brute materiality. So the relationship between it, and character, has to be more complicated and unstable than the usual, commonsense notions tend to allow. Mind does not dominate world in Faulkner's work, any more than world merely dictates the terms of the mind. Between life and landscape, character and climate, there is active dialogue, collaboration and conflict: created out of habit or simple need.

Something of this dialogue is registered in that moment in *The Hamlet* when Flem Snopes has just arranged for the wild Texas ponies to be sold to the gullible locals of Frenchman's Bend. As the untameable animals scatter in all directions, causing havoc, V.K. Ratcliff and his companions fetch Will Varner to help the injured Henry Armstid. "They went up the road in a body," the narrator observes,

> treading the moon-blanched dust in the tremulous April night murmurous with the moving of sap and the wet bursting of burgeoning leaf and bud and constant with the thin and urgent cries and the brief and fading burst of galloping horses ...
>
> * * *
>
> ... The moon was new high overhead, a pearled and mazy yawn in the soft sky, the ultimate ends of which rolled onward, whorl on whorl, beyond the pale stars and by pale stars surrounded ... Then the pear tree came in sight. It rose in mazed and silver immobility like exploding snow; the mockingbird still sang in it. "Look at that tree," Varner said. "It ought to make this year, sho."
>
> "Corn'll make this year too," one said.
>
> "A moon like this is good for every growing thing outen earth," Varner said. "I mind when me and Mrs. Varner was expecting Eula. Already had a mess of children and maybe ought to quit then. But I wanted some more gals ... there was an old woman told my mammy once that if a woman showed her belly to the full moon after she had done caught, it would be a gal. So Mrs. Varner taken and laid every night with the moon on her nekid belly, until it fulled and after. I could lay my ear to her belly and hear Eula kicking and scrouging like all get-out, feeling the moon."
>
> "You mean it actually worked sho enough, Uncle Will?" the other said. "Hah," Varner said. "You might try it. You get enough women showing their nekid bellies to the moon or the sun either ... and more than likely after a while there will be something you can lay your ear and listen to ..."
>
> * * *
>
> ... there was a brief rapid thunder of hooves on wooden planking.
>
> "There's another one on the creek bridge," one said.
>
> "They are going to come out even on them things after all," Varner said. "They'll get the money back in exercise and relaxation. You take a man that aint got no other relaxation all year long except dodging mule-dung up and down a field furrow. And a night like this ... is good for him. It'll make him sleep tomorrow night anyhow, provided he gets back home by then."[3]

---

[2] William Faulkner, *Requien for a Nun* (1951; London: Chatto & Windus, 1953 edition), pp. 202, 231. See also, *Absalom, Absalom!* (1936; London: Chatto & Windus, 1937 edition), p. 361.

[3] William Faulkner, *The Hamlet* (London: Chatto & Windus, 1940), pp. 305-8.

At first, it may seem that the conversation and activities of the characters here are in awkward contrast to the disconcerning beauty of their surroundings. However, as Michael Millgate has commented, despite their distance from the ornate splendour of the narrator's language, these people are clearly not unaffected by what they see. Varner's ready deployment of folklore is in itself a dialogic reading of nature: a communal attempt to interpret the perceived rhythms of day, month, and year that is given a sharply personal edge by his bawdy humour. The voice of his culture, registered in the inherited folk wisdom ("A moon like this is good for every growing thing"), engages with the extravagant voice of the narrator ("the moon ... a pearled and mazy yawn"), and with a more personal voice compounded of memory and comedy. All of these, in turn, engage with the fluid voices of the countryside—the song of the mockingbird, the galloping hooves, "the tremulous April night murmurous with the moving of sap"—so as to produce a feeling, not of unity, still less of the imposition of one voice on another, but of a complex, fertile engagement of opposites. "The novel," Michael Bakhtin has observed, "is ... multiform in style and variform in speech and voice." And here the multiplicity of style and variety of voice extend from "nature" through "culture" to the individual to project a creative inter-relationship in which each element possesses its own identity while being involved in contact with the other elements, and in mutual shaping. Varner himself seems to be shrewdly aware that the anarchic energy of the "almost musical" cries and hoof-beats is somehow in keeping with the tremblings and murmurings of the night: the rueful pursuers of the ponies will at least have an adventure to talk about for years to come. And the reader, taking a cue from him, may intuit a further, underlying relation betweeen the fecundity of nature, represented by the Spring night, the ponies, the story of Eula's conception and after, and the ravishing sexuality of Eula herself—who appears, shortly before the passage just quoted, looking through a window, "full in the moon ... the strong faint lift of breasts beneath marblelike fall of garment."[4] Faulkner brings these things together, just as he does the voices of the episode, but he never collapses them into some spurious notion of harmony. Nature, culture, and human nature are separated out and given their different languages, so that the reader can all the more easily see the moments of sympathy and connection between them, *and* take the measure of their difference.

Another way of putting this is to say that, here and elsewhere in his work, what Faulkner does, effectively, is to introduce instability into what is often seen as the most stable, and stabilising, of relationships: that between a human being and the earth. In the passage I quoted—and, even more, in the episode of the Texas ponies from which it comes—Faulkner permits different voices to collude and conflict: among them, the voice of Will Varner, the voice of folkloric wisdom, the voice of a more sophisticated narrator, and the "voices" of nature. As a result, event and environment are not perceived as stable: a scene from provincial life, say, located in appropriately pastoral

---

[4] Ibid., p. 306. See also, Michael Millgate, *The Achievement of William Faulkner* (London: Macmillan, 1966), p. 190; Mikhail Bakhtin, *The Dialogic Imagination*, edited and translated by Caryl Emerson and Michael Holquist (Austin, Texas: University of Texas Press, 1981), p. 261.

surroundings. On the contrary, they are seen in terms of a collision: a play, or conflict, between different specific forces that are themselves unstable and variable—subject not only to inter-action but to change. None of the relations here is represented as fixed: there is continual flux and reflux, as the different narrative voices shift between different forms of exchange. The voices, the languages remain distinct, of course, but they engage with each other: Faulkner's simple, fundamental point is that different ways of talking, and different systems of exchange, meet and inter-act in that general process we call history—and in the particular moments of contact inscribed in the text.

This instability I am talking about is more than just a matter, though, of Faulkner's insistence on the collaborative nature of the creation of landscape, a sense of place—or of his emphasis on the fluctuating nature of the intimacies between man, or woman, and the earth. A further and deeper factor at work here has to do with the novelist's feeling for the history of the land. Faulkner thinks historically, even when it comes to his encounter with the earth; and, for him, that history is marked in particular by the assumptions of possession and dispossession. Nobody owns the land: that—as so many people have observed—is Faulkner's initial premise. The point is made insistently throughout his work, for example, in the story of the "education" of Ike McCaslin in *Go Down, Moses*—or in the description of "Uncle Buck" and "Uncle Buddy" in *The Unvanquished*, two members of the McCaslin clan who (we are told)

> believed that the land did not belong to the people but that people belonged to land and that the earth would permit them to live on and out of it only so long as they behaved and that if they did not behave right, it would shake them off just like a dog getting rid of fleas.[5]

So, not unnaturally, one of Faulkner's narrative preoccupations became the assumption of power over nature: the belief, or delusion, shared by generations that they have thoroughly possessed and permanently named the places they inhabit, the delusion that they have done this, that is, rather than just passed over them and given them passing identification. The ironies implicit in Faulkner's fictional interrogation of this belief were made the sharper because Faulkner tended to share that belief himself: as a landowner and, more important, as the man who laid claim to being "Sole Owner & Proprietor" (as he put it) of Yoknapatawpha County. Like so much elke in Faulkner's work, the idea or illusion of ownership exists there as both symptom and explanation: as something to be interrogated, through the lives of characters like Thomas Sutpen or Flem Snopes, but as something that also shapes the narratives those characters inhabit. That idea, we could say, is both an object and a means of knowledge in Faulkner's writing since Faulkner's relation to the land of Yoknapatawpha was analogous to that of his characters. Claiming to possess it, he was in fact possessed by it; wanting to appropriate it, he could do no more than inhabit it temporarily. Like the

---

[5] William Faulkner, *The Unvanquished* (1938; London: Chatto & Windus, 1955 edition), p. 36. The phrase "WILLIAM FAULKNER, Sole Owner & Proprietor" appears on the map of Yoknapatawpha County that Faulkner drew for *Absalom, Absalom!* For an interesting recent discussion of Faulkner's notions of ownership see Philip Weinstein, *Faulkner's Subject: A Cosmos No One Owns* (Cambridge: Cambridge University Press, 1992).

land to which the label "Sutpen's Hundred" is attached in *Absalom, Absalom!*, it existed apart from any specific acts of naming, all pretensions to ownership and control. It was inertly, and continually, resistant to fixed signs.

The assumption of power over nature links up closely, in Faulkner's work, with the assumption of power and proprietorial control over human nature, witnessed in historical injustices towards the members of two races. As a Mississippian, Faulkner had particular reasons for linking the fact of the land to the idea of betrayal: massive land claims, the dispossession of Native Americans and the claim to possession of African Americans were all marked and related features of the state's history. Between 1820 and 1832, huge land cessions amounting to two-thirds of the state were wrung from the Choctaws and Chickasaws by what one historian has called a combination of "bribery and drink," and "threats and promises ... of only two alternatives—extinction or forcible removal."[6] These transactions set Mississippi on a different road that led not only to secession and civil war but, afterwards, to an insularity remarkable for its extent and persistence. In the short term, there was a massive explosion of cheap public land and a speculative farming population. During the "flush times" between 1830 and 1840, the state population as a whole increased 175 percent, while the slave population grew 197 percent: by 1840, for the first time, black people outnumbered whites in Mississippi. However, in the long term, towns failed to develop, industry was stifled, education remained dormant: in short, a pattern was set that for a century after 1830 would keep Mississippi one of the most rural states in the nation. Of course, other states seized land from the Indians and experienced booms in speculation and slavery. But the speed, scale, and consequences of the flush times in Mississippi were unusually—although not uniquely—dramatic. So it is hardly surprising that, as a native son of Mississippi and a peculiarly alert one, Faulkner should have registered the tangled, tentacular relationship between man (or woman) and land. The vicissitudes of history were something written into his surroundings, promoting instabilities that seemed to be as much a matter of place, really, as of time.

Something of the way history was inscribed in geography for Faulkner is registered in two of his stories that deal with the complex, ironic relationship between

---

[6] John Ray Skates, *Mississippi* (New York: Random House, 1979), pp. 80-1. See also, pp. 83, 87-9. "The land is inimical to the white man," Faulkner argued once, "because of the unjust way in which it was taken from Ikkemotubbe and his people. That happened by treaty, which President Jackson established with the Chickasaws and the Choctaws, in which they would take land in Oklahoma in exchange for their Mississippi land, and they were paid for it, but they were compelled to leave it, either to leave on—to follow a chimera in the West or to stay there in a condition even worse than the Negro slave, in isolation. There are a few of them still in Mississippi, but they are a good deal like animals in a zoo: they have no place in the culture, in the economy, unless they become white men, and they have in some cases mixed with white people and their own conditions have vanished, or they have mixed with Negroes and they have descended into the Negroes' condition of semi-peonage." When a member of the group to whom he addressed these remarks declared, "And ... they [the Choctaws and Chickasaws] never owned the land. The land was never theirs." Faulkner responded, "That's right. The Indians held the land communally, a few of them that were wise enough to see which way the wind was blowing would get government patents for the land." *Faulkner in the University: Class Conferences at the University of Virginia 1947-1958* edited by Frederick L. Gwynn and Joseph L. Blotner (Charlottesville, Va.: University of Virginia Press, 1959), pp. 43-4.

red, white, and black people in Yoknapatawpha, "Red Leaves" and "A Justice." "Red Leaves" concentrates on the autumn of the Old Days, the time of the Native Americans in the county. Issetibbeha, the Man, has just died and his black body servant has fled, in order to escape the traditional burial of the slave with the dead chief. With this story of escape and pursuit acting as the narrative spine, the anonymous narrator then comes back into earlier times to recall the arrival of black slaves among the Chickasaws. To the Chickasaw Indians, we are told, their newly acquired human property seemed

> remote, inscrutable. [The slaves] were like a single octopus. They were like the roots of a huge tree uncovered, the earth broken momentarily upon the writhen, thick fetid tangle of its lightless and ourtraged life.[7]

The intensely poetic conceit hardly seems out of place. This is partly because of the ritualistic quality of the narrative. Faulkner may be intent on establishing the past as something vitally connected to the present, but he also wishes to respect its specificity and radical difference; and one convenient way of doing this is through an oracular, shaman-like style of storytelling. The conceit has a more particular relevance here, however, since it expresses the sense of violation, natural forces disrupted and disturbed, that characterises this era of exploration, enslavement, and conquest. The reader is continually reminded of the frontier as a site of struggle and confusion, where trophies and status have become blurred, unpredictable, and faintly ominous. Issetibbeha, for instance, owns "ten thousand acres of matchless parklike forest where deer grazed like domestic cattle," a "herd of blacks for which he had no use at all," "a gilt bed ... and a pair of slippers with red heels" brought back from a trip to Paris; and he lives in a rotting shell of a steamboat which slaves have hauled twelve miles overland, its "carving glinting momentarily and fading through the mould in figures cabalistic and profound." A similar conflict of cultural icons is notable in the representation of the escaped slave: who, we are told, wears

> a pair of dungaree pants bought by Indians from white men, and an amulet slung on a thong about his hips. The amulet consisted of one half of a mother-of-pearl lorgnon which Issetibbeha had brought back from Paris and the skull of a cottonmouth mocassin. He had killed the snake himself and eaten it, save the poison head.[8]

The tensions between the residual culture of the Chickasaws, and the emergent culture of the whites, is neatly caught here and then expanded in the larger terms of the story. Most of "the People" (as the tribe is called) observe the rituals of the hunt. However, Moketubbe, Issetibbeha's son, prefers wearing the red slippers to engagement in strenuous, ritualistic practices; and, in any event, *this* rite is contaminated by the simple fact that the hunt is for a commodity, a human being reduced to property. As the useless trinkets Issetibbeha brings back from Paris indicate, the tribe has already surrendered to the white man's world of exchange value; and it has virtually abandoned

---

[7] William Faulkner, "Red Leaves," in *Collected Stories*, p. 315. See also, pp. 320, 324.
[8] Ibid., p. 330.

hunting as a source of physical and spiritual sustenance in favour of the white man's ideology of ownership and trade. The escaped slave, we learn, had once eaten a rat, which he had caught easily since it had been "civilised, by association with man reft of its inherent cunning of limb and eye"; and the People have come to resemble that rat, corrupted by association with a culture that will, in any case, supplant them. The lesson of possession, of land and slaves, is one they have learned without, it seems, much deliberation or even desire; and it will lead, eventually, to their dispossession by the men who have been their teachers—distant, enigmatic creatures who seem to have won the struggle between cultures even before it has begun.

One of the triumphs of a story like "Red Leaves," I think, is that implicitly it takes cognizance of a crucial problem in the representation of the history of a land: the problem, that is, of disclosing that past as separate and yet also a precondition of the present—of uncovering both connection and difference. The Native American past of Yoknapatawpha speaks with its own voice in "Red Leaves," its strangeness registered among other things in the strangeness *it* perceives in the figure of the white man, a scarcely decipherable source of trinkets, whisky, and odd new customs like finance and ownership. But it speaks in a language not unrelated to our own, uncovering traces of a struggle that was and is the grounds of our existence. It speaks to us, in short, in terms that reconstitute it as what Fredric Jameson would call a vital episode "in a single vast unfinished plot"[9]—and as the necessary, and bloody, prehistory of the present.

In "A Justice," this sense of the process by which history is written into geography—of the past inhering in place and of that past as at once intimate and strange—all this is closer to the surface of the narrative because, as so often in Faulkner's work, the act of telling, "old tales and talking," becomes a paradigm of the way we reconstitute the history of a land—and the way we situate ourselves as historical beings. The levels of telling in "A Justice" are several. Quentin Compson is the narrator and he tells a story that he heard, as a boy, from Sam Fathers who, in turn, heard it from Herman Basket, one of the People. It is set in the last, corrupted era of Choctaw (in later stories, Chickasaw) life as it began to be disrupted by contact with white culture; and it is a tale of origins, concerning Sam's birth and naming. The genealogy of which "A Justice" tells is a radically mixed one. Sam was born, he himself, Quentin, and we learn, of a black slave woman by a Choctaw warrior named Crawfish-ford, much to the chagrin of the slave woman's black husband. The rivalry between Crawfish-ford and the husband supplies much of the narrative substance: a rivalry that is given an ingenious resolution by the then chief of the tribe, Ikke-motubbe—or Doom, as he came to be called. His solution to the problem is to require Crawfish-ford to build a palisade fence around the slave woman's house to keep its young builder out; and, apparantly, this makeshift "justice" works. Sam's complexion may be suspiciously copper-coloured and his origins dubious—hence his initial name, Had-Two-Fathers—but the next child born to the woman is as black as could be

---

[9] Fredric Jameson, *The Political Unconscious: Narrative as a Socially Symbolic Act* (Ithaca, N.Y.: Cornell University Press,1981), p. 17.

wished, and clearly begotten by the woman's husband. Quentin's response to this narrative, when he first hears it, is uncertain to the point of incomprehension: "I was just twelve then," he recalls, "and to me the story did not seem to have got anywhere, to have had point or end." But, as he re-tells it, the older Quentin remembers his conviction that he would one day understand the significance of what he had heard: that he would not always have the experience but miss the meaning. "Grandfather called me again," he informs us:

> This time I got up. The sun was already beyond the peach orchard ...
>   * * *
> "What were you and Sam talking about?" Grandfather said.
> We went on, in that strange, faintly sinister suspension of twilight in which I believed I could still see Sam Fathers back there, sitting on his wooden block, definite, immobile, and complete, like something looked upon after a long time in a preservative bath in a museum. That was it. I was just twelve then, and I would have to wait until I had passed on and through and beyond the suspension of twilight. Then I knew that I would know. But then Sam Fathers would be dead.
> "Nothing, sir," I said. "We were just talking."[10]

Whether Quentin, at any age, begins to *know* the significance of what has been said remains dubious. He seems to be trapped in the voices and stories of the past, mastered by the narratives of his place, rather than mastering them. But if this tale of origins seems strangely opaque to the twelve-year-old Quentin, and even to the older Quentin who remembers it, the lines of meaning are clearer to us the readers, while by no means transparent: the different tellings are locked in, at some point, to a single vast unfinished plot, a repressed history of conflict and division. The first and most obvious conflict is that between youth and age, innocence and experience: reflected not only in the contrast between the young Quentin and the older. When offered a glimpse of the authentic and ugly realities of frontier life, the young boy's initial response is one of incomprehension and denial. The older Quentin, the one whose telling frames the tale, never gets beyond this into conscious knowing, still less into understanding of the *historical* dimensions of what has been told. But there is a quality of recognition, however internalised, a repressed acknowledgement of the forces of disruption and death, that leaves its surface traces in, for instance, the closing image of Sam Fathers immobile "like something ... in a museum." The penultimate sentence, "But then Sam Fathers would be dead," may come as a shock, but it has been prepared for in this story of "the old days" that reaches its conclusion at the moment of twilight. This may be a tale of origins but it is also a tale of endings, and the one thing Quentin certainly learns—even if this is an intuition rather than an acknowledged thought—is that in his beginning is his end—the one too closely tied to the other, really, for comfort.

A more radical division than this, in the sense that Quentin himself can neither resolve it nor ever manages to understand it, is the sexual one—which carries with it bitter intimations of the dual role of woman as taboo and commodity. The offence

---

[10] William Faulkner, "A Justice," in *Collected Stories*, pp. 359-60. See also, *Absalom, Absalom!*, p. 303. For the possibly autobiographical origins of this story see, John Faulkner, *My Brother Bill: An Affectionate Reminiscence* (New York: Trident Press, 1963), p. 65.

Crawfish-ford commits is not just that he crosses the colour line but that he violates the property rights of another man since in this irredeemably patriarchal society one person is deemed to "belong" to another—even if both, in turn "belong" to a third party—because she is a woman and the wife of the other. These rights are eventually protected by the fences men are accustomed to build around their property to mark out their territorial rights; and the fence is built sufficiently high to prevent trespass. With his rights confirmed, the husband can then set about his proper, male business of securing a successor, and this time there can be no problem of paternity. The sanctity of woman has been affirmed for the fundamental reason that the integrity of the line of succession, the *male* line, would otherwise be in doubt. In a matriarchal culture, tangible proof of legitimacy is possible: in a patriarchal one, that proof must always remain abstract and symbolic, based on "a justice" that positions woman as temple and chattel—denied access to all but one, particular man. The ironic implications of this spill over in several directions. There is, first, the analogous presumption of possession of one race over another: the two slaves are, after all, the property of the chief who administers justice. Quite apart from adding to the judicial confusion (is the woman primarily in the ownership of her husband or her master?), this serves to situate the whole business of justice itself as an historical phenomenon. Doom, the chief, is resolving a problem he has helped to create. By bringing slaves into his tribe, including the two at the centre of the dispute, he has helped introduce (or, at least, reinforce) the concept of a human being as securible property on which the case against Crawfish-ford rests. The law, in this sense, serves to buttress and perpetuate a system that commodifies relations, turning them into a matter of contract; and the principal agent of the law not only supports that system, he is also one of its authors and main beneficiaries.

The third division or conflict in "A Justice" is, unsurprisingly, the racial one. Sam Fathers problematic racial origins and identity supply the occasion of the narrative. Sam "lived with the Negroes," we are told,

> and they—the white people; the Negroes called him a blue-gum—called him a Negro. But he wasn't a Negro. That's what I'm going to tell about.[11]

Quentin tells about this in telling the story Sam told him and was told in turn. Sam tells of the problem, too, in the very act of telling anything: "he talked like a nigger," Quentin says, "but his skin wasn't quite the colour of a light nigger and his nose and his mouth and his chin were not nigger nose and mouth and chin."[12] In a superficial sense, this problem is solved when we learn who Sam's father was. But this hardly makes the younger Quentin feel more comfortable or knowledgeable; and the older Quentin still remembers Sam as an enigmatic, hieratic figure—"like something ... in a museum," representing secrets from the past shrouded in mystery. Not everything in the past is mysterious, of course. Sam has a remarkably frank way of dealing with

---

[11] Faulkner, "A Justice," p. 343.
[12] Ibid., p. 344. See also, "A Courtship," in *Collected Stories*, p. 361.

some subjects that makes those subjects painfully clear: "a Choctaw chief," he instructs the young Quentin, "sold my mammy to your great-grandpappy." The facts of bondage, possession and dispossession, and the corruption of one culture by another: these are all indisputable facts of early Mississippi life, the story discloses, facts that have shaped the land and contaminated relations ever since. There is, however, a difference between the raw, originary state of relations between people, and between people and land, and their subsequent state, if for no other reason, then because those were the old times before (as it is put in another story) "Issetibbeha and General Jackson met and buried sticks and signed a paper, and ... ran a line through the woods." Intervening accumulations of history, measured here by cumulative layers of old tales and talking, mark off the gap between the time Had-Two-Fathers was born and the moment when the older Quentin looks back at his younger self travelling home in twilight. The past is another country, then ... And yet, and yet: it shares its borders with the present. As the "two fathers" of Sam and the two selves, the two narrative presences of Quentin indicate, the tragic divisions of yesterday are structurally related to those of today. The fissures between the races that scar the very identity of the narrators and the land that situates them, these are part of one, developing story, one unending history of internecine struggle that is embedded—but not buried—in the earth of Yoknapatawpha. It is no wonder, then, that the words with which "A Justice" ends set a claim to knowledge ("I would know" later, claims Quentin) in tension with an admission of ignorance ("Nothing, sir," he tells his grandfather): it is precisely this, Faulkner intimates, that the simultaneous identity and difference of the past demands. We *can* know the past of a place, and can imaginatively participate in it, because its processes form a continuity with our own. But what we know, among other things, is its otherness: the past is not the present—not the place as we know it now—not least because it has shaped the present—and the place we know now—and so helped to determine what we are.

In what is, deservedly, one of the most famous passages in Faulkner's work, in *The Town*, Gavin Stevens describes the view from a ridge "on beyond Seminary Hill"—from which, he says, "you see all Yoknapatawpha in the dying last of day beneath you." "And you stand suzerain and solitary above the whole sum of your life," Stevens declares towards the beginning of this passage.

> First is Jefferson, the centre ... beyond it, enclosing it, spreads the County ... the cradle of your nativity and of the men and women who made you, the record and chronicle of your native land proffered for your perusal in ring by concentric ring like the ripples on living water above the dreamless slumber of your past.[13]

The passage as a whole is often read as a final testament, a farewell tribute from Faulkner to his apocryphal county just before he abjured the rough magic of his craft. Gavin Stevens is not Faulkner, of course, but what he says here does have a resonance that probably springs from autobiographical origins. Faulkner does seem

---

[13] William Faulkner, *The Town* (1957; London: Chatto & Windus, 1958 edition), p. 272. See also, pp. 273, 274.

to be trying to fulfil a need here, to stake a final claim to his land. Quite apart from the sheer uncertainty of Faulkner's attitude towards ideas of mastery and possession, however, what I would like to stress about this verbal landscape is the speed with which the speaker moves from space to time as he calls the roll of all those who (as he puts it) lie "supine beneath you, stratified and superposed, osseous and durable," from "old Issetibbeha, the wild Chickasaw king" to the names of later eras—"Sutpen and Sartoris and Compson," "McCallum and Gowrie and Frazier." The roll is called in a way that reminds the reader of stories that have been told and, equally, of those that remain untold, if only because, as the narrator admits, "the tragedy of life is, it must be premature, inconclusive and inconcludable, in order to be life." All this sums up, much better than I can, what I have been trying to suggest here about landscape in Faulkner. How geography is indelibly attached to history in the Yoknapatawpha fiction. How the sense of place is vitally connected to the sense of the past (a past that is seen as simultaneously intimate and alien). And how both, in turn, are seen as a product of human creativity, a continuing process of exchange. I began by saying that geography matters in Southern writing, and matters with a particular ferocity in Faulkner's work. Not the least reason it matters in Faulkner's work, I think, is because (like so much else in that work) it is seen as a site of struggle: an object *and* a tool in that debated, that continuing conflict of voices (and much else) through which we define not only *where* we are but *who* we are.

FROM REGIONAL BEARS TO NATIONAL MYTHS
THE REWRITING OF WILLIAM FAULKNER

Gene M. Moore, University of Amsterdam

The distinction between regional and national discourse is not something inherent in a writer's work, but a construction based on the various contexts against and within which a work can be read. "Region" and "nation" are distinctions made not only in writing, but also in reading. The forces that shape the discourse of a region or a nation are historically and socially contingent, and they also shape the images in terms of which writers come to see themselves. William Faulkner provides a particularly apt case to illustrate this process of construction. There has long been no doubt that Faulkner is a great "American" novelist; Frederick R. Karl's biography of Faulkner is even entitled *William Faulkner: American Writer* (1989). After he achieved international fame with the Nobel Prize in 1950, Faulkner was sent by the State Department on trips to Japan and elsewhere as a cultural spokesman for national American values. Yet for many years, throughout most of his writing career, Faulkner had been ignored or dismissed as a Southern regionalist with a morbid penchant for stories of miscegenation and violence, like a kind of up-market Erskine Caldwell. *Sanctuary*, with its notorious "corncob rape," was the novel for which he was best known throughout the thirties and early forties; by 1945 it was the only one of his more than fifteen novels that was still in print. The story of Faulkner's spectacular rise from obscurity to the Nobel Prize within five years has often been told, but I would like to examine the extent to which this rebirth of appreciation depended on a cultural "rewriting" of Faulkner from a regional writer into an artist of national stature.

By common consent, the first major step in the construction of Faulkner's reputation was the publication of Malcolm Cowley's *Portable Faulkner* by the Viking Press in 1946, which for the first time placed Faulkner's stories and fragments from his novels in chronological sequence, and made it possible to see that Faulkner had accomplished a task worthy of a Balzac or a Zola by creating a historical chronicle and a sociological map of the South from the earliest days of exploration (the 1820s, the time of Balzac's Paris) up to the present. Yet in spite of Cowley's deep admiration and respect for the historical depth and complexity of Faulkner's achievement, he regarded Faulkner chiefly as a Southern writer. As he wrote in the Introduction to his Portable edition:

> Faulkner performed a labor of imagination that has not been equaled in our time, and a double labor: first, to invent a Mississippi county that was like a mythical kingdom, but was complete and living in all its details; second, to make his story of Yoknapatawpha County stand as a parable or legend of all the Deep South. (2)

In speaking of a "mythical kingdom" that "liv[es] in all its details," Cowley would seem to be describing values that are beyond the realm of merely regional, or indeed, for that matter, of national or international claims. Robert Penn Warren, reviewing Cowley's volume, declared that "It is important ... that Faulkner's work be regarded not in terms of the South against the North, but in terms of issues which are common to our modern world" (Schwartz 26). And yet, for Cowley, the serious artistic value of this "mythical kingdom" was based primarily on the way in which it stood for the history or legend of a region: Faulkner's mythical kingdom was deemed important not for its universality, but because it was exemplary and typical of the Deep South.

The "completeness" of Faulkner's kingdom was possible because of the relative cultural homogeneity of the rural South, which maintained a stable, traditional Anglo-Saxon and black population that had not attracted immigrants like the Eastern and Western coasts, or like the cities generally. The bitterness following the Civil War intensified the Southern sense of place, and made it a point of honour for sons and daughters to stay at home and avoid contamination from Northerners, Yankees, or foreigners. In effect, the humiliating loss of the Civil War constituted the South as a region more intensely and passionately than other parts of the nation, and elevated this sense of regional patriotism and xenophobia into an essential element of the code of Southern honour, along with courage, racism, and religious fundamentalism. This cultural insularity made possible the preservation of a collective cultural memory, a legend and obligation that could be passed on for as many as six generations, and which came to constitute an increasingly heavy and complex burden in an era of improved travel and communications with the outside world. From the beginning of his career, Faulkner had often confronted his narrators or protagonists with experience of the wider world beyond the South: for example, Quentin Compson goes off to Harvard and relives the murder of Charles Bon in a student room in Cambridge before committing suicide; Gavin Stevens receives a doctorate from Heidelberg; and Linda Snopes Kohl brings the ideals and methods of the Spanish Civil War back to the streets of Jefferson. In this sense the elements of a latent "national" consciousness were never absent from Faulkner's work; and this ultra regional patriotism was strengthened by the national call to arms in the First and Second World Wars, where Southerners could reconcile their need to prove their valour with a cause that was defined primarily by "Yankees" (and this accommodation was made easier by the fact that racial segregation in the American armed forces was not ended until 1948, well after the end of the Second World War). These international conflicts also forced Faulkner to reconsider the question of Southern identity as embodied in his characters. Still, despite early appreciation in France by Sartre and André Malraux, Faulkner was primarily known as a regional novelist of the exotic rural South before the publication of Cowley's anthology.

Lawrence H. Schwartz, in a fascinating book entitled *Creating Faulkner's Reputation: The Politics of Modern Literary Criticism* (1988), has traced in detail the stages by which Faulkner was "rewritten" or redefined in the period from 1945 until he was awarded the Nobel Prize in 1950. Schwartz shows how Faulkner's precipitous rise to fame was aided not only by Cowley's anthology, but also by a fortunate combination of other commercial and political factors. As Americans entered into the postwar political leadership of the Western world and sought to define a national culture worthy of their dominant position, New Critics and New York intellectuals shared a common need to find and celebrate a truly native writer who was untainted by previous flirtations with either fascism (like Pound or Thomas Wolfe) or Communism (like Steinbeck or Hemingway). Faulkner's "aloofness" came to seem a warrant of his political integrity. The postwar "paperback revolution" also helped Faulkner, by keeping him in print in twenty-five-cent editions with lurid covers hinting at cheap sex and violence. Schwartz notes that when the editors of the New American Library decided to publish Faulkner, they had difficulty finding a bound copy of *The Wild Palms* or *The Unvanquished* to use as a copy-text! Faulkner had never been able to support himself and his family on his writing alone, and he did not begin to earn money for his publishers until after the war.

Schwartz explores the cultural politics that led to the "creation" of Faulkner's reputation as a national writer, but this process can also be examined in terms of his individual works. The seven stories in *Go Down, Moses* (1942), which Faulkner called his "race-relations" novel (and which the *MLA Bibliography* still finds it difficult to classify either as a novel or as a collection of stories), provide useful examples of the conflicts and paradoxes involved in establishing the claims of regional or national discourse. Like the Sartorises of *Flags in the Dust*, the Sutpens of *Absalom, Absalom!* and the Compsons of *The Sound and the Fury*, the McCaslins of *Go Down, Moses* embody the pride and degradation of one of the first families of Yoknapatawpha County, with the important difference that the McCaslin clan is divided into a complex double lineage that is both black and white. As we learn in chapter four of "The Bear," the founding patriarch, Lucius Quintus Carothers McCaslin, who died in 1837, had three white children by his unnamed wife, but also three children by his female slaves, committing not only rape and miscegenation but also incest, since his own illegitimate daughter would grow up in slavery to become the mother of another of his children. This child, a boy known as Tomasina's Terrel or Tomey's Turl, is hunted with dogs in the first story of *Go Down, Moses*, when he runs away to visit a neighbouring slave girl, who is finally won in a poker game between their masters. What we are not told at this point in the story, and do not fully discover until "The Bear," is that Tomey's Turl is both half-brother and half-nephew to the twins Theophilus and Amodeus (known as Uncle Buck and Uncle Buddy), and that he is also three-fourths white. This adds a piquant irony to his son Lucas Beauchamp's pride in the fact that he is descended, like Isaac McCaslin, from a male line and not from the "distaff side."

It is curious that the behaviour of the founding patriarch, Lucius Quintus Carothers McCaslin, is honoured throughout the book: whites and blacks alike claim him as the origin of their pride and dignity. The point that his descendants are necessarily lesser men is made in the story "The Fire and the Hearth," when Cass Edmonds is bested by Lucas Beauchamp when he attempts to take Lucas's wife Molly into his own house to nurse his motherless baby. The division between the black and white descendants culminates in the awkward scene in the story "Delta Autumn" where Uncle Ike, now an old man in his seventies on one of his last hunting trips, discovers that his cousin,

Roth Edmonds, has had an illegitimate son by the great-granddaughter of Tomey's Turl without ever realising either that his mistress was his cousin or that she was black. The girl arrives unexpectedly with her baby, and in the culminating scene, Uncle Ike pays the girl off and sends her away, on the grounds that his country is not yet prepared to accept the idea of a mixed marriage: *"Maybe in a thousand or two thousand years in America*, he thought. *But not now! Not now!"* (361). The fact that Uncle Ike's rejection of the girl is founded on a national sense of propriety, and not a regional one, is all the more significant when we recall that earlier in the same story, Ike McCaslin has been speaking up for America's involvement in the Second World War against the skepticism of his younger listeners:

> "This country is a little mite stronger than any one man or group of men, outside of it or even inside of it either. I reckon, when the time comes and some of you have done got tired of hollering we are whipped if we dont go to war and some more are hollering we are whipped if we do, it will cope with one Austrian paper-hanger, no matter what he will be calling himself. My pappy and some other better men than any of them you named tried once to tear it in two with a war, and they failed." (338-39)

Yet this same patriotic invocation of national spirit (most of the novel was written in 1941, before Pearl Harbor) breaks down before the barrier of race, which continues to tear blood-relationships in two. Why does Ike, half of whose family is black, help Roth Edmonds to reject the girl? Is his cry of "Not now!" based on an acceptance of racism, and if so, how can a racist be credited with giving voice to a national discourse? Faulkner was questioned about this very passage by a student at the University of Virginia, and his reply shows the extent to which, by 1958, he had come to see himself as a spokesman for national rather than regional values. The questioner said, "I was wondering how you might apply that [passage] to the present-day conditions that have happened since the writing of the story, with the Supreme Court decision and what not." Faulkner answered:

> "He used 'a thousand or two thousand years' in his despair. He had seen a condition which was intolerable, which shouldn't be but it was, and he was saying in effect that this must be changed, this cannot go on, but I'm too old to do anything about it, that maybe in a thousand years somebody will be young enough and strong enough to do something about it. That was all he meant by the numbers. But I think that he saw ... that a condition like that is intolerable, not so much intolerable to man's sense of justice, but maybe intolerable to the condition, that any country has reached the point where if it is to endure, it must have no inner conflicts based on a wrong, a basic human wrong." (*University*, 46)

There is, I think, an element of faltering apologetics in Faulkner's explanation which exemplifies the difficulty of moving from regional to national claims. To begin with, it is difficult to believe that Ike, who is more than willing to suffer physical discomfort to revisit what is left of the Big Woods, feels "too old" to stand up for what is right. Perhaps in refusing to inherit the McCaslin lands he felt that he had adequately renounced the wrongs of ownership and of slavery, and had no further stake in righting an intolerable and fundamental wrong. In this respect Ike McCaslin remains, understandably, a regional character, a latter-day frontiersman whose identity is bound up with his profound love of the unspoiled wilderness, but who is out of his depth in trying to deal with the complexities of the corrupt and complex world that has come to replace the simple courage and endurance of hunters. His treatment of the girl is barbaric by any but regional standards, as when he tells her, "You sound like you have been to college even. You sound almost like a Northerner even." Finally, when he realizes that she is not white (because she says her aunt "took in washing"), we are told: "He cried, not loud, in a voice of amazement, pity, and outrage: 'You're a nigger!'" And she answers with calm dignity: "Yes. ... James Beauchamp—you called him Tennie's Jim though he had a name—was my grandfather. I said you were Uncle Isaac" (360-61).

If half of *Go Down, Moses* deals with race-relations, the other half deals with the fate or doom of the wilderness, as personified in the bear named Old Ben, which Ike McCaslin hunts under the spiritual tutelage of Sam Fathers, himself the last Indian in Faulkner's world, the noble son of a Negro slave and a Chickasaw chief. This hunting saga clearly has universal echoes, as a latter-day version of the story of Theseus and the Minotaur, or Saint George and the Dragon, or Hemingway's fisherman in *The Old Man and the Sea*, or indeed any combat in which a wild beast is slain in order to preserve the possibility of human dignity and civilisation. The death of the bear is also the death of Sam Fathers, of the dog Lion, and of the Big Woods as a way of life. In a gesture that no one understands, Ike McCaslin honours their memory by refusing to accept the land that is his inheritance. In a reversal of Robert Frost's updating of the doctrine of manifest destiny with the claim that "The land was ours before we were the land's," Uncle Ike feels that the woods are indeed his, but he knows better than to pretend to own them. Ownership is the secret curse of all the McCaslins: the twin brothers Uncle Buck and Uncle Buddy defy convention by letting their slaves sleep in their unfinished plantation house while they themselves share far less pretentious accommodations. They carefully lock the front door of the big house each night for form's sake, while the Negroes are already crawling out the empty door- and window-frames at the rear. These twin brothers, Ike's father and uncle, are among the first to develop a plan to liberate their slaves (or their black cousins) even before the Civil War. Ownership also frustrates the efforts of Hubert Beauchamp, Ike's maternal grandfather, to leave a legacy of gold coins in a silver cup: when the cup is finally exposed to view, it turns out to be only an old coffee pot filled with a handful of copper coins and a pile of paper IOUs. The message of Uncle Ike would seem to be that the land could only be ours *before* we tried to claim it, and that all ownership, whether of land or of people, can only result in corruption.

In conclusion, Faulkner's stature as a national writer was facilitated not only by the political and commercial circumstances chronicled by Schwartz, but also by his own fictional attempts to bring his regional characters into conflict with national values that were geographically broader or historically deeper. In *Go Down, Moses* these areas of confrontation which serve to define the gap between regional and national discourse include the wilderness of the Big Bottom, as a hunter's paradise and a timeless reference anchored in the earliest beginnings of the land; topical references to the Second World War as a renewed occasion for national pride and frontier values; and finally also the rejection of the mother with "nigger blood" who returns from the

North or the West tainted with college education and an illegitimate child. The extent to which Ike McCaslin remains caught in a condition of intolerable injustice marks both Faulkner's fidelity to a historical moment and the limits of his ability to accommodate the Southern code of honour fully into a national ethos. Uncle Ike may be a great hunter with a profound respect for the other races mixed in Sam Fathers, but he has no faith in his nation's ability to accept a mixed marriage that might at last begin to transcend and destroy the racial barrier that divides the McCaslins against themselves.

WORKS CITED

Cowley, Malcolm, ed., *The Portable Faulkner*. New York: Viking Press, 1946.

Faulkner, William, *Go Down, Moses*. 1942. New York: Modern Library, 1955.

Gwynn, Frederick L., and Joseph L. Blotner, eds., *Faulkner in the University*. New York: Vintage, 1959.

Karl, Frederick R., *William Faulkner: American Writer*. New York: Weidenfeld & Nicolson, 1989.

Schwartz, Lawrence H., *Creating Faulkner's Reputation: The Politics of Modern Literary Criticism*. Knoxville: University of Tennessee Press, 1988.

DECONSTRUCTING THE "NECESSARY" WORLD SOUTHERN DEFENSIVE NARRATIVE AND THE CHILDHOOD AUTOBIOGRAPHY

Ineke Bockting, University of Amsterdam / Université d'Orléans

1. Introduction

This discussion of narratives of the American South situates itself in the interface between history and literature, and approaches the theme "the writing of region" by looking at an area that Rupert Vance referred to as "the deepest South" and James C. Cobb called "the most Southern place on earth": the Mississippi Delta. I hope to show in what sense this region is a written construct, but we will see especially how and by whom it was "deconstructed" in order to free its unwritten aspects.

In his article "The Historical Dimension," published in the collection *The Burden of Southern History* (1960), the well-known Southern historian C. Vann Woodward concerns himself with the interface between literature and history in the specific context of the American South. He argues that what Southern history and Southern literature have in common is an intense preoccupation with the past, never perhaps put into words more eloquently than by William Faulkner's character Gavin Stevens in *Requiem for a Nun*: "The past is never dead. It's not even past" (Faulkner, *Requiem* 80). Therefore, Woodward argues, the Southern historian should stop arrogantly pretending to know it all, but "make his bow," as he puts it, to the Southern man of letters (Woodward 27). Woodward mentions, of course, Faulkner's masterpiece *Absalom, Absalom!*, which is, in fact, a test case.

My discussion will take some of its material from this wonderful novel *Absalom, Absalom!*, which presents itself as a "multiple historiography," in which three generations of speakers from a small Mississippi town ponder the history of their region through different accounts of the collapse of the planter's dynasty of the Sutpen family. But I will also be concerned with another genre, which is right there in the interface between history and literature: the autobiography, and, more specifically, the Southern childhood autobiography. We will be concerned with the question of how the childhood autobiography deconstructs the "necessary world" of the South. Let us begin, therefore, by exploring some aspects of this "necessary world," in the interface between history and literature.

2. The "necessary world" of the South: Faulkner's *Absalom, Absalom!*

The place to start a discussion of the interface between history and literature is perhaps Hayden White's body of theory concerning the writing of history. Briefly, just to create a context for us here, to White historical events present themselves to the "percipient eye" as "stories waiting to be told, waiting to be narrated" (White 6); this because it is the most natural, the most universal, the most human impulse to give meaning to events by putting them into a story-form, whereby "story-form" implies a beginning-middle-end structure, a texture or fabric that holds these together, and a perspective from which the events are narrated.

Writers of history, White argues, have at various times rejected this story-form. The annalists, first of all, have in their writings neither a beginning-middle-end structure or texture, nor a perspective. These writings are, in fact, simply lists of events: births, deaths, good crops, bad crops, floods, fires, and the comings and goings of people. In contrast, the chroniclers do show in their writings some sort of a beginning-middle-end structure, as well as a certain fabric: a theme such as the life of a king, a people, a town, an institution, or a great undertaking such as a war or a crusade. It is this theme, of course, that dictates the inclusion or exclusion of events.

But although it "often seems to wish to tell a story, aspires to narrativity," White argues, the chronicle "typically fails to achieve it" (White 5), because what it still does not possess is a perspective, a point of view, a social centre that would give the account ethical and moral significance. Such a social center is necessarily a center of power, embodied by tradition, heritage, law, authority, and bringing in all the tensions, the conflicts and the struggles—as well as their solutions—that are the subjects of narratives. It is ultimately the question of morality—the question of the "rightness" or "wrongness" of events—that is involved here. Thus, as White puts is: "every historical narrative has as its latent or manifest purpose the desire to moralise the events of which it treats" (White 14); in other words, it is the giving-in to a desire to moralise that makes a chronicle into a real story of the past.

This desire to moralise, in fact, is behind the different accounts of the past in Faulkner's *Absalom, Absalom!* Had these accounts been produced in annal form, they might have read:

1860 Henry Sutpen and Charles Bon leave Jefferson, Mississippi

1865 Henry Sutpen kills Charles Bon

Thus they would have presented two unrelated events with perhaps other unrelated events before, after, and in between. However, in the different accounts in the novel, these events all read something more like:

1860 Henry Sutpen leaves home with his friend Charles Bon, repudiating his birthright

1865 Henry Sutpen kills his sister Judith's fiancé Charles Bon

Such entries are in themselves already stories in embryo form (White 14), because the additions "his sister Judith's fiancé" and "repudiating his birthright" already bring in issues of power: heritage, tradition, authority. What the accounts seem to strive for, then, is to become true narratives with a judgement on historical events: was the repudiation justified? Was the murder perhaps unavoidable? We see this clearly in *Absalom, Absalom!*, whose speakers all seem forced to ask the question of "why?" This question preempts the desire to moralise; that is, why *is* it that Henry Sutpen repudiated his birthright, an issue which is at the heart of the collapse of the Sutpen dynasty. To fulfill his or her desire, each of the speakers of *Absalom, Absalom!* is forced to provide his or her own closure.

For Miss Rosa Coldfield, the first and oldest speaker in the novel, the answer to the question of why Henry repudiated his birthright is extremely simple: Henry left Sutpen's Hundred, refusing to be his father's heir because his father—Thomas Sutpen—was a "brute," even if she uses more lady-like words:

> He wasn't a gentleman.
> He wasn't even a gentleman.
> No: not even a gentleman ...
> (Faulkner, *Absalom* 13, 13, 15)

This explanation of the repudiation is based on her own experience with this "brute," a man who had the nerve to propose to her—a young Southern lady—to mate and wait and see if the product would be a male, who could then become the new heir for Thomas Sutpen after Henry had turned his back on him, and then perhaps get married.

Miss Rosa's story is "a desperate narration," the adjective used by Roger Salomon in his work on the mock heroic, and originally taken from James Joyce. Miss Rosa is indeed a typical heroine of a mock-heroic tale, like Quixote trying to live in a world that no longer allows for her kind of heroism (see also Wyatt-Brown 1994). Her "desperate narration" is a narrative of justification and disclaiming of responsibility that seems to turn the sequence of cause and effect as we normally think of them around. The insult that she had to suffer makes it necessary for Miss Rosa to "create" the world of the past in this way; her goal, in the end, is to create a "usable past" for herself. The outrageous move by the "brute" to ask her to supply him with a new heir was the effect of Henry's repudiation of his birthright, but it becomes in Miss Rosa's mind its cause.

For the speaker of the next generation—Mr. Jason Compson, the son of Thomas Sutpen's only friend—the desire for closure shows itself quite differently. Throughout Mr. Compson's text, we find Henry's repudiation explained as follows:

> Because Henry loved Bon.
> Because he loved Bon.
> Yes, he loved Bon ...

he loved grieved and killed, still grieving and, I believe, still loving Bon ...
(110, 111, 118, 119)[1]

It is, as with Miss Rosa's text, the degree of repetition that gives the narration its
"desperate" quality. But this quality shows itself in other ways as well.

Mr. Compson "knows," for instance, that the love between the two young men
was reciprocal, so that Bon's fiancée Judith, Henry's sister, is not even important as
a person. Let me show the tremendous force with which Mr. Compson creates this
"necessary world." While in his account to his son Quentin he first tells us that Judith
was "*perhaps* ... merely the shadow, the woman vessel with which to consummate the
love whose actual object was the youth [Henry] ..." (133; my emphasis), not much
later he already adds confidently, "*as I said before*, it was not Judith who was the
object of Bon's love. ... She was just the blank shape, the empty vessel ..." (148; my
emphasis). Not only has Mr. Compson completely forgotten the hesitation he had felt
before—signalled by the word "perhaps"—he also uses the simple past construction "as
I said before" where he might have used the present perfect "as I have said before,"
thus cutting off any effects of his earlier statement upon the present state of affairs.

Let us turn to the second "why" that stands in the way of the kind of closure that
would make a moral judgement possible and satisfy the desires of the different
speakers of *Absalom, Absalom!*: the question of why Henry Sutpen killed his best
friend and fiancé of his sister Judith. For Mr. Compson the reason is that Charles Bon
was intending bigamy; as Compson creates the story, Bon already had a wife—an
octoroon who enjoyed a high status in New Orleans—and Henry, who had heard about
the marriage, felt he had to stop his friend from making his sister "a sort of junior
partner in a harem" (147).

Yet, at the same time, this closure does not satisfy Mr. Compson, even if he
cannot quite put his finger on the reason for this. His own narration, in fact, is "just
incredible" to him: "it just does not explain." Ella Schoenberg has argued that Mr.
Compson, as a lawyer, should have realised that Bon's marriage to an octoroon woman
in New Orleans would simply have been void in Mississippi, where marriages between
the races were forbidden (Schoenberg 44). But even if this is so, the decisive question
is, of course, still whether Henry knew this. I believe, rather, that Mr. Compson
comes close to realising here that his "desperate narration" is related not to the original
events so much as to the turmoil of his own personality and time.

What, finally, about the third generation of tellers: Mr. Compson's eldest son
Quentin, familiar from the earlier novel *The Sound and the Fury*, and his roommate
at Harvard University, the young Canadian Shrevlin McCannon? What comes out of
their combined desire for closure is that Charles Bon is, in fact, Henry's half-brother,
and that therefore Henry has to prevent incest in addition to bigamy. What critics have
often failed to notice, however, is that at this point there is a difference between the

---

[1] For a fuller discussion of these passages, see Ineke Bockting, *Character and Personality in the Novels
of William Faulkner: A Study in Psychostylistics*. (New York: University Press of America, 1995) chapter
V.

stories of Quentin and Shreve, even if Faulkner wrote: "it might have been either of them and was in a sense both: both thinking as one" (378). While Shreve speaks, only Quentin's nonverbal behavior is presented: sitting "hunched in his chair, his hands thrust into his pockets as if he were trying to hug himself warm between his arms, looking somehow fragile and even wan in the lamplight" (367); "his hands in his trousers pockets, his shoulders hugged inward and hunched, his faced lowered" (405).

Theirs is not one desire all the way through, because while Quentin is stuck on the idea that Bon had wanted to commit incest with his sister, Shreve is free to move beyond this more superficial closure, to the question of the "why" beyond it. For him the question is no longer: "Why did Henry kill Bon?" He is satisfied that the reason was that Bon intended to marry Henry's only sister. For Shreve the question becomes: "Why was Bon set on marrying her in the first place?" Those readers who are familiar with *The Sound and the Fury* know why Quentin is unable to move beyond the closure of incest.[2] In any case, it is Shrevlin McCannon, the outsider, who arrives at another closure: for him Bon intended to marry Henry's sister in a final effort to force his father into acknowledging him as his son.

The text that Shreve ascribes to Bon is full of allusions to this strategy: "[Charles] stopped and said, right quiet: *All right. I want to go to bed with who might be my sister. All right* and then forgot that too. Because he didn't have time. That is, he didn't have anything else but time, because he had to wait. But not for her. That was all fixed. It was the other" (407). The "other" is, of course, Thomas Sutpen, the father who has refused to acknowledge his eldest son. As Shreve sees it, Bon waits for "a sign" more and more desperately as time progresses:

> Maybe he thought it would be in the mail bag each time the nigger rode over from Sutpen's Hundred and Henry believing it was the letter from her that he was waiting for when what he was thinking was *Maybe he will write it then. He would just have to write "I am your father. Burn this" and I would do it. Or if not that, a sheet a scrap of paper with the one word "Charles" in his hand, and I would know what he meant and he would not even have to ask me to burn it. Or a lock of his hair or a paring from his finger nail and I would know them.* ... And it did not come, and his letter went to her every two weeks and hers came back to him, and maybe he thought *If one of mine to her should come back to me unopened then. That would be a sign.* And that didn't happen: and then Henry began to talk about

---

[2] Naturally, one can choose to read the books as separate stories, and the characters as different people, but linking them does add extra meaning and does not have to result in misreadings. Estella Schoenberg has provided a time-table that convincingly shows the interlocking of the two novels. The shared chronology of *The Sound and the Fury* and *Absalom, Absalom!* and the closeness in time of the important events have also been noted by Cleanth Brooks (1979) and Paul Ragan (1986). After all, it is in the summer of 1909, in *The Sound and the Fury*, that Quentin tries unsuccessfully to face up to his sister's lover Dalton Ames. His father tries to convince him that Caddy's behaviour is not worth his despair, and advises him to go back to Harvard a little earlier than he had planned, in order to forget about her. Quentin is not taken seriously, and even the "confession" of his incest with Caddy and the announcement of his plans to commit suicide do not shake his depressed and alcoholic father into action. It is only one month later, in September of the same year, and on the eve of his departure for Harvard, that Quentin hears Miss Rosa's story and talks to his father afterwards. This same night, Quentin accompanies Miss Rosa to the old ruin of Sutpen's Hundred, where he speaks to Henry (*Absalom, Absalom!*). Quentin then spends the following Christmas and New Year at home with his family (*The Sound and the Fury*), so that he has only just returned to Harvard when his father's letter informs him of the death of Miss Rosa. He then spends the night talking about the Sutpens with his roommate Shreve (*Absalom, Absalom!*).

his stopping at Sutpen's Hundred for a day or so on his way home and he said all right to it, said *It will be Henry who will get the letter, the letter saying it is inconvenient for me to come at that time; so apparently he does not intend to acknowledge me as his son, but at least I shall have forced him to admit that I am.* (407, 408)

Charles Bon believes, against his better judgment, that the war will have changed his father and shown him some real values: "*what I believe probably is that war, suffering, these four years of keeping his men alive and able ... will have changed him (which I know that it does not do) to where he will say to me not: Forgive me: but: You are my oldest son. Protect your sister; never see either of us again*" (433).

Indeed, Bon is perfectly willing, in Shreve's view, to give up Judith as soon as he has accomplished his goal:

Yes. Yes. I will renounce her; I will renounce love and all; that will be cheap, cheap, even though he say to me "never look upon my face again; take my love and my acknowledgement in secret, and go" I will do that; I will not even demand to know of him what it was my mother did that justified his action towards her and me. (408)

He will not even have to ask me; I will just touch flesh with him and I will say it myself: You will not need to worry; she shall never see me again. (435)

But this second version of the story, in which Charles Bon turns out to be Henry's brother and the danger therefore is incest, does not explain enough either. Probably, incest is not quite bad enough in the defeatist atmosphere of the final stages of the war. Henry is even able to tell his father that he is prepared to let his half-brother marry their sister: "*when you dont have God and honor and pride, nothing matters except that there is the old mindless meat that dont even care if it was defeat or victory, that wont even die, that will be out in the woods and fields, grubbing up roots and weeds.—Yes. I have decided. Brother or not, I have decided. I will. I will*" (442).

Thus, Shreve must search for a more satisfying solution, which he finds in a third version of the story, in which Charles Bon is not just any half-brother of Henry Sutpen, but a mulatto one, born out of Sutpen's early marriage to a very lightly coloured mulatto woman who passes for white. In the story that is now constructed, Henry had to prevent not only bigamy and incest, but also miscegenation. Shreve has Sutpen play this last trump card by telling Henry that Charles is a mulatto and therefore should be prevented from marrying Judith: "*He must not marry her, Henry. His mother's father told me that her mother had been a Spanish woman. I believed him; it was not until after he was born that I found out that his mother was part negro*" (443). When Charles finally hears this version, his desperation reaches a quiet culmination: "*He didn't need to tell you I am a nigger to stop me. He could have stopped me without that, Henry*" (445), after which he effectively forces Henry to kill him.

We can see clearly, here, that the problem is an elementary and universal, psychological one: the son seeking the father's acknowledgement. But by having imagined Charles Bon as a black man, the young Canadian has also made it into a fundamentally Southern problem, one about which the Southern writer and social critic Lillian Smith has written:

When children came from these secret unions they were rarely acknowledged by their white fathers. Usually they were wholly rejected, though now and then they were secretly clung to. Most of us know stories of a white man in our community who chose not to reject his mixed children but educated them instead and helped them find a decent life for themselves. Sometimes he left these children's names in his will and posthumously made amends for human relations which in life he had not the courage to honor. This is one of the brighter threads weaving through the dark evil design of the history of the intimate life of the two races.

But these acknowledgments, though important to remember, have been few. The stark ugly fact is that millions of children have been rejected by their white fathers and white kin and left to battle alone the giants that stalk our culture. Little ghosts playing and laughing and weeping on the edge of the southern memory can be a haunting thing....

This mass rejection of children has been a heavy thing on our region's conscience. Like a dead weight dropped in water it lies deep in the ooze of the old and forgotten, but when talk of change is heard, it stirs restlessly as if still alive in its hiding place and is felt by minds innocent of participating in the original sin but who for involved reasons have identified themselves with it. (Smith 124-125)

Such minds "innocent of the original sin" yet having "identified themselves with it" obviously include those of the young Southerner Quentin Compson and even the equally young Canadian Shrevlin McCannon.

The "necessary world" of Thomas Sutpen—as created by Quentin and Shreve—combines the narratives of justification, of undoing, of self-victimisation and of the disclaiming of responsibility that the repertoire of the region provides: "I provided for him"; "if I had done an injustice, I had done what I could to rectify it"; "they deliberately withheld it [the knowledge that his first wife was black] from me." But it is especially Shreve who exposes the elementary needs of the son who loses out against this "necessary world" of the father: the son's essential failure to "deconstruct" the world that the defences of the father have created. It is my purpose now to look at some texts that were more successful in this, and that can be found in the childhood autobiography as it was written in the South.

3. Deconstructing the "necessary world": the childhood autobiography

Scholars and readers alike have been astonished by the sheer number of childhood autobiographies that the twentieth-century South has produced, and many have asked the question why this should be the case.[3] In his introduction to *A Southern Renaissance*, Richard King has written:

---

[3] A short list might include, apart from the ones discussed in this article, Mamie Field, *Lemon Swamp and Other Places*; Florence King, *Confessions of a Failed Southern Lady*; William Alexander Percy, *Lanterns on the Levee*; Willie Morris, *North Towards Home*; Harry Crews, *A Childhood: The Biography of a Place*; Eudora Welty, *One Writer's Beginnings*; Maya Angelou, *I Know Why the Caged Bird Sings*; Clifton Taulbert, *Once Upon a Time when We Were Colored*; Pauli Murray, *Song in a Weary Throat*; Virginia Foster Durr, *Outside the Magic Circle*; Melton McLaurin, *Separate Pasts: Growing up White in the Segregated South*; and Marita Golden, *Migrations of the Heart*. One could add to these autobiographies those novels that contain a good deal of autobiographical material, such as Alice Walker's *Meridian* and Zora Neale Hurston's *Their Eyes Were Watching God*.

> Much of the writing about the South, particularly by Southerners, has been intensely autobiographical, even confessional. It seemed time to draw back and try to make sense of the cultural context within which Southern writers and intellectuals—and articulate Southerners in general—have tried to formulate their ambivalent feelings about the region. (King ix)

Lillian Smith's *Killers of the Dream*, from which I quoted above, is certainly not a straightforward autobiography. King has called it "an autobiography of sorts, or better a meditation upon the intersection of personal and regional experience." But precisely because it has this double focus is it a good starting-point for a discussion of how the genre of the childhood autobiography exposes the "necessary world" of the Southerner, in which there is no room for relations between people of different colours.

All the important childhood autobiographies, Lynn Bloom has argued, "deal with the pervasive experience of racial segregation and its searing effects on blacks and whites alike" (Bloom 113). They all refer to a time when, with the "shock of disbelief," the young child makes the discovery of difference. This shock often causes a denial: it took Smith more than thirty years to drag up an experience that had been "wiped out of" her memory by guilt. This is the memory of Janie, a little girl who had been mistaken for white and had lived with the Smith family for close to a month before her "true color" was discovered and she was sent back to the "colored town." Smith notes the discussion that took place between her and little Janie at the time:

> "Are you white?" she said.
> "I"m white," I replied, "and my sister is white. And you"re colored. And white and colored can"t live together because my mother says so."
> "Why?" Janie whispered.
> "Because they can"t," I said. (Smith 37)

The problem is that the grown-ups are unable to respond, and through their confusion show their guilt; "don't ask me again, ever again, about this!" (37) Smith's mother answers to her insistent questions as to why Janie cannot even come to play any more.

Although she does justify herself to Janie with the help of her mother's words, Lillian Smith knows that something is very wrong. She feels betrayed, and it is here that the deconstruction of the "necessary world" of the parents takes its shape: "something was wrong with a world that tells you that love is good and people are important and then forces you to deny love and to humiliate people" (39). Textually, this deconstruction is clear in the memory of yet an earlier experience, in which Smith was forced to forsake the love of the woman who had been her nurse:

> I *knew* that my old nurse who had cared for me through long months of illness, who had given me refuge when a little sister took my place as the baby of the family, who soothed, fed me, delighted me with her stories and games, let me fall asleep on her deep warm breast, was not worthy of the passionate love I felt for her but must be given instead a half-smiled-at affection similar to that which one feels for one's dog. I *knew* but I never believed it. ... (28-29; my emphasis).

The attributive verb *knew*, in the first and last sentence of this passage, is a factive, which means that in its unmarked form it signals consent. In other words, the speaker indicates that she agrees with the assertion made in the attribution itself, which in this case presents the "necessary world" of her parents' defences, a world in which the black woman knows her place and the child "knows" it too.

However, this rational consent of the young child, who at birth cannot help entering the "necessary world" of its caretakers, is paired with an emotional distance from this same world, as signaled by the attributive verb phrase *did not believe*. The "shock of disbelief" caused by the experience entails the loss of more than one important "other": the beloved black person as well as the parents, both of whom are unable to answer the question "why?" It is here that a split in the mind between knowing and believing is created: a form of schizophrenia on a cultural basis, which is also one of the stylistic hallmarks of a great writer of fiction: William Faulkner. As a matter of fact, it is *the* way in which Faulkner explores "the problems of the human heart in conflict with itself" (Fant and Ashley 51).[4]

All autobiographies, William Andrews writes, recall "a time in early life when each viewed the racial other through the undifferentiated perspective of childhood," but only the white children "were privileged to grow up with a myth of a homogeneous past in which, insofar as a child could tell, there were no racial barriers to their access to the pleasures of life" (Andrews 52). Of course, the "shock of disbelief" hits the children of colour the hardest, as they suddenly see how their world is cut in half. Here is the decisive moment for Anne Moody in her autobiography *Coming of Age in Mississippi*:

> Every Saturday evening Mama would take us to the movies. The Negroes sat upstairs in the balcony and the whites sat downstairs. One Saturday we arrived at the movies at the same time as the white children. When we saw each other, we ran and met. ... We were standing in the white lobby with our friends, when Mama came in and saw us. "C'mon! C'mon!" she yelled, pushing Adline face on into the door.... "I told you "bout running up in these stores and things like you own 'em!" she shouted, dragging me through the door. When we got outside, we stood there crying, and we could hear the white children crying inside the white lobby. After that, Mama didn"t even let us stay at the movies. She carried us right home.
>
> All the way back to our house, Mama kept telling us that we couldn"t sit downstairs, we couldn"t do this or that with white children. Up until that time I had never really thought about it. After all, we were playing together. I knew that we were going to separate schools and all, but I never knew why....
>
> Every time I tried to talk to Mama about white people she got mad. (Moody 37-38)

A similar experience can be found in Richard Wright's *Black Boy*:

> I soon made myself a nuisance by asking far too many questions of everybody. Every happening in the neighborhood, no matter how trivial, became my business. It was in this manner that I first stumbled upon the relations between whites and blacks, and what I learned frightened me. ... And when word circulated among the black people of the neighborhood that a "black" boy had been severely beaten by a "white" man, I felt that the "white" man had had a right to beat the "black" boy, for I naïvely assumed that the "white" man must have been the "black" boy's father. And did not all fathers, like my father, have the right to beat their children? ... But when my mother told me that the "white" man was not the father of the "black" boy, was no kin to him at all, I was puzzled.
> "Then why did the 'white' man whip the 'black' boy?" I asked my mother.

---

[4] See Charles Bon's words in an earlier quotation: "*what I believe probably is that war, suffering ... will have changed him (which I know that it does not do)*" (1987:432; my emphasis).

"The 'white' man did not *whip* the 'black' boy," my mother told me. "He *beat* the 'black' boy."
"But why?"
"You're too young to understand." (Wright 30-31)

Here, as in the texts of Anne Moody and Lillian Smith, it is the inability of grown-ups to put the "necessary world" up for questioning that makes the child achieve the emotional distance that will lead to the deconstruction of this world.

4. Conclusion

The childhood autobiography is in a way a natural genre for the deconstruction of the "necessary world," because it sees a critique of the South as part of a natural process of growing up. However, Bloom writes: "black and white, these autobiographers grew up in a changing South, and their works reflect not only their intellectual superiority to the adults, black and white, who tried to acculturate them to the segregationist status quo, but also the changing mores and values of the twentieth century" (Bloom 114). I would add: they not only "reflect" these changes, but actively helped to bring them about.

Anne Moody finds out, however, how hard it can be to deconstruct the "necessary world" even after it has formally become obsolete. After almost having given her life in the struggle for the desegregation of public transport, she finds her people still sitting as if segregated in the coloured waiting-room, making her cry out: "Don't you know that you have been desegregated?" Change is often dangerous and always difficult, even, and perhaps especially, for those who will eventually benefit from it most. It is fortunate, though, that the childhood autobiography of the South, in the 1940s, '50s and '60s, by tapping into the Civil Rights Movement gave its historiographies perspectives that could no longer be ignored.

Bibliography

Andrews, William L., "In Search of a Common Identity: The Self and the South in Four Mississippi Autobiographies." *Southern Review* 24:1 (1988): 47-62.

Bloom, Lynn Z., "Coming of Age in the Segregated South: Autobiographies of Twentieth-Century Childhoods, Black and White." *Home Ground: Southern Autobiography*, J. Bill Berry, ed. Columbia: University of Missouri Press, 1991.

Bockting, Ineke, *Character and Personality in the Novels of William Faulkner; A Study in Psychostylistics*. New York: University Press of America, 1995.

Brooks, Cleanth, *William Faulkner: Towards Yoknapatawpha and Beyond*. New Haven: Yale University Press, 1979.

Cobb, James C., *The Most Southern Place on Earth: The Mississippi Delta and the Roots of Regional Identity*. Oxford: Oxford University Press, 1992.

Fant, Joseph L. and Robert Ashley, eds., *Faulkner at West Point*. New York: Random House, 1964.

Faulkner, William, *Requiem for a Nun*. (1951) New York: Vintage, 1975.

Faulkner, William, *Absalom, Absalom!* (1936) New York: Vintage, 1987.

King, Richard H., *A Southern Renaissance: The Cultural Awakening of the American South, 1930-1955*. Oxford: Oxford University Press, 1980.

Moody, Anne, *Coming of Age in Mississippi*. (1968) New York: Dell, 1976.

Ragan, David Paul, "'That Tragedy Is Second-Hand': Quentin, Henry, and the Ending of *Absalom, Absalom!*" *Mississippi Quarterly* 39:3 (1986): 336-350.

Salomon, Roger, *Desperate Storytelling: Post-Romantic Elaborations of the Mock-Heroic Mode*. Athens: University of Georgia Press, 1987.

Schoenberg, Estella, *Old Tales and Talking: Quentin Compson in William Faulkner's* Absalom, Absalom! *and Related Works*. Jackson: The University Press of Mississippi, 1977.

Smith, Lillian, *Killers of the Dream*. (1949) New York: Norton, 1978.

White, Hayden, "The Value of Narrativity in the Representation of Reality," *in: The Content of Form*. (1987) Baltimore: Johns Hopkins University Press, 1992.

Woodward, C. Vann, "The Historical Dimension," in: *The Burden of Southern History*. (1960) Baton Rouge: Louisiana State University Press, 1989.

Wright, Richard, *Black Boy*. (1937) New York: Signet, 1963.

Wyatt-Brown, Bertram, *The House of Percy: Honor, Imagination, and Melancholy in a Southern Family*. Oxford: Oxford University Press, 1994.

POLITICAL IDENTITIES IN CONTEMPORARY CHICANA LITERATURE: HELENA MARÍA VIRAMONTES'S VISIONS OF THE U.S. THIRD WORLD[1]

Sonia Saldívar-Hull, University of California, Los Angeles

As contemporary Chicana feminist writers recognise the urgency of dealing with misogynist traditions within Mexican American culture, the political realities faced by U.S. people of Mexican descent additionally demand that they expose institutionalised racism and record the people's struggle against economic exploitation. The Chicana feminist writers whose works I currently examine in my forthcoming book, *Feminism on the Border*, acknowledge the often vast historical, class, racial and ethnic differences among women living on the geopolitical border between the United States and Mexico. They also build on the inroads that Chicano Movimiento writers like Angela de Hoyos accomplished in the late 1960s and early 70s. These contemporary Chicana feminist writers express a political consciousness that extends and complicates the boundaries of American literary production. The type of Chicana feminism that I locate in the literary production of several contemporary Chicana writers such as Sandra Cisneros, Gloria Anzaldúa, and Helena María Viramontes' explodes the false dichotomy between the aesthetic and the political. These writers and their texts build on the traditions of activism and as a result produce cultural artifacts that put literature to work.

The above phrase, putting "literature to work" is one that I adapted from Nobel Peace Prize medalist Rigoberta Menchú's realisation that her notoriety as Nobel Prize recipient provided new audiences other that the usual ones who already knew of her and her people's struggles. "Conocí que podia poner la medalla a trabajar" noted Menchú in a lecture to an audience of students, faculty, and Latino community members at the University of California at Los Angeles in June, 1993. She graciously thanked the Chicano and Chicana community for sponsoring her lecture and noted her debt to the Mexican people for providing refuge for her Guatemalan comrades in their struggle against the Guatemalan government. She illustrated the power of symbol making when she revealed her reason for choosing the museum of the Templo Mayor in Mexico City as the site where her Peace Prize medal would rest until the indigenous peoples of Guatemala can once again claim the land they inhabited for centuries before "el disastre," the European conquest of the Americas.

---

[1] I would like to thank Professors Teresa McKenna and Norma Cantú for their gracious comments on earlier versions of this essay.

While the Nobel recognition indeed opened more doors for Menchú in her project of publicising the atrocities committed upon the indigenous peoples of her country, to the rest of the world, her well-known testimonial, *Me Llamo Rigoberta Menchú, Y Asi Me Nació La Conciencia* (1983), provides an example of how literary production can engage in this type of explicit political work. In the public lectures which she offers throughout the United States, Menchú speaks of the continued struggles of indigenous peoples throughout the Americas. In that sense, the Americans of Mexican descent living in the United States (some for five generations, some more recent immigrants) are included in Menchú's vision of indigenous struggles.

In that tradition of indigenous American literatures that defies a reductive classification of the marginalised literatures of the Americas as regionalism but insists on problematising the complex identities of gender, race, and ethnicity, we find East Los Angeles-born Helena María Viramontes, a Chicana feminist writer who produces a discourse that also puts literature to work. Her discourse is written in a sparse language and utilises a non-linear narrative form that affirms its ties to Native American literature rather than to the dominant U.S. traditions of literary expression. In Viramontes's first publication, *The Moths and Other Stories* (1985), this partisan literature that takes as a major theme women's struggles within patriarchal Mexican and Mexican American customs also provides the complex short story, "The Cariboo Cafe," in which the unprepared reader enters the text as an alien to a refugee culture, the people who in the 1983 foreword to *This Bridge Called My Back* Cherríe Moraga represented as "Refugees of a World on Fire."[2] Viramontes crafts a fractured narrative that reflects the disorientation that mainly Latino immigrant workers feel when subjected to life in a country that controls their labour but does not value their existence as human beings. The Third World U.S. city represented in this narrative reflects the geopolitical space of a Chicana and Chicano Los Angeles that exists as a police state for these U.S. Mexicans as well as for the undocumented Central American immigrant workers.

In the same Viramontes collection, the narrative "Neighbors" presents yet another complex view of life in contemporary Los Angeles. Scenes of a 73 year-old woman, Aura, whose body no longer obeys her strong mind's commands, mingle with Viramontes's always sociologically aware analyses of the urban landscape. She transports the reader to a world where the neighbourhood's young men cannot find jobs, a world whose postmodern pretensions does not include them. In cities like L.A., urban renewal plans design skyscrapers and freeways that decimate the *barrio* and replace it with enclaves of the unemployed army of surplus labour. While it has become fashionable to represent the young men of the Chicano neighbourhoods as *cholos*, or gang members—"homeboys," to use a self-identifier—the multivalent irony remains that these "homeboys" exist as deterritorialised subjects of an "America" that refuses to acknowledge Chicano and Chicana identity as indigenous to the geographic area.

---

[2] See my analysis of "The Cariboo Cafe" in "Feminism on the Border: From Gender Politics to Geopolitics" in *Criticism in the Borderlands*. A more detailed version of that essay appears in my forthcoming book.

In "Neighbors," Aura's deteriorating body figures as the metaphor of the violated neighbourhood. Wracked by pain, she feels "miserable and cornered," and begins "cursing her body, herself for such weakness" (107). The long-time native of the neighbourhood suffers a physical pain that makes her "begin to hate." With the constant howl of police sirens in the background, Aura, the barrio, internalises the hatred that dominant society breeds. She harbors resentment and grows suspicious of anyone new to the neighbourhood. When another old woman appears on her porch looking for Fierro, the man who has lived in the house behind Aura's house for thirty years, Aura's suspicion of any outsiders induces the visitor to produce proof of her right to visit Fierro. In Viramontes's words, "[the visitor] began rummaging through her bags like one looking for proof of one's birth at a border crossing" (103). While this visitor is never named in the story, she figures as a central force in the narrative. Wearing a badly mended dress, unwashed, and "with a distinct scent accompanying her," the apparently homeless woman signifies, if not Death, *La Muerte*, herself, then certainly the harbinger of death. She wears a lopsided cotton wig, so we might read her as *La Pelona*, another cultural marker of impending death.

Viramontes presents Aura as the fractured aura of the Chicano neighbourhood that internalises the racism of the dominant media—the press, as well as such Hollywood movies as "Falling Down" that can only imagine Chicano youth as *cholos*, as violent homeboys. The old woman is still mentally alert but her deteriorating body that throbs with arthritis drives her to a state of hatred. As we enter the soul of Aura, we observe her self-loathing:

> She began to hate. She hated her body, the ticking of the hen-shaped clock which hung above the stove or the way the dogs howled at the police sirens. She hated the way her fingers distorted her hand so that she could not even grasp a glass of water. But most of all she hated the laughter and the loud music which came from the boys who stood around the candied-apple red Impala with the tape deck on full blast. They laughed and drank and threw beer cans in her yard while she burned with fever. The pain made her so desperate with intolerance, that she struggled to her porch steps, tears moistening her eyes, and pleaded with the boys. "Por favor ... Don't you have homes?" The boys, Toastie and Ruben, remind her: "We *are* home!" (108).

With this ironic reply, the Chicanos assert a claim to their land. The young men fight each other to defend the turf, the territory to which the hegemonic group confines them. Bound by these other borderlines, these young men remain locked into a terrain that additionally imprisons them in fixed positions as the sub-proletariat. Viramontes's insistence on that word, "home," recognises the displacement of the border dweller; "home" signifies the state of homelessness for women such as Aura as well as for the lost, undereducated young men of the Chicano urban barrios in the United States.

In this political narrative about aging, about violence, about fear, the children of the barrio "gather ... in small groups to lose themselves in the abyss of defeat, to find temporary solace among each other" (102). When Aura betrays that site of solace by involving the police in what is a minor infringement on her need for silence and solitude, Viramontes brings home to the reader the police state under which many Chicano communities live. The military police are not only in some far-off Latin American country, but in our U.S. neighbourhoods:

Her feeling of revenge had overcome her pain momentarily, but when the police arrived, she fully realized her mistake. The five cars zeroed in on their target, halting like tanks in a cartoon. The police jumped out in military formation, ready for combat. The neighbors began emerging from behind their doors and fences to watch the red lights flashing against the policemen's batons. When the boys were lined up, spread-eagled for the search, Toastie made a run for it, leaping over Aura's wrought iron fence and falling hard on a rosebush. His face scratched and bleeding, he ran towards her door, and for a moment Aura was sure he wanted to kill her. It was not until he lunged for the door that she was able to see the desperation and confusion, the fear in his eyes, and he screamed at the top of his lungs while pounding on her door, the vowels of the one word melting into a howl, he screamed to her, "Pleeeeeeeease." He pounded on the door please. She pressed her hands against her ears until his howl was abruptly silenced by a dull thud. When the two policemen dragged him down the porch steps, she could hear the creak of their thick leather belts rubbing against their bullets. She began to cry. (108-9)

Like "The Cariboo Cafe," "Neighbors" ends with the image of a gun. While Viramontes's feminist texts refuse closure, in "Cariboo" one cannot imagine the policeman not shooting the refugee woman. In "Neighbors," however, Aura's fatal error occurs when she calls the police (the militia of the hegemonic group) to the barrio in an attempt to ensure her safety. Viramontes forces us to rethink simple dichotomies: in the Chicana/o homeland, who is the enemy, who is our ally? Are the young men of the neighbourhood Aura's enemies? Are the police her allies? Can we read Aura's loaded gun, intended for Toastie and Ruben, as a sign of resistance? Against whom do the Aura's resist? Against whom do they rage? Have the Auras of Chicana/o neighbourhoods been so incorporated by the dominant group that they internalise their racism and blame the disenfranchised, the under-educated, the under-employed young men of the barrio for all their problems?

If Aura does indeed shoot the gun at the visitor whom I earlier identified as *la pelona*, Aura denies for herself and for her neighbours the possibility of a peaceful death. *La pelona's* visit to the neighbourhood has earlier enacted an ancient ritual, easing the old man Fierro to a natural death at the end of a long, if not peaceful, life. With Aura's loaded gun, violence from within its ranks entraps the Chicano/Chicana neighbourhood as much as violence from the dominating group and their police enforcers. Clearly, Aura's loaded gun in a contemporary Chicano/a neighbourhood is not the same weapon that Américo Paredes evoked in his oppositional text, *With His Pistol in His Hand*.

In her forthcoming work, *Paris Rats in L.A.: A Novel in Short Stories*, Viramontes takes us back to this metropolitan barrio to reclaim it along with its women and men. Instead of the media oversimplifications of the barrio as a war zone of gang violence, she presents the barrio as township, the barrio as home, and its young men and women in admittedly violent gangs, but she gives us the reasons (or *unreason*) for this violence. She offers us insights into the process whereby our children, our young women and men, are condemned to lives on the margins, on the borders, of the United States.

In the title story, "Paris Rats in L.A.," Viramontes introduces her ten-year-old narrator, Ofelia, also known as "Champ," and her brother, Gregorio. In Gregorio, Viramontes lifts the mask of hostility that young Chicanos wear in their wars against each other and against the outside world. As poet of the urban barrio, Viramontes's young narrator brings her beloved brother to life:

His pendelton shirt hangs on him, but it's ironed real smooth though he's been out all night, and buttoned to the neck and wrists even when it's so hot. He always looks mad and jest real mean, though I think he ain't, but everybody kinda moves away like they're ascared of the big scar that streets down from his cheek to his neck cuz he ain't ascared of no knife, no gun, no nuthin'; and nobody says anything when he smokes a camel on the bus even when you're not supposed to. He's got spiders for eyes and so's everybody, Fox and Horse and stuff, call him Spider, but I can't on account he says to me: "My name is Gregorio, remember that Champ, remember." And to me, he's the most handsomest man in the world. (1-2)

Viramontes gives a name, a face, and ultimately, humanity to people who the dominant group prefers to keep anonymous, sinister, and therefore easier to either kill on the street or disappear into the labyrinth of the U.S. prison system. Spider is the male subject constructed by the hegemonic group; Gregorio is that subject uncovered, he gains identity with his sister's demolition of the false stereotypes within which young Chicanos like him have been rendered invisible.

Since only two of the stories in this collection have been published, "Miss Clairol" and "Tears on My Pillow," I will limit the rest of my analysis to "Tears on My Pillow." Here, Viramontes shows how Ofelia negotiates the gendered spaces of the barrio. Ofelia is left alone in her Terrace Flats project apartment while her mother Arlene, an urban proletarian, labours in a garment sweatshop and returns dead tired, the noise of industrial sewing machines ringing in her ears hours after leaving the factory.

Ofelia names her anxiety as a burning. The child's stomach burns as she observes her community: wife beating and killing, neglected children, exhausted women and men whose labours fuel the consumption of luxuries by the upper classes in cities like Los Angeles. One cannot ignore the other images that a burning Los Angeles currently evokes: the fires of the Rodney King uprising as well as the other fires in the hills over Malibu sent by that mysterious phenomenon, El Niño, fueled by the Santa Ana winds, or, as some whisper, perhaps urban guerrillas.

In the same way that the stories "Paris Rats in L.A." and "Spider's Face" give substance, voice, and identity to the barrio Chicanos, this story gives the female gendered subject, the Chicana Ofelia, visibility and a multilayered identity. Opening the narrative with the ten-year-old child's variant of the *Llorona* folktale, what emerges is a "native" Chicana's perspective of the historical moment from which we can start theorising the political in Viramontes's text.

In an interview, "The Problem of Cultural Self-Representation," Gayatri Spivak suggests that we ask the literary texts that we examine as cultural critics "in what way, in what contexts, under what kinds of race and class situations, gender is used as what sort of signifier to cover over what kinds of things" (52). In the Chicano context, the legend of *La Llorona* typically functions as a masculinist tale that illustrates women's innate depravity and treachery. But one of Viramontes's accomplishments in this very short story of only five pages is the *un*-covering of male privilege within the Chicano cultural context. Rendered in the vernacular, young Ofelia's version of *La Llorona* opens Viramontes's narrative:

Mama María learned me about La Llorona. La Llorona is the one who doing all the crying I been hearing all this time with no one to tell me who it was til Mama Maria. She told me La Lauren's [llorona] this mama, see, who killed her kids. Something like that. How does it goes? Something like there's this girl and some soldiers take her husband away and she goes to the jail to look for him, asses why these soldiers took him. And she gots I don't member how many kids all crying cause their daddy's gone, you know. And the soldier being mean and stupid and the devil inside him ..., he points a gun to her head and says, "I gonna kill you." But she looks at him and says, "Do me the favor." That's like something Arlene would say, you know. But the girl, she don't know when to stop. "You kill everything so go ahead and kill me," she tells the soldier, "but first kill my kids cause I don't want 'em hungry and sick and lone without no 'ama or 'apa or TV." So the devil says "Okay," and shoots all the kids, bang, bang, bang. But you know what? He don't kill her. Cold shot, huh? She goes coocoo and escapes from the nut house. ... And to this day, the girl all dressed up in black like Mama Maria cause she killed her kids and she walks up and down City Terrace with no feet, crying and crying and looking for her kids. For reallies, late in the dark night only" (110).

When we trace the legend of *La Llorona*, we find that this tale actually chronicles the historical moment of violence against the indigenous female subject in the Americas. The popular tradition of *La Llorona* for many Chicana/os, however, covers up this original moment of colonial contact with the aboriginal women in the sixteenth century.

In his study of "Mexican Legendry and the Rise of the Mestizo," Américo Paredes states that "legends are ego-supporting devices." He continues:

They may appeal to the group or to individuals by affording them pride, dignity, and self-esteem: local or national heroes to identify with, for example ... Whether in doing so they validate or challenge the social structure, ease tensions or exacerbate them is besides the point. (98)

Paredes correctly points out that "frustration and defeat" feed the ego as do "victory and conformity." He examines Mexican legends in order to construct the uniquely *Mexican* national character of the mestizo, that is: "the distinctive blend of Spaniard and Indian, with contribution by the Negro and other ethnic groups ..." (98). The legend of *La Llorona* contains such a story of mestizaje, of miscegenation, which Paredes locates within Hernan Cortes's conquest of Mexico.

A thorough review of the different variants of the legend and its relationship to the historical figure of La Malinche would demand more space than is appropriate here; however, suffice it to say that an audience more familiar with European narratives than with Aztec or other indigenous tales of the Americas can find analogies, as Paredes does, in Euripides's *Medea* or Puccini's *Madame Butterfly* (103). The legend transposes European traditions about women's vengeance against men onto indigenous pre-Columbian myths. Paredes states:

the literary legend of *La Llorona* struck deep roots in Mexican tradition because it was grafted on an Indian legend cycle about the supernatural woman who seduces men when they are out alone on the roads or working in the fields. At times she destroys her lovers after giving herself to them, but often she is helpful as well as passionate and may make a man's fortune or help him raise a fine crop of corn. She is *matlacihua* or Woman of the Nets among the Nahuatl speakers, and other language groups such as the Mexes and the Populucas know her by other names. As *la segua*, she has been reported as far north as Texas, and she is also known as far south as Panama. (103)

Jose Limón, in "La Llorona, the Third Legend of Greater Mexico," believes that *La Llorona,* after La Malinche and La Virgen de Guadalupe, is the "third, comparatively unacknowledged, major female symbol of Greater Mexican socio-cultural life" (2). He grounds her story in "concrete historical experience," drawing on marxist and feminist theories. He agrees with Bacil Kirtley that the legend also grafts her into "another distinctive Indian legend, that of Cihuacoatl, the Aztec goddess, who, according to Sahagun, appeared in the night crying out for dead children" (10). According to Limón:

> What the Europeans seem to add are the motifs of (1) a woman with children (2) betrayed by an adulterous lover, their father, followed by (3) insane revenge infanticide in which she is typically the killer concluding with her anguished repentance during which she cries for her children ... the indigenous peoples seem to add (1) an *Indian* woman sometimes in a flowing white dress, (2) crying *in the night*, (3) near a body of water (an important element in Aztec mythology), and (4) meeting people, mostly men who are shocked when they see her. (11)

As Limón asserts, a source for the legend emerges in Aztec mythology. Ten years before the Conquest there were visions and sightings, omens, according to Fray Bernardino de Sahagun's *Historia General de las cosas de Nueva España*. Sahagun notes that

> people heard a weeping woman night after night. She passed by in the middle of the night, wailing and crying out in a loud voice, "My children, we must flee far away from this city!" At other times she cried" "My children, where shall I take you?" (cited in *Broken Spears*, 6).

According to Diego Muñoz Camargo, in *Historia de Tlaxcala,*

> the people heard in the night the voice of a weeping woman, who sobbed and sighed and drowned herself in her tears. This woman cried: "O my sons, we are lost ...!" Or she cried: "O my sons, where can I hide you ...?" (cited in *Broken Spears*, 9-10).

If these versions, allegedly narrated by native informants to Spanish chroniclers, authorise the *Llorona* legend as having to do with conquest, with imperialism, with the violence inflicted on the indigenous Americans, then Viramontes maps out how a contemporary Chicanita bears witness to the conquest of her own world in the East Los Angeles barrio. Ofelia transforms the story that her grandmother, Mama María, tells when the child's lived experience in the City Terrace government housing projects spills over to her *Llorona* narrative. The child's variant testifies to the moment of violence against the male and female mestizo and mestiza subjects in the United States Borderlands. Hers is a variant that un-covers her cultural, class and gendered positions.

The tears on Ofelia's pillow mark her construction by patriarchal culture as a weeping (hysterical?) woman, *una Llorona*. But in contemporary Chicana feminist discourse, Ofelia's tears cry out for her powerful cultural and ancestral link to the indigenous earth goddess, Cihuacoatl, "who wept and called out in the night" (*Broken Spears*, 12). Rather than being drowned by an insane mother, this Ofelia, whose link to Shakespeare's drowned woman resonates to the reader but is radically transformed, drowns herself only in figurative tears as she witnesses the brutality and violence in her neighbourhood. Rather than the European figure of the insane, rejected, victimised Ophelia, the Chicana representation of the female subject lives to tell the tale. Again, drawing on Spivak's textual strategies in "The Post-Colonial Critic," I propose that if sanctioned infanticide is the regulative psychobiography for the indigenous or *mestiza* woman in the *Americas*, then Ofelia's powerful revision of the cultural script portends the possible transformations that occur when Chicanas produce alternative cultural self-representations (71).

Ofelia begins her *Llorona* narrative with the familiar version that blames the woman for the murder of the children. But her memory of the *cuento* clashes against the realities of her life. Surrounded by other refugee families in the Terrace Flats government housing projects, families possibly from Latin American countries where *desaparecidos* is a noun referring to men and women who resist the hegemonic group, Ofelia retells the story as a tale of *desaparecidos*. The husband is not the Spanish con-quistador who seduces the *India,* the indigenous woman, and attempts to take his children back to work the land in Spain, this husband is imprisoned. Like so many *Guatemaltecos* or *Salvadoreños* in their countries, or Chicanos in U.S. prisons for various unjust reasons, the father in Ofelia's version is blameless.

La Llorona confronts the imperialist soldier, and in spite of her resistance and confrontation (or because of it?) he murders her children. The soldier kills her children to establish his supremacy and to ensure her submission. Her defeat is translated by the child Ofelia as going "coocoo." Then there is a break in the narrative which mimics the slippage in the historical memory of a people who dis-remember the violence of the conquest. It was not a traitorous Malintzin Tenépal nor a hysterical *Llorona* bent on insane revenge who kills her *hijos*, who commits infanticide, but the occupying *soldados* intent on complete conquest and the submission of the indigenous peoples. Only after Ofelia establishes a different version, gives a different point of view, does the child narrator slip back to the more familiar androcentric, hegemonic tale that blames the woman for the infanticide, that blames the conquered for the conquest. The popular narrative intrudes with an ending that Ofelia does not recognise from her own experience.

But there is much more to this Viramontes narrative. She demolishes the popular narrative of *La Llorona* when the City Terrace women's identities as single parents emerge, all with different ways and with different levels of success in *raising* children, not drowning them. Ofelia swears that she has heard *la Llorona* in her neighbourhood. Indeed, as Ofelia's mother, Arlene, knows, what Ofelia hears is not legend but the real cries of the neighbour woman, Lil Mary G., who endures beatings by her man and who is eventually murdered by him. City Terrace is no Aztlán, the mythical homeland of the Aztec natives and the utopian dreamland of the Chicano nationalists of the 1960s and 70s. For Lil Mary G., her daughter Veronica, for Arlene, Ofelia, and Gregorio, Aztlán does not exist.

Ultimately, what Viramontes captures in "Tears on My Pillow" is the political problematic of the gendered subject in the Chicana and Chicano cultural arena. The Chicana narrator un-covers the missing memory of the imperialist moment of violence against the indigenous women in the sixteenth century. But she also confronts the clash within her own world in City Terrace, in the Chicano "homeland." Women are blamed and beaten by their kinsmen and exploited by postmodern capitalism. While Viramontes offers an alternative version of the moment of contact with the European conquerors, the soldiers of Ofelia's *llorona* narrative, in this story, she cannot offer a moment of liberatory self-realisation.

"Tears on My Pillow" ends with Ofelia watching her mother's preparations for a night out at a local club, the Palladium, a release from Arlene's mind-numbing work-week at the factory. Ofelia thinks that Veronica's loss of her mother must be the worst thing that can happen to anyone and innocently links Lil Mary G.'s death with Arlene's repeated absences through the necessities of her position as exploited labour and through Arlene's after-hours benign neglect: "They just disappear, leaving you alone all ascared with your burns and La Llorona hungry for you" (115).

Ofelia burns with the anxiety of reincorporation by that master narrative, the tale of *La Llorona*. Irresolution, or the refusal of closure in Viramontes's political text, signals a complex project currently being undertaken by Chicana feminist writers, critics, and cultural workers that undercuts old stereotypes and opens up new possibilities for empowerment through the self-representation of Chicanas by Chicanas, women who insist on a self-identifier that marks their political subjectivity as feminist as well as working-class-identified.

Works Cited

Kirtley, Bacil F., "La Llorona and Related Theme," *Western Folklore* 19 (1960): 155-168.

Leon-Portilla, Miguel. *The Broken Spears: The Aztec Account of the Conquest of Mexico*.

Limón, José, "*La Llorona*, the Third Legend of Greater Mexico: Cultural Symbols, Women, and the Political Unconscious." Lecture presented at the Renato Rosaldo Lecture Series, University of Arizona, Tucson, Arizona, 26 July 1985.

Menchú, Rigoberta, *I ... Rigoberta Menchú: An Indian Woman in Guatemala*. Ed. Elisabeth Burgos-Debray Trans. Ann Wright. London: Verso, 1984.

Moraga Cherríe, and Gloria Anzaldúa, eds., *This Bridge Called My Back: Writings by Radical Women of Color*. 2nd ed. New York: Kitchen Table: Women of Color Press, 1983.

Paredes, Américo. *With His Pistol in His Hand: A Border Ballad and Its Hero*. Austin: University of Texas Press, 1958.

——, "Mexican Legendry and the Rise of the Mestizo: A Survey," American Folk Legend: A Symposium. Ed. Wayland D. Hand. Berkeley and Los Angeles: University of California Press, 1971, pp. 97-107.

Saldívar-Hull, Sonia, "Feminism on the Border: From Gender Politics to Geopolitics," *Criticism in the Borderlands: Studies in Chicano Literature, Culture, and Ideology*. Ed. Héctor Calderón and José David Saldívar. Durham, N.C.: Duke University Press, 1991, pp. 203-20.

——, *Feminism on the Border: Contemporary Chicana Writers*. Forthcoming, University of California Press.

Spivak, Gayatri Chakravorty, "The Problem of Cultural Self-representation," *The Post-Colonial Critic: Interviews, Strategies, Dialogues*. Ed. Sarah Harasym. New York and London: Routledge, 1990, pp. 50-58.

Viramontes, Helena María, *The Moths and Other Stories*. Houston: Arte Público P, 1985.

——, *Paris Rats in L.A. and Other Stories*. Unpublished manuscript, forthcoming.

——, "Tears on My Pillow," In Charles Tatum, ed. *New Chicana /Chicano Writing*. Tucson: University of Arizona Press, 1992, pp. 110-115.

——, "Miss Clairol," *The Americas Review* 15 (Fall/Winter 1987): 101-105.

THE NATIONALIST MODEL FOR AMERICAN ETHNIC NARRATIVE

Peter Carafiol, Portland State University

I want to start by recounting two far-flung moments in American ethnic history. The second is from Booker T. Washington—the first is more recent. It comes from the *New York Times News Service*, February 2, 1994, the day after Deval Patrick was appointed Assistant Attorney General for Civil Rights. I offer it as a pointedly concentrated rendering of a familiar piece of the cultural liturgy. "Patrick's entire life," the *Times* intones, "has been one of overcoming obstacles. His rise from poverty to success is the kind of story that even some conservatives would cheer."[1] The significance of this formula is precisely in its brevity. Its short-hand and unselfconscious reference to terms that are elaborated in countless texts, and its deliberate association of those terms with "conservative," which is to say self-consciously "American" identities, suggests how thoroughly settled these terms are, by now, in our vocabularies. Only the barest hint is necessary since the operative language is so deeply embedded in the cultural code.

The generic story of self-creation in America condensed by the *Times* is a simple and familiar one. A boy—if not a boy then we would have what might be called an "unauthorised account"; the terms and implications would change, as would the narrative strategies and generic conventions that amount to experiments in making sense of the conflicting terms involved—a *boy*, then, is born into obscure poverty. But, taking full advantage of such opportunities as life offers, and by dint of native abilities, hard work, and good character, he leaves his low past behind and achieves the solid American success he had barely dreamed for himself. The potency of this script is reflected in its broad use—so common as to seem almost natural, a cultural habit, a routine. As the official organising interpretations and shaping ideal for numberless American narratives from Franklin's fragmented "Memoirs" to Nixon's, it has remained so powerful in our culture—even long after it had been made an object of parody by the militantly disillusioned like Nathaniel West—precisely because it embodies in *individual* terms the past and future of the nation. Patrick's appointment is so resonant because it encourages us to associate that promise of personal success and fulfillment with a "civil right."

The second incident, from near the end of Booker T. Washington's work of Auto-Mythography, *Up From Slavery*, relates what I take to be the defining moment of the book.[2] Travelling by train in Georgia, Washington is invited to sit with two white

---

[1] Steven A. Holmes, *New York Times News Service* in *The Oregonian*, 2 February 1944: A16.
[2] Booker T. Washington, *Up From Slavery* (New York: Lancer Books, 1968), pp. 171-72.

Bostonian women of his acquaintance in a car full of white Georgia men. To Washington's discomfort and the obvious dismay of the Georgians, one of the women orders a meal, and unable to get away, Washington rushes through his dinner under the glare of Southern eyes. Afterwards, Washington moves apprehensively to the smoking car to find out how things stand. But, once there, he is surprised to be greeted cordially all round because, in the interim, it had become known, as he says, "who I was."

This triumphant moment comes, as triumph must in these ritual dramatisations of cultural progress, near the end not just of the book, but of years of struggle and suffering during most of which the world was indifferent to Washington's presence and just before the narrative turns away from personal memoir to recite a litany of public accomplishment and (especially) recognition represented most prominently by the text of his Speech at the Atlanta Exposition, which the account presents in full as documentary evidence of the "recognition" dramatised in the railroad car encounter.

It is the point of such key narrative moments to seem definitive—brief, bold assertions of unqualified personal identity, marking as they do the relationship between, in this case, Washington and the surrounding culture. This apparent simplicity, however, only covers up conflicts inevitable to communication around and about ethnic boundary lines, conflicts that could be said to define such boundaries through the formative intersection of rhetorical forms, linguistic and social. Huck Finn's famous "I'll go to Hell," for example, presents itself as subversive, but as James Cox has persuasively argued, Huck's repudiation of his own culture's values actually reinforces the ethical assumptions of Twain's post-Civil War audience and thus demonstrates both the futility of Huck's quest for "freedom," and the speciousness of the idealised notion of "freedom" he seeks. The doubleness of this ostensibly definitive statement receives its fullest and fully appropriate expression in what has often been seen as the Phelps Farm "farce" that follows. Washington's moment, as I shall suggest below, conceals a similarly convoluted dance of desire for and dissent from larger cultural norms.

In this essay, I want to look briefly at the composition of individual identity and of a specifically "ethnic" identity in Horatio Alger's *Ragged Dick*, Booker T. Washington's *Up From Slavery*, and Richard Wright's *Native Son*. Each of these works has been a model for the nature and construction of ethnic identity in America. Each has been a springboard for generalisations about the conditions of an American "Character"—and it is that connection between "ethnic" and "American" identities I want to focus on here. I'm interested in what these texts have to say about narratives that take ethnos for a subject in the American context, including the critical narratives of ethnicity produced by literary scholars. I want to use them to suggest some of the interrelationships between critiques of the subject and the problems posed by ethnic boundaries as writers draw and redraw them. Read both in and against the context of revisionist discourses, these works yield problematic and even ideologically uncomfortable understandings of the interplay of self and culture, of individual and ethnos. Among other things, they prompt us to ask what the construction of the ethnic self within a larger hegemonic culture suggests about the integrity or the "otherness" of our own cultural identities and the institutions we construct around them with our fictive and critical accounts?

Their ambiguous relations to the tradition implicate these narratives of personal identity in the influential narrative strategies that have defined America and its writing in an equally ambivalent opposition to the European tradition. The story of America, in its myriad manifestations and as told for various purposes, has been an effort to represent original identity against the background of an established authoritative tradition. This is its particular importance to the construction of narratives that play on self-discovery, creation, invention, development like those I am dealing with here. American Literary Studies offers a particularly instructive study in critical versions of such narratives since American literary studies has always depended on at once defining and effacing ethnic identity. In *The American Ideal*, I argued that the idea of "America" has—particularly in literary studies—been a strategy for asserting difference without having to explain it.[3] As "America" subsumes particulars within its overarching and literally unquestionable unity, it has represented an "other" world within worldly experience, an analog of, and a temporal substitute for, the divine order toward which Christian history aspired.

Perched awkwardly and self-consciously on the outskirts of British culture, all American literature has been regional literature, by which I also mean that it is literature from the margin, alienated from yet unavoidably supplicant to an established dominant literary tradition, the product of a colonial culture and people, and thus a literature of ethnos. In short, American literature is ethnic literature. It is ethnic not because its authors are members of a repressed minority, but because its narrative forms and rhetorical strategies speak to and from its marginal position, and are the same as, could even be said to have provided the models for, the narratives we more typically think of as ethnic that followed. In their zeal to distinguish American texts from British, American cultural rhetoricians imagined a powerful model for ethnocentric self-creation, and set the terms that subsequent ethnic narratives have worked with and against.

The tradition of critical writing that comprises American Literary Scholarship, both before and after its professional institutionalisation in the last quarter of the nineteenth century, constructed a coherent literary tradition to incarnate and legitimate the national identity, and at the same time, justify its own professional existence. From its first exemplars in nineteenth-century literary scholarship, the "American" tradition of literary study can be seen as early instance of what has become, in more recent academic discourse, a ritualistic invocation of "change." Like the Lutheran dissent from Catholicism, the secession of American literature from the British tradition was only the first step toward unbounded future fracturing. In that sense, monolithic as American Literary Scholarship may seem to its modern dissenters, its initiation into the institution of literary studies more than a century ago prefigured and paved the way for what their proponents usually consider "post-modernist" programmes of canonical revision and diversity. In the realm of scholarship, American literary studies opened new rhetorical territory. The embryonic narrative of "America" appeared at the end

---

[3] Peter Carafiol, *The American Ideal: Literary History as a Worldly Activity* (New York: Oxford UP, 1991).

of the fifteenth century as a necessarily ambivalent early strategy for dealing with the authority of historical experience.[4] The historiography incarnated in that narrative reimagined apocalyptic or revolutionary change as the fulfillment of received values, and on earth in the New Eden rather than in heaven. On that Christian model, the stories of American identity have dramatised a crossing from the European past to the New World American future in which former identities are sloughed off as if they had never been, leaving essential identities untouched. Four hundred years later, in the developing field of American Literary Scholarship, that meant accommodating while claiming to abandon the past and making the new tolerable by bringing it within the existing horizon of critical understanding and social desire—specifically, at the time, the longing for national unity and security after the Civil War, a longing that seemed particularly acute amidst the crushing world-wide depression of the 1870s and after that generated social unrest in the U.S. and violence throughout Europe.

The idea of "America" has been a way of *assuming* cultural, historical, and narrative coherence, and in the process, of constraining the interpretation of facts and of texts. In scholarship, it has produced a tradition of critical writing that I have described elsewhere as the Rhetoric of Revisionism.[5] In faithful imitation of the New World settlers' claims to have left the Old behind, each initiative in American Literary Scholarship repudiates its own professional past in this way, and in that same gesture, reiterates it. Even at their most conventional, they are narratives of dissent, at their most rebellious, aspirants to the tradition. Each has depended on forgetting the central fact that its revolutionary posture is a rhetorical *norm* in the field. The remarkable persistence of the narrative of America as a strategy for assuming a double position vis-à-vis tradition reappears in the place "America" takes in contemporary academic conversations about ethnicity, where it represents—Janus-like— both the repressive and failed past and the idealised all-embracing future. In this period of what Umberto Eco might call Hypercritique, it is not surprising that traditional narratives of American identity and the established assumptions of American literary scholarship have all, finally, begun to quiver under critical scrutiny. Such is the pace of critical turnover that, in the past few years, even the next generation of dissent, the exclusivist notion of ethnicity that justified the early inroads of ethnic writing into the tradition has already been subjected to the same critique that's being directed at exclusivist models of literary nationalism. Yet, as in American Literary Scholarship, it is still a powerful,

---

[4] William C. Spengemann most recently discusses the implications of "America" for developments in English language and literature in *A New World of Words: Redefining Early American Literature* (New Haven: Yale University Press, 1994). That work enforces the point that the narrative characteristics I am describing have, for a long time, been famously associated with Romantic writing in general, a point which, as Spengemann shows, suggests that "American" narratives are not confined within the national boundaries or to the citizenry of the United States, but are a world-wide response to post-medieval conditions, prominent among them the idea of a "New World." The other direction in with this cuts is to expand, as I try to do here, the horizon of texts to which the writing conventionally considered ethnic may be connected. Even the insistence of such writing on its own difference—especially that insistence—is not different.

[5] See my earlier essays "After American Literature," *American Literary History* 4.3 (1992): 539-549, and "Changing the World: The Rhetoric of Revisionism," *ADE Bulletin* Spring 1992: 61-68.

an essential question whether the critique of ethnicity will take a form as superficial and cosmetic as it so far has in American Literary Studies while more fundamental questions are ignored or short-circuited.

Both the conflict and the progress of critical accounts among prominent scholars of ethnic literature reenact the problems of the attempt to tell an ethnic story against the all-absorbing background of American narratives that have, in effect, already covered and thus occupied, laid claim to, the same ground. The contrasting and shifting approaches of, say, Werner Sollors and Henry Louis Gates toward the very nature of ethnicity and ethnic study represent alternate strategies that reflect the ambivalent terms of ethnic cultural coherence, and their conflicting political implications and aims echo long-standing debates among Americanists about the unity in diversity of American cultural and literary traditions. My point here is not that there is something "wrong" with the critical rhetoric of ethnicity. On the contrary, I take its features simply as examples of the way critical arguments depend on dominant and pervasive surrounding rhetorics, professional or cultural. The movements performed by the criticism of ethnicity mark both developmental stages in its own professional initiation and the reiterated forms of revisionist rhetoric. The contradictions implicit in particular formulations reflect the doubleness of American literary discourse and of the genres of critical writing—Ethnic, Feminist, New Historicist—that huddle, however awkwardly, under that rubric—dancing nervously between stasis and change, eternity and history, an increasingly strenuous dance under conditions such as our own when the *desire* for change coexists with cynicism about any particular effort to realise it.

Alger's and Washington's books promise social change and the willed production of a better world. They present themselves as stories of boundaries and of the crossing of boundaries, of new identities achieved and old ones abandoned. The boundaries they describe define the conditions of ethnos, laying out the values by which one ethnic group distinguishes itself from its "other" and thus, implicitly, the terms required for a successful initiation into membership. These fables of crossing model the resolution of social divisions, imply the flexibility of ethnos, and affirm the desirability of new membership and of change itself at the same time that they reaffirm existing values and beliefs. The new identity achieved by an individual figures the character of the repeatedly renewed ethnic order. As stories of ethnic identity, *Ragged Dick* and *Up From Slavery* recapitulate and legitimate, in their different ways, the rhetoric of American national identity. Of course, just as the official interpretation of Franklin's *Autobiography* depends on ignoring most of his text—and indeed, just as the official understanding of American Literature depends on ignoring most of the texts in the United States, or by American citizens, much less those written in "America"—the embracing description of the American success story has for the most part ignored the complexities of Alger's and Washington's works, complexities that make them more interesting and provoking than propaganda tracts for the American dream. As these works reveal the fractured boundaries of the multi-layered American social structure, they interrogate not just traditional notions of American cultural coherence (by now, one hopes, that move has lost its power to startle), but also the particular arrangement of ethnic boundaries that have composed the social order and formulated debate about ethnic difference in America.

As Alger's work shows, these conflicts are not restricted to narratives of race, but characterise rhetorics of ethnos, of crossing and power, of social construction in general. *Ragged Dick* tells its story of ethnos, however, from the inside rather than from the margin, and thus is bent on affirming its own middle-class identity. Thus, contrary to the usual "rags to riches" characterisations of the Alger tales, Dick is not seeking admission to the capitalist aristocracy. Modelling an appropriate personal modesty and the democratic instincts that define a truly American spirit, even while he is still Ragged Dick in *fact*, the grimy shoeshine boy who sleeps in cardboard boxes longs only to be respectable, worthy of induction into the middle class that (for the purposes of the book) defines the nation. He stars in a reassuringly ritualistic drama of self-discovery composed in the conventional terms of the established culture. There is nothing threatening or subversive about this initiation across social classes. And the fact that Dick is helped along at every stage by agents of the Ethnos he wants to join—barely concealed avatars of his own future self—simply reflects the unspeakable importance of his progress to the cultural self-image.[6]

Ragged Dick works hard to make "class" look like a permeable boundary. And it is obviously in the interest of the middle-class ethnos to present it that way. According to the tale, all Dick needs to achieve respectability are a bath, a new suit of clothes, a certain refinement of manners, a modicum of education, and a clearer understanding that he might actually achieve these things by throwing off his old ways. This emphasis on the superficial is possible precisely because "character," an essential trait, is at the heart of Dick's ability to move into the respectable classes, as it was at the heart of the discourse surrounding American national identity in the third quarter of the nineteenth century. Dick's movement from shoeshine boy to respectable citizen requires only superficial fine tuning because he possessed the only really essential and intrinsic trait all along. From the first page of the text, when Dick is rousted out of his flimsy cardboard abode by a passing porter who recognises right away that "there's some good in you, Dick [once Dick has declared his honesty the Porter miraculously knows his name], after all." "There was," the narrator adds, "something about Dick that made him attractive."[7] It is this appearance, rather than the heroic deeds that are popularly associated with the success of Alger heroes, that gets Dick his first break —the responsibility of showing a respectable middle-class youth around New York— "he looks honest," the Father says, "He has an open face, and I think can be depended upon."[8] And repeatedly in moments of crisis—when Dick is accused of trying to pass a bad bill, or of robbing a "middle-aged woman" on the trolley—his honest expression reassures those in authority that he can not be guilty. The point here is not just that Dick's initiation among the respectable depends on this innate character unrelated to background or experience (although it does) and, therefore, could not really, as the

---

[6] Horatio Alger, *Ragged Dick* (New York: Collier, 1962).
[7] *Ragged Dick*, p. 2.
[8] *Ragged Dick*, p. 55.

book promises, simply be imitated by those with similar aspirations. The point is that this essential, this inner, trait must *manifest* itself on the outside as well. Dick's face advertises his worthiness for membership. There is no need to fear a mistake. In the commercial ethos of this book, unifying Spirit must become material, a motif the American and the Christian stories (by no coincidence) share. No longer a marker of strictly otherworldly worth, it is a worldly form of social currency.

The desirability of these changes is never in doubt. There is no hint that Dick might be losing anything by leaving his old associations behind, since it is hard to image poverty as Dick initially embodies it as a desirable state or the poor as a group with which even its own members are particularly eager to identify.[9] His friend Frank's obligatory democratic assertion that "you are none the worse for being a bootblack" is belied by the narrative's pervasive disdain for the lower classes.[10] Nothing in the narrative is allowed to impede or cloud Dick's deliberate ascent from poverty, a change that Dick unaccountably says "reminds me of Cinderella ... when she was changed into a fairy princess."[11] This fairy-tale analogy is unaccountable simply because there is absolutely nothing magical about what Dick does, and the materiality of it, as accumulation and work—core middle-class values—is both means and end in one. Dick's apparent ethnocentric feat, in the midst of his transformation, that he might be seen by his old crowd as putting on airs is less an expression of class solidarity than of middle-class distaste for aristocratic snobbery. His assimilation into the group of respectable adults—older versions of Dick who made their own way over the ground he is travelling and who help him out as he later helps out others in his old place, portrays society as a spiritual rather than a worldly order, one produced not by contingent experience, acts in the world, but by spiritual identities independent of worldly circumstances. Dick's experience redefines "middle class culture" as, in effect, a latter day "gathered church" of the respectable. As in the gathered churches of seventeenth-century New England, members are brought together by the common spirit (now of honesty and uprightness) they share even though, in a nineteenth-century spirit of enterprise, they turn their energies toward expanding their numbers by helping new initiates along the material path to full membership. In this narrative of self-revision, Dick both changes and does not change. Becoming a member of the new ethnos is the process of stripping away the inessential to more fully enact what he has always been.

As Dick marches toward the inevitably successful end of this cultural self-celebration there lingers the question of what he gives up, the "value" of the past that is scapegoated in this narrative as it always is in revisionist accounts, and of the character he has had to sacrifice to join the "respectable" club. Like Twain's vernacular characters, Dick wields an ironic humour and his own characteristic idiom to puncture the posing and pretension that has taken on particularly threatening impli-

---

[9] For a discussion of the problems of imagining an identify around some affirmative model of poverty, see John Guillory, *Cultural Capital: The Problem of Literary Canon Formation* (Chicago: University of Chicago Press, 1993), p. 13.

[10] *Ragged Dick*, p. 72.

[11] *Ragged Dick*, p. 58.

cations in an increasingly anonymous and predatory urban commercial culture. In this nineteenth-century American version of the venerable debate between country and town, the terms have gotten mixed. The town is still sophisticated and experienced, but now low-class and unrefined, while the country embodies both upper-class refinement and a bumpkin-like naiveté. As middle-class America's new urban hero, Dick must have, in effect, two identities at once, one (described from the dominant perspective as "superficial" and changeable), is also the most attractive and effective. This personality, rather than the proper little clerk he becomes, is the reason Dick is so attractive a character, one worth building a story around. The other is "essential" but also undistinguishing—it is a "character" (like that ascribed to the Nation as its principle of coherence) but not an individual and (as we see it in the other boys) helpless.

More than anything else, it is Dick's language that identifies and "otherises" him. It locates Dick in a different ethnos as the speaker of a foreign language. That language articulates a unique personal identity, distinct from the honest "Character" that identifies him as a candidate for conversion, and not, like that "Character," an abstract principle that can span apparent lines of ethnos precisely because it is shared universally by all the "respectable" alike. Dick's anti-formal speech, his personal linguistic style, distinguishes him even from his own lower-class companions, and makes him, literally, incomprehensible to his new middle-class friends. Because of his peculiar individual style, he is variously called "a queer boy," "a character," "a queer chap." "What a chap you are," says his friend Frank, and little Ida Greyson [Dick's symbolic love interest] calls him a "droll boy"—"What a funny boy you are."[12] By which, of course, they all mean that he is really very "strange," very "other," though in the nicest possible way.

Yet Dick's "drollery" is more than merely entertaining. However inessential and hence disposable traits associated with his lower class self might seem on the highroad to the middle class, as tools for surviving in nineteenth-century society they are not, functionally speaking, merely superficial. On the contrary, they are essential not just to the interest of his character and of the narrative, but to the very social promise that is the book's premise and aim, a promise embodied in Dick's "democratic" union of the "common" and the respectable. Articulated in that "droll" language, it had made him both a source of strength to lower-class youths who shared his ambition but not his characteristically positive humour and the champion of less experienced middle-class youths whose greater refinement made them prey to urban frauds. And, combined with the new character that he has put on with his new clothes, Dick's lower-class street smarts give him almost magical power to turn aside threats from pickpockets, swindlers, and sharp business practitioners that would have made easy victims of his well-bred middle-class companions. In effect, his lower-class experience puts him in a position to save the middle-class characters who are busy saving him from the lower class. This power is central to the issue that, after the promise of progress, most

---

[12] *Ragged Dick*, p. 145.

preoccupies *Ragged Dick*: the terrifying increase in the possibilities for crime and unethical and predatory business practices in the dizzying urban life, a society so large that personal relationships cannot possibly provide security. This is what Dick gives up when he shucks his old identity.

Whatever their uses, however, vernacular characters are, typically, subversive of the very middle-class values Dick is longing to assume. So, along with his "new life," Dick puts on a new identity and a new language, keeping the old one only as a humorous style, a sort of vernacular joke that condescendingly insists on the distance between classes rather than bridging it. In the process, he gives up the most characteristic, the most interesting, entertaining, and powerful part of himself. Consequently, however unambiguously desirable the transformation may have seemed at the start, by the time Alger works his way to the conclusion of *Ragged Dick*, the social success that had provided the narrative with its reason for being also demands the silent sacrifice of personal distinction to a commercial standard. Gaining official acceptance, Ragged Dick fades away into "Richard Hunter, Esq., a young gentleman on the way to fame and fortune" and thus into the common values of commodity culture that substitutes dollars for style. More importantly, this transformation jettisons the only powers in the book that have successfully opposed the divisive and exploitative energies of urban capitalism—the dark underbelly of nineteenth-century progress and the great implicit obsession of Alger's work.

Alger's "American success" storyline reappears relatively unchanged in Booker T. Washington's *Up From Slavery*. But, unlike Alger's story, Washington's work has not (and not accidentally), for all its centrality and influence, been taken as a paradigm of American experience. Although critical response to Washington's book, as to his life, has been mixed over the years, and much less than favourable since the 1960s as African-American difference has taken over from integration as the dominant model of multi-ethnic relations, there is, I believe, something to be gained by taking the work, as much as possible, in its own terms rather than taxing Washington for failing to write the book we would like to imagine we would have in his place. Although criticism has often seen Washington as dupe or shill, he ought also to be viewed as a consummate rhetorician, one who knew his audience and its attitudes all too well. On that view, the repression of identity and of feeling (anger and bitterness) that could be said not just to characterise, but very nearly to constitute the text, looks very much like the self-discipline Washington exercised throughout his life. From one end of the book to the other, Washington describes his willingness to do anything to get what he wants. In the context of late nineteenth-century racism and its social consequences, ignoring or denying his own feelings and self-respect can reasonably be considered trivial prices to pay, and it seems inevitable that the composition of his "life" would inscribe those same traits. Responding to the overwhelming racial repressions of the time, *Up From Slavery* sets modest goals. It seeks only to allay white racial paranoia and elicit a benign neglect so that the negro might ultimately "lift himself up" to equality, though (pointedly) not social integration, with whites. With this end in view, the true national evil is not racism but blame, all trace of which must be eradicated. The resulting social dynamic is more rigorously Naturalistic than anything in Norris or Dreiser. Slaves and slave-owners are all alike "victims of the system of slavery" that "the Nation unhappily [and in the passive voice] had engrafted on it at that time."[13] Amidst such universal yet agentless victimage, blame, however improbably, is impossible, and thus neither Washington nor, as we are told, any other Black has ever felt any anger or bitterness toward whites.

The unfolding of Washington's narrative moves spasmodically between his desire to elicit sympathy by presenting the poverty and deprivation of southern negroes and his desire to avoid offence. He wants, in short, to induce sympathy without inducing guilt. That conflict leads to the retractions that end so many of his chapters. What might be called the abstract governing principles expressed in the final paragraphs of these chapters oddly deny the particular facts that make up both the substance of the narrative and the (pasteurised) reality of life in the South. For example, having described the appalling conditions of "colored" life around Tuskegee, Washington leaves his readers with the reassurance that "in giving all these descriptions ... I wish my readers to keep in mind the fact that there were many encouraging exceptions [though they are never presented] to the conditions which I have described," and he justifies even relating these distressing facts as an effort to highlight "the encouraging changes that have taken place" since the time he describes.[14] Even when pain *must* be assigned to Slavery and its consequences, Washington does so according to an inverting economy of the spirit rather than to one of the body—an almost perverse appropriation of familiar Christian rhetoric. Injustices perpetrated on Negroes by Whites redound upon the perpetrators, Washington argues. "The most harmful effect of the practice to which the people in certain sections of the South have felt themselves compelled to resort, in order to get rid of the force of the Negroes' ballot, is not wholly in the wrong done to the Negro, but in the permanent injury to the morals of the white man. The wrong to the Negro is temporary, but to the morals of the white man the injury is permanent." This piece of revisionist moral history is the more extreme since Washington is describing the consequences here not just of restrictive voting laws, "cheating," and perjury, but of lynching. These passages engage the narrative in an odd self-cancelling dance typical of the revisionist rhetoric of ethnicity, one that is performed in similar ways by (as I have suggested) *Ragged Dick* and by *Native Son*.

However it may appear to modern eyes, in its own terms Washington's outlook is optimistic—earnest effort, we are repeatedly told, *will* bring its reward. Despite the burdens imposed by the history of slavery and the episodic determinism of his own account, Washington's world is plastic. The instrument of change, however, is not revolutionary or economic—it is a matter of character, of discipline. The attitude of whites toward blacks can be changed, but only if blacks violate white expectations through a superhuman conformity to their values, and those values define the limits of the world's plasticity. This plea for a place within the existing order is both the aim and the success of the work. *Up From Slavery* encourages whites to reimagine blacks

---

[13] *Up From Slavery*, p. 10.
[14] *Up From Slavery*, p. 120.

in a beneficial (though not redemptive) way. And in 1900, *that*, Washington suggests, was the best that could be hoped.

In the process, Washington's rigorous rhetoric not only displays but insists on the boundaries between blacks and whites, rather than trying to cross them. While Dick's struggles earn him the right to disappear into the middle-class norm, Washington's success has made him stick out, not just from society at large but even especially from other blacks. Washington's final persona, the public figure who has earned "recognition," and can therefore eat in a railroad dining car with whites, reveals no connection to the still unregenerate earlier versions of his self (uneducated negroes) he claims to represent. Like St. Augustine, he has miraculously undergone an apocalyptic change, the very apocalypse he cannot imagine for society at large, one that transubstantiates and thus abandons his own history, his ethnic past, by inscribing it in a revisionist narrative.

Not only is Washington unique, rather than representative, from the first, he does not actually cross the boundaries that divide the races and enter, as Dick does, a new ethnos. He takes on, instead, a special status—recognition—of but not in the white world and that status depends not on his individual personality, but on a persona that is only nominally "his." Even his ultimate recognition comes exclusively in white terms. The fact that white strangers on a train knew "who I was" begs just the question *Up From Slavery* most represses: just who might that actually be? One unexamined implication of the line is that, as regards his "recognition," who he *was* is more important than who he *is*. It is his past identity as a slave, rather than his current character, that makes him remarkable and the object of public notice. Incarnating his own prescription, he has achieved social recognition as that negro who has so excelled in conformity to white values, and thus is so unlike the rest of the race, as to be admissible to the forms of the white world. He is the official negro, the representative of his race to the white world precisely because, like other mythic American figures (Franklin, Whitman, Lincoln), he's at once so exceptional and so ordinary. The distance he repeatedly measures between himself and other blacks—by his disdain for their less refined manners, his accounts of his own extraordinary trials, his inability to explain his success apart from intrinsic character traits that might be unique to *him*—only confirms white views of the negro by presenting Washington's experience as inimitable. His special status *and* his narrative speak to the inferiority of other members of the race as much as to their potential, and in fact might be seen as enabling their continued exclusion—that, after all, being the historical work of tokenism.

Like other narratives of ethnos, *Up From Slavery* pretends that race can be a permeable boundary akin to class in Alger. For Washington, however, the superficial that worked so to Dick's advantage is the insurmountable problem, the definer of boundaries. In effect, while in the revisionist discourse of class the essential becomes superficial—Dick's essential character shows in his face—in the revisionist discourse of race the superficial becomes the most essential. It is perhaps the most inescapable feature of Washington's condition that he can never be (mis)taken for the paradigmatic American. Washington's status as "representative" is necessary if the narrative is to claim a larger cultural, rather than a merely personal, significance. But, especially in light of his "essential" uniqueness from the first, it can only be attributed to a biological similarity that really substantial change, a genuine crossing of boundaries, would, somehow, have to erase. Unlike Dick, Washington is necessarily "alone," a unique being to be "recognised," rather than to be embraced by a new ethnos. The alienation Washington's uniqueness creates from "his" people also mirrors his unbridgeable distance from the whites whose culture he has acquired. He is not, cannot be, in either world. In contrast to Dick, the Washington of *Up From Slavery* is and must always be a show piece. His identity does not depend on reputation, it *is* a reputation. In the rhetoric of crossing offered by his book, it is unthinkable for Washington to be made part of the white ethnos—he travels there on the visa of his notoriety.

The American narrative, in its ambivalence to its own European past, articulated American identity as both hermetic and (in a subtext that seems clearer to us than to its original authors) an extension of the dominant European culture. Like that of this revisionist American narrative, the work of Ethnic narrative is double: to define both the self and the other. But more importantly, texts seeking inclusion from the margin, like Washington's, define the self *as* other. To gain entry into the dominant discourse, these narratives must "otherise" the marginal self to make it fit into that "other" world to which they aspire. These two works, *Ragged Dick* and *Up From Slavery*, seem so conservative, so familiar, because they reiterate the terms of the dominant culture in the very process of, and even as a strategy for, dissenting from it. This self-effacement in order to assume dominant values is the most remarkably alienating characteristic of this genre of revisionist rhetoric. Characters like Booker T. Washington and Ragged Dick echo each other as they reflect the powerful transubstantiation upon which the American narrative depends: the faith that the common present harbours a transcendent destiny, the perfected future of mankind—a faith that finds continuing voice among Americanist culture critics.

Narratives of ethnos typically present the appearance of crossing in order to bolster social optimism and place the narrative (and the society it constructs) in the modern world of progress, the world of "America," casting themselves as vehicles of ethnic aspiration in a hospitable and sympathetic world. But, whatever else they may be—and despite their own promises—these narratives of ethnicity are not models for *crossing* ethnic boundaries. Despite their claims to foster social progress in the spirit of an American culture not shackled to and by social strata, in these works no crossing occurs. On the contrary, *Ragged Dick* and *Up From Slavery* ethnocentrically insist on the taking of sides and reinforce the necessity of boundaries. That conflict between the need to represent and the need to cross characterises both Washington's condition and revisionist narrative in general. In this respect, his own narrative conditions make him a particularly forceful expression of the rhetoric of ethnicity in general, poised between an irretrievable past and an unattainable future. In that position, they must do double duty in a second, and still more important, sense. Representing change, but unable to embrace it, they advertise the mythic *promise* of change in a system the very terms of which make change impossible. Most crucially, they domesticate the very idea of change by reading it as the ideal fulfillment of existing assumptions.

I want to turn now to *Native Son*, which seems to me to provoke change of a different sort and in a different way.[15] From the first, this book has been drafted into any number of available interpretive frames. I'd like to suggest that it is a subversive recruit, one that breaks those frames down and then leaves itself open, as a book of ethnos that can't be comfortably fitted with any ready ethnic "moral." Unlike Washington's, Bigger's world is not plastic, not open, not even to the possibility of fulfilling white expectations—intentionally at least. It is a world not even of obstacles, but of an unremitting, a crushing, poverty of options. Bigger's inarticulate longing for purposeful action that would define his "being" in the world can have no expression. Denied the ability to act, he stares heavenward toward the plane that represents, at once, his desire for a place in the world through action and his desire to transcend it. Even Bigger's desire for self-defining action is precisely matched by an overwhelming fear of any action that might strip him of his protective anonymity, thrust him into vulnerable relief, burden him with a responsibility that, personally void, he cannot possible sustain. Consequently, Bigger hates and fears everything, not just the forces that prevent action, but also those (like his family) that he cannot act *for*. Fear of action: fear of no action. Living this hopeless conflict, Bigger is left with only hysteria and a sort of spontaneous explosion of behaviours, involuntary responses to what Wright calls the "rhythms of his life: indifference and violence"—sweeping the pool balls dramatically but ineffectually around the table, leaping at Gus because he reflects Bigger's own fear of the white man—actions unreasoned, unmotivated, more cathartic than practical.[16] He rigorously denies even his own existence, for if he were to acknowledge it, he would either have to destroy the world that gives him existence but denies him expression or, alternatively, destroy himself. Constantly confronted with impossible situations in which he must do what he fears, must act but cannot, Bigger's universal hatred turns to spasmodic violence. Permitted no acceptable action, all Bigger can do is rebel against action itself ("The moment a situation became so that it exacted something of him, he rebelled").[17] Crushed under universal prohibitions, the only behaviours open to him are criminal or accidental, or both.

Hating the rules that subjugate him, Bigger cannot imagine any others. When Jan and Mary ignore the taboos against egalitarian Black/white social relations, he can only assume it must be some kind of joke at his expense, or worse, a trap. Their clumsy and inevitably condescending attempts at kindness only return Bigger to the end of all his ventures into life: "He felt he had no physical existence at all right then; he was something he hated. ... At that moment he felt toward Jan and Mary a dumb, cold, inarticulate hate."[18] Mindless, dead, speechless, bodiless—all Bigger knows is that he lacks something, that he feels incomplete. A gun, a knife, a car complete him, and violence makes him forget his hate, which is also his fear.

---

[15] Richard Wright, *Native Son* (New York: Harper & Brothers, 1940, rep. 1966).
[16] *Native Son*, p. 31.
[17] *Native Son*, p. 44.
[18] *Native Son*, p. 67-8.

These conditions place Bigger so far outside the game of "recognition" Washington plays, that he can only count as an ironic commentary on it. Of course, on the one hand, insofar as the boundaries of his identity are defined by white culture, the Washington of *Up From Slavery* is incongruously kin to the various characters attributed to Bigger Thomas. Yet apart from the stereotyped identities created for him by whites, Bigger is simply void, and in that sense, he could be said to express the view of self that is left out in Washington's account. Bigger is the black experience Washington's myth of the self leaves behind and can never really represent, the black self that isn't Washington's unique exemplary Negro. The conditions of crossing are altered here, a major consequence of white capitalist hegemony to make everything "black" undesirable in the same terms that "poor" is for Alger. Bigger cannot stop being black by exercising intrinsic virtues and learning good grammar like Dick, or by exercising discipline and assuming white values like Washington. That he can't cross racial boundaries is a statement not just about extrinsic social barriers or about his character, but also about the terms of his existence. Bigger cannot *make* himself anything any more than he can *do* anything. Unlike Dick and Washington, he isn't special from the first. There are no successful versions of himself to help him, instead his would-be "benefactors" are clearly slumming, and in Bigger's world being "recognised" is not fulfillment, it is death.

To Bigger's imagination, killing looks like a way to make a place for himself in the world, and he brandishes his vaunted willingness to kill as a way of dominating others. But, when killing is a reality rather than a fantasy like the movies that shape his impossible desires, when Bigger actually kills Mary, it is just another spasmodic and unconscious act imposed on him by his own terror of the "white." Mary's death is the natural result of Bigger's fear in the face of white power, produced by an unconscious contraction of the muscles in terror at the possibility of being discovered in a white girl's bedroom. But, however similar in its causes to his earlier acts of reflex violence, the consequences are crucially different. Mary's corpse is material testimony that, for the first time, he has done something the white world must notice. And in a sense that might seem still more bizarre had we not just seen Washington's example, that possibility of recognition (however skewed) looks, to Bigger's eye, something like an identity. The recognition his acts give him in white newspapers gives him the same satisfaction it gave Washington (a fact that represents the perversity of Bigger's position), and it is no more accurate. But it is far more dangerous. As far as the world (and he) is concerned, Bigger is alive for the first time, alive to the only world that counts—the white world of action—and he assumes for himself a new character befitting his new residence. As a naturalised citizen in that world, he imagines, he has to "do better," and is bothered that he should have gotten more money out of it; he should have *planned* it.[19]

As the subsequent action inexorably shows, Bigger's life, even in this moment of personal triumph, is self-cancelling. With one act, Bigger both gives himself life and

---

[19] *Native Son*, p. 123.

declares himself dead, gives himself a place in the world for the first time and goes out of it entirely, kills and commits suicide. All his longing, after the fact, for purposeful action is a gross self-deception, not to mention a capitulation to the assumptions of the white world he hates and that now wants to kill him. In the first place, he was not, as I have suggested, even *responsible* for Mary's murder. He just did it. And his wish that he had planned it better is pathetic illusion. As it turns out, he was actually relatively safe as long as he stuck to purposeless action, partly because purposeless action makes no sense to a society that gives scope to motives. But the purposeful action into which his new sense of "self" lures him assures his destruction. When he tries to act intentionally, tries to actually *do* something for himself, first to cover up and then to profit from his crime, he calls his own doom down upon him. It is essential to Bigger's particular act of self-expression that he cannot and must not express it. In his contradictory efforts to render his acts inconsequential by destroying Mary's body and to profit from her death, he rouses the sleeping beast—the one to which Washington spent a lifetime singing lullabies—and its eye is upon him.[20]

When it finally comes, his capture only dramatises externally and explicitly the internal and implicit imprisonment that has been the defining experience of Bigger's life. Despite Bigger's newly coined but specious self-respect, his actual crime does not even exist in that white view. The world refuses even to *mis*construe his actions as murder, much less as what they were, or to hate and kill him for himself, since that would require some acknowledgment of his self-lessness. Instead it casts him in an old, familiar, and in its way comfortably racist story, making him embody stereotyped fears of Black sexual threat. It appears there not as murder, but as a "sex crime" that "excludes him from the world" and pronounces his "death sentence." This misreading of his defining act "meant a wiping out of his life even before his capture." And it will kill him for that, for what he did not do (rape) rather than for what he (sort of) did.

Worse still, those on the other side, those who want to help him—Max, Jan—don't understand him any better than anyone else. Each tries to cast Bigger in his own pet moral or political drama. Sympathy and hatred alike, it seems, reflect ideological preconceptions. But worst of all, amidst all this dehumanisation, Bigger himself is no different from the rest, and ends up adopting their views as his own. Following Jan's lead, Bigger justifies his own actions by assuming they must have had a purpose—or, more accurately, he assumes that he had a purpose, a direction, an organising self,

---

[20] The murder of Bessie, which many readers would see as intentional and thus inconsistent with the portrait of Bigger I am sketching here seems to me, on the contrary, the most inescapable example of Bigger's hopeless position, trapped between incompatible and equally impossible options. While the killing lacks the reflex detachment of Mary's murder, the text takes great pains to inscribe it into the same dynamic of optionlessness, of the impossibility of purposeful action, that dominates the rest of the book and Bigger's life. The section in which Bigger is trying to figure out what he must do about the not particularly useful or trustworthy Bessie is repeatedly punctuated by variants of the line "he can't take her with him and he can't leave her behind." This reiteration reminds him and us, in an almost incantatory way, that Bigger has no route of effective action. The result, throughout the book, is inaction or aborted actions. Deprived of productive options, Bigger botches killing Bessie, just as the rest of his life is a botch. He kills Mary without trying; he cannot kill Bessie (effectively) when he tries, and once again, this failure, built as it is into the dynamic of his life, contributes to his capture and death.

because he acted. In a world without meaning or purpose, a world where the concentrated essence and meaning of his life has been its essential meaninglessness, he buys into the reassuring white view that actions are securely connected to purpose—that the world is a coherent place. Like Dick (unselfconsciously) and Washington (with great determination), all Bigger's efforts to imagine a "self" for himself echo assumptions that are alien to him. Even his imaginary selves are imagined by others. Bigger Thomas doesn't know "who I was" and efforts to answer that question are always and only efforts to answer it for him, and thus demonstrate its unanswerability in the traditional terms the attempts assume. Apart from these impositions, there is nothing to see, and Bigger subjects himself even to death in terms composed on cliché models, rather than imagining (as he could not do) his exteriority to all available terms.

Bigger's starkly self-contradictory experience embodies Wright's paradoxical efforts to write a book that both is and is not about black life, an effort that generates a text that exceeds the conventional categories of ethnicity. "Bigger was not black all the time, he was white too," Wright wrote.[21] Wright wanted to stress "that part of him which is part of all Negroes and all whites," claiming that "neither Bigger nor I resided fully in either camp."[22] Bigger's problem is not being a "black" self *in* a white world, but being any self at all. His stake is not so much in black ethnos as in his own fear. Inside and outside in the novel have lost clear meaning amidst universal emptiness and blindness—the black man and culture are mutually alienated, mutually blind to their own and their respective "others'" lack of any innerdirectedness. Bigger Thomas does not learn and if he did it would do no good. But neither does anyone else. *Native Son* displays a cultural blindness, an impermeability so absolute that it amounts to fixity for all its characters. In this book, none dwell free and thus the text rewrites the ethnic rhetoric of oppositions. I'm not suggesting by this that Wright's black and whites are "equal" in power, and all equally victims (as Washington would have it), even of blindness. Such quietist claims, like their revisionist alternatives, miss the sense in which *Native Son* revises the conventional models of identity and agency that drive traditional narratives of ethnicity, confusing, in the process, the boundaries that parcel out power, which becomes a sort of Foucauldian pervasiveness, rather than an instrument of will.

As a result, Wright's text is subversive in a still broader sense than opposition to prevailing social arrangements of power would entail. Wright refuses to fulfill revisionist expectations by offering any viable substitute for blindness, imposed identities, and emptiness. *Native Son* will not move a step from the inhuman initial conditions it posits. It carries the Naturalist subordination of individuals to culture beyond the conservatively determinist implications writers like Norris were prepared to envision, displaying not only the hopeless progress toward disaster of a character victimised by vast forces far beyond his meagre capacities, like McTeague, but also the pitiful self-deception of Bigger Thomas in accepting that disaster, explaining his own fate in the

---

[21] "How 'Bigger' was Born," *Native Son*, p. xiv.
[22] "How 'Bigger' was Born," *Native Son*, p. xxiv.

very terms that doomed him, and using that explanation as a source of pathetic comfort.

For Bigger, being black is unacceptable, being white is impossible. *Native Son* discomposes the cultural categories, the ideological vocabularies, that made Alger's and Washington's works possible, refusing the available vocabularies of revision along with those of oppression. *Native Son* explodes the pretence not just of permeability, but of received vocabularies of ethnic boundary. Its world would seem to be most radical expression of boundaries, but actually it dissolves them. The figure for the colour "line" in *Native Son* is a circle like Pascal's God, its centre is everywhere and its circumference nowhere. Not less pervasive or powerful, but less binary, oppositional, neatly definable—less congruent with lines of personal identity.

By diffusing the idealist centre of revisionist narratives, Wright's example speaks to contemporary critical questions about the role of texts in cultural change. Conventional tales of social change like *Ragged Dick* and *Up From Slavery* make "crossing" possible by assuming intrinsic and eternal traits, a spiritual identity, shared universally by community members. These narratives portray abandonment—of old identities, of history—as essential to progress. The spiritual model of social identity they feature both justifies that abandonment and drowns out unreconciled voices even as it assures that the old world will appear essentially unchanged in the new. Wright, however, cannot imagine an easy transition between antiseptically opposed worlds. Bigger lacks the spirit—individual and cultural—that made social order imaginable for Alger and Washington, with the catastrophic results for him that we see. His life is made meaningful to others only as they impose their own universalising assumptions to domesticate his otherness. And Bigger's challenge to these traditional models of social progress also challenges those who would compose a contemporary narrative of social progress—fictive or critical.

His disaster opens questions about the imagining of new social orders, the reimaging of cultural coherence consistent with a rigorous critique of totalising narratives that have had growing prominence in recent critical discussions, but have their foundation in "American" discourse. The contemporary criticism of diversity, of which American Literary Scholarship was an ancestor, has unquestionably contributed to the breakdown of faith in idealist critical models. Yet, that same focus continues, as it has throughout the long history of the "America" debate, to frustrate the coherence that supports collective action. Americans have, understandably enough, been preoccupied, as they tried to construct their nation, with ethnos, with understanding themselves as a community, rather than as a ragtag collection of races, creeds, and opinions. In literary studies, American ethnocentrism has precisely been a striving for a way of defining and collecting works under a corporate identity. It has, in fact, been the triumph of the eternally revisionist narrative of America that it has done this successfully for so long, bringing alien groups under its umbrella and making them glad to be there. This inclusiveness, however, depended on idealist models of personal and corporate identity that now seem to many more destructive than creative and thus no longer useful either for society or, more narrowly, for new critical projects.

Yet, repudiating oppressive orders, the vocabulary of diversity, constructed as it must necessarily be out of the ethnocentric vocabulary it rejects, offers no strategy for motivating collective action to replace the ones it would abandon. It suggests no contemporary terms, nothing so powerful as the old appeals to "our common humanity," or to the fact that we are "all sinners alike," to explain why we should treat those who are "other," those who are different from ourselves, as we would treat those we accept as members of our community. What, in the absence of traditional religious and moral values can preserve principles like egalitarianism after the demise of their eighteenth-century liberal rationales? What enforces the desire for trans-ethnic understanding after foundational justifications are discarded? What strategies do we have or can we construct for fulfilling the founding model, *e pluribus unum*, but in contemporary terms not of unity but of productive action in our diversity?

An emphasis on the rhetoricity of ethnocentrism refocuses attention on the role of literature in cultural change by reminding us that changing the terms of culture, the forms of life, is a matter of the kind of rhetorical reweaving undertaken by *Native Son*. Though it may seem merely tautological, still it may be therapeutic to say that narratives of race, critical and fictive, are constituted in the language of race—the only language they have available to them. Thus, they are subject to and shaped by its features, its distinctions, the limits and possibilities of its established implications, the unspeakably complex web of verbal interrelations that comprise a vocabulary, and that vocabulary is itself enmeshed in the much larger linguistic web that articulates the forms of life. On this view, the rich are "rich" and the poor "poor." Blacks are "black," not by biology or conditions, but by virtue of all the familiar uses that word finds among speakers of the language. If they are not "negro" or "black" but "African-American," then those new words self-consciously carry old freight. As Alger, Washington, and Wright collectively suggest, ethnic boundaries so construed cannot be crossed, since as *matters* of definition, they are, *by* definition, impermeable. That is their purpose. To actually cross them would mean, for example, to become "white," and although that is essentially what Washington has been accused of, we have seen that avoiding just such a "crossing" was the scrupulous preoccupation of his text. Revisionist accounts seeking inclusion, as Alger's and Washington's did, operate within the existing revisionist vocabulary of change and the new and thereby end up reiterating and reinforcing familiar boundaries. The gestures of these narratives are, themselves, reiterated in critical and theoretical approaches to the subject because these approaches, in their turn, also are constituted out of the rhetorical features of ethnic discourse, the terms that have been employed to debate the subject, the very forms, that is, that debate seeks to change. This circularity is critical to mainstream/margin discourse.

Yet in all this talk of circularity and the immersion of revisionist impulses in the tradition, I don't mean to peddle pessimism about the possibility of change. In fact, I'm more inclined to see change as unavoidable than as impossible. And, despite the claims of Walter Michaels and others, there is no theoretical reason a narrative, and thus a society, cannot "escape" its existing conditions, alter its own forms. Though, as Stanley Fish has so often said, it cannot do so just by wanting to. While works like Alger's offer the comfort of conventional reading, books like *Native Son* are important precisely as they give us an unfamiliar and therefore necessarily uncomfortable one, one that confuses and thus confronts our own usual terms. The exercise of that confronting is at once an implicit critique, a clearing of old understandings from the ground and an early rhetorical move toward constructing new social forms. On the evidence of such texts, texts that treat writing as a matter of imaginatively recomposing the borders of language that are also the borders of ideologies, social change might be aided with acts of composing new vocabularies. If boundaries cannot be crossed, they can be redefined. This is, however, both a long-term and a freakish process.

Just what to do with texts, even if this is true, still looks like a tough question to many critics. The principal lesson pressed home by the dizzying complex of critical debates over this issue is that we have not, so far at least, developed particularly satisfactory accounts of the relationships scholars are trying to explain. The job of connecting literature with other discourses, of describing the larger cultural implications of individual texts, of connecting particular rhetorical acts with cultural rhetorics, of weaving multiple ethnic voices into a society is bigger than the one recent historicist critics of American literature have undertaken.

In this connection, it is a particularly ironic commonplace that instruments of innovation tend, for the most part, to go unrecognised by those schooled in the old vocabulary, who have taken innovative vocabularies that revise traditional boundaries for everything from bad writing to shopworn wisdom. A test of the success of any developing criticism might be how effectively it deals with the "other" not just as a matter of learning to "respect differences" and certainly not by domesticating it in familiar narratives, whether oppressive or redemptive. Like Columbus in the "New World" the characters in *Native Son*, whether "racist" or "progressive," insistently see what is not there and prompt Bigger to do so as well. Bigger Thomas assumes he has an identity because he acted, just as America has been assumed to have an "identity"—a coherent national character—because it attained political nationhood. Each of these fantasies appeals to the same venerable and powerful interpretive habit (rather than merely to a particular cultural prejudice), an ethnocentric way of understanding that insists on inscribing the "other" into familiar accounts of the self and the known. That interpretive ethnocentrism is common both to critical interpretation of the textually new and to the ethnocentric treatment of "other" groups. *Native Son* subjects such interpretation to ironic critique and lays bare its implications as a social model. Thus *Native Son* can be read as unmasking the interpretive assumptions that stand behind both the discourse of "America" and ethnic discourses. Readers committed to articulating a more socially engaged literary studies might take a cue from this detailed and rigorous refusal of traditional sides in ethnic debate and of the familiar, even comfortable, postures toward ethnicity they entail. In this light, alternative interpretive projects might be entertained less for their perceived consistency or inconsistency with particular ideological positions, than for whether they promote new vocabularies and thus provoke us to understand not just something we did not know, but something we did not know we *needed* to know. By diverging from received forms, texts like *Native Son* penetrate the sometimes dark and tortuous paths of cultural change. In our current circumstances, readers cannot afford to disregard the transformative potentials of such excursions into unknown cultural forms or of the critical reconstructions they can inspire. Such works are, it seems to me, indispensable resources in the effort to articulate substantial cultural revision and thus to assist the future in its coming.

3. POPULAR CULTURE PERSPECTIVES

REGIONS OF THE SOUL
ETHNOGRAPHY AS NARRATIVE

John Peacock, Maryland Institute College of Art

In 1643, Roger Williams, founder of Rhode Island, wrote in his ethnography *Key into the Language of America* of a late night discussion he had "before the chief sachem or prince of the [Indian] country, with his archpriests, and many others in full assembly." Their topic: where does the soul go after death? At the point when the account begins, Williams, having retired to his blanket within earshot of the campfire but not yet asleep, continues to listen in on the discussion of the indefatigable Indians. His own line of reasoning has been taken up by no less an authoritative figure than the sachem Miantonomi. Another Indian, an unnamed Quinnicut, has heard Williams's previous discourse with the sachem and now defends the traditional Indian point of view after the white man has apparently gone to sleep. He argues that souls "went not up to heaven or down to hell" as the white man claimed, for, the Quinnicut continues, "our fathers have told us that our souls go to the southwest," the region of abundant corn harvests. Against this analogy between natural and spiritual life, the sachem representing Williams's point of view responds with convincing logic. "How do you know yourself that your souls go to the southwest?" Miantonomi demands. "Did you ever see a soul go thither?" The Indian representing the native point of view adopts the same skepticism in reply: "When did he (naming [Williams]), see a soul go to heaven or hell?" It is at this point that chief Miantonomi cuts through all this appeal to empirical observation and ends the thrust and parry of debate with an appeal to the authority of the written word: the white man doesn't have to rely on the evidence of his senses, the chief says, for "he hath books and writings, and one which God himself made, concerning men's souls, and may well know more than we that have none, but take all upon trust from our forefathers" (198-199).

Much better known than Williams's narrative is a twentieth-century account by Claude Lévi-Strauss of his first contact with some Nambikwara Indians in the Mato Grosso in Brazil:

> [By] evening there were seventy-five people in all. Many of the natives seemed never to have seen a white man, and their more than dubious welcome combined with their leader's extreme nervousness. Neither we nor the Indians felt at all at our ease and we had to lie, like the Nambikwaras, on the bare ground. No one slept: we kept, all night long, a polite watch upon one another.
>
> It would have been rash to prolong the adventure, and [the next day] I suggested to the leader that we should get down to our exchange [of gifts, a traditional diplomatic gesture for reducing hostility]. ... It was then that there occurred an extraordinary incident which forces me to go back a little in time. That the Nambikwara could not write goes without saying. I distributed pencils and paper among them, none the less, as I had done with the Caduveo. Their leader was the only one among them to have understood what writing was for.

And now, no sooner was everyone assembled than he drew forth from a basket a piece of paper covered with scribbled lines and pretended to read from it. With a show of hesitation he looked up and down his 'list' for the objects to be given in exchange for his people's presents. So-and-so was to receive a machete in return for his bow and arrows, and another a string of beads in return for his necklaces—and so on for two solid hours. What was he hoping for? To deceive himself, perhaps; but, even more, to amaze his companions and persuade them that his intermediary was responsible for the exchanges. He had allied himself with the white man, as equal with equal, and could now share in his secrets. We were in a hurry to get away, since there would obviously be a moment of real danger, at which all the marvels I had brought would have been handed over. (*Tristes Tropiques*, 88-89)

These two accounts reflect the different roles often ascribed to writing in the two periods when Williams and Lévi-Strauss were writing. In Williams's narrative the power of writing exemplifies the power of the sacred word, of scripture, to refer to that most absent referent, the departed soul. In Lévi-Strauss's narrative, the power of writing is quintessentially the power not of scripture but of scrip, of money, to refer to absent goods and, therefore, implies Lévi-Strauss, the power to be instrumental in the capitalisation of traditional, face-to-face bartering economies.

Despite different conclusions, there are similarities in the way the two accounts are narrated that attest to a tradition of discourse linking them. In both, white men admit responsibility for exposing Indians to writing for the first time, though neither claims to have actually taught them how to write. Instead of imposing this cultural practice on the Indians, each means to report something he has learned from them about the nature of writing—a lesson about its significance and power—something that only the leaders among the Indians have understood. Whether appearing to be asleep in Williams's case or being under the obvious protection of the chief in Lévi-Strauss's, their roles as non-participating narrators appear to keep them from influencing the Indian. If a chief ends up in both stories representing the white man's point of view about writing, the carefully distanced role of the narrator implies that these chiefs have discovered the essence of writing for themselves without having been indoctrinated. Thus, Williams and Lévi-Strauss try to establish the objectivity of what their stories say about writing.

Besides defining the narrator's unobtrusive participation, Williams and Lévi-Strauss employ other narrative strategies to buttress the illusion that their accounts are objective. One would think that a completely linear and continuous narration would best contribute to this effect. But what if something preceding the Indian's discovery seemed to qualify its spontaneity and suggest on the contrary that the Indian's earlier interaction with the white man had predisposed him to conclude as he later did about writing? One might expect a narrator who was determined to preserve the appearance of not influencing the Indian to delete any preliminaries that might suggest otherwise. But then readers might have difficulty believing that the Indian discovered the essence of writing with no previous discussion whatsoever, that his discovery was completely and absolutely spontaneous. The narrator has to draw a fine line, therefore, making it seem neither as if he had previously influenced the Indian nor as if the Indian had understood writing upon his very first encounter with it.

Williams and Lévi-Strauss resolve this dilemma with narrative strategies that are by no means the same but that are comparable. Lévi-Strauss's strategy is more familiar to modern readers and thus easier to understand. He concedes that before the chief made such a decisive use of the appearance of being able to write, the chief and his people had earlier received pencils and paper from the anthropologist, the chief being "the only one among them to have understood what writing was for." Instead of narrating this first, however, in the order the events actually occurred, Lévi-Strauss inserts it in the middle of narrating the later event. He interrupts himself in order to fill in this necessary background, which, as he puts it, "forces me to go back a little in time" (88). Thus the reader gathers that the chief has had enough familiarity with writing to later exploit it as he does, but the point of nonlinear narration, as modern readers implicitly recognise, is to break the chain of causality suggested by linear sequence. Lévi-Strauss describes events in the reverse order in which they occurred so as to avoid the impression of having predisposed the chief.

Roger Williams's audience shared modern readers' conventional understanding that linearity suggests causality, but Williams did not reverse the order of narration to suggest a non-causal relation between events. How then did he solve the problem that his narrative shares with Lévi-Strauss's of showing that the Indian knew enough without the white man actually teaching him to make his spontaneous and therefore cross-culturally objective conclusion about the meaning of writing? In order to answer this question, we have to analyse a part of Williams's *Key* more closely.

Like Lévi-Strauss, Williams admits that the main incident followed his own preliminary interaction with the Indians (198). Unlike Lévi-Strauss, however, Williams does not directly report what actually transpired earlier between himself and Miantonomi. He only suggests it indirectly by prefacing his account with a dialogue in the form of one of the vocabulary exercises that make up a large part of his book and give it part of its ostensible purpose as a bilingual language key for introducing Williams's English audience to the Algonquin language. The exercise contains two lists of phrases, one in Algonquin horizontally opposite its English translation. As in many modern language teaching exercises, the lists read vertically like dialogues between unidentified members of the different cultures. The particular list that precedes the narrative about writing concludes with a fictitious Indian asking "*Who told you?*" about heaven and his white interlocutor answering "*God's book or Writing*" (198).

How different it would have been if, instead of giving this dialogue the form of a vocabulary exercise, Williams had inserted it into his narrative as his own discussion with Miantonomi. But after suggesting through the vocabulary exercise what one might typically say to convert an Indian, Williams does not contextualise such a dialogue as his own particular remarks to Miantonomi and instead omits what he actually did say to the chief. He thus presents a missionary scene in general as a prologue to the narrative about writing but does not present himself in particular as preaching the significance of scripture to the Indian. Williams manipulates the formal discontinuity between the vocabulary exercise and his narrative in order to achieve the same illusion of not predisposing the Indian that Lévi-Strauss achieves by intercalating nonlinear narrative elements.

How do these techniques contribute to the overall effects of the two works? This time we begin with Williams.

By appearing simply to present the factual account of an untaught Indian who had without urging understood the essence of Christian doctrine and the scriptural means for representing it, Williams's narrative attested to something universal rather than culturally or even nationally specific about Christianity. This was the message that Williams was preaching not to the Indians (whose salvation he did not think he could assure) but to his white readers, especially those orthodox New England Puritans who interpreted scripture as prophesying that the destination of elect souls was a particular city on a hill in Massachusetts. Williams thought this elect nation idea to be as parochial as the Indian belief that the destination of the soul was someplace in the southwest. He was trying to deconstruct the elect nation, to unwrite any particular geographic region of the soul. The point was that if an unregenerate and uncivilised savage could overcome his own parochialism and glimpse the Bible's universal message that election concerned persons and not place, why couldn't Williams's English readers with all their civilisation do the same? Thus Miantonomi's objective cross-cultural testimony to the true superiority of scripture over oral tradition became the text for Williams's implicit sermon (made explicit elsewhere in his book) about the false sense of superiority over the Indians that his Puritan readers derived from being literate and otherwise cultured. Only by appearing not to preach to the Indian could Williams effectively preach this sermon to his white audience. His role as narrator was thus fundamentally ironic in that he effectively denied he was preaching to one audience in order to do just that to another.

This irony was not appreciated by New England magistrates who banished Williams for, among other things, his notions about Indians and Indian-white relations. While Williams thought the Bible superior to oral tradition as an authority for the soul's spiritual rather than national or regional destiny, in worldly contexts he denied that writing was superior to Indian traditions such as the use of wampum belts to record land claims and territorial treaties. These were frequently disputed among Indians and whites not only because of different recording methods but also because of different assumptions about land use and ownership. Northeastern tribes sometimes allowed Europeans to move onto lands that had been partly cleared for hunting purposes less apparent to European eyes than agriculture or manufacturing. Rather than permanently occupying land (as European nations did), northeastern tribes seasonally shared it—a practice for conserving game and avoiding tribal war (Day 329-345; Bennet 369-397). On the basis of their experience with each other, Indians assumed that their land treaties with Europeans did not commit them to quit the land altogether. Europeans—with different economies and therefore different assumptions about property—often did not disabuse Indians until after treaties had been signed, at which point European customs were clarified and enforced (Jennings 80-82; Eisinger 260-328; Hallett 34-37). Williams understood Indian practices and denied that the English were any more justified in seizing Indian deer parks than they would be in seizing the unoccupied English hunting parks of their king. He argued that Massachusetts land treaties with Indians should be renegotiated with additional payments to the Indians for land taken from them. The important Bay Puritan leader John Cotton listed this argument as subverting the government of the colony when Cotton made his case for Williams's banishment to Rhode Island.

Albeit for different reasons than Williams's contemporaries, modern readers have not tended to appreciate the ironies in his perspective either. They concentrate on Williams the missionary or Williams the ethnographer and ignore the discrepancy or explain is as a contradiction in the man and as an incoherence in his work. Thus, according to Perry Miller,

> The fact that the book has no formal continuity, that it consists merely of a list of words and phrases punctuated by seemingly random observations, has prevented it from being studied by any but anthropologists (who certify its scientific reliability). (54-55)

Miller was right to criticise ethnographers for misreading Williams by extracting what they thought were reliable facts about the Indians and forgetting about or bracketing the religious message. Miller, however, misread him in the opposite way by emphasising the *Key* as an evangelical tract and downplaying the fact that it was "in structure, simply a dictionary" (54). Neither approach appreciated the ironic effect Williams achieved. The effect of making vocabulary lists frame apparently objective narrative fragments was to make ambiguous the relations between several kinds of discourse—reportage, pedagogy, and preaching.

There is a comparably ironic style in Lévi-Strauss's *Tristes Tropiques*. Even though his major premise that writing involves more misrepresentation than speech seems the reverse of Williams's, there are so many qualifications on other levels that the two accounts really complement each other not just in ironic methods but in ironic effects.

As with Williams, it is easy to misread Lévi-Strauss as downright equivocal. He cites preliterate kingdoms in ancient Africa and pre-Columbian America as exceptions to his main thesis that the exploitation of hundreds of thousands of people requires an extensive system of written records. Moreover, from the same field work that provides the incident of the Indians' first exposure to writing comes an equally well-known incident contesting the distinction between the power of writing and the innocence of speech. The Indians' belief in the power of the spoken word is demonstrated when several little girls, angry at their playmates, go to the anthropologist and whisper their enemies' names in his ear so as to harm them by violating the taboo on speaking proper names. Lévi-Strauss cannot resist encouraging his young informants also to reveal the proper names of adults in the tribe at the same time. He recognises that speech, like writing, is a reservoir in which information deemed very significant can be withheld, released, or otherwise manipulated in ways that have powerful consequences, as defined by a culture (270). Of course, Lévi-Strauss clarifies that writing affords the means to *systematise* exploitation, not the prerequisites for exploitation *per se*, which obviously antedate writing.

Because of such attempts to shade blacks and whites into grays, *Tristes Tropiques* is as full of tonal, temporal and structural discontinuities as Williams's *Key*. The same statement or event may have contradictory implications within such a discontinuous narrative. Like Williams, Lévi-Strauss often shifts from description to reflection in order to elucidate a greater similarity out of a particular difference. The purpose is not to collapse differences but to maintain them in tension with similarities. The irony is that a difference on one level may be a similarity on another. To distinguish cultures with and without writing, for example, is descriptively accurate yet false as a basis for one culture thinking itself morally superior to another. This is Williams's particular point, and Lévi-Strauss enlarges upon it as a modern anthropologist who begins with all kinds of descriptive differences between peoples with and without writing and then proceeds to discover a deep structure of cognitive rather than religious similarities.

Any writer can reach different conclusions in the same work if he or she carefully contextualises them in different ways. They may emerge in the difference between narrative and speculation, or simply in the difference between the time of event and the time of retrospective narration. Both Williams and Lévi-Strauss frame their works as remembrances of things past, or, as Williams puts it, as a "private help to my own memory" (83). The result of such a strategy is that the narrator is ironically often able to say one thing and receive credit for something quite different, if for no other reason than that the audience recognises him as two people: the person who participated in the temporally and spatially distant events and the person who is now re-telling them. The narrator can handle his temporal distance from the events he recounts so as actually to enhance rather than undermine their believability. This is the principle of all kinds of narratives—Gothic, modernist, autobiographical, journalistic, and, I would argue, ethnographic—that the narrator relates through the distance of his own dim recollections or as a patchwork of points of view and intercalated tales.

Perhaps the ultimate irony in each work is an irony of multiple strategies and not just multiple contexts. Each employs parts of two essential and in some respects opposed strategies: one strategy aims to eliminate the observer's subjective distortion of the data. This strategy attempts to make the observer invisible and generic, and has influenced conventions in science and literary realism. The particular form of observer distortion that the ethnographer as writer must mask is the ethnocentric partiality with which any ethnographer inevitably tends to view another culture in terms of his or her own. Ethnography, like many other forms of narrative, must strategically disguise its author's point of view as an adequate and not just partial vision or reality, which is to say, as a vision that seems to be imposed on neither reader nor character. In ethnographic narratives the characters are native informants, and the ethnographer's perspective seems objective only if he disguises it as theirs. Both Williams and Lévi-Strauss recede behind their informants so as to show they have not controlled or distorted the native point of view.

The other strategy, on the contrary, is to acknowledge the participation and effect of the observer, to emphasise the authenticity of his unique perspective as well as his problems in describing his data and communicating with his audience. This strategy has influenced alternative scientific and aesthetic methods—the Heisenberg uncertainty principle in physics, impressionism and psychological realism in art and literature. The apparent discontinuities in Williams's and Lévi-Strauss's texts—the mixture of styles and tones and the nonlinear sequence—are deliberately impressionistic and unscientific.

Both authors show signs of being unable or unwilling to control the presentation of their data in some important respects.

Williams and Lévi-Strauss thus draw on and reject parts of two interpretative strategies. They differ from traditional scientific procedures which make a great distinction between the uncontrolled randomness (therefore representativeness) of the data collected, and the controlled (therefore objective) interpretation of the data. Instead of totally following the strategy of controlled and standardised interpretative procedures, both authors combine this strategy with the contrary one of exercising as little control in some respects over presentation and interpretation as over the raw data in general. Thus, they imply that there is no distinction between observation and interpretation. Their ethnographies are themselves presented almost as data, and the effect to be achieved from giving this impression is two-fold and again partly contradictory. On the one hand, the native sources seem to emerge with greater immediacy when they do not appear to be mediated by a controlled interpretive procedure. On the other, the observer himself, by drawing attention to his subjective and uncontrolled lack of procedure, makes himself an object of study to his audience rather than the controlling lens through which he claims to see clearly—a claim that sometimes leads to the criticism that the author is in fact looking through either dark, or rose-colored glasses. Williams and Lévi-Strauss head off this criticism by not claiming to be entirely objective in the first place. One all-important proviso for their inherently ironic narrative strategy being accepted and believed is that it must clearly distinguish itself from accounts that are meant to be either purely objective or purely subjective.

In conclusion, Williams and Lévi-Strauss, while not typical, clarify by their extremity the problem of ethnography considered as a form of narrative. The ethnographer typically writes in a state of rhetorical contradiction. On the one hand, as scientist, he claims to give an accurate, objective representation of a different culture so as to push the frontier of scientific debate about cultural differences and similarities a little closer to the approximate truth. On the other, the ethnographer has few of either the advantages or disadvantages of the laboratory scientist: data are not as easily and frequently submitted for replication and other controls of the scientific procedure; instead, ethnographies are usually governed by the conventions of naturalistic study, deriving their truth value from the fact or appearance of as little methodological distortion of the data as possible, which means rendering the native subject in his own terms and context. A valid procedural rawness derives from the ethnographer's having been on the scene and having left it unchanged—a myth that is strategically important to embrace implicitly or explicitly in any ethnography that makes a strong claim to advance the pursuit of truth.

Thus ethnography—like many other forms of narrative—fixes its author on the horns of a dilemma. What relation to the native subject does the ethnographer seem to convey: that of a detached western scientist/missionary labeling the native as part of a typology of cultures, or that of a fellow traveler in the wilderness? Neither position is entirely to be believed. Together they make a preposterous and impossible combination. Only through an implicitly ironic narrative strategy can the ethnographer, like any writer, be for real.

WORKS CITED

Bennett, M.K., "The Food Economy of the New England Indians, 1605-1675." *Journal of Political Economy* 63 (1955): 369-397.

Day, Gordon M., "The Indian as an Ecological Factor in the Northeastern Forest." *Ecology* 34 (1953): 329-345.

Eisinger, Chester E., "The Puritans' Justification for Taking the Land." *Essex Institute Historical Collection* 84 (1948): 286-328.

Hallett, L.F., "The Colonial Invasion of Hereditary Lands." *Bulletin of the Massachusetts Archaeological Society* 20 (1959): 34-37.

Jennings, Francis, *The Invasion of American: Indians, Colonialization, and the Cant of Conquest*. New York: Norton, 1975.

Lévi-Strauss, Claude, *Tristes Tropiques*. Trans. John Russell. New York: Criterion Books, 1961.

Miller, Perry, *Roger Williams: His Contribution to the American Tradition*. 1953. New York: Atheneum, 1962.

Williams, Roger, *A Key into the Language of America*. Ed. J.H. Trumbull. *The Complete Writings of Roger Williams*. New York: Russell and Russell, 1963. Vol. 1.

MAPPING THE COLOUR LINE
THE WPA GUIDEBOOK TO NORTH CAROLINA*

Christine Bold, University of Guelph

The WPA guidebooks are often considered primary documents of 1930s' regionalism, comprehensive inventories of States and cities, amassed by unemployed writers who, under federal sponsorship, developed a sympathetic eye for the hitherto neglected figures of their localities.[1] In this "phenomenal democracy of retrospection" lies their value: the North Carolina guide, for example, is still marketed as "A State Treasure."[2] Yet if we read along the trajectory of the guidebooks' production, textualisation, and reception, both process and product appear anything but seamless. Especially in the South, the guidebooks became the ground on which interest groups at the federal, regional, and local levels played out their warring agendas. In itemising the States' routes and sights, the guides also map the limits of cultural insiderism, by demarcating the social identifications and relations central to membership in the South's "imagined community."[3]

Within the South, North Carolina was a notably intense site of image-making. Added to traditional North-South tensions and New Deal struggles over federal *versus* state authority was the particular institutional weight put on North Carolina within the Federal Writers' Project. Henry Alsberg, National Director of the Project, put great stock in the liberal sociology of the University of North Carolina at Chapel Hill as a source and model for guidebook production. Eventually he established Chapel Hill as the regional office with responsibility for State and regional productions throughout the

---

* I wish to thank the members of my women's writing group at the University of Guelph—Susan Brown, Diana Brydon, Donna Palmateer Pennee, and Ann Wilson—for their invaluable responses to an earlier draft of this essay. Research for this essay was made possible by generous grants from the Social Sciences and Humanities Research Council of Canada and from the United States Embassy in Canada.

[1] Institutional history of the Federal Writers' Project generally is culled from Jerrold M. Hirsch, "Portrait of America: The Federal Writers' Project in an intellectual and cultural context" (Ph.D. diss., University of North Carolina at Chapel Hill, 1984); Kathleen O'Connor McKinzie, "Writers on Relief: 1935-42" (Ph.D. diss., Indiana University, 1970); Jerre Mangione, *The Dream and the Deal: The Federal Writers' Project, 1935-42* (Boston: Little, Brown, 1972); Monty Noam Penkower, *The Federal Writers' Project: A Study in Government Patronage of the Arts* (Urbana: University of Illinois Press, 1977).

[2] William Stott, *Documentary Expression and Thirties America*, rev. ed. (New York: Oxford University Press, 1985), p. 114; the designation of the guidebook appears in the introduction—"An Introduction to a State Treasure"—to the most recent edition (*North Carolina: The WPA Guide to the Old North State* [Columbia: University of South Carolina Press, 1998] [v]).

[3] Benedict Anderson, *Imagined Communities: The Origins and Spread of Nationalism* (London: Verso, 1983).

entire South. The pressures and tensions which emerged in North Carolina were always intricated in larger issues of Southern identity and autonomy.[4]

Production of *North Carolina: A Guide to the Old North State* (1939) was ideologically riven in at least three directions, into a triangulation marked geographically by Washington DC, Asheville, and Chapel Hill. Washington was the location of the national office of the Federal Writers' Project, staffed primarily by East Coast intellectuals. The Washington editors had a distinct agenda: they promoted the expression of regional diversity and cultural difference regulated by presentational grids and emphases which were centrally controlled. To that end, the national editors insisted on retaining final approval over guidebook copy, and they made greater and lesser editorial interventions over language, regional priorities, the representation of racial and ethnic diversity, the politics of class, and the claims of local against professionalised knowledges.[5] What they sought, in short, was local colour cut to the cloth of New Deal designs.

They met with fierce resistance from Edwin Bjorkman, State Director of the North Carolina Writers' Project, who established his office in Asheville, in the western end of the State. Bjorkman's qualifications for the position came from his long career as newspaperman, critic, translator and creative writer. He was not, however, a native Southerner but a Swedish immigrant first to Minnesota then to New York City and finally to North Carolina just ten years before the Project began.[6] Perhaps because he was an incomer, Bjorkman was highly sensitive to local opinion. He solicited information and advice from local architects, amateur historians, public officials, and patriotic organisations in preference to academic sources, and he came to style himself

---

[4] The archival papers on which this analysis is based are as follows: The Federal Writers' Project, William Terry Couch Papers, No. 3709 in the Southern Historical Collection, The Library of The University of North Carolina at Chapel Hill (abbreviated as FWP, SHC 3709); the William Terry Couch Papers, No. 3825 in the Southern Historical Collection, The Library of The University of North Carolina at Chapel Hill (Couch, SHC 3825); the University of North Carolina Press Records, in University Archives, Manuscripts Department, The University of North Carolina Library, Chapel Hill (UNCP); the North Carolina Writers' Project, WPA General Records, Division of Archives and History, North Carolina Department of Cultural Resources (NCWP); the Work Projects Administration Federal Writers' Project Central Office Records, Record Group 69, National Archives and Records Administration, Washington DC (WPA NARA, 69); the Work Projects Administration Central Correspondence Files, Record Group 69, National Archives and Records Administration, Washington DC (CCF NARA, 69); the Work Projects Administration Division of Information, Record Group 69, National Archives and Records Administration, Washington DC (DoI NARA, 69); the Records of U.S. Work Projects Administration: Federal Writers' Project, Library of Congress Manuscripts Division, Washington DC (LC FWP). I have gleaned additional details from Jerrold Maury Hirsch, "Culture on Relief: The Federal Writers' Project in North Carolina, 1935-42," M.A. thesis, University of North Carolina at Chapel Hill, 1973, and from the histories of the Federal Writers' Project cited above.

[5] For detailed examples of negotiations between DC and State offices over the Missouri guidebooks and the "Road" series of tour books, see Christine Bold, "Mapping Out America: The W.P.A. American Guide Series and the American Scene in the 1930s," in *Modern American Landscapes*, eds. Robert Lawson-Peebles and Mick Gidley (Amsterdam: Free University Press, 1995), and "The View from the Road: Katharine Kellock's New Deal Guidebooks," *American Studies* 29 (1988): 5-29.

[6] William S. Powell, ed., *Dictionary of North Carolina Biography*, vol. 1 (Chapel Hill: University of North Carolina Press, 1979), p. 163; Hirsch, "Culture on Relief," pp. 9-13.

protector of local interests and "local knowledge" against Washington's incursions.[7] Bjorkman insisted: "Most states undoubtedly are peculiar, but this one more than most. The people here are almost morbidly independent and jealous of their rights of self-determination. They are willing to accept favors from the Federal Government but only on their own conditions."[8] For their part, much as Washington trumpeted the value of the local, they would not countenance Bjorkman's version of localism, believing him blinded by self-importance, what they called his "God-complex."[9] Bjorkman's estimation of his environment was borne out, however, when he was attacked in local letters to New Deal officials as "Bjorkman the Swede," this "alien," "this tactless ill-humoured foreigner."[10]

Mediating the stalemate between Asheville and Washington was William T. Couch, Director of the University of North Carolina Press in Chapel Hill. Couch was well known as a promoter of Southern liberalism and a supporter of the sociological reformism which marked intellectual activity at Chapel Hill. He was appointed Associate State Director by Alsberg, in the belief that he would promote Washington's agenda and thereby save the North Carolina Project.[11] Couch differed from Bjorkman in that he solicited academic contributions from his Chapel Hill colleagues, preferring "specialised knowledge" over Bjorkman's reliance on local expertise; Couch was also much more prepared to publish the critiques of Southern economic inequities and social injustices to which academic investigation often led. On the other hand, Bjorkman and Couch agreed that it was the State's fundamental right to define its own cultural heritage. Couch was raised in Virginia and North Carolina; his academic training was grounded in a deep emotional and intellectual commitment to the South's distinctive identity.[12] The more immersed he became in the guidebook project, the more deeply he resented Washington's centralisation of power until, in late 1939, he resigned in an eruption of charges, legal challenges and investigation by the FBI.[13]

This triangulation of interests issued in a series of confrontations over the representation of local sites and conditions. Particularly fierce battles developed over African-American subjects. Sterling Brown, National Negro Affairs Editor, tried to effect a reconceptualisation of African-Americans among White Southern officials: he and his fellow editors demanded that North Carolina increase its employment of Blacks; they inserted draft copy which expanded the volume and detail of material on

---

[7] See, for example, North Carolina Bulletin #11, Bjorkman to All District Supervisors, 24 Jan. 1936 (WPA NARA, 69, Entry 1, Box 36); Letter, Bjorkman to Alsberg, 19 June 1936 (FWP, SHC 3709, Folder 1); Letter, Bjorkman to Mr. Santford Martin, 4 March 1937 (FWP, SHC 3709, Folder 1).

[8] Letter, Bjorkman to Alsberg, 3 Dec. 1937 (WPA NARA, 69, Entry 13, Box 114).

[9] Letter, Katharine Kellock to Alsberg, 4 Feb. 1936 (WPA NARA, 69, Entry 6, Box 61).

[10] Letter, Mrs. Samuel H. Hines to Alsberg, 10 Nov. 1936 (WPA NARA, 69, Entry 1, Box 37).

[11] See, for example, Letter, Alsberg to Bjorkman, 25 May 1936 (WPA NARA, 69, Entry 13, Box 114); Letter, Alsberg to Couch, 9 July 1937 (WPA NARA, 69, Entry 13, Box 114).

[12] Daniel Joseph Singal, *The War Within: From Victorian to Modernist Thought in the South, 1919-45* (Chapel Hill: The University of North Carolina Press, 1982), p. 267ff.

[13] Letter, Couch to Blanche M. Ralston, 23 Oct. 1939 (FWP, SHC 3709, Folder 8); Minutes, Meeting of the Board of Governors of the University of North Carolina Press, 14 May 1940 (UNCP, Subgroup 1, Folder 1).

Blacks (to improve what Brown termed "unrecognisable" city descriptions); and they insisted that Black music and folklore be treated as distinct cultural achievements (not borrowings from Whites).[14] Bjorkman argued that such centralist dictates were foreign to local conditions. Great local offence would be caused by extensive attention to the Black population, and local authorities were not prepared to assign originary status to Black culture.[15] While Couch was more liberal on African-American content than Bjorkman, the two erected a common front in resisting Washington's pressure to hire Blacks. They argued that local African-Americans lacked the appropriate expertise, to the point that they established one of the most discriminatory Project employment records across the country (worse by far, for example, than the conservative, Deep South state of Georgia).[16] In this instance, "local knowledge" was invoked as a device for excluding the voices of the lowest underclass and thus controlling the signs of regional distinction.

The textual imprint of these editorial confrontations is heavily masked in the guidebook's presentation. Like all the volumes in The American Guide Series, *North Carolina* is prefaced by a signed letter from the State Governor, stressing: "This Guide presents a complete view of the State, her people, the historical background, and a complete inventory of the resources of North Carolina, all compiled in one volume." The very constructedness of the publication is played down in, for example, the publicity statement that "In 1935, the United States of America sat itself down, took its pen in hand, and started to write a book. ... It is the only time when a nation has written its autobiography."[17]

Framing the guidebook with a sketch of its production, however, enables what Edward Said calls "contrapuntal reading," reading for both the inclusions and exclusions, to recover the "structures of attitude and reference" regulating the published text.[18] From this perspective, internal State tensions are reproduced in the guide's epistemological split. All guidebooks were divided into three parts: a section of expository essays on the State's history, geography, economics and the like; then detailed descriptions of the State's largest cities and towns; and finally a series of tours crisscrossing the state. In the North Carolina production, the essays became Couch's preserve: the majority were written by academics, often Chapel Hill colleagues, and Couch retained considerable editorial prerogative.[19] In these essays, the State is represented by statistical information, socio-economic analysis, and a historical and geographical sweep available only to the academic or professionalised perspective, all

---

[14] See, for example, Editorial Report on Elizabeth City, by SAB [Sterling A. Brown], 23 October 1937 (LC FWP, A323); Ed. Report on Wilmington, SAB, 25 Oct. 1937 (LC FWP, A323); Letter, Henry Alsberg to Edwin Bjorkman, 26 April 1938 (FWP, SHC 3709, Folder 2).

[15] See, for example, Letter, Bjorkman to Alsberg, 13 Dec. 1937 (WPA NARA, 69, Entry 13, Box 114); Letter, Bjorkman to Alsberg, 1 Sept. 1938 (WPA NARA, 69, Entry 13, Box 114).

[16] See, for example, Letter, Couch to Alsberg, 4 December 1936 (FWP, SHC 3709, Folder 1); Memorandum, Office on Negro Affairs to Couch, 19 Oct. 1938 (FWP, SHC 3709, Folder 3).

[17] Durham *Herald-Sun*, 9 Nov. 1941 (and elsewhere).

[18] Edward Said, *Culture and Imperialism* (N.Y.: Alfred A. Knopf, 1993), p. 66.

[19] See, for example, Letter, Bjorkman to Couch, 13 Jan. 1937 (FWP, SHC 3709, Folder 1).

delivered in measured tones which fold exposures of rural destitution and racial discrimination undramatically into a coherent narrative.

Knowledge takes a distinctly different form in the back end of the guidebook, which was marshalled by Bjorkman and his assistants, with heavy editorial intervention by Washington.[20] In the city descriptions and tours, history is made up of legend, tradition, supposition—not the carefully documented findings of the academic—and the local scene throngs with wildly different orders of information. Ripleyesque items—a smattering of mummified and revived corpses around the State, the adjoining married quarters of Siamese twins, the pet rooster named after the Apostle Paul—jostle side-by-side with tales of vicious Ku Klux Klan activity, violent strike-breaking in Gastonia and Marion, taxonomies of natural and industrial production, and sites of Revolutionary, Civil War, and American Indian battles. By one paradigm, the State is understood as a causally connected narrative; by the other, it is a ragbag of almost random incidents and tales.

At the same time, the front and back ends of the guidebook do work together, particularly to lay North Carolina's claims to prominence on the national stage: an emphasis achieved by Bjorkman and Couch's common front, against Washington's agenda. Clearly, a framework of national standards shapes academic analysis: the opening essays' dense narratives are regularly punctuated by comparisons on the national scale: North Carolina, we are told, is the home of the first State university in America, "second only to Massachusetts in the production of cotton textiles" (72), and site of the putative first declaration of independence in the Thirteen Colonies. Special emphasis is given to Sir Walter Raleigh's attempted settlements in what became Dare County, "birthplace of the Nation (1584) and of aviation (1903)" (294). Within the cities' and tours' throng of miscellaneous information, the one constant feature is the "George Washington Slept Here" syndrome. Countless sites are identified by their association with figures of national significance: the birthplaces of Presidents, Congressmen, and Signers of the Declaration of Independence; the stopping places of Revolutionary, Confederate, and Union Generals; and sites visited by Presidents Taft, Polk, Jackson, Johnson, Wilson, and, of course, Washington: innumerable cities, towns, houses, inns, and farms made consequential by Washington's inconsequential acts (discovering that he had mislaid his powder puff at Smithfield [380], for example, and resting under a tree near Hampstead [287]). There is even the town of Washington which he did not visit, but of which it is noted: "The George Washington Bicentennial Commission established the fact that of the 422 cities and towns in the Nation named for George Washington, this town was the first" (284). These insistent markers provide what Karal Ann Marling calls "material intimacy with important figures and great events of the past"; Washington, of course, is a figure central to the construction and maintenance of *national* identity.[21] The guidebook quietly rewrites history, not only renaming what it calls "the War between the States" (the term "Civil War" appears

---

[20] See, for example, Letter, Alsberg to Couch, 15 June 1937 (FWP, SHC 3709, Folder 2).

[21] Karal Ann Marling, *George Washington Slept Here: Colonial Revivals and American Culture, 1876-1986* (Cambridge: Harvard University Press, 1988), p. 18.

nowhere in the guidebook), but documenting for North Carolina a central position in any narrative of national formation.

In positioning North Carolina as the ground against which the nation took shape, the guidebook circumscribes national identity with a colour line so deeply inscribed in the textual structure and so camouflaged in the language as to render it almost unchallengeable. In doing so, the guidebook contributes to what Toni Morrison identifies as the "Africanism" which "provided the staging ground and arena for the elaboration of the quintessential American identity," "a particular 'Americanness' that is separate from and unaccountable to this [black] presence."[22] Morrison's analysis is directed at the canon of American literature, with its elaborate tropes and figures; her remarks ring equally true, however, for the more taxonomic and prosaic register of the guidebook.

The guidebook essays consistently employ the rhetoric of balance in representing the State's racial record, stating: "In education, social welfare, and economic advance much has been done for and by Negroes in North Carolina. It is likewise true that much more remains to be done" (57). But shaping this measured articulation is what can only be termed textual segregation: once Blacks have been removed to a separate essay, other essays are free to note the State's "progress" or the benefits for "everyone" without acknowledging the racial specificity of those terms.

That the negotiations between Washington and North Carolina did *not* lead to a negotiated or balanced racial representation is particularly evident in the city and tours material. When information was transferred from Washington to North Carolina—that is, from one cultural matrix to another—its political meaning and textual function were radically transformed. When Black editors in Washington insisted on details of Black history and contemporary life, they were encouraging North Carolina writers and editors to reconceptualise African-Americans as agents in the State's culture. The ways in which Bjorkman and his assistants more or less reluctantly incorporated this material, however, marginalised blacks as named absences, a people without lived culture or history. Repeatedly, in city descriptions, we are told that blacks make up 52% of the population—or 37% or 26%—yet they are frequently removed to a single paragraph, characterised in group terms without further differentiation or detail. In the Charlotte description, for example, we are told: "Lying between South McDowell and South Brevard Streets is Blue Heaven, typical of the sections inhabited by the poorer Negroes" (159). A comparison with John Spivak's lengthy, excoriating exposé of Blue Heaven, in his 1936 study *America Faces the Barricades*, suggests that the appeal to typicality was the guidebook's means of escape from the details of harsh reality.[23]

Tour descriptions repeatedly reify Blacks by incorporating them into the landscape: local colour (in two senses), rather than agents acting against a scenic backdrop. Repeatedly, buildings are described as "Negro dwellings" or "Negro cabins," as if inanimate buildings possessed racial characteristics which the guidebook

---

[22] Toni Morrison, *Playing in the Dark: Whiteness and the Literary Imagination* (N.Y.: Random House-Vintage, 1993), pp. 44, 5.

[23] John L. Spivak, *America Faces the Barricades* (N.Y.: Covici Friede, 1936), pp. 28-30.

TYPICAL WRECK NEAR HATTERAS

ONLY NEGRO COAST GUARD CREW, PEA ISLAND STATION

Illustration 1

could fix. These sites then function to map the black presence as a margin, a sideshow
to the main route: on tour 8, "Between Oxford and Creedmoor the route passes"—we
might want to say *bypasses*—"the homes of white and Negro tenant farmers and
traverses fields of tobacco and corn"; on tour 16, the directions read: "Left from
Pineville on paved US 521 across a bridge beside a small Negro cabin, **1 m.**; L. 220
yards off the highway is the SITE OF THE BIRTHPLACE OF JAMES KNOX POLK
(1795-1849), 11th President of the United States" (406-07). This process of quiet
objectification is perhaps most recognisable in Tour 1A: "PEA ISLAND STATION
(*open*), **15 m.**, is the only one in the Coast Guard service manned by Negroes. In the
surf nearby is the rusty boiler of a grounded Confederate blockade runner" (300). The
implied equivalency between the wreck and the Black workers as tourist sites is
reinforced by a page of illustrations: "Typical Wreck Near Hatteras" and "Only Negro
Coast Guard Crew, Pea Island Station" (Ill. 1).

If the guidebook is textually fissured by the colour line, so too is its information
marked by other cultural fault lines. There is the racial line which seals American
Indian material safely into the categories of military history and romantic legend; the
gender line which allows a sizeable number of references to women as individuals but
disallows the recognition of women as a social and political category; and the poverty
line which pushes tenant farmers, sharecroppers, and textile workers to the edges of
North Carolina's story, too. It is not that the guide is uninterested in cultural
difference: the Winston-Salem description devotes pages to the history, politics,
education, and culture of the Moravian settlers. It is that, as the guidebook increasingly
takes on the accents of commonsensical, "unmediated" observation, it is increasingly
incapable of acknowledging the inequities of race and class.

What is textually repressed, however, can be seen to return in the illustrations.
The positioning of racial "others" in the clusters of photographs insists on that which
the written text repeatedly denies: that is, their originary role in North Carolina's
culture. See, for example, the opening series titled "Historical" (Ills. 2-7). As the
series of photographs unfolds, it moves determinedly away from the Cherokee "types,"
left behind as the stuff of history, with their archeological sites ("Tuscarora Graves,
Louisburg"; "Indian Mound, Mt. Gilead") and rituals ("Cherokee Ball Game";
"Cherokee Bear Dance"). We move into the individualised names of military heroes
and statesmen (Cornwallis, General Greene, Andrew Johnson, Governor Zebulon B.
Vance), then, triumphantly, to the mark of North Carolina's progress into modernity,
with the Wright brothers' technological coup. Similarly, the gathering labelled
"Industrial and Agricultural" opens with pictorial representations of black workers,
the raw end of the production cycle, aestheticised in photographs by Mrs Bayard
Wootten, Couch's favourite local photographer (Ill. 8).[24] As the illustrations represent
the increasingly industrialised stages, black faces disappear, in images of the cotton
industry, then the tobacco industry (Ill. 9-10). African-Americans reappear only in a

---

[24] On Couch's support for Wootten, see Field Report, by Darel McConkey, 2 Nov. 1936 (WPA
NARA, 69, Entry 6, Box 61); on Bjorkman's resistance to her employment, see Letter, Bjorkman to
Alsberg, 6 Nov. 1936 (WPA NARA, 69, Entry 1, Box 36).

CHEROKEE TYPES

Illustration 2

TUSCARORA GRAVES, LOUISBURG

CHEROKEE GORGET
B. S. COLBURN COLLECTION

INDIAN MOUND, MT. GILEAD

Illustration 3

CHEROKEE BALL GAME

CHEROKEE BEAR DANCE

Illustration 4

BLOCKHOUSE AT FORT RALEIGH   CORNWALLIS' HEADQUARTERS, WILMINGTO

STATUE OF GENERAL GREENE, GUILFORD COURTHOUSE MILITARY PARK

Illustration 5

BIRTHPLACE OF ANDREW JOHNSON, RALEIGH

BIRTHPLACE OF GOV. ZEBULON B. VANCE

Illustration 6

GLIDER FLIGHT BY WRIGHT BROTHERS, KILL DEVIL HILL.

WRIGHT BROTHERS' MONUMENT, NAGS HEAD

Illustration 7

Illustration 8

UNLOADING COTTON AT GIN, SMITHFIELD

POWER LOOM IN COTTON MILL

Illustration 9

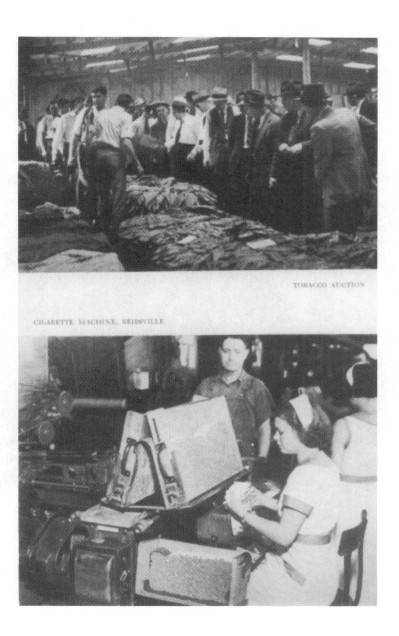

Illustration 10

DARKIES SHELLING CORN

Illustration 11

final, "Miscellaneous" grouping, aestheticised again well outside the progressive, industrial cycle ("Darkies Shelling Corn," Ill. 11). If these groups of illustrations leave Cherokees and Black workers behind, of course, they also entrench them as the beginning: there would be no North Carolina history without Cherokees, no cotton industry without Blacks. Seeking to be the ground of the nation, the guidebook presents material which can be understood to ground North Carolina's identity in the very "others" who are elsewhere removed to the margins of the State.

The reception of the North Carolina guidebook, as I read it, only inscribed these emphases more deeply into the larger discursive field produced by the American Guide Series. Both local and national newspapers welcomed the guidebook as an official record, fixing the State's cultural identity for posterity. Interest was intense: a flood of editorials, reviews, and letters in North Carolina's press counted pages allotted to localities, crowed over the rehearsal of local accomplishments, and testily corrected errors of local fact.[25]

One of Sterling Brown's main objections was that guidebook copy always oriented itself, rhetorically, towards a white readership: the agency of Blacks, as travellers or readers, erased yet again.[26] Tellingly enough, the one sustained note of dissension within the generally celebratory reception occurred in response to African-American material. In the brief description of the small town of Rockingham, the guidebook matched population to copy in unusually close proportions. One paragraph sketched the town's history and industry, then the second paragraph read:

> In Rockingham, Saturday is still "Negro day." The Negro population of the section is almost as large as the white. Since they live mostly on the cotton plantations, where the land is level, the rows long, and the summer sun scorching, Rockingham grants them one day to call their own. The carnival spirit prevails as whole families stroll about in their best clothes. In picking time cotton hands discuss the price of cotton and the wages planters are paying for labor in order to bargain with their overseers. (351)

As soon as the guidebook appeared, the Rockingham *Post Dispatch* rushed out a response titled "Shameful":

> On page 351 is a grossly unfair and false description of Rockingham. If this sort of reading matter depicts other towns as inaccurately as it does Rockingham, then the book should be consigned to the furnace. It certainly should not be circulated in this or any other State.

The review proceeds to quote only the second paragraph of the Rockingham description, commenting:

---

[25] See, for example, Dare County *Times,* 27 Oct. 1939; Elizabeth City *Daily Advance*, 6 Oct., 13 Oct. 1939; Chowan *Herald*, 12 Oct. 1939; Roanoke Rapids *Herald*, Oct. 1939; Sanford *Herald*, 16 Oct. 1939; *The Franklin Press & The Highlands Maconian*, Oct. 1939; Nash County *News*, Oct. 1939; Winston-Salem *Journal*, 29 Dec. 1939. Bjorkman responded publicly to some newspaper criticisms in the Elizabeth City *Daily Advance,* 10 Nov. 1939 and the Greensboro *Daily News*, 5 Nov. 1939.

[26] See, for example, Editorial Report on Elizabeth City, SAB, 23 October 1937 (LC FWP, A323).

Can you imagine any group or individual writing or sponsoring any such tripe as that? And to think the Government has PAID some smart-alec WPA writer for such a libel!
 It is disgraceful.[27]

Letters were fired off to New Deal officials in Washington, while the Greensboro *Daily News* and the Richmond County *Journal* kept up the public pressure: "What we are ashamed of is the fact that WPA writers who authored the book in question are so dumb, so ignorant, so simple that the only thing they see when they come to Rockingham is the parade of negroes strolling up and down the street on Saturday."[28] What the guidebook saw, or failed to see, was clearly an issue of intense political interest to a wide constituency.

Although the WPA guidebooks are oft-cited as one of the most authentic demonstrations of 1930s' regionalism, clearly they were far from spontaneous expressions of regional diversity. I read the guidebooks as very particular products of a political dynamic. In the case of North Carolina—a distinctively liberal State—the convergence of federal authority and the expectation of comprehensive taxonomy put pressure on socio-political fault lines which then indelibly marked the representation of cultural identity. Because so many communities felt that their interests were at stake in those representations, popular debate mushroomed in response to the guidebooks. Much broader attention was afforded this debate over Southern culture, for example, than that—more familiar to academics—pitting Chapel Hill liberal sociology against Vanderbilt aesthetic Agrarianism.

The generic specificity of the guidebooks is suggested by William Couch's other work in the Federal Writers' Project. Once Couch escaped the particular array of pressures which converged on *North Carolina*, he produced work much more consistent with his reputation as a liberal on race relations, in his roles as publisher and spokesman on various interracial commissions throughout the 1930s. In 1939—the year of *North Carolina*'s publication—Couch published *These Are Our Lives*, a volume of life histories told mainly by poor Black and White rural and industrial workers to members of the Writers' Project in North Carolina, Tennessee, and Georgia.[29] While this volume had its own constraints and mediations, it did foreground and individualise the African-Americans and the poor thrust to the edges of the guidebook, and it respected the skills of Project employees whom Couch had judged too inexpert for guidebook work. No longer constrained by federal and generic expectations, the southern Project could produce another imagined community.

---

[27] Rockingham *Post-Dispatch*, 12 Oct. 1939.

[28] Richmond County *Journal*, 18 Oct. 1939; see also Greensboro *Daily News*, 13 Oct., 14 Oct., 29 Oct. 1939.

[29] *These Are Our Lives: As Told by the People and Written by Members of the Federal Writers' Project of the Works Progress Administration in North Carolina, Tennessee, and Georgia* (Chapel Hill: University of North Carolina Press, 1939).

LOCAL NOIR: PUTTING SOUTHERN LOUISIANA ON THE MAP IN THE CRIME FICTION OF JAMES LEE BURKE

Anneke Leenhouts

Since 1987 James Lee Burke has published, in rapid succession, six novels set mostly in and around the town of New Iberia in southern Louisiana and centring on the life and career of Cajun police detective Dave Robicheaux. Like Burke's previous novels - of which only *The Lost Get-Back Boogie* (1978), having acquired a certain cult status, is likely to be familiar to a wider audience—they are largely in the social-realist tradition, confirming, if such confirmation were needed, that crime fiction, as fellow author Gregory McDonald has expressed it in *The Craft of Crime*,

> really is the greatest opportunity that a typewriter gives you for social criticism. ... The mystery novel happens in the streets and in homes and in families, and instead of great long explanations as to why the telephones don't work or why a certain government bureaucracy doesn't work or why the buses don't work, you *see* that the telephones and the government bureaucracy and the hospital system are not working.[1]

Burke, moreover, clearly draws inspiration from the hard-boiled fiction tradition popularised in the American pulp magazines of the 1920s and '30s, most notably *Black Mask*, a tradition in which tough detectives, in the words of Julian Symons in *Bloody Murder*, "inherited the radical feeling occasionally found in the dime novels ... and their rise reflected the increasing violence of American society, and the misery of the depression years."[2] His detective fiction can be called realistic in the sense of Raymond Chandler's definition of realism in "The Simple Art of Murder," which lays down that:

> The realist in murder writes of a world in which gangsters can rule nations and almost rule cities, in which hotels ... and celebrated restaurants are owned by men who made their money out of brothels ... where a judge with a cellar full of bootleg liquor can send a man to jail for having a pint in his pocket, where the mayor of your town may have condoned murder as an instrument of money-making, where no man can walk down a dark street in safety because law and order are things we talk about but refrain from practising ... where the hold-up men may have friends with long guns, [and] the police may not like your testimony ...[3]

[1] Gregory McDonald in John C. Carr, *The Craft of Crime: Conversations with Crime Writers* (Boston: Houghton Mifflin, 1983), p. 113.

[2] Julian Symons, *Bloody Murder; From the Detective Story to the Crime Novel: A History* (1972; rev. ed. Harmondsworth: Penguin Books, 1974), p. 140.

[3] Raymond Chandler, *Pearls Are a Nuisance* (Harmondsworth: Penguin Books, 1969), p. 194.

Though Dave Robicheaux is a policeman, working first for the New Orleans Police Department and subsequently for the sheriff's department in New Iberia, Burke's novels are a long way from being standard police procedurals. Almost invariably, Robicheaux becomes involved in his cases accidentally: finding the body of a young black girl in a bayou while on a fishing trip in *The Neon Rain;* diving for a crashed plane in *Heaven's Prisoners* to save the little girl who is to become his adopted daughter, and discovering four instead of the subsequently reported three corpses on board; a call by a friend in need, that traditional private eye's stand-by, in *Black Cherry Blues*; accepting an undercover mission for the DEA in *A Morning for Flamingos*; more personal associations in *A Stained White Radiance*; the arrest for drunk driving of a film star in *In the Electric Mist with Confederate Dead*. Chance involves him in plots that soon become multi-stranded and multi-levelled, frequently involving the DEA, the FBI, even the CIA. Robicheaux himself is a maverick cop, forever testing the restrictions imposed by the organisations that employ him, occasionally getting himself suspended as a result or else resigning in disillusionment. Very little of the novels is taken up by regular police work and there is little station atmosphere. While the crimes Robicheaux winds up investigating generally do get solved, albeit not always in an orthodox or even expected manner, as integral to the plots of the novels as the criminal cases are the landscape Robicheaux travels and the people he encounters, the whole combining into the novelist's assessment of the state of things in contemporary southern Louisiana.

At the end of *The Neon Rain*, the first novel of the series, Dave Robicheaux resigns from the New Orleans Police Department after fourteen years' service, most recently as a homicide detective in the First District, which includes the French Quarter. He uses his retirement money to buy a boat-rental and bait business in his native New Iberia, and goes to live with his new, second wife in the house his father built "out of cypress and oak. ... the wood[, which] had never been painted ... dark and hard as iron ... the beams ... notched and jointed with pegs."[4] As he has his boat towed up the Bayou Teche and into the town, Robicheaux, we are told, "watched yesterday steal upon [him]—the black people in straw hats, cane-fishing for goggle-eye perch, the smoke drifting out through the trees from barbecue fires, the college-age kids at fish-fries and crab-boils in the city park, the red leaves that tumbled out of the sky and settled like a whisper on the bayou's surface."[5] The scene seems set for a rural idyll, with the safe haven of New Iberia offered as a counterpoint to the violence and squalor of New Orleans, yet Burke's subsequent novels make it clear that the simpler, safer world of Robicheaux's nostalgia-induced imagery is largely illusory. The house his father built is invaded by gunmen, who kill his wife while she is asleep; Robicheaux himself is assaulted on one of his rental boats and in his bait shop, and at one point it is not safe for his adopted daughter, Alafair, to take the school bus.

---

[4] James Lee Burke, *Black Cherry Blues* (1989; New York: Avon Books, 1990), p. 7. Further references in the text to BCB.
[5] James Lee Burke, *The Neon Rain* (1987; London: Vintage, 1991), p. 239. Further references in the text to NR.

On the one hand, Burke establishes the specificity of his southern Louisiana setting in descriptions of its more familiar and appealing aspects: its lush bayou landscape; the hot-house climate of its summers, when almost every afternoon "within minutes the barometer would drop, the air would suddenly turn cool and smell like ozone and gun metal and fish spawning, the wind would begin to blow out of the south and straighten the moss on the dead cypress trees ... and swell and ruffle the pecan trees in my front yard; then a sheet of gray rain would move out of the marsh";[6] the attractive architecture and urban landscape of East Main Street in New Iberia, which runs parallel with Bayou Teche and "begins at the old brick post office and the Shadows, an 1831 plantation home that you often see on calendars and in motion pictures set in the antebellum South, and runs through a long corridor of spreading live oaks, whose trunk and root systems are so enormous that the city has long given up trying to contain them with cement and bricks";[7] or St. Charles Avenue in New Orleans, "covered by a canopy of enormous oak trees and lined on each side by old, iron-scrolled brick homes and antebellum mansions with columned porches and pike-fenced yards filled with hibiscus, blooming myrtle and oleander, bamboo and giant philodendron";[8] familiar tourist attractions such as Jackson Square and the French Market in New Orleans, the Cajun tradition of *fais dodo*, the music of cajun and zydeco bands, and, above all, Louisiana food, from chicory coffee and *beignets* at the Café du Monde through shrimp and oyster po' boy sandwiches, fried catfish, barbecued chicken with *sauce piquante*, *boudin*, and dirty rice to oysters on the half shell, gumbo, and crawfish *étouffée*.

In this appealing southern Louisiana, Robicheaux fishes, both for pleasure and profit, observes magnificent sunsets, has a keen eye for the wildlife of the bayous, stops off for coffee at the Café du Monde whenever he is in New Orleans. Yet underlying it all is the inexorable reality of the region, depression-gripped since the oil boom ended and saturated with drugs. "Over the years," Robicheaux says,

> I had seen all the dark players get [here] in one form or another: the oil and chemical companies who drained and polluted the wetlands; the developers who could turn sugarcane acreage and pecan orchards into miles of tract homes and shopping malls ... the Mafia, who operated out of New Orleans and brought us prostitution, slot machines, control of at least two big labor unions, and finally narcotics. (SWR, 30)

The world Robicheaux typically moves in is one conveniently ignored by Louisiana tourist boards. A representative slice of it is the Atchafalaya basin, which is defined as "the place to go if you don't fit anywhere else. ... Twenty minutes from Baton Rouge or an hour and a half from New Orleans, you can punch a hole in the dimension and drop back down into ... [a] South that you thought had been eaten up by the

---

[6] James Lee Burke, *In the Electric Mist with Confederate Dead* (New York: Hyperion, 1993), pp. 40-41. Further references in the text to EMCD.

[7] James Lee Burke, *A Stained White Radiance* (1992; New York: Avon Books, 1993), p. 47. Further references in the text to SWR.

[8] James Lee Burke, *Heaven's Prisoners* (1988; London: Vintage, 1990), p. 231. Further references in the text to HP.

developers of Sunbelt suburbs," (SWR, 144-45) a place inhabited by "Cajuns, red-bones, roustabouts, pipeliners, rednecks whose shrinking piece of American geography is identified only by a battered pickup, a tape deck playing Waylon, and a twelve-pack of Jax" (BCB, 3).

The Robicheaux novels, true to the radical tradition of detective fiction, offer few illusions about police work or its lasting benefits to society. Reflecting on his career in New Orleans, Robicheaux concludes that, "I don't think my participation in what politicians call 'the war on crime' ever made much difference. New Orleans is no safer town. ... Why? Narcotics is one answer. Maybe another is the fact that in fourteen years I never turned the key on a slumlord or on a zoning board member who owned interests in pornographic theaters and massage parlors" (HP, 75). In Burke's novels, money can buy power and respectability, and in a state with a long tradition of legal and political corruption such as Louisiana, the collusion of its wealthiest and most powerful forces is implicitly assumed. The Star Drilling Company in *Black Cherry Blues* is as willing to condone murder by its employees in the furtherance of its own interests as any criminal organisation, while those grown rich in the drugs trade present themselves as businessmen. A lot of their drugs money is laundered and invested in legitimate or semi-legitimate enterprises; Julie Balboni owns a recording studio and is in "the entertainment business," putting up part of the financing of a Hollywood costume drama in *In the Electric Mist with Confederate Dead*; Bubba Rocque of *Heaven's Prisoners* tells Robicheaux: "I own a lot of business. I got a dozen oyster boats, I got a fish-packing house in New Iberia and one in Morgan City. I own seafood restaurants in Lafayette and Lake Charles, I own three clubs and an escort agency in New Orleans" (HP, 89) .

Of Robicheaux himself it is said time and again that he is not "on the pad," but the novels are not openly condemnatory of his New Orleans partner, Cletus Purcell, whose reputation as a cop is such that, "All you had to do was mention to a pimp or house creep or jack roller that Cletus Purcell would like to interview him, and he would be on the next bus or plane to Miami,"[9] and whose career in the police force comes to an abrupt end when he accepts $10.000 to kill a potential witness in a federal case. Law enforcement reality is that the police, only too aware of their own limited powers, for the most part "unconsciously target the most available and inept ... addicts, street dealers, petty thieves, hookers and a few of their johns, storefront fences, and the obviously deranged and violent ..." (HP, 254) and their methods are often far from orthodox: witnesses, potential suspects, and likely sources of information are inti-midated, assaulted, even accidentally killed. When, on rare occasions, there is a chance of convicting a big player, as in the case of Drew Sonnier filing charges against Joey Gouza in *A Stained White Radiance*, few people are concerned about the veracity of her (in fact false) statement, for,

---

[9] James Lee Burke, *A Morning for Flamingos* (1990; New York: Avon Books, 1991), p. 67. Further references in the text to MFF.

unfortunately for him, nobody cares if a guy like Joey is innocent. People want him put away in a cage for a long time, and they don't care how it's done. The prosecutor will probably get a new political career out of it, his lawyers will get rich on his appeals while he's chopping sugarcane at Angola, his wife and mistresses will clean out his bank accounts and sell everything he owns, and his hired stooges will go to work for his competitors and forget they ever heard of him." (SWR, 183)

With the exception of *Black Cherry Blues*, which has its main action in Montana and focusses on an oil exploration company's unscrupulous fight against environmentalist activists, the Robicheaux novels all have to do in one way or another with organised crime in Louisiana and its principal activities, the importation and distribution of drugs, extortion, gambling, and prostitution, with a couple of sidelines such as illegal immigration and the shipping of arms to right-wing extremists in nearby Central America thrown in for good measure. Controlling these activities are Louisiana-born Italians along with more recent arrivals from Colombia and Nicaragua, men who live on large properties in exclusive suburbs fronting on Lake Ponchartrain and, irony of ironies, worry about the crime situation in New Orleans. "'We used to have understandings with the city,'" Julie Balboni complains in *In the Electric Mist with Confederate Dead*. "'Everybody knew the rules. ... [now] take a walk past the Desire or St. Thomas project and see what happens. People get killed in Audubon Park, for God's sake'" (28). At the other end of the scale are the perpetrators of the type of crime these men worry about, "fifteen year-old kids in the projects dealing rock, girls, guns, Mexican brown, crank, you name it, the Italians won't fool with it, it's too uncontrollable" (105) .

Burke makes it clear that, in southern Louisiana's criminal economy as much as in the official one, blacks occupy the lower tiers. The picture he paints is one of a place of iniquity and unresolved racial tension, where the relatives of murder victims live in country shacks and crumbling apartment blocks while successful criminals such as Bubba Rocque can acquire "a ruined antebellum home on the Vermillion River outside of Lafayette and ... [spend] a quarter-million dollars rebuilding it" (HP, 85). In the course of duty Robicheaux visits rural poor black people, who live in "weathered, paintless shacks along a dirt road on the back of a corporate sugar plantation. ... [without] glass in the windows ... [t]he walls ... insulated with pages from the Sears catalog" (NR, 24), or at a crossroads out in New Iberia parish, "the shacks ... gray and paintless, the galleries sagging, the privies knocked together from tar paper, scrap lumber, and roofing tin" (MFF, 25). The fact that the Robicheaux novels by and large steer clear of black-on-black crime and its implications—the only black criminal Robicheaux pursues is an illegal immigrant from Haiti called Toot (presumably from *tonton macoute*), who is one of the killers of his wife—is itself indicative of the certainty that despite all changes for the better, the lives of black people continue to count for less than those of their white counterparts. The comparative lack of interest in violent crime within the black community, high homicide rates notwithstanding, stands as perhaps the clearest legacy of the days of segregation. For, as Edward L. Ayers has pointed out in *Vengeance and Justice*, "studies of homicide from the early twentieth century (and ever since) show the same pattern: most homicides in the South involved a black assailant and a black victim."[10]

Considering their geographical location, Burke's stories are short on black characters, but racial undertones are ever present. Thus the current sheriff of New Iberia, a man who used to be in the dry-cleaning business and an active member of the local chamber of commerce, is spoken of as a vast improvement over the stereotypical, racist southern sheriff of Robicheaux's youth, a man who "was not bothered by the bordellos on Railroad Avenue and the slot machines all over Iberia parish. ... [and who would] tip his John B. Stetson hat to a white lady on Main, and talk to an elderly Negro woman as though she were a post" (HP, 55) Robicheaux is also quick to acknowledge other changes for the better: "the laws of segregation were gone; kids didn't go nigger-knocking on Saturday nights; the Ku Klux Klan didn't burn crosses all over Plaquemines Parish" (HP, 163). Burke is at pains throughout to stress Robicheaux's non-racialist outlook. His problems in *The Neon Rain* stem in large measure from his interest in the cause of death of a supposedly drowned black girl considered expendable by the drug dealers who killed her and the Cataouache Sheriff's office alike. His egalitarian pedigree is established in *In the Electric Mist with Confederate Dead*, where we learn of an incident in 1957 when Dave Robicheaux, stringing cables in the Atcha-falaya marsh to pay his way through college, watched the summary execution of a black prisoner, and of what happened afterwards:

> Later, I told the [work] party chief, the sheriff's department, and finally anybody who would listen to me, about what I had seen. But their interest was short-lived; no body was ever found in the area, nor was any black man from around there ever reported as missing. As time passed, I tried to convince myself that the man in chains had eluded his tormentors. ... At age nineteen I did not want to accept the possibility that a man's murder could be treated with the social significance of a hangnail ... snipped off someone's finger. (EMCD, 11)

Tante Lemon in *A Morning for Flamingos* pays him what must be the ultimate compliment when she says that, "'Mr. Dave a white man, but he don't never lie'" (MFF, 49). Robicheaux is willing to take the time and trouble to question the conviction for murder of Tee Beau Latiolais in *A Morning for Flamingos*, and to accept that Tante Lemon, his grandmother, may be speaking the truth when she provides him with an alibi, rather than dismissing her words out of hand as the police and the prosecutor's office have done. Yet earlier Tante Lemon has summed up what still continues to be a fundamental truth: "'You a white man. Colored folk ain't never gonna be your bidness'" (MFF, 29). Nowhere is this reflected more clearly than in Robicheaux's relationship with Batist, the black man who helps him run his boat-rental business and who is probably his closest male associate: Burke portrays Batist as a man of great physical strength and tremendous loyalty, but he rarely goes further than that. The reader encounters Batist only in the white world of Robicheaux's boat business and

---

[10] Edward L. Ayers, *Vengeance and Justice: Crime and Punishment in the 19th-Century American South* (New York: Oxford University Press, 1984), p. 241.

in the context of Robicheaux's recollections of the French speaking world of his youth, which Batist, who is illiterate, remains far closer to than Robicheaux himself, who has a college degree and has become fully integrated in English speaking, American Louisiana. For all that Robicheaux trusts Batist with his own life and that of his family, leaving his daughter in Batist's care when he goes in search of his wife's killers in *Heaven's Prisoners*, in their everyday relationship he sometimes has trouble avoiding sounding paternalistic, as when he has to explain to his daughter why Batist is so upset about her pet raccoon having eaten some Milky Ways from the bait shop he manages: "'Batist grew up poor and uneducated and never learned to read and write....he has to make an "X" when he signs for a delivery and he can't count the receipts at the end of the day. So he concentrates on things that he can do well....Then [your raccoon] gets loose and makes a big mess of the shelves....in Batist's mind he's let us down'" (SWR, 237). While the underlying message is that Robicheaux, by adopting her, has saved Alafair from a fate very like Batist's in her own native village in the mountains of El Salvador, it also establishes that he accepts Batist's condition.

Burke explores the dilemmas of race most specifically in *A Stained White Radiance*, where Robicheaux goes to great lengths, including legally suspect ones, to prove that racist politician Bobby Earle (who is clearly modelled on Louisiana's David Duke) is tied to the Mob and/or the "jailhouse nazis" of the Aryan Brotherhood, two of whom have murdered a New Iberia deputy. Going to the state capitol building in Baton Rouge, Robicheaux observes the political realities of his state when he sees "the regard with which Bobby Earle was treated by many of his peers, the warm handshakes, the pats on the arm and shoulder, the expression of gentlemanly goodwill by men who should have known better," and is reminded of "the deference sometimes shown to a small-town poolroom bully or redneck police chief" (181). Similarly, he watches Earle's electoral constituency at a rally and concludes that,

> these were not ordinary small-town blue-collar people. This was the permanent underclass, the ones who tried to hold on daily to their shrinking bit of redneck geography. ... They jealously guarded their jobs from blacks and Vietnamese refugees, whom they saw as a vast and hungry army about to descend upon their women, their schools, even their clapboard church houses, where they were assured every Sunday and Wednesday night that the bitterness and fear that characterized their lives had nothing to do with what they had been born to, or what they had chosen for themselves. (292)

The policeman in Robicheaux ultimately winds up saving Earle's life (significantly, with Batist's assistance) when deranged Verise Sonnier mistakes him for his son Weldon and tries to shoot him; the liberal in him has to accept, albeit reluctantly, that Bobby Earle is neither funded by the drugs syndicates nor involved with the bikers of the AB, but simply is "out there by consent."

Burke uses the crime novel as a vehicle to examine the social and economic dynamics of a particular region. The character of Dave Robicheaux and his liberal agenda are set off against the violent, macho world of his police work. Burke is particularly interested in the economics of crime, and he stresses the deprived socio-economic backgrounds of its perpetrators and victims alike. The stripper Robin Gaddis in

Heaven's Prisoners, for instance, is the product of "a three-generation case history that was a study in institutional failure and human inadequacy" (HP, 21); Cherry LeBlanc in *In the Electric Mist with Confederate Dead,* busted at sixteen for prostitution, dead at nineteen at the hands of a sadistic serial killer, to Robicheaux's mind "wasn't born a prostitute or the kind of girl who would be passed from hand to hand. ... Others had helped her get there. My first vote would be for the father, the child molester, in Mamou" (37). Criminals by and large come out of "the great body of psychologically misshapen people" Robicheaux refers to as "The Pool":

> Members of The Pool leave behind warehouses of official paperwork as evidence that they have occupied the planet for a certain period of time. Their names are entered early on in welfare case histories, child-abuse investigation, clinic admissions for rat bites and malnutrition. Later on these same people provide jobs for an army of truant officers, psychologists, public defenders, juvenile probation officers, ambulance attendants, emergency-room personnel, street cops, prosecutors, jailers, prison guards, alcohol- and drug-treatment counselors, bail bondsmen, adult parole authorities, and the county morticians who put the final punctuation mark in their files. (SWR, 76)

It is worth noting here that Burke suggests that Robicheaux's understanding of the world of The Pool is at least in part innate. Robicheaux is a "recovering alcoholic," in AA parlance, and he gets locked up in jail on several occasions when drunk and once while falsely accused of murder. His nickname, Streak, is for the white streak in his black hair, which has its origins in a vitamin deficiency in his youth. Given that his poor-white father was illiterate and occasionally jailed for fighting in bars when drunk, and that his mother ran off with a *bourée* dealer, the implication is that Robicheaux narrowly escaped being one of the statistics himself.

In *The World of the Thriller,* Ralph Harper observes: "There is no question but that the thriller represents a taming, a simplification, and a setting to rights of the most serious evils and perils, and it does so in a manner which revives our confidence in a misused and discredited humanity, by the coincidence of luck and virtue."[11] The hero is not only "offered an opportunity to right wrongs or to stem the tide of chaos, but the almost impossible also happens—the hero succeeds."[12] Gregory McDonald has put forward a similar line of argument: "our lives are chaotic and we have to have the belief that we can make sense out of them, that we can order them, and more simply than other literary forms the mystery novel does order chaos. For the most part, things come out O.K. in the end and all the lines are tied."[13] The southern Louisiana world in which Burke's Dave Robicheaux makes his home arguably is more complex than that. Though Robicheaux is instrumental in solving murders and other, mostly drugs-related crimes, and the perpetrators of these crimes by and large wind up dead or in prison, there is little illusion of "the most serious evils and perils" being set to rights or all the lines being tied together. "Having been raised in Louisiana, I had always

---

[11] Ralph Harper, *The World of the Thriller,* (1969; Baltimore: Johns Hopkins University Press, 1974), p. 9.

[12] Ibid., p. 12.

[13] Carr, p. 113.

thought that politics was the province of moral invalids," Robicheaux informs the reader in *The Neon Rain* (108), and the subsequent novels only go to reinforce this view. It is telling that the person Robicheaux most fully explores the concept of personal honour and moral responsibility with is none other than Confederate general John Bell Hood, who makes a number of supernatural appearances in *In the Electric Mist with Confederate Dead*. "'Maybe we have so much collective guilt as a society that we fear to punish our individual members,'" Robicheaux suggests (EMCD, 271). Natural beauty and cultural diversity, both of which Burke's southern Louisiana is amply supplied with, cannot conceal that the combination of corrupt government and geographical proximity to the drugs producing countries of Latin America has turned the region into a dangerous and violent place becoming progressively unsafer. Perhaps for that reason, Robicheaux's real successes have little to do with combatting organised crime or bringing guilty men to justice; rather, they are small-scale, personal triumphs of hope over experience: helping Robin Gaddis kick her drug addiction, saving two teenage runaways from the clutches of a child molester at the New Orleans bus depot late at night, and, above all, adopting Alafair. If Robicheaux does not quite match up to the image Raymond Chandler memorably defined in "The Simple Art of Murder" —"a man ... who is not himself mean, who is neither tarnished nor afraid. ... a complete man and a common man and yet an unusual man.... a man of honour, by instinct, by inevitability.... the best man in his world and a good enough man for any world ..."[14]—it is at least in part because the rules of the game have undergone some fundamental changes. In a landscape whose local colour, on closer inspection, proves overwhelmingly *noir*, Robicheaux, the author makes it clear, is the best we are likely to get.

---

[14] Chandler, p. 198.

OWEN WISTER AND EMERGENT DISCOURSES
OF THE AMERICAN WEST

John Dorst, University of Wyoming

There is a joke, one of those hardy perennials that has been in circulation for a long time, which goes as follows: Two Easterners are on a auto tour of the American West. They decide one morning to take a quick drive over to a range of mountains that appear to loom just a little way up the road. Expecting a short trip, they are dismayed to find themselves traveling many miles without seeming to come any closer to their goal. Finally, they see up ahead an old man sitting on a roadside fence. As they pull over, they notice he is an Indian and that he is sitting there staring off toward the mountains they've been driving toward for hours. One of the tourists leans out the window and says, "Excuse me, can you tell me how far it is to those mountains?" No response. The old man sits silently, staring off into the distance. "Pardon me," the tourist tries again, raising his voice a few notches, "but can you tell us how long it will take us to get to those mountains up ahead?" Again, the old Indian doesn't even acknowledge his presence. Finally, the traveller leans way out the window and tries the question once more, shouting at the top of his voice. Getting no response a third time, he pulls his head back in and says to his companion, "Well, I guess that old man is a lot farther away than we thought."

It is an article of faith among folklorists, who spend much of their time in the serious study of things most people don't consider particularly meaningful, that even such a seemingly trivial little item as this joke might have lurking within it considerable cultural significance. The claim I would make, in fact, is that this brief comic narrative is a surprisingly concentrated expression of the issues I will be expanding upon in what follows.

The humour turns upon two comic misperceptions. The Eastern tourists, modern analogues to the tenderfoot or greenhorn of an earlier day, misread the landscape, having no experience with its deceptive qualities. And they also misperceive the old man, always identified as an Indian in the versions I've heard. Deluded in thinking the mountains are nearby when they really are far away, they also make the mirror image mistake of assuming the old man is far off, when of course he is right next to them and hears everything they say. With eyes fixed on the distant landscape, this silent observer "sees" the tourists for what they are. He is, in effect, watching them without their being aware of it. And what he is watching is the comic spectacle of their faulty act of looking.

My point is that in this one joke we have a rather complicated scenario which encompasses many of the discursive relationships characteristic of our current historical moment. In particular, it maps a geometry of relationships based on acts of looking. Its themes are deceived vision and, in the person of the silent Indian, a kind of covert observation of what is itself a visual experience. This arrangement of what in its simplest formulation can be characterised as "looking at the activity of looking" is at the heart of a social order where the commodified spectacle and touristic experience are increasingly central. The joke is overtly about the foolishness of Eastern tourists, but more fundamentally it is an allegory of the "tourist gaze" itself.[1]

Although this little parable of the modern tourist mode applies widely to the advanced consumer culture most of us inhabit, the fact that it is set in the American West is not entirely accidental. Perhaps more than any other American region, the far West is constructed in terms of visual experience. And this has been so for a long time. In what follows I will focus on one moment in the history of that construction—one that seems to me particularly important, namely, the moment of Owen Wister's classic Western romance *The Virginian: A Horseman of the Plains*, published in 1902.[2] Widely acknowledged as a watershed in American cultural history, or at least in the cultural history of the American West, this text has not been viewed in relationship to the conditions of cultural production that were emergent at the time of its publication and that have become increasingly pervasive in the course of the twentieth century. In particular, its relationship to what would become the modern touristic "gaze" has gone unremarked.

A convenient way to begin establishing this link is to notice that an early episode in the novel offers some striking parallels to the modern joke I began with. The book opens with the arrival by train of the Eastern tenderfoot in the remote frontier settlement of Medicine Bow, Wyoming Territory. The story's eponymous cowboy hero is there waiting to convey the visitor 263 miles by wagon to the ranch of his host. Like the auto tourists in the joke, the newcomer is expecting a short ride from the railhead to Judge Henry's Sunk Creek spread. He is astonished to discover the distance before him. After spending the night in town, he and his cowboy guide set off toward, as he describes it, the "vast horizon." Five miles out of town he looks back and is amazed by the sight: "There was Medicine Bow, seemingly a stone's throw behind us." A half hour later, there it still is, a little smaller, but "visible in every feature, like something seen through the wrong end of a field glass."[3] These observations lead to a whole comic episode in which the Virginian regales his new companion with increasingly outrageous exaggerations premised on the notion that the distinctively regional qualities of light and air give the West a special visual quality, which he refers to in his Southern drawl as "a mos' deceivin' atmospheah."

Although the garrulous cowboy hero seems the virtual opposite of the silent Indian, they actually occupy something of the same structural position in the two narratives. They are the superior observers of the deceived or confused visual experiences

---

[1] I borrow this apt term from the title of John Urry's book, *The Tourist Gaze: Leisure and Travel in Contemporary Society* (London: Sage Publications, 1990).

[2] Owen Wister, *The Virginian: A Horseman of the Plains* (New York: Macmillan, 1902). All quotations are taken from the annotated Penguin edition (New York, 1988).

[3] Wister, p. 38.

of new arrivals. The episode in the novel could be seen as the inaugural arrival scene of the emblematic tourist in the Western landscape, the greenhorn narrator being the direct ancestor of the latter-day sightseers.

But it is not just in the overtly touristic themes of this one episode in Wister's novel that the emergent gaze of a modern visual discourse is evident. The book is suffused throughout with themes, motifs, and structures that herald a modern "text of the American West," a text organised around what was in Wister's day a new discourse of looking. It is a discourse characterised by such things as the marring or occlusion of vision, fantastic feats of observation, covert surveillance, and the realisation that seemingly passive objects of looking are actually active subjects capable of looking back. Elements such as these have become pervasive in our advanced consumer culture, as is especially evident in forms of touristic experience. It is Wister's moment as an important point of emergence of this discourse that is my main concern here.

Perhaps the single most important passage in *The Virginian* for a consideration of this issue is also notable as the book's most overtly violent episode:

> He made no answer, but mounted Pedro; and the failing pony walked mechanically forward, while the Virginian, puzzled, stood looking after him. Balaam seemed without purpose of going anywhere, and stopped in a moment. Suddenly he was at work at something. This sight was odd and new to look at. For a few seconds it had no meaning to the Virginian as he watched. Then his mind grasped the horror, too late. Even with his cry of execration and the tiger spring that he gave to stop Balaam, the monstrosity was wrought. Pedro sank motionless, his head rolling flat on the earth.[4]

Without more context, of course, we can't understand exactly what is going on here. But even with that fuller story supplied, there is still a little slippage at the heart of this passage that we can't fully understand unless we place it in a context much larger than *The Virginian* as a bounded narrative. What does the rancher Balaam actually do to the horse Pedro? We are never told explicitly. It doesn't take much looking to find out that what Wister intends here is that the brutal rancher gouges out the pony's eye. But just given what's in the text, we might remain as guileless and mystified a spectator as the momentarily paralysed Virginian.

It doesn't take too much further investigation to find that this episode, like several others in the novel, had a previous existence as a magazine story,[5] and before that it appeared in Wister's Western journal of 1889, presented there as an account of a very disturbing personal experience. Apparently, while Wister was on one of his Wyoming visits, his temporary host, a rancher named Tisdale, enlisted the Easterner's aid in moving some horses. In a fit of rage at a played-out pony, Tisdale actually performed the hideous act, and in the privacy of his journal Wister does not shrink from a more graphic description.

What I want to pull up for closer inspection in this episode is the obvious importance it places on the eye, both literally and figuratively. Doing so gets us away

---

[4] Wister, p. 240.

[5] *Virginian*, explanatory note 56, pp. 444-45.

from considerations of the individual author's experience and intention and gives us access to larger patterns in cultural history. In this scene a creature is brutally blinded, though the act itself is withheld from our view, and the Virginian is set up, at least momentarily, as a spectator. We see him physically passive, but engaged in a particular kind of looking—a seeming fascination at this sight that was "odd and new to look at." His perplexity is followed by sudden recognition at the unveiling of this act of violence against vision.

Although Wister's novel includes a lynching, the now archetypal shoot-out on mainstreet, and sundry other moments of swift action, this blinding episode is by far the most graphically violent passage in the whole book. The climactic showdown with Trampas is positively lyrical by comparison. And it is not just, or even mostly, Pedro's blinding that makes this moment so violent. That event is immediately followed by the Virginian's reaction:

> Then vengeance like a blast struck Balaam. The Virginian hurled him to the ground, lifted and hurled him again, lifted him and beat his face and struck his jaw. The man's strong ox-like fighting availed nothing. He fended his eyes as best he could against these sledge-hammer blows of justice. He felt blindly for his pistol. That arm was caught and wrenched backward, and crushed and doubled. He seemed to hear his own bones, and set up a hideous screaming of hate and pain. Then the pistol at last came out, and together with the hand that grasped it was instantly stamped into the dust. Once again the creature was lifted and slung so that he lay across Pedro's saddle a blurred, dingy, wet pulp. Vengeance had come and gone. The man and the horse were motionless. Around them, silence seemed to gather like a witness.[6]

Here again, we have violence against the eyes, resulting in this case in a temporary blindness. And the spectacle has been given a jurisprudential slant. The "blows of justice" rain down and the spectatorship takes the legal (and sacral?) form of "witnessing."

One could go on at considerable length about the expanding circle of visual and ocular imagery deployed in this inaugural text in the modern tradition of Western romance. I'll only mention, though, that this scene of horse maiming is used rather effectively as the lead-in to the plot development that provides the heretofore episodic story with a more continuous narrative thread. Let me just note that in the next set of events a new context and structure of looking is set up. The Virginian and Balaam, who soon comes around from his beating, proceed with the journey they are on. But, unbeknownst to them, they have come under the gaze of some unseen watchers, later identified as a small band of renegade Indians (unspecified as to tribe or in any other way) who have not returned to the "southern reservation" after the hunting season. We never actually "see" them and they remain a *deus ex machina* in the intermittently creaky plot.

Here then a reversed structure of looking is established in which the spectators rather than the spectacle are rendered invisible. And violence is now a function of the gaze itself, rather than a feature of the spectacle observed. In the Pedro episode the eye

---

[6] Wister, p. 240.

is the object of attack; here the gaze is hostile. Again, the physical act of violence occurs off stage and all we see is the result, the Virginian, wounded in an Indian ambush, lying close to death at a pool conveniently near the home of his schoolmarm sweetheart. She finds him in this state, saves him, and nurses him back to health, in the process enacting with him a whole other geometry of looking, one that comes to Wister ready-made from preexisting romance traditions.

It is not my intention here to attempt a neat sorting of what seem to me the very complex discourses of looking operating throughout *The Virginian*. For one thing, these operations are not tidy. It is in the nature of discourses, as I'm using the term, that they spill into and out of particular texts and violate the conventional boundaries we use to organise literary history. My point is simply that the discursive formations evident in Wister's text, a seminal text in the modern construction of the American West, have a great deal to do with a new tourist gaze that was emerging in the decades just prior to the turn of the century. I am working on the assumption that tourism in our advanced consumer culture, and more specifically, the tourism of the American Far West, has itself developed an immensely complex discourse of looking in which the packaging, managing, exchanging and, above all, commodifying of the gaze are at the core of a massive social enterprise. And I believe the historical moment Wister occupies (reflects, anticipates, exemplifies, etc.) is one where the shift toward this modern discourse is taking definite shape. *The Virginian* registers this development both overtly and covertly.

For readers not familiar with Wister's personal history, I need to point out that my leap from *The Virginian* to emergent elements of the modern touristic gaze is not taken completely without the net of direct historical connection. Wister's own career in the West itself inscribes a touristic trajectory that may not be strictly chronological, but that does offer some conceptual order. Wister was, first of all, one of those Gilded Age health tourists sent off to find vigor and renewed strength of mind after some sort of nervous collapse brought on by the pressures of an increasingly perplexing world in the urban East. For Wister it seems to have been the anticipation of beginning his professional legal studies that helped precipitate a breakdown, and it was no less a personage than S. Weir Mitchell who in 1885 sent him on a health-giving Western tour to Wyoming (then a Territory). Very quickly Wister took on the Western garb and paraphernalia of another tourist mode, the 19th century hunter-tourist. This was in fact a well-established role by the time Wister first adopted it. Leisured Eastern and European, mostly British, sportsmen came with a mode of looking well represented in Wister's journals of his early years in the West: weather, landscape vistas (in Wister's case lyrically described), the far view in search of quarry, the stalking view that discovers the accessible target and, finally, at least by implication, the view down the sights of the rifle, the view that transforms the act of looking into violent intervention and appropriation of a tangible artifact—the souvenir trophy.

And it is worth pointing out in passing that this gaze of the hunter-tourist has much in common with the entrepreneurial, appropriating gaze of the developer, land speculator, and scientific resource survey. It's no accident that, as Earl Pomeroy pointed out long ago, more than a few of these elite hunter-tourists invested, and in some cases took up residence, in the West, buying large ranches and participating in the cattle boom that was completing its moment of crisis just at the time Wister was making his earliest visits.[7] Wister's famous hero is notable, as more than a few people have pointed out, for crossing a class boundary to take his place among this rancher elite, which he does with the special insight of the working cowboy who recognises that a way of life is coming to a close. The Virginian's response to these new conditions is to establish a fenced ranch of the sort that is to become the norm in the industrialised West, happily in his case a ranch with its own coal deposits, which he realises will become a valuable commodity when the railroad finally makes it to the more remote settlements.

Wister's own career took a different turn. By the early 1890s he had crossed a cultural boundary between the leisured hunter-tourist who went West to engage in the healthful, manly pursuits of outdoor sportsmanship, and the literary tourist intent on giving an account of the West precisely at a moment of radical transformation, a transformation that he could only see, like his contemporary Frederick Jackson Turner, as a kind of loss or diminution. Wister began writing his Western stories in 1891 and contracted with *Harper's* magazine in 1893 for a series of them, launching a career that would culminate about a decade later in his paradigmatic Western romance.

What I want to propose here is that this shift in Wister's own tourist gaze marks a much larger transformation in the discourse of looking at the American West, one which we still are working with—and working out—in touristic experience today. The same year that Wister began writing about the West he carried with him on what had become almost annual visits to Wyoming (by then a state) his first roll-film Kodak box camera. Introduced to the general market only the year previous, the model he apparently took could capture up to 100 shots and required none of the technical knowledge of wet-plate photography that had dominated before Eastman's innovations of the 1880s.[8] In short, Wister was of the first generation of so-called *Kodakers*, the avant-garde of what would become mass, truly touristic, snap-shot photographers.

Whereas in his early journals we sometimes find Wister regretting his lack of the painterly skills that would allow him to capture visually a landscape that defied verbal description, after 1891 he can be heard to express what has become a universal tourist lament: "I wish I'd had my camera with me." But more significant for my purposes than this shift in technology is Wister's embodiment of a deeper shift in the discourse of looking. We begin to hear him unreflexively acknowledging a new set of relationships of seeing that constitute fundamental conditions of possibility for modern tourism.

Before the moment I'm trying to identify here, the ways of touristic looking in the West were premised on what we might call monadic experience—one subject confronting one object of visual perception, most typically, of course, the Western landscape. One eye views one scene according to one received set of visual conventions:

---

[7] Earl Pomeroy, *In Search of the Golden West: The Tourist in Western America* (New York: Knopf, 1957).

[8] Mark L. Gardner, *The Western Photography of Owen Wister* (Master's thesis, University of Wyoming, 1985).

be they the art-historical conventions of the picturesque or the sublime, or those of the scientist, the sportsman, or the resource surveyor, to name a few. There is now a fairly deep literature on these monadic ways of looking.[9] While the object of observation in some of these modes might be problematic in its defiance of the conventions applied to it, as interestingly examined by Anne Farrar Hyde in her book *An American Vision*,[10] in all of them the eye stays fixed and uncomplicated. What we see happening in Wister is the problematisation of the eye itself. The gaze, represented most concretely in an emergent tourist apparatus of looking, fractures, dissociates, turns back upon itself in a new visual geometry of viewing positions. The monadic look is displaced by a new social space defined by an exchange of gazes, a new economy of looking.

In this new discourse at least three positions of looking are the minimal requisite: a spectacle somehow already prepared to be looked at, an audience of spectators, and, most importantly, an encompassing gaze that, metaphorically speaking, "looks down" upon what is already a scene of looking, a gaze that exists to look at another act of looking.

A concrete example, again drawn from Wister, will illustrate my point. In his July 18, 1891, journal, a month to the day after he witnessed the real life horse maiming that would become the Pedro episode in *The Virginian*, Wister reports a visit to Warm Springs Canyon, near the town of Dubois, Wyoming. He is thoroughly enchanted by this remarkable site, a deep gorge in which are to be seen two natural rock bridges. "It is impossible to get down to the water there," he tells us, "but we shall try tomorrow, for I greatly desire a photograph of this place." Later he makes it down, with much difficulty, and is not disappointed by the experience. And at this point he expresses the kind of sentiment that reflects a modern touristic way of looking:

> ... thank the Lord, it is nameless and unknown save to Indians, cowboys, and horse thieves.... Some day, no doubt when civilization crawls here, this poor creek with its cañon and natural bridges will echo with the howling of the summer mob, who will have easy paths made for them, and staircases, and elevators perhaps too. There will be signposts directing you to Minerva Terrace, Calypso Garden, Siren Grotto, for every unfortunate ledge and point will be saddled with a baleful name rotten with inappropriateness. I hope at least some of the photographs I took will succeed.[11]

The unintentional irony is perhaps obvious. Wister here enacts in a couple of sentences the structure of looking I'm trying to identify. He relates to this site in what will fast become a conventionally touristic fashion. He finds his way, after difficult

---

[9] Two important examples are William Goetzman, *Exploration and Empire* (New York: Norton, 1966), pp. 199-228, 333-352, 603-648; and Peter B. Hales, *William Henry Jackson and the Transformation of the American Landscape* (Philadelphia: Temple University Press, 1988).

[10] Anne Farrar Hyde, *An American Vision: Far Western Landscape and National Culture, 1820-1920* (New York: New York University Press, 1990).

[11] Wister's Western journals are housed in the archives of the American Heritage Center, University of Wyoming.

travel, to a viewing position from which he can "mark"[12] the site with the tourist snapshot. But virtually at the same time he adopts in his imagination a viewing position outside his own act and from which he views the anticipated tourist hordes who will come to view the site once it has been packaged more conveniently. That his prediction about this particular place has not (yet) been confirmed is beside the point. At issue here is the dissociation of the gaze, its splitting so to speak, into a look that directly confronts and records the site, and a look that gazes down from a superior position at this first sort of looking. Although he misrecognises himself as belonging to the "authentic" Western company of Indians, cowboys and horse thieves who know of this place, his Kodak is in fact the badge of his membership in that large company yet to come. His camera belongs to the set of artifacts—the stairs, the elevator, the pre-packaged and named views and natural features—that accommodate the "summer mob." This doubleness of gaze is confirmed by Wister the very next month, when he visits the falls of the Yellowstone River. He draws heavily on the conventions of the sublime to describe his reaction to this site, a mode appropriate to earlier touristic perceptions of the West, but immediately thereafter he deplores the presence of common tourists, now real and not imagined, who "scuttle through here like mice." Wister's journal here constructs him in two viewing positions simultaneously, one looking at the site and one looking at the *act* of looking at the site. The basic structure allows for many variations, subtleties, and complexities that continue to work themselves out in the massive tourist project so central to our own historical moment.

I have suggested here that Wister's most important literary work, usually treated as the Ur-document of a new American mythology, maybe the definitive American mythology, also encodes, however indirectly or symbolically, a kind of crisis in the history of looking, looking, that is, as a cultural apparatus. The very fact that in *The Virginian* violence directed toward vision is so vividly depicted as a spectacle can be understood as a symptom or displaced expression of this larger crisis. The passage in which the unnamed and unseen Indians are gazing from a locus of covert surveillance, hardly a new motif, situates them, ironically, in the position of super-viewers looking down onto a scene already constructed in terms of spectatorship, thus bringing them into the new space of looking I've been talking about. With the development of the film Western this structural positioning of Indians will take on particular prominence. The parallels to the Easterner joke are, I hope, obvious.

The very absence of a direct description of Pedro's blinding implies yet another layer of spectatorship, that is, the genteel audience of mostly female romance readers who in fact played a large part in the immediate, spectacular success of Wister's novel. All of these literary elements, and more besides, along with Wister's construction of his own experiences in the West suggest to me that we are here in the presence of a collective phenomenon that marks an important cultural shift in the discourse of looking, its touristic manifestations providing the most tangible, and perhaps central, instance. My interest in Wister is as a representative, though largely unacknowledged

---

[12] The importance of the touristic activity of "marking" sites is addressed in Dean MacCannell's seminal study, *The Tourist: A New Theory of the Leisure Class* (New York: Schocken Books, 1976; rev. ed., 1989).

figure in the early development of these structures of looking that have become today a massive and dominant apparatus, the one through which we cannot help but see the landscape and history of the West as a region that is thoroughly "written."

A NEW WEST, OR A NEW WESTERN

Andrea Scheele

On the cover of Thomas McGuane's novel *Nobody's Angel*, published in 1982, an excerpt from a review of the book in the *Los Angeles Times* says: "The thinking man's Western." The quotation implies that a Western for a thinking man is exceptional and since the excerpt is used for promotional ends it also implies that there exists a market for thinking man's Westerns. Obviously, the discursive construct of the West has changed. I will attempt to describe the changes in the views of the West by looking at Owen Wister's *The Virginian*[1] and at Thomas McGuane's *Nobody's Angel*. [2] The Western was greatly influenced by Owen Wister's *The Virginian*, published in 1902, a novel that provided an escape from daily reality—instead of giving food for thought. I will describe the cultural background of *The Virginian* and the influence of the novel on the understanding of the West. Subsequently, I will show how the narrative voice in *Nobody's Angel* tries to liberate itself from the narrative pattern established by *The Virginian*.

 The Virginian appeared only nine years after Frederick Jackson Turner had presented his essay "The Significance of the Frontier in American History." Turner was only thirty-two years old at the time, and not well known. Owen Wister, who was in Chicago to visit the Columbian Exposition at the time of Turner's presentation, did not attend the meeting. Only in retrospect was Turner's speech seen as a major event. Had Wister heard Turner, he would have been, as Darwin Payne describes it, "fascinated and pleased, especially noting the similarities of their ideas."[3] The notion that the frontier experience was essential in the shaping of a truly American character had a strong appeal to Wister, as it did to Turner. Turner proclaimed life on the edge between civilisation and wilderness a uniquely American experience and argued that the improvisations required for daily living on the frontier had created a unique national character.

 When Turner gave his speech the frontier no longer existed. The disappearance of the frontier, he says, "marks the closing of a great historic movement," because "[u]p to our own day American history has been in a large degree the history of the

---

[1] Owen Wister, *The Virginian: A Horseman of the Plains*, (1902; New York: Viking Penguin, 1988).

[2] Thomas McGuane, *Nobody's Angel* (1982; New York: Random House, 1994).

[3] Darwin Payne, *Owen Wister: Chronicler of the West, Gentleman of the East* (Dallas, TX: Southern Methodist U P, 1985), p. 139.

colonisation of the Great West."[4] The clearly nationalistic tone of the Frontier thesis was shared by many of Turner's contemporaries, among them Owen Wister and his friends Theodore Roosevelt and Frederic Remington. The Civil War and its aftermath, mass immigration, and the expansion of the United States by the colonisation of the West instigated their search for a national character and an epic to unite the Republic.

In the American consciousness the West had been both a place of the mind and a place of physical reality. It was a place to which one could escape and start a new life away from established society. In this West man could renew his bond with nature and purify himself. The West was, therefore, a place of hope and fulfillment. Turner's Frontier Thesis allowed for a revival of the mythic rhetoric of the West.

Wister wrote *The Virginian* after the closing of the frontier, but in his novel he went back to the period of the cattle frontier. He fused the image of the cowboy with the existing myth of regeneration. The protaganist, the Virginian, incorporated Wister's ideal American, an Easterner who was reborn in a virgin land, and a new prototype of the West, the cowboy, who lived on the frontier.

The West at the turn of the nineteenth century was accessible by train. Wister, Roosevelt, and Remington visited the West and admired the region for its splendid landscapes. Their admiration for the West was based on its physical reality. They expressed the desire to preserve part of the United States in its pristine state—a desire imbued with the longing for a new Eden.

The awe inspired by the beauty of the West, however, only extends to its geographical landscape and denies its social one. The Turner Thesis considers only the experience of white male settlers, and leaves out the experience of the Indian peoples, Hispanics, Chinese, and other ethnic groups populating the West, and it virtually ignored the role women played on the frontier. As Limerick notes, "the basic theme of Western American history has been the convergence of diverse people, encounters among people of wildly [sic] different backgrounds."[5] Turner did not account for the multi-ethnic character of the West, and neither did Wister. On the contrary, their celebration of the West, apart from being based on admiration for the West's physical beauty, was a rejection of an American East marked by industrialisation, immigration, urbanisation, reform movements, and a new and more prominent role for women. Instead of adapting a discourse that captured these Eastern developments, Wister's and Remington's cowboys, and Roosevelt's and Turner's noble frontier men reestablished white male supremacy in a mythic West. From this point of view, their interest in the West was an escape from modern America which began to take shape at the turn of the century.

The new role of women in society threatened the complete domination of social life by men. Men were forced to reconsider their roles and reinvent their identities.

---

[4] Frederick Jackson Turner, "The Significance of the American Frontier in American History," *Major Problems in the History of the American West*, ed. Clyde A. Milner II (Lexington. MA: Heath, 1989), p. 2.

[5] Patricia Nelson Limerick, "The Rendezvous Model of Western History," *Beyond the Mythic West*, gen. ed. Stewart L. Udall (Salt Lake City: Gibbs Smith, 1990), p. 37.

Instead of assimilating, Wister chose to escape in a celebration of manhood. *The Virginian* reinvents men's domination of society through a reestablishment of the dominant male. The novel set an example for thousands of movies and novels in which the celebration of manhood was constantly repeated and reinforced.

Wister dedicated the novel to Theodore Roosevelt, who in 1901 had become President of the United States. Roosevelt promoted a political symbolism in which the triumphant march of a superior white civilisation into the West played a leading role. Remington interpreted this West in his paintings, and Wister captured it in his fiction. Central to their work was the notion of the West as a place "where people rediscovered the most important values of life."[6] According to Wister, the moral values that had made possible the creation of the United States were decaying in the East, but were resuscitated in the truly American environment epitomised by the frontier.

The West in *The Virginian* is a picture rather than a milieu. It is a cowboy West without cows. Many critics have pointed to the absence of cattle in *The Virginian*. The Virginian never smells of cows or gets tired because of hard work. His problems have nothing to do with the hardships of the life of a cowboy, but are related to moral conflicts. Cawelti points out that "[t]he element that most clearly defines the Western is the symbolic landscape in which the story takes place and the influence this landscape has on the character and actions of the hero" (193). Wister's portrayal of Wyoming creates a mythic reality. Cawelti argues that "[d]espite the fact that [the novel] is permeated with stereotypical characters and unlikely situations" the reader is willing to go along with the story because its "fantasy world seems so complete and interesting in itself that it is still possible to enter into an effective escapist identification with the protagonist" (19).

Folsom even observes that Wister presents the West as a place that Easterners do not comprehend and that therefore has a "mythic dimension to them."[7] The contrast between the Eastern narrator and the Virginian emphasises the remoteness of the West, physically and mentally. Mogen notes: "To those outside of the West the region is one of vast indistinct contours with great landscapes of mountain and plain and lone heroic figures."[8] The fact that the construct of the West portrays the region as an indistinct place with stereotyped figures allows the reader to enter a mythic land, a land providing escape from the daily reality of the East.

Wister is interested in a transformation of Easterners and in the resurrection of the true American, who in his opinion is white. He does not construct an image of the West in which different peoples merge. Although the frontier will disappear and the geographical West will become civilised—and, according to Wister, corrupted like the East—the imagined West of Wister remains untouched. *The Virginian*, therefore,

---

[6] John C. Cawelti, *Adventure, Mystery, and Romance: Formula Stories as Art and Popular Culture* (Chicago: The University of Chicago Press, 1976), p. 218.

[7] James C. Folsom, *The American Western Novel* (New Haven: College and University Press, 1966), p. 107.

[8] David Mogen, "Owen Wister's Cowboy Heroes," *The Western: A Collection of Critical Essays*, ed. James K. Folsom (Englewood Cliffs, N.J.: Prentice-Hall, 1979), p. 203.

functions as a reminder of Wister's moral America and still provides a model for his ideal of spiritual renewal.

The myth of the frontier still stirs the popular imagination. The mythical image of the frontier is optimistic and nationalist, and it ignores the brutal conquest of the West or glorifies it. As a result politicians gladly evoke the frontier to stress their belief in America. John F. Kennedy made it a key word of the speech in which he accepted the presidential nomination at the Democratic convention in 1960. Ronald Reagan said in his second inaugural speech: "A settler pushes West and sings a song, and the song echoes out forever and fills the unknowing air. It is the American sound. It is hopeful, big-hearted, idealistic, daring, decent, and fair. That's our heritage, that's our song."[9]

Although the myth of the West as narrated by Turner and Wister persists, contemporary writers and historians attempt to change the discourse about the West. They try to come to terms with a demythologised West; they no longer evoke the rhetoric of the frontier, but strive to give meaning to a land *without* a frontier.

Thomas McGuane's *Nobody's Angel* describes a West in which the disparity between the heroic, mythic West and the dispirited reality of the West are cause for despair. This West has become, as McGuane puts it, "a wreck."[10] McGuane's first novels are set in the north woods of Michigan and in Key West, Florida. *Nobody's Angel* is the first of McGuane's novels to be set in the West. All three places are "extreme outposts of civilisation."[11] The novels' settings mirror their overall theme of depicting life at the fringe of society. McGuane's protagonists seek out the freedom of the frontier; they are attracted by the frontier myth promising a second chance in life. They follow in the footsteps of the Virginian, but, eventually, must admit the frontier no longer exists. The frontier myth becomes a harmful illusion. Henry Nash Smith notes,

> history cannot happen—that is, men cannot engage in purposive group behavior—without images which simultaneously express collective desires and impose coherence on the infinitely numerous and infinitely varied data of experience. These images are never, of course, exact reproductions of the physical and social environment. They cannot motivate and direct action unless they are drastic simplifications, yet if the impulse toward clarity of form is not controlled by some process of verification, symbols and myths can become dangerous by inciting behavior grossly inappropriate to the given historical situation.[12]

---

[9] *Public Papers of the Presidents of the United States: Ronald Reagan, 1985, Book 1* (Washington: United States Government Printing Office, 1988), p. 58.

[10] Quoted in Russell Martin, "Writers of the Purple Sage," *The New York Times Magazine*, 27 December 1981: 18.

[11] Jerome Klinkowitz, *The New American Novel of Manners: The Fiction of Richard Yates, Dan Wakefield, and Thomas McGuane* (Athens: The University of Georgia Press, 1986), p. 12.

[12] Henry Nash Smith, *Virgin Land: The American West as Symbol and Myth* (Cambridge: Harvard University Press, 1973), p. ix.

In *Nobody's Angel*, the protagonist, Patrick Fitzpatrick, explores the meaning of the frontier myth in today's West and finds that the masculine model of the cowboy is not applicable to contemporary romance.

Nobody's Angel is technically a third-person novel, but the voice is not the voice of a narrator. It is the voice of Patrick Fitzpatrick, observing himself from various angles and exploring different narrative styles, to find out which roles he is willing or able to play. Jon Wallace notes that Patrick "generally speaks as a narrator *about* himself, but sometimes he speaks in a narrative voice *as* himself."[13] By employing different styles Patrick changes his relation not only to himself but also to the Western myth. He changes from hero to anti-hero in an attempt to make sense of his life through language. He tries to come to terms with the discrepancy between the mythic and the geographical West, and questions the discursive construct of the West as it is presented in the mythical Western. Wallace argues that in discovering himself, Patrick "*is* just talking to hear himself talk, and the paragraph *is* supposed to be just sound —the sound of a voice in search of an appropriate tone. Or way of being. This is what *Nobody's Angel* is all about: the search for style, and therefore presence" (110).

Nobody's Angel creates a fragmented world in order to illustrate the West without the frontier; a West surfeited with styles. *The Virginian*, and every Western thereafter, defined the formalised narrative of the West. Patrick Fitzpatrick consciously dissects the elements of this narrative in order to define his emotional self. The style of the Western has become useless and restrictive for Patrick Fitzpatrick. He seeks to present his own contemporary drama by "sweeping out the old conventional notions of the West" (Klinkowitz 12).

Like the protaganist in *The Virginian*, Patrick tries to discover himself in relation to several other characters. The characters in *Nobody's Angel* are the same ones whose appearance or absence is essential to the formula Western as it is typified by *The Virginian*. Patrick gives substance to these personae because he is not able to cope with their one-dimensionality in the Western. Patrick longs for meaning because he needs to convince himself of his own existence. The Virginian proves in his actions in relation to the other characters in *The Virginian*, Molly, Trampas, and the Judge, that he is a true American. Patrick, however, finds out that he is unable to connect with his surroundings and people around him. His attempt to deconstruct the myth of the West makes him just another hero in it, changing the elements of the narrative to align them with the world he sees around him. He is unable to escape from its formula, he is caught up in the masculine world of the Western where he does not belong: "He wasn't a captain or a cowboy. He thought for a moment, literally thought, about what he had set out for; and he knew one thing: he was superfluous" (223).

Nobody's Angel is a novel of manners in which the characters define themselves by their dress, their drinks, and foremost by their discourse. Patrick Fitzpatrick's world is made up of voices and soundbites. Klinkowitz observes that McGuane describes "lifestyles that are determined by words and images, actions that are dictated

---

[13] Jon Wallace, *The Politics of Style: Language as Theme in the Fiction of Berger, McGuane, and McPherson* (Durango, Colorado: Hollowbrook, 1992), p. 111.

by what has been read and seen, patterns of behaviour in which life is edited and fictionalised" (i). In *The Virginian*, manners matter because they show how an American should live. In *Nobody's Angel*, manners are not the focus of attention, but elements of the narrative scrutinised for their compositional value. Klinkowitz points out that "the effect of this new interest in signs and systems is to focus attention on the page. The novel of *manners* now becomes the *novel* of manners, with both writerly and readerly self-consciousness for the forms involved" (8). For example, when Patrick and his girlfriend, Claire, go to a local disco the music tells the story of their ending love:

> They danced from cheating to trucks to lost love to faded love again, which seemed sadder than lost love, to the green grass of home, double beds, jobs you could shove, a ride to San Antone, yellow roses, the Other One, caring and trees. Claire put her arms around him and began to cry. She said, "Oh baby, do something." When the first, most ardent wave had passed over him, he thought, and not without fear or confusion but still shot through with ardor, This is it. (209)

Patrick fails to give the distinct form to his life that would convince him of his existence; as it is, he is unable to see himself apart from the broadcast myth of life and love in the West.

A rereading of *The Virginian* reveals that Wister carefully drafted an epic in which his ideas about a united white male America were formulated. His hero was meant to set an example for his fellow countrymen, who just like Wister himself were apprehensive about the future of the Republic. *The Virginian* takes the reader into a new country. *Nobody's Angel* forces the reader to compare that country with the West that is constructed by Patrick Fitzpatrick's voice and to make sense of the discrepancies between the two constructs. In *Nobody's Angel* the West is no longer a place where freedom and manhood can be found. McGuane's cowboy roams around the country with a saddle in the trunk of his car; the image of a self-reliant man on a horse in the "high lonesome" has made way for a substitute image reflecting the decline of the West. The protagonist, Patrick Fitzpatrick, fails to come to terms with his surroundings because he is chained to a myth in which he cannot exist. He wants to live in a world where not only white men but also women and Indians have a place. He cannot find the words to construct such a world, because he is caught in the formula of the Western. His return to Europe at the end of the novel shows that he is trapped in the escapist theme of the Western. In a reversal of a stock motif in American literature, he goes East instead of West. No longer able to live within the cowboy code and unable to find an alternative, he retreats into a man's world, the army, and a relationship with a woman who exists only in his mind. Because he has not found possibilities for self-fulfillment, he cannot answer the quintessential question the novel of development poses: what does it mean to be a man and how does one arrive at that point? Patrick makes clear that the impact of the West on the American consciousness has changed; his deconstruction of the Western creates a new Western, one that no longer provides an escape but keeps the protagonist chained to a language that makes no sense to him.

Patrick lives with the expectation of renewal, but discovers that there is no frontier available in the contemporary West. The implications of the closed frontier finally sink in, almost a century after the superintendent of the census announced that America's frontier era had come to an end. Patrick has to reinvent himself and face reality. The literature of the West, however, gives him no clues for a description of his personal experience. It is a literature made up of stale images and soundbites from popular Western novels, radio and film. McGuane criticises America by drawing attention to the escapist theme in literature. The loss of the frontier compels America to reinvent its Western literature. This literature will construct a new discourse and formula to describe the West. Wister did not want to do so and saddled literature with a harmful myth, because it was, in Henry Nash Smith's words, not "controlled by some process of verification and incited behavior grossly inappropriate for the given historical situation." It was harmful for women and coloured people, and, ironically, in the end also for white men as well. A comparative reading of the novels reveals that the new discourse will have to construct an image of the West that includes all of these people and is concerned with how to live best in a West without frontier.

THE SOUTHERN AND THE WESTERN
WRITING REGION AND NATION IN HOLLYWOOD CINEMA

James I. Deutsch, University of Leipzich

When it comes to celluloid regions, the one that invariably stands out is the American West: the only region in the U.S. to have an entire genre of film (known, of course, as the Western) devoted to its exposition. Similarly, when it comes to the topic of genre film—generally defined as "familiar, essentially one-dimensional characters acting out a predictable story pattern within a familiar setting" (Schatz 6)—the Western also stands out. Several scholarly books have catalogued the total number of Hollywood genres, ranging from six (Solomon) to eighteen (Gehring), but the Western is one of the few that has made its way onto every one of the lists. It is sometimes forgotten, however, that these film genres were not instantly established at the dawn of movie history roughly one hundred years ago. Rather, they emerged only several decades later in the 1910s and 1920s as the Hollywood studios began to standardise and stabilise their production, following the model of the industrial assembly line in order to realise greater profits.

In this article, I would like to discuss some of the similarities and differences between two incipient Hollywood genres during those early years, the Southern and the Western, each of them vying to symbolise the birth of the American nation as a whole through the fictional representation of one particular region. By the early 1940s, the undisputed winner of this competition was the Western film, which meant that writing the celluloid region of the West became on a symbolic level the writing of the nation. The Southern film, on the other hand, came to symbolise not the nation as a whole, but its dark and exotic, often dangerous, underside, a region that by its distinctive history and culture was marked as irredeemably separate from the rest of the country.

Much has already been written about the Western film, so its characteristics are familiar:

1) It is set circa 1865 to 1890, i.e., after the Civil War has ended, but before the closing of the frontier. According to Frederick Jackson Turner's study of the 1890 U.S. Census (made famous in his 1893 paper on "The Significance of the Frontier in American History"), 1890 was the first year in which the unsettled areas of the West no longer formed a continuous line of frontier, thereby marking "the closing of a great historic moment" in American history (Turner 1). It is very doubtful that many Hollywood producers had ever read Turner's thesis, much less the report by the Superintendent of the Census, but they instinctively understood the same idea.

2) It is set in the sparsely settled West: not in the cities, such as Denver, San Francisco, or Kansas City, but in the picturesque landscapes of broad expanses and

isolated communities, e.g., the red rocks of Monument Valley or the soaring snow-capped peaks of the Grand Tetons. Because the land is still only sparsely settled, Western film audiences can witness the very arrival of civilisation. Film after film provides the viewer with a continual reenactment and re-creation of the years of frontier settlement, taking place exactly "at the meeting point between savagery and civilisation" (Turner 3).

3) Frequently, the plot centres on a conflict between these two competing powers, civilisation (usually represented by the forces of social order, such as homesteaders and settlers, the community and its marshall, the cavalry, and the railroad) versus the forces of savagery (usually represented by the Indians or by renegade outlaws and desperadoes). This is an epic moment of confrontation in the history of American civilisation, when savagery and lawlessness are in decline, and when civilisation and social order are advancing.

4) The Western film hero is often a figure caught between these two forces of civilisation and savagery. He (and the masculine pronoun is used here deliberately) is usually identified with nature, free and spontaneous. He is not yet tied down by civilisation or domesticity (e.g., fences, houses, excessive laws and legalisms, culture, and refinement). Nor is he a savage; even if certain legalistic officials may regard the hero as an outlaw, it is usually because he has been unjustly accused. The Western hero does not wear eastern clothes that are mass-produced and store-bought. He does not work for the railroad; he is usually neither a homesteader nor a settler. Indeed, he seldom seems to make a living of any kind; despite his frequent status as a cowboy, he is rarely seen mending fences or punching cattle. Rather he is the quintessential self-made man, self-reliant, and independent. All he has is his horse, his gun, and one set of clothes. Nevertheless, he is not regarded as poor or exploited, living as he does, out in the purity of nature. When the settlers arrive, the hero either a) must move further and further west, further away from the homesteads and towns of civilisation, or b) he may choose to ally himself with the forces of social order against the forces of savagery and chaos, even though in so doing he helps to bring about the taming and eventual disappearance of the Wild West. This is the great paradox of the pioneer Western hero. When he makes the West safe for settlers, he must either surrender his independence and self-reliance, or move out to where the land is more free, where there are no fences, where the buffalo roam, where the deer and the antelope play, where seldom is heard a discouraging word, and the skies are not cloudy all day: home on the range, not home in the town.

The Southern film, as it first emerged around 1915, shares many characteristics with the Western film genre:

1) It has a precise setting in time, roughly 1852 to 1877, i.e., from the after-effects of the Compromise of 1850 (such as the publication of *Uncle Tom's Cabin* in 1852) through the years of the Civil War and up to the end of Reconstruction and the removal of federal troops from the South following the contested election of 1876.

2) It has an equally precise setting in space, namely the eleven states of the former Confederacy, and most frequently in the small towns and plantation regions of the South.

3) The plot centres on the same symbolic conflict as in the Western, i.e., between the two forces of civilisation and savagery. The difference is that in the Southern film the forces of civilisation are represented by the Southern aristocracy, i.e., the white planter class of educated ladies and gentlemen, and often also their loyal and trust-worthy house servants—what used to be known (in politically incorrect terms) as the faithful darky. The forces of savagery in the Southern are represented by a variety of individuals: blacks who are not faithful but who are uppity, usually portrayed as uneducated and coarse field hands; intrusive Northerners who lack the Southerner's manners and refinement, and who depending on the exact setting in time may be radical ante-bellum abolitionists whose rigid arrogance prevents them from properly understanding the ways of Southern civilisation, Union soldiers and renegades who do not care to understand the ways of the South, or radical post-bellum carpetbaggers whose narrow-minded vindictiveness prevents them also from properly understanding the ways of Southern civilisation.

4) The Southern film hero, like the Western film hero, helps to bring about the victory of civilisation over the forces of savagery. The difference is that Southern heroes are invariably members of the plantation aristocracy, and with the assistance of their faithful darkies, they are able to overcome the potentially destructive forces of uppity blacks and intrusive Northerners (abolitionists, soldiers, and carpetbaggers), in order to create a new society, one that is regionally Southern in its roots and past, but that is also newly national and quintessentially American in its future.

The best-known example of the Southern is D.W. Griffith's epic film, *The Birth of a Nation* (1915). So many of the genre's essential ingredients are present that the film can be considered a model, if not also a warehouse (in which all items are abun-dantly in stock), of the Southern film genre. The film's opening scenes establish the South as an idyllic and bucolic civilisation, with whites and blacks co-existing harmo-niously. Indeed, the blacks are so happy and also so childlike that they can't help but sing and dance for their strong but benevolent white masters. This ante-bellum Southern harmony, however, is soon to be disrupted by misguided radicals and abo-litionists from the intrusive North. Following defeat in the Civil War, the film's central protagonist, a Confederate veteran named Ben Cameron, returns to his shattered home-land, the small town of Piedmont now rendered dangerous and chaotic by the savagery of Northern carpetbaggers in league with uppity blacks. Aided by his loyal darkies (referred to as "Faithful Souls" in the film's intertitles), Cameron rallies the forces of order, represented here primarily by the riders of the Ku Klux Klan, wearing white robes with Christian crosses, to defend civilisation against the forces of savagery. So dangerous are the film's savages, most notably the rampaging hordes of African-American troops, that ex-Confederates have even joined together with ex-Yankees to fight side-by-side for civilisation (and the purity of white women) in a small log cabin. The film's final scene reaffirms this reconciliation of North and South, as Ben Cameron is joined in marriage to Elsie Stoneman, the daughter of a Radical Repub-lican. The two formerly antagonistic regions are thus reunited symbolically in the birth of a new nation, which the filmmaker enhances by superimposing on them the image of the Prince of Peace in the City of God. Based on Thomas Dixon's novel, Griffith's original film title was *The Clansman*, but acting on Dixon's suggestion after the film was first previewed in Los Angeles, the title was changed to represent Griffith's idealistic dream that Northerners and Southerners had put aside their sectional differences after the Civil War and had joined together to create a new nation. Writing the story of the region became for Griffith the writing of the nation.

The Birth of a Nation is certainly the best known, but it was just one of numerous Southerns produced at this time. A few months later in 1915, for example, came the film *Marse Covington*, which covers roughly the same period of time, starting just before the Civil War when Covington Halliday is given a Negro servant, Dan, who calls him Marse Covington. Covington serves in the war as a Confederate captain, and returns afterwards to his ruined homeland. The faithful darky Dan, however, refuses to take his freedom, and remains on the Halliday plantation to share in Covington's misfortunes, which include being cheated out of his property by unscrupulous Northerners, and reduced to standing in bread lines. By the end of the film, however, Covington unites with an honest Yankee named Walter Lewis, who reclaims the deed to the Halliday plantation, and marries Covington's daughter, thus once again symbolising the new union of North and South and the birth of a new nation.

A third example of the early Southern film is *Miss Dulcie from Dixie* (1919), in which the titular Dulcie Culpepper hopes to reconcile her father, the proud Confederate Colonel Culpepper, with her uncle John, who was disowned by the family when he married a Northern woman before the Civil War. The reuniting of North and South is in fact engineered by Dulcie's loyal mammy, the faithful darky who brings not only Uncle John back to the Culpepper plantation where he is reconciled with his brother, but also Uncle John's stepson, Orrin Castleton, who naturally becomes Miss Dulcie's husband, as per the usual resolution of the Southern film.

The writing of the Southern, as I've described the film genre, was calculated of course to appeal to both Northerners and Southerners, to illustrate the ways in which the writing of a new nation, the United States, was delivered out of the devastation wrought by the Civil War. The theme still had popular appeal as late as the mid-1930s, most notably in two Shirley Temple film vehicles, *The Littlest Rebel* (1935) and *The Little Colonel* (1935). In both cases, the precocious ringlet-haired moppet, with the help of the usual faithful darkies (played in both films by Bill "Bojangles" Robinson), brings together previously warring parties representing the North and the South.

Indeed, the Southern might have become a more enduring film genre, had the representation of the new nation not been more successfully rendered with the writing of another region, namely the West. The Western film genre had several advantages over the Southern:

1) The West for the most part had been ideologically neutral during the War Between the States, and therefore lacked the potentially divisive political implications of a Southern protagonist or a Southern setting.

2) The racial theme of the faithful darky, which was not necessarily inappropriate to the philosophy of Booker T. Washington's "Atlanta Compromise" of 1895, i.e., to "cast down your buckets where you are," and accommodate yourself to a racist society, was found to be much less appropriate following Washington's death in 1915,

and the subsequent ascendance of more assertive African-American leaders. Although many Westerns were in fact equally racist in their stereotypical depictions of various Indian tribes, it should be noted that Native Americans were much less politically assertive at the time, indeed were not even granted U.S. citizenship until 1924.

In any case, the most telling advantage of the Western film was that it could not only expropriate the Southern's reconciliation of North and South, but could also situate this new birth of a new nation in a region more ideologically and politically neutral—and thus with more box-office potential—namely, the American West.

Perhaps the most influential of the Westerns with this theme of North-South reconciliation is also the one with the most distinguished heritage: *The Virginian*, based on Owen Wister's novel of 1902, which has been adapted for film no less than four times: in 1914 (starring Dustin Farnum), 1923 (Kenneth Harlan), 1929 (Gary Cooper), and 1946 (Joel McCrea). The title character, of course, comes from the capital state of the former Confederacy, and still carries with him some of the South's sense of honour and nobility. And the match he makes from the North, Miss Molly Stark Wood, comes from Vermont, perhaps the most Yankee of states. Significantly, they are wed neither in the North nor the South, but in the New West, the "wild Cattle Land," where the "open sky [would] shine down on them," and where "their feet should tread" upon the "frontier soil" (Wister 276). Their union in marriage, held in the cattle-rustling territory of Wyoming, thus improves upon the reconciliation of North and South found in Southern films like *The Birth of a Nation* by symbolising in addition the advance of American civilisation into the formerly lawless West.

This formula of Northerners and Southerners together fighting the forces of savagery in order to further the advance of civilisation is utilised in numerous other Westerns, including two of the most famous examples of the film genre, *Stagecoach* (1939) and *Shane* (1953). In *Stagecoach*, the North is represented by Doc Boone, not only bearing a name meant to conjure up the American frontier tradition of Daniel Boone, but also bearing the experience of having fought with Union General Phil Sheridan during the Civil War. The South is represented by a mysterious ex-Confederate known simply as Hatfield, a notorious gambler in the West, but actually the son of Judge Greenfield, an aristocratic Virginian. Early in the film, Boone and Hatfield reveal their mutual antagonism by strongly disagreeing on Civil War terminology. When Boone refers to "the War of the Rebellion," the phrase that may have been politically correct in the North but was certainly not so in the South, Hatfield counters, "You mean the War for the Southern Confederacy, sir." But Boone firmly insists, "I mean nothing of the kind, sir." Later in the stagecoach, the two nearly come to blows when Hatfield complains that the smoke from Boone's cigar is disturbing Lucy Mallory, a fellow aristocratic Virginian. "A gentleman doesn't smoke in the presence of a lady," proclaims Hatfield self-righteously. In response, Boone suggests that Hatfield may not be much of a gentleman himself, judging from the bullet that the doctor removed three weeks ago from the back of one of Hatfield's gambling victims. These sectional rivalries are forgotten, however, when it comes to fighting off the savage menace of Geronimo and his Apache warriors. In a scene that calls to mind the finale of *The Birth of a Nation*, in which Union and Confederate veterans joined together to repel the savagery of marauding African-American troops, Boone and Hatfield are likewise united in battle. The similarity between the two films is further underscored by an identical use of close-ups to show that the white defenders are prepared to kill their virginal girls and women rather than let them fall into the hands of the lustful non-whites.

In *Shane* (1953), the homesteaders who have joined together to fight off the lawless and savage Rykers include a proud ex-Confederate known as Stonewall Jackson Torrey and his opposite number, a homesteader named Yank Potts, who early in the film delights in taunting Torrey by playing "Marching Through Georgia" (as in General Sherman's march) on his harmonica. But these regional rivalries are overcome by the birth of a new nation on the Western frontier, shown most vividly in the scene where all the homesteaders—men, women, and small children, Northerners, Southerners, and newly arrived immigrants, to judge from their foreign accents—are gathered together under an American flag waving in the breeze on the Fourth of July. In contrast to these homesteader families advancing the course of civilisation in the West, the lawless Rykers have no women and children among them. The film's subtext of triumphant American patriotism is further solidified by the name assigned to this villainous ranching family that wishes to expand its land holdings by running the homesteaders off the sparsely settled landscape. In Jack Schaefer's 1949 source novel, the ranchers' name is Fletcher, but in the film they are known as Ryker, a homonym for *Reicher*, as in Third Reicher. During World War II, filmmaker George Stevens had seen firsthand the horrors of the Nazis in places like Dachau, so it is no coincidence that he should label the villains in the only Western film he ever made as expansionist-minded Nazis seeking *Lebensraum*. A further association is that the Rykers/ Reichers terrorise the local homesteaders by hiring a cold-blooded gunman (played by Jack Palance) who is dressed in black and deliberately linked in the film with actual bolts of lightning, not unlike members of Adolf Hitler's *Schutzstaffel* or SS, which used lightning as one of its symbols. The only individual who can defeat this savage menace is the Western hero Shane, who temporarily gives up his independence—even to the point of taking off his gun and wearing store-bought clothes—in order to ally himself with the families of flag-waving homesteaders. But in the end, the Western hero must put his gun and his buckskin clothes back on, in order to wipe out the villains. Then he rides back into the mountains, into the purity of nature, from which he came.

But while the Western was forging ahead with this kind of one-hundred-percent Americanism, what had become of the Southern film genre?

Next to *The Birth of a Nation*, the most famous Southern is *Gone with the Wind* (1939), which adheres to the conventions and formulas of the genre most of the way through the film. In terms of time and place, for instance, *Gone with the Wind* follows the formula by beginning in the plantation South before the Civil War. The film's written prologue sets the stage:

> There was a land of Cavaliers and Cotton Fields called the Old South. ... Here in this pretty world Gallantry took its last bow. ... Here was the last ever to be seen of Knights and their ladies fair, of Master and of Slave. ... Look for it only in books for it is no more than a dream remembered. A Civilization gone with the wind.

As per the usual formula, however, the forces of savagery—in the form of the Civil War and Reconstruction—invade this idyll of civilisation. In terms of characters, *Gone with the Wind* contains not only the usual stock figures of aristocratic Southerners (e.g., the gallant cavaliers and their ladies fair) in opposition to intrusive Northerners (including carpetbaggers and marauding soldiers), but also the usual opposition of faithful darkies versus uppity blacks. Indeed, for playing the most quintessential of loyal Mammies, Hattie McDaniel was the first African-American to win an Academy Award. However, *Gone with the Wind* significantly chooses not to equate the writing of region with the writing of nation. There is no noticeable reunification of North and South in the end, not even a reconciliation of the film's two independent but also strikingly self-entered protagonists, Rhett Butler and Scarlett O'Hara, played by Clark Gable and Vivien Leigh. Scarlett's proclamation that "tomorrow is another day" bespeaks no greater cause than her own Southern pride and prejudice.

The many descendants of *Gone with the Wind* are therefore regionally Southern without also being symbolically national. Whereas many of the early Southerns had hoped to promote a new national unity, nearly all of the later Southerns harbor no such ambitions. Instead, they foster so much of a sectional and separatist identity that they seem to defy any association—much less any kind of reconciliation—with the North. Typical of this group are the films that bring Scarlett O'Hara's manipulative Southern belle up to date and therefore out of the 1852-1877 time period. The best-known examples include Lillian Hellman's *The Little Foxes* (1941), starring Bette Davis as the domineering Regina, but particularly also the film adaptations of Tennessee Williams' plays, such as *A Streetcar Named Desire* (1951), in which Vivien Leigh appears again, but now with a name of a different colour, Blanche instead of Scarlett, indicating the loss over time of her Southern ardour and fervour.

The other direction in which the Southern film developed, again reinforcing a separate regional identity, is that of the so-called Southern Gothic: a South filled with freaks and grotesques, sometimes harmless, but more often dangerous, if not also degenerate and depraved, posing a serious threat to the well-being of more mainstream (and not identifiably Southern) America. Because they make no claims regarding the advancement of American civilisation, the Southern Gothic films all but abandon the nineteenth-century settings of the earlier Southern films.

Perhaps the best example of this phenomenon is *Deliverance* (1972), based on a celebrated novel by James Dickey. Four men from the modern city (an unnamed Atlanta) take a weekend canoe trip down one of the South's last remaining wild rivers. But disaster—in the form of vicious and sadistic Appalachian mountaineers—intervenes, leaving one member of the party dead, another brutally sodomised, and the lives of the other two dramatically altered. Although the film follows Dickey's novel quite closely, it diverges from its source in several significant ways, all of which tend to exaggerate the Gothic depravity of the Southern region. Sympathetic remarks in the novel—such as one character's "there are songs in those hills that collectors have never put on tape" (40) and "There's lots of music, it's practically coming out of the trees. Everybody plays something: the guitar, the banjo, the autoharp, the spoons, the dulcimer ... These are good people" (45)—are noticeably absent from the film version.

Take also, for example, the famous scene in the film known as "dueling banjos," though strictly speaking it is one banjo against one guitar, the banjo played by a young mountaineer, the guitar by Drew, one of the city men, indeed the one who later is killed. In Dickey's novel, the banjo player has a name, Lonnie, and although his physical description is unflattering—he is depicted by the author as "an albino boy with pink eyes like a rabbit's," with one eye staring "off at a furious and complicated angle"—there is nothing sinister or dangerous about him (58). Indeed, in the novel, Drew and Lonnie join their instruments together, leaning close to each other, a pose that would seem to call cinematographically for a two-shot. But in the film version, the scene has no two-shots. Instead, the camera cuts back and forth between the two musicians, and is staged so that the boy—who is accorded no name in the film—is seated on the porch, remaining aloof and above Drew standing below him. When the song ends, Drew extends his hand in a friendly gesture of musical appreciation and camaraderie, but the boy rudely and ominously turns his head away from Drew, never even acknowledging the offer of Drew's handshake. Moreover, the filmmakers seem to have scoured the area for one of the strangest specimens of Southern mountaineers they could find. Although not quite a pink-eyed albino, the boy has a flat forehead, almond-shaped eyes, jug ears, and a moronic grin. When one of the city men mutters, "Talk about genetic deficiencies," the movie viewer hears an insult that is not in the novel, albeit one that is probably in the minds of many members of the movie audience. In these early scenes from the film version of *Deliverance*, the country folk are mostly bizarre curiosities, not yet life-threatening. It is not until the next day, on the river, that the four city men encounter the truly dangerous Southerners, two mountaineers with rifles, who for no apparent reason rape one of the four and are about to start on a second, when they are counter-attacked by the other two canoeists.

Even more dangerous are the Southerners in *Easy Rider* (1969), admittedly not a true Southern film, but one that by virtue of its enormous popularity had a significant influence on the genre. The Southerners portrayed in *Easy Rider* first beat to death the easy-going lawyer named George who is accompanying the two protagonists; and then in the film's final scene use a shotgun to kill Wyatt and Billy, who are peacefully riding their motorcycles in Louisiana along the Mississippi River. With names that reverberate out of Western history (Wyatt Earp and Billy the Kid) and wearing appropriate costumes (American red-white-and-blue for Wyatt and fringed buckskin for Billy), the two protagonists are clearly meant to symbolise the promise of America. Wyatt and Billy, in fact, literally ride out of the fabled West: leaving first California and then the red-rock landscapes of northern Arizona, in search of themselves and their country, before they are destroyed by the narrow-minded hatred of the Southern region. Numerous other examples could be cited from Hollywood films of the 1970s and 1980s, including *The Texas Chainsaw Massacre* (1974), *Macon County Line* (1974), *Return to Macon County* (1975), and the ironically titled *Southern Comfort* (1981), but the point is that the forces of savagery in the Southern film are no longer restricted to intrusive Northerners or uppity blacks who inhabit the South. Rather, the savagery resides in the people who are themselves the most Southern and seemingly representative of their region.

Admittedly, the Western film genre had also undergone significant change by the 1970s and 1980s. A cycle of revisionist Westerns, such as *Little Big Man* (1970), *The Ballad of Cable Hogue* (1970), *McCabe and Mrs. Miller* (1971), *Buffalo Bill and the Indians* (1976), and others had deliberately challenged the conventions of the genre. Sometimes the action was set after the presumed close of the frontier in 1890, and sometimes the lines between the forces of savagery and the forces of civilisation were deliberately blurred, so that traditional heroes like George Armstrong Custer were depicted as dangerous psychopaths, while traditional villains like the Cheyenne and Sioux were portrayed as considerably more civilised than their white counterparts. Although often acclaimed by critics and scholars, the revisionist Westerns generally failed at the box-office, in large part because they did not match the expectations of the mass audience. Having grown accustomed to what a generic Western should look like, American audiences were reluctant to accept the counter-generic revisions of the 1970s.

One consequence was that the Western film had practically vanished from the scene by the early 1980s. Rather than produce an anti-genre film that was likely to flop, Hollywood executives tended either to avoid the Western altogether, or to place it in another generic setting, such as the urban city or outer space, where its most important characteristics (e.g., clear-cut lines between savagery and civilisation) could continue in recognisable form. Thus, true fans of Westerns could be satisfied during these relatively dry years by urban thrillers like *Assault on Precinct Thirteen* (1976), essentially a remake of *Rio Bravo* (1959); *Hardcore* (1979), a remake of *The Searchers* (1956); or any of the films in the Dirty Harry series. Similar examples from the science-fiction genre include *Battle Beyond the Stars* (1980), a remake of *The Magnificent Seven* (1960), which in turn was a remake of *The Seven Samurai* (1954); *Outland* (1981), a remake of *High Noon* (1952); and even *Star Wars* (1977), which copies scenes from *The Searchers*. In the 1990s, the genuine Western film may be currently in remission, but its characteristics seem to survive in other forms.

To summarise, the initial attempts at writing the Southern region as the American nation, as exemplified by such early influential films as *The Birth of a Nation*, were subsequently abandoned by Hollywood filmmakers. Particularly after *Gone with the Wind*, an equally influential film that did not opt for postwar reconciliation with the North, filmmakers increasingly employed the South as an exotic and often dangerous setting, one that was marked by its distinctive history, culture, and inhabitants as irredeemably separate from the rest of the country. In seeking another American cultural region to inscribe metaphorically as the nation, Hollywood turned instead to the West, creating in the characters, settings, and narratives of the Western film genre a perpetual reenactment of civilisation's triumph and the subsequent "birth of a nation."

WORKS CITED

The Birth of a Nation. Dir. D.W. Griffith. Epoch Producing Corp., 1915.

Deliverance. Dir. John Boorman. Warner Bros. Pictures, 1972.

Dickey, James. *Deliverance*. Boston: Houghton Mifflin, 1970.

Easy Rider. Dir. Dennis Hopper. Columbia Pictures, 1969.

Gehring, Wes, ed. *Handbook of American Film Genres*. Westport: Greenwood, 1988.

Gone with the Wind. Dir. Victor Fleming. Metro-Goldwyn-Mayer, 1939.

Marse Covington. Dir. Edwin Carewe. Metro Pictures Corp., 1915.

Miss Dulcie from Dixie. Dir. Joseph Gleason. Vitagraph Co., 1919.

Schatz, Thomas. *Hollywood Genres: Formulas, Filmmaking, and the Studio System*. New York: Random, 1981.

Shane. Dir. George Stevens. Paramount Pictures, 1953.

Stagecoach. Dir. John Ford. United Artists, 1939.

Solomon, Stanley. *Beyond Formula: American Film Genres*. New York: Harcourt Brace Jovanovich, 1976.

Turner, Frederick Jackson. "The Significance of the Frontier in American History," In: *The Frontier in American History*. New York: Henry Holt, 1920, 1-38.

Wister, Owen. *The Virginian*. 1902. New York: NAL, 1979.

WRITING ALASKA, WRITING THE NATION
"NORTHERN EXPOSURE" AND THE QUEST FOR A NEW AMERICA

Esther Romeyn and Jack Kugelmass

Introduction

In the early 1980s, scholarship on nations and nationalism underwent a decisive transformation by the publication of three seminal works which, from different perspectives, introduced the concept of the nation as an imaginative construct. Eric Hobsbawm's and Terence Ranger's edited volume *The Invention of Tradition* (1983) analysed the ways in which governments and political movements, through rituals, folklore, or myths, "invent" traditions in order to imbue the novel political formation of the nation with a sense of historical continuity; Benedict Anderson, in his *Imagined Communities* (1983) stressed the centrality of the mass print media of the 19th century —the novel and the daily newspaper—in enabling the popular "imagining" of the nation as a community; while George Mosse's *Nationalism and Sexuality* (1985) placed 19th century bourgeois norms of sexual behavior and morality at the center of this collective envisioning.[1] Together, these works stimulated what might be called a paradigm shift in the study of nation by demonstrating the relevance of textual analysis to the study of nation which traditionally has been the province of history as well as the more empirically oriented disciplines of sociology and political science.

The models put forward by these studies have since been applied to different historical contexts (the "post-colonial" instead of the 19th century), nations (non-Western instead of European), social groups ("minority" groups instead of the middle classes), solidarities (regional instead of national), and sexualities (homosexual instead of heterosexual).[2] And although most scholarly work has concentrated on literary creations, the 20th century rise of new media such as radio, film, and televison, has stimulated some scholars to examine the construction of national identity in these media

---

[1] Eric Hobsbawm and Terence Ranger, eds., *The Invention of Tradition* (Cambridge: Cambridge University Press, 1983); Benedict Anderson, *Imagined Communities: Reflections on the Origins and Spread of Nationalism* (London: Verso, 1983); George L. Mosse, *Nationalism and Sexuality: Middle Class Morality and Sexual Norms in Modern Europe* (Madison: University of Wisconsin Press, 1985).

[2] See for instance Barbara Harlow, *Resistance Literature* (New York: Methuen, 1987); Fredric Jameson, "Third World Literature in the Era of Multinational Capital," *Social Text* 5 (Fall 1986): 65-88; David Cairns and Shawn Richards, *Writing Ireland: Colonialism, Nationalism and Culture* (Manchester: Manchester University Press, 1988); Homi Bhabha, ed., *Nation and Narration* (London and New York: Routledge, 1990).

as well.[3] In this essay, we turn our attention to American television, and in particular to the contemporary teledrama *Northern Exposure* which has been airing in weekly installments since the fall of 1990. Initially receiving mixed reviews, the show has come to be regarded as one of the most innovative in contemporary television. Moreover, as we will argue, the show's playful engagement with regional, ethnic and sexual "difference" constitutes a striking "reimagining" of the American nation.

"Kanukadee"

Joel Fleischman, an expatriate New York Jew, is at home with his object of hate/romance, Maggie O'Connel, an expatriate upper class Detroiter. Both are now living in Cicely, Alaska, she seeking the daring life of an Alaskan bush pilot, he for the duration of three years in servitude to the state which paid his medical school tuition. Maggie, who is fixing Joel's sink (she is also his landlady) asks him why there's still bread in the house given the fact that Passover is approaching. Joel corrects her pronounciation of "khumets," the Hebrew/Yiddish word for leavened foods, and asks, in his usual sarcastic voice, what she knows about Passover. Maggie explains that, since she intends to surprise him with a seder, she has been reading up on the subject. Joel is not too thrilled.

> Joel: "You know, it would be like me wanting to have an Easter egg Party for you or something."
> Maggie: "What's wrong with that?" ... "I don't get it. I'm just trying to give you part of your culture."

Irritated she stomps out of the house.

The next scene finds Joel fishing with Chris, the local philosopher and d.j. with a mail order divinity degree, and Ed, a Native American film buff. In the middle of a diatribe on women, Joel hooks a fish which we shortly learn is no fish at all, but the local Native American version of the Loch Ness monster, Kanukadee, or "Gunee," as those familiar with the monster call it. Encouraged by the townspeople, Joel ensconces himself for a fight with the beast, and when all have gone off to sleep and Joel is completely alone, his line begins to pull. Joel climbs into a boat and is drawn to the middle of the lake. Frightened, he offers to let Kanukadee go if it takes him back to shore. It doesn't respond. Suddenly, a human form dressed in a dark suit and white shirt drags itself up into the boat. The form turns out to be a familiar face from Queens, New York.

> Joel: "Rabbi Schulman! ... What are you doing here?"
> Rabbi: "Looking for guidance."

---

[3] For example Ella Shohat, *Israeli Cinema: East/West and the Politics of Representation* (Austin: University of Texas Press, 1987); George Lipsitz, "The Meaning of Memory: Family, Class, and Ethnicity in Early Network Television," in *Time Passages: Collective Memory and American Popular Culture* (Minneapolis: University of Minnesota Press, 1990).

Joel: "In East Loon Lake?"
Rabbi: "You go where the search takes you."

The rabbi explains that he has been dismissed by his congregation because of his opposition to the hire of a female cantor insisting on "gender free" services.

Joel: "What's it like down there?"
Rabbi: "It's dark, Joel. It's dark and it's deep."

When Joel prepares to cut the line and head back to the shore, the rabbi admonishes him not to. Explaining the centrality of fish imagery in Judeo-Christian tradition, he suggests that Joel might have hooked onto "something big." He then continues to ask Joel about his life. Joel talks about Maggie O'Connel.

Rabbi: "That's a nice Jewish name. Are you serious?"
Joel: "Well, we started out hating each other and now she wants to cook me Passover dinner."
Rabbi: "Really? That's very nice.... That's not nice?"
Joel: "To tell you the truth, it makes me very uncomfortable."

Suddenly, the boat starts rocking heavily, there is a deep roar, and the two men are thrown overboard by a huge wave. In the next scene, they find themselves in a tunnel, clearly walled by skeletal ribbings. Realising that they are now "inside the belly of the beast," Joel suggests that they avoid being "slimed to death" by stomach acids and recommends making a colon-rectal exit. As they walk the rabbi tries to make sense out of what has happened, and concludes that the key must lie in the story of Jonah.

Rabbi: "I mean, think about it for a minute. Why was Jonah swallowed by the whale in the first place? The Lord said: 'Go to Nineveh. Cry out against their wickedness!' Instead, Jonah hops a boat and goes to Tarshish. The Lord raises a ruckus, Jonah gets the heave ho. What's the meaning behind all of this?"
Joel: "Next time go to Nineveh."
Rabbi: "Responsibility. Jonah was trying to avoid his responsibility."

By this time the two men have reached what appears to be a New York City subway stile, and after Joel jumps the obstacle (he gives the rabbi his only token) they find themselves seated in a stalled graffiti-covered subway car. They each turn contemplative. The rabbi decides that it is his duty to stick with his congregation, and perhaps to be more sensitive in the future. Joel asks the rabbi if he should have Passover with Maggie.

Rabbi: "She might be your Nineveh, Joel. What you're running away from. And it may not be my field, but, maybe, by denying her Passover, you're denying her intimacy."

Joel then proposes a scenario in which he and Maggie would decide to get married and Maggie would convert, and inquires what the rabbi would think of that.

Rabbi: "The cutting edge of me says, go and be happy and follow wherever it leads you. My gut says, go and find a nice Jewish girl. We live in a very confusing age, Joel. Here we are, as close to the

Almighty as we're likely to get in this life and still there's no clarity. I mean, do you hear any voices? The Lord spoke to Moses directly. There was no allegory involved."

As the rabbi finishes speaking the train starts moving.

Joel awakens at the side of the lake, the focus of concern of the locals, who have found his boat smashed to pieces. In the final scene, the community is gathered at Joel's to read the Passover Haggadah, with Joel presiding. Marilyn, his Native American assistant, reads: "The *karpes* (bitter herbs) represents our gratitude to God for the bounty of the earth. We dip it in salt water to remind us of the tears our ancestors shed when we were slaves in the land of Egypt."

Magic realism

With *Northern Exposure*, its two creators, Joshua Brand and John Falsey, confirm an already well-established reputation for offbeat and innovative television programming which includes the previous hit series *St. Elsewhere*, and *I'll Fly Away*. The key to the team's trademark success in pursuing unconventional storylines on prime time television lies in its strategy of targeting a television audience of upper income, well-educated professionals. Highly coveted by advertisers because of its selective viewing habits and enough disposable income, this audience insures the Brand/Falsey productions the sponsorhip of elite corporations such as Saturn and American Express.[4]

While *Northern Exposure* stands out for its cinematic approach to photography and script, and its occasional use of such postmodern dramatic techniques as the creation of ontological confusion (in one episode key characters break the "fourth wall" by commenting that the storyline being pursued is not a viable one), its most innovative dimension lies not in dramatic technique or in technical experimentation, but in the selection of its subjects and in the conventions of its storytelling. And here the show's setting, small town Alaska, is the key to an artistic playfulness rarely seen on prime time television.

As the last frontier, Cicely, Alaska, attracts a medley of peculiar types. The show's central character, Joel Fleischman, is far more the anti-hero than the hero. A somewhat nerdy, upwardly mobile child of lower middle class origin, Joel is frequently portrayed as downright obnoxious. With his Republican sympathies, materialistic orientation and preoccupation with cutting edge science, he is also completely uncaptivated by the romance of the frontier. Opposite him plays the beautiful and combative Maggie O'Connel, who has sought refuge from her upper class Detroit background in the adventurous downscale life of an Alaskan bush pilot. The two make an unlikely

---

[4] Mark Schapiro, "How a Couple of Bookish Guys Made Good on TV," *New York Times* 12 Jan. 1992, Section 2: 29. Indeed, the key characters of *Northern Exposure* have established lucrative sidelines as actors in commercials for creditcards, cars and fast-food chains. Interestingly, in their endorsements of these various products they seem almost to be "in character."

couple and the ups and downs of their relationship provides an important subplot running through the show.

Chris, another central character whose good looks and folksy wisdom make him an ideal candidate for *raisonneur*, comes to Cicely with the stigmatised past of a former prison inmate. The show's other frontierspersons include Maurice Minifield, a stocky, bull-like ex-astronaut and local entrepreneur. His great plans for Cicely's future and his somewhat pretentious connoisseurship of art, collectibles, fine wines and food stand in contrast to his humbling experiences on the romantic front, including the loss of his woman to his former best friend, the town's tavern owner Holling Vincoeur. Unlike Maurice, Holling lacks all pretenses. His primary hobby is making paint-by-number oil paintings and he is absolutely unattuned to the subtleties of gourmet taste. A deracinated 63-years-old French Canadian, he is married to the 18-year-old, hip, teen lingo·user Shelly Tambo, proud citizen of Saskatchewan, Canada.

Cicely further counts among its residents Marilyn Whirlwind, Joel's Native American receptionist; Ed Chigliak, an aspiring Native American filmmaker and shaman in training; and Ruth Ann, a Harley-driving grandmother who, disappointed with the conventional lifestyles of her children, decided to start a new life for herself on the frontier and now runs the town's grocery store. Others make periodic appearances—a gay couple who own an upscale bed-and-breakfast; a Viet-vet gourmet chef whose wild physical appearance and rude manners make Joel Fleischman's New York sarcasm seem like upper crust civility; and various transients including a Tolstoy-spouting Muscovite, travelling salespeople and dentists, local native Americans, Bernard, the Afro- American "soul" brother of Chris, and a number of former suitors (or their ghosts) of Maggie O'Connell.

The show's location in Alaska provides an explanation for the unconventionality of its individual characters. Indeed, the region sets the stage for, and explains much of, the equally unconventional dramatic action. In one episode, the Aurora Borealis attracts plane loads of Japanese couples determined to conceive under auspicious conditions; in another, the Northern light, and the consequent absence of nightly darkness has everyone hopping with excessive physical and sexual energy. And on the last frontier, one expects such expressions of individualism as Chris's construction of a giant catapult with which he intends to toss a living cow (in the end he settles for a beat-up piano).

This commitment to sense of place makes the show unique in the cultural landscape of American television. Most sitcoms and teledramas (*Roseanne*, *Thirty-Something*, or *Murphy Brown*) are about relatively homogeneous communities, distinguished by class, profession, race or lifestyle, which exist "somewhere" in media space. While locations are mentioned, place generally remains invisible and has no bearing on the plot. But even shows which are place-specific such as *L.A. Law*, *St. Elsewhere*, *NYPD Blue* or *Dallas*, tend to conflate place with class and/or lifestyle —upscale yuppies, professionals, the post-60s 60s generation. In these shows, place typically has a veneer-like quality. *NYPD Blue*, for example, one of the few successful new shows of the '94 season, sandwiches each segment of its plot with stunning cinematic montages of New York City, but the stories themselves and the characters portrayed are devoid of any real connection to the city.

Place, of course, is a problematic element in commercial media. All television shows have to incorporate a certain amount of ethnographic detail in order to situate their plots and present believable motivations for central characters. But too much attention to regional or local peculiarities carries certain risks. Viewers may like the suggestion of being transported to some other place when they switch on a show, but they may not be willing to expend too much effort in getting familiar with the turf. Producers therefore are content to rely upon a restricted economy of signs to emplace plots and characters. In *Cheers* for example, Boston is evoked through one regional type—a Bostonian-speaking postman—an occasional reference to a local baseball or hockey team, and opening and closing shots of the bar within a Bostonesque streetscape. Beyond that the bar is meant to evoke any "place where everyone knows your name."

But *Northern Exposure* is different. It employs a remarkable intensity of emplacement that cements the storylines, and provides a basis for their lyrical and offbeat quality. Alaska itself, wild, pristine and bountiful, inspires the breaking of convention, and adds a magical dimension to everyone's life. In one episode for instance, Joel discovers a frozen mammoth. Realising that the animal may be one of the largest of its species ever found in North America he convinces a highly sceptical paleontologist in Anchorage to fly to Cicely to examine the specimen. When they reach the site, however, the mammoth seems to have vanished into thin air. Joel later discovers that an elderly resident named Walter, after awaiting the opportunity for years, has finally managed to free the carcass from its icy cage, and has butchered the beast in order to supplement his meat supply. When Joel expresses his outrage at this cavalier attitude towards scientific finds, Walter indicates that numerous other specimens have found their way into the local native diet! In Cicely, the extraordinary is perceived by all locals as utterly ordinary.

This same dimension legitimises the show's excursions into magic realism. Most strikingly employed in such episodes as "Kanukadee," the show continually transgresses the boundaries of the "real" by representing ghosts, apparitions, dreams, and local Indian spirits with the same veracity as flesh and blood characters.

Tour d'horizon

While this dedication to ethnographic localism provides *Northern Exposure* with a license for innovative cinematography and experimental storytelling, it also enables the show to explore cultural difference. As we argued before, most American sitcoms and television dramas focus on relatively homogeneous communities. This applies even to the few shows that do highlight difference—programmes intended for African-American or Asian-American audiences usually have a cast composed mostly of members of the same ethnic group. In *Northern Exposure,* however, difference is multiplied by the magnet of the frontier, so that many different kinds of people coexist within a specific, regional space.

The effect of this is to create a heteroglossia which is unparalelled in contemporary American television. Indeed, it seems to hark back to the urban, ethnic, working-class situation comedies of early network television, which sought to integrate an ethnically and socially diverse audience into the hegemonic fold of an white, consumerist, middle class culture.[5] But perhaps more significantly, the diversity which characterises *Northern Exposure* finds its closest model in an earlier medium of communication, the 19th-century novel. It is this connection that brings into perspective the show's particular strategy of constructing the nation.

As Timothy Brennan explains, the Russian literary scholar Mikhail Bakhtin coined the term "heteroglossia" in the context of his investigation into the nation-forming role of the novel. It referred to the fact that

> It was in the novel that, for the first time, previously foreign languages met each other on the same terrain, forming an unsettled mixture of ideas and styles, themselves representing previously distinct peoples now forced to create the rationale for a common life.[6]

The novel modelled itself on the genre of the epic. But while the epic, centered around a hero of mythical descent, functioned as a purely ritual means of "affirming a people," the novel transformed the epic's rhetoric of beginning and origins to serve the political purpose of "creating a people."[7] If in the epic the hero travels the extremities of the known world, the netherworld, and the Eternal World, in the novel, as Benedict Anderson has observed, the "movement of a solitary hero through a sociological landscape ... fuses the world inside the novel with the world outside."[8] The hero's "*tour d'horizon*" through a landscape which is clearly "bounded," "objectifies" differences of region, ethnicity, race, and class into a composite mixture of different languages, jargons and styles, and incorporates these differences within the bounded space of the novel, which represents the bounded space of the nation. It thus enables the "imagining" of the (composite) nation as a community, in spite of the heterogeneity of its population and its internal inequalities.[9]

Northern Exposure exhibits a similar metaphorical syllogism: Cicely is Alaska, and Alaska is America. Here, as in the novel, the picaresque hero, the New Yorker Joel—a modern-day (and therefore diminished) descendant of the epic hero—traverses a continent (the first episode of the show has him on the plane heading west from New York) and in his tour d'horizon links the otherwise separate boundaries of the nation.

---

[5] On this point, see George Lipsitz, "The Meaning of Memory: Family, Class and Ethnicity in Early Network Television," in *Time Passages: Collective Memory and American Popular Culture* (Minneapolis: University of Minnesota Press, 1990).

[6] Timothy Brennan, "The National Longing for Form," in Homi K. Bhabha, ed., *Nation and Narration* (London and New York: Routledge, 1990), p. 50.

[7] Ibidem.

[8] Benedict Anderson, quoted in Brennan, "The National Longing for Form," p.50.

[9] See Brennan, pp.50-51; Benedict Anderson, *Imagined Communities: Reflections on the Origin and Spread of Nationalism* (London: Verso, 1983), p.16.

Represented by the different characters of the show, east and west coast, north and south, frontier and civilisation, margin and center converge in Cicely. By thus creating a space of conjuncture for different kinds of people, classes and subcultures, the show sets the stage for its reimagining of the American nation.

Perhaps, there is nothing surprising in this parody of the 19th-century novel: television, a predominantly "writerly" medium, has overtaken the print media as a primary means of communicating information, and increasingly has shown an ability to create imaginary worlds every bit as vibrant as those found in older modes of communication.[10] But *Northern Exposure*'s parody of the politics of the genre at first seems somewhat anachronistic. In the post-Vietnam Empire Blues, national narratives have lost much of their credibility. Liberal movements in the country, rejecting the "totalising" perspective of earlier, consensus-oriented narratives of American national identity, have espoused "multiculturalism" in an attempt to do justice to the diversity of the American nation. This tendency is reflected not only in the reform of school- and college curricula, and in particular in the teaching of American history and literature, but American authors increasingly identify themselves (or are identified by critics) in terms of the "multicultural" categories of ethnicity, race, gender and region, and rather than constructing the nation, are concerned with the writing of separate ethnic regions (or they write the nation as ethnic regions). The epic "national" hero has been transformed into the "ethnic" hero of Philip Roth, Toni Morrison or Gerald Vizenor. Moreover, television networks, following the directives of "niche-marketing," increasingly divide their audiences in terms of gender, class, race, or age, in effect exhibiting a multiculturalism inspired not by political correctness but by market imperatives.

Postmodern, Post Empire U.S.A., then, is experiencing a crisis of identity that finds little synthetic formulation in contemporary literary or media culture. But if what literary critic Homi Bhabha has called the "pedagogical" discourse of the nation, that discourse which formulates sacred origins, tradition and descent,[11] has proven to be too static to respond to current challenges to its authority, and to re-form itself according to contemporary needs, television is potentially well suited to fill that void. The repetitious and ad hoc nature of television—conveying what George Lipsitz describes as "a sense of living in an infinitely renewable present"[12]—leaves it potentially very well prepared to function as the second mode of discursive address through which Homi Bhabha sees the nation being written: the "performative" discourse of the "people." This discourse functions as a "daily plebiscite," a repetitive act of voluntary consent by the people who form the nation's body politic. In its improvised nature, this "performative" mode of address is sufficiently adaptable to survey what happens at the

---

[10] For an interesting discussion of television's increasing dominance over film as a medium of serious social and artistic expression, see Bernard Weinraub, "In Sheer Quality, TV Is Elbowing Hollywood Aside," *New York Times*, 14 February 1995, B1-2.

[11] Homi K. Bhabha, "DissemiNation: Time, Narrative, and the Margins of the Modern Nation," in Homi K. Bhabha, ed., *Nation and Narration* (London and New York: Routledge, 1990), p. 305.

[12] George Lipsitz, "The Meaning of Memory," p. 41.

margins of the nation, and to contain emergent threats of difference, which cannot be instantaneously integrated into the pedagogical national discourse, within its narrative bounds.[13]

It is this exploratory yet containing discourse of the nation that the writers of *Northern Exposure* set out to create. In the words of Joshua Brand: "We view Alaska as a state of mind, a place our imagination needs to have exist."[14] And it is no coincidence that they create this place for a predominantly white, middle class, educated and upwardly mobile audience, a segment of the population that has heavily invested in the idea of the nation as cultural smorgasbord.

Wholesome provincialism

What, then, is the discursive strategy of *Northern Exposure*? How does it write the American nation? As we have already suggested, the show attempts to represent its *tour d'horizon* of the American nation from an ethnographic, multi-cultural perspective. This multi-culturalism, however, is not separatist but dialogic in orientation: in Cicely, different cultural perspectives interpellate each other. In a tribute to local Indians, Thanksgiving is also the Day of the Dead, which natives celebrate by throwing ripe tomatoes at non-natives, most of whom learn to take the abuse in good spirit. Only Joel Fleischman has trouble with it, arguing that "he's not white, but Jewish." In another episode Fleischman learns that Indian ways of expressing displeasure are often through silence, and the silence of his assistant Marilyn forces him to accept the gift of one of his patients—adoption into a local tribe. Even if Joel protests that he "already belongs to a tribe," that he's Jewish and that "Jews are a very tribal people," he has to learn that his allegiance to his ethnicity does not exclude the exploration of other identities.

The acceptance of difference is an underlying ethic of the show, and this tolerance implies an acceptance of the difference within oneself. Joel must accept Maggie O'Connel's offer to make him a Passover seder; in another episode, Joel must accept the local community as the appropriate one to form the ritual quorum for reciting the kaddish—the Jewish prayer for the dead; Maurice, as conservative as they come—a man undoubtedly inspired by the manly heroics of John Wayne—must make his peace with the local gay couple and attend their wedding; Holling and Shelly have their own squabbles over cultural difference when Shelly becomes an ardent Canadian patriot after she considers the benefits of the Canadian health-care system for her newborn baby, and discovers that Holling is no longer Canadian and scarcely feels much connection to his native Quebec—he can't even remember the province's motto "*Je me souviens.*" When Shelly leaves with the baby to attend a winter fest in British Columbia, Holling heads after her by snowmobile, and drives onto the festival grounds singing a Canadianised version of "This Land Is Your Land" as a love song to Shelly.

---

[13] Bhabha, pp.293-297.
[14] Matt Roush, "'Exposure' Casts an Offbeat Comic Spell," USA Today, Monday, 8 April 1991, 3D.

Little wonder that one reviewer described *Northern Exposure* as an "Alice-in-Wonderland flight of imagination."[15]

In the words of one of its producers, *Northern Exposure* conjures up "a 'non-judgmental universe' of unconventional characters in a clash of cultures."[16] It is through the dialogical interpellation of cultural identities that the residents of Cicely arrive at a mutual comprehensibility[17] which establishes the "common ground" without which the community cannot exist. But what does this common ground ultimately stand for? Cicely represents a universe where, even as the residents espouse their separate identities, cultural boundaries are permeable.

On a conceptual level, this particular interpretation of the prescription *e pluribus unum*, is worked out most explicitly in the intersection of different folklores, particularly Jewish and Native American.[18] Ever since the Romantic era, folklore has been a well-tested medium for delineating a "Volk" and distinguishing the genus of one group from that of another. But in Cicely folklore is neither exclusive nor exclusionary. In one episode, for instance, Joel hears his assistant Marilyn use a word that sounds like the Yiddish word *shmeykhl*, or smile. Astounded he tries to discover the link between his own "native" culture and the people among whom he now lives, and discovers that a Jewish trader had spent time among the Indians a century ago and had made his way into their verbal lore. Leaving it ambiguous whether Joel has actually discovered or simply imagined this link, the show's writers are quick to pull a Borscht Belt gag when a Native American chef at Holling's bar mentions to Joel that he once heard Buddy Hackett on the Carson show talking about altekakers (in Yiddish literally meaning "old crapper" and figuratively standing for "decrepit old men") and that altekoke is a Tlingit term for "revered one"!

But nowhere is the mutual interpellation of different folklores more poetic than in the "Kanukadee" episode. This complex magic realist tale reveals the show's particular take on multiculturalism. Joel, the somewhat deracinated Jew aspiring to yuppiedom, must travel thousands of miles away from his ethnic community in order to touch base with the mythic structures of his own people. (His rabbi follows a similar itinerary!) And he does so while simultaneously experiencing those of a Native American culture. On the frontier the immigrant becomes native, becomes American, but in the new America becoming American tolerates, even promotes ethnicity, albeit without ghettoisation.

---

[15] Schapiro, p. 29.

[16] Ibidem.

[17] See Brennan, p. 49.

[18] Folklore has been a crucial ingredient in the "invention" of national traditions ever since the Romantic Era conceived folk tales and customs as the repository of the essence of a "people." In appropriating the folklore traditions of different ethnic groups, *Northern Exposure* borrows the same strategy, this time to reimagine an America of "harmoniously coexisting and overlapping ethnic groups." Werner Sollors, *Beyond Ethnicity, Consent and Descent in American Culture* (New York: Oxford University Press, 1986) p. 194.

In this sense, Cicely, Alaska, provides the staging ground for what Werner Sollors terms the "ethics of wholesome provincialism."[19] It stands as a metaphor for a nation which steers a middle course between the excesses of ethnocentrism and deracination, in which mutual cultural intelligibility is the proper alternative to ethnic separatism on the one hand, and cultural homogeneity on the other.[20] This "wholesome provincialism" is redemptive on more than one level. Stressing "vision" over status or money, it is "conceived as a way to realise true individuality."[21] Joel, the healer, needs to be cured not only of a stodgy tribalism, but also of his materialism, and has to accept that being a town doctor in Alaska is ethically superior to living the good life as an Upper East Side doctor catering to the wealthy. But Joel is not the only one redeemed in this show. By allowing his fellow townspeople to participate in his culture he provides others with a mythic framework that has served his own people well over several millennia. The Native American Marilyn Whirlwind, for instance, can experience the redemptive thrust of the seder.

The commingling of mythologies and folklore, then, creates a vast pool of cultural resources through which old wounds and divisions within the nation, too, are healed. But in this vision of a "unified structure"[22] of the nation, a structure that is redemptive and harmonious, there is no place for ethnic conflict. And as Brand and Falsey admit, their interest is in "exploring the different cultures rather than focusing on the clashes."[23] In its exploration of the relationship between Native Americans, Jews, and various "whites" in an Alaskan frontier community, the show consciously circumvents what is arguably the most explosive and divisive issue in American national culture today, the issue of race and ethnic conflict. And this is why the show could not possibly have been situated in a cosmopolitan, multicultural, urban setting such as New York City. In a replay of the Frontier Thesis, *Northern Exposure* finds the cauldron of American nationhood far away from the decay of civilisation.[24] Only on the Alaskan frontier can the show legitimately portray its only Afro- American not as part of the "hood," but as as much of an individual as anyone else, and, more significantly, as the straight, even nerdy, Republican "soul" brother of Chris, which makes him already

---

[19] Sollors goes on to describe this as an idealised diversity which defines a good ethnic attitude as a "new," an acquired, or an achieved identity, located between the ancient narrowness of a hierarchical old-world orientation (embodied by the nationalist spirit ...) and the dangers of homogenisation by total assimilation ...; or ... between an identity based exclusively on divisive descent and one primarily founded on bland universalist consent." (Sollors, pp. 190-191).

[20] Sollors, p. 190.

[21] Sollors, p. 194.

[22] Sollors, p. 193.

[23] Schapiro, p. 34.

[24] Indeed, what is particularly striking in shows of comparable caliber, such as *NYPD Blue*, a police series set in New York, or *L.A. Law*, about a law firm in Los Angeles, is that if these shows exhibit a metaphorical syllogism similar to that of *Northern Exposure*, and are as much about the nation as they are about a particular city, the nation they write is hardly a reimagining of America. The worlds they portray are corrupt and crime ridden, with the possibility of redemption only present to the degree that people stay out of trouble.

half white. Moreover, the show also subverts white/Native American conflict: acts of Native protest are represented as purely symbolic and ludic.

In shying away from any overtly political issues, then, *Northern Exposure* reveals the limitations of its redemptive vision, a vision which is, after all, the dreamscape of an audience of young, urban professionals.

A minor language

Until now we have read *Northern Exposure* as an American text. However, the show contains a subversive Jewish subtext as well. Not only is the lead character Jewish and do various episodes explore issues that are of particular concern to Jews, they do so from a decidedly Jewish perspective. This becomes particularly clear in an episode which aired early in the 1994/95 season and in which, in response to the apparent popularity of the Kanukadee episode, Rabbi Schulman makes a comeback. Timed to coincide with the Jewish New Year, the show takes as its subject the theme of Yom Kippur—the concepts of repentance and the casting off of sins.

In the New Year episode three storylines are intertwined. The first centers on Maurice's efforts to woo a visiting English Lady by arranging a traditional English fox hunt, complete with imported fox, in her honor. Unfortunately for Maurice, the fox escapes and finds refuge with Ruth-Ann, who gives it sanctuary. In the second story, Holling is trying to cope with his guilt feelings for not having been a good father for a wayward grown-up daughter whose existence he had only discovered recently, and whom he has invited to Cicely in order "to make amends somehow and start over again." The daughter, however, cashes in the plane ticket he has sent her, leaving Holling dejectedly musing to Ed that "I've created a hole in the world that I cannot repair."

In the third story, Joel is preparing for the upcoming Yom Kippur fast by gorging himself at Holling's Bar, while his lunch companion, Ed, watches curiously. When Ed asks for the meaning of the holy day, Joel explains the orginal custom of placing the sins of the community onto a goat that is then sent into the desert. The story makes a strong impression on Ed, who, as a shaman in training, is eager to broaden his knowledge of healing practices. To him, it suggests a way to help both Holling and Maurice. In the course of the episode, Ed proposes to Holling that, as shaman, he would like to take on the role of scapegoat/fox, in order to enable Maurice to proceed with his hunt, and absolve Holling from the sin of having abandoned his daughter.

Meanwhile, the official healer Joel is (as usual) extremely rude towards a number of his fellow townspeople. He gets into a row with Maggie who berates him for having fired his assistant Marilyn for taking a few days off without adequate prior notice. When Maggie stomps off, we see the mouth on an adjacent totem pole move, and hear it sigh "Oy, Joel" in the voice of Rabbi Schulman. In a subsequent scene, Schulman makes his physical appearance (in his underwear but wearing a Pharisee hat), while Joel is still in bed. Holding a pile of video casettes, the rabbi summons Joel to the television in the living room and explains that he represents "the spirit of Yom Kippur past." He proceeds to show scenes from the past year (in fact from past episodes) in which Joel's rudeness stands out, and suggests that Joel may not have been sufficiently repentant for his transgressions.

Next, the rabbi appears dressed in a white skull cap and a *talis*, or prayer shawl. He announces that he's now the spirit of Yom Kippur present, and while explaining that repentance is not like "washing your hands," takes Joel to visit scenes that represent the consequences of his inconsiderate actions of that same day. Finally Rabbi Schulman reappears dressed in black and shows Joel his business card "Schulman Brothers Mortuary Inc. Services, Cremations, Chapel. *Se Habla Espanol*" (a comical nod to multiculturalism?). As the spirit of Yom Kippur to come, the rabbi shows Joel how little his future departure from Cicely will be mourned by the local residents. Joel then starts pleading to change his fate.

The rabbi responds by blowing a shofar and ahead in the distance the gates of prayer (a reference to the main Yom Kippur prayer) begin to close. Joel runs frantically, begging for mercy and swearing that he will change, but the gates shut just before he reaches them. He awakes screaming and hearing the shofar now tranformed into the bugle sound of the hunt that is taking place in the woods outside his cabin. Finding out from Ed, who comes to his window panting from running (he's playing the fox/scapegoat), that Yom Kippur is not yet past, Joel hastens to make amends with the townspeople.

In the final scene, Joel sits alone on a hill overlooking a pristine landscape. As the sun sets, and he is about to break his fast, the voice of Rabbi Schulman intones the final Yom Kippur prayer, while a clarinet plays a Jewish melody in the background.

On one level, the meditation on the meaning of repentance and the nature of "healing" that constitutes the theme of this episode, seems merely to provide an opportunity for the series' by now familiar strategy of creating a common ground through the mutual interpellation of different folklores and belief systems. But what emerges with particular poignancy in this episode, is how deeply Jewish this common ground is. By parodying Dickens' *A Christmas Carol*, the Yom Kippur story consciously transforms that most cherished example of popular Christian storytelling into a Jewish tale. But Jewish mythology also provides the healing structure for Ed. And while the proclivity towards syncretism the show attributes to Native Americans is designed to suggest a "healthy" ethnicity, it is Jewish mythology that provides the ultimate framework for redemption.

It is this subtext that positions the show as a "minor literature," which Gilles Deleuze and Félix Guattari define as that literature which a minority constructs within a major language.[25] By inflecting the dominant language and culture from within, a minor literature effects a "dismantling or demolition of forms and categories that determine the 'great literature' ..."[26] and enables a "reterritorialization," a reinscription of a formerly marginalised position into the center of a culture. *Northern*

---

[25] Gilles Deleuze and Félix Guattari, *Kafka: Toward a Minor Literature* (Minneapolis: University of Minnesota Press, 1986) p. 16.

[26] Deleuze and Guattari, p. xix.

Exposure does something very similar. Indeed, the implications of the show's minority perspective become abundantly clear during the 1994/95 season, in an episode which takes the strategy of "deterritorialisation" and "reterritorialisation" to its logical extreme. Confronted by the need to find a plausible termination of Joel's role in the show (Rob Morrow, the actor who plays Joel, decided to withdraw in order to pursue a movie career), the writers ignore what would have been the most predictable scenario: that of Joel settling back into his comfortable yuppie life style in New York, with Maggie at his side. Instead, the love-hate relationship between the two, which in previous episodes had finally been consummated and had even led to a projected marriage, blows up and leads to a mutual recognition of their fundamental incompatibility, in this case highlighted by a satirical reference to outgroup stereotypes (Joel decides that he cannot live with a woman who sleeps next to a loaded gun, especially when that gun inexplicably starts going off by itself, while for Maggie Joel's squeamishness becomes the breaking point).

After having toyed with the possibility of inter-faith relationships and inter-marriage for the entire duration of the show (Joel's conversation with Rabbi Schulman in the Kanukadee episode being the most philosophical discussion of the dilemmas involved), the Brand/Falsey team opts out of a commonplace story of mutual accom-modation with its implication of Jewish assimilation. By doing so, the writers suggest that there are limits to the degree of "intermingling" of cultures, after all. These limits had already been hinted at, most notably in an episode in which Joel tries out having a Christmas tree, realises that the ritual has no meaning for him, and drags the tree to Maggie's lawn where he installs it as a surprise gift to her.

In taking this non-assimilationist perspective, *Northern Exposure* stands in stark contrast to other television dramas which feature Jewish main characters. The Christmas episodes of "Thirtysomething," for instance, resolve an initial conflict between Jewish and Christian traditions in the inter-faith household of Michael and Hope into a situation of coexistance and mutual enrichment. Moreover, *Northern Exposure*'s refusal to see Christian tradition as the center of American culture is underlined by the fact that in Cicely, the community celebrates Christmas not by staging a Christian nativity play, but by re-enacting the Native American origin myth of the birth of the Raven. The center that *Northern Exposure* posits as the grounding structure of its reconstructed American nation, then, is formed by a mythical kinship between two groups of "Others" in American culture: Jews and Native Americans.[27] This kinship not only exists in the friendship between the medical doctor Joel and the healer Ed, who are virtual doubles of each other. It is made even more explicit in episodes such as "Kanukadee" and "Yom Kippur" and in such events as Joel's adoption into a local tribe and his discovery of the use of Yiddish terms by his Native assistant. Indeed, this latter episode points to a Jewish presence in the area of Cicely long before his own arrival or that of his fellow non-native settlers. It is in episodes

---

[27] It is significant that in this scenario Native Americans take the place of Afro-Americans, the traditional allies of the Jewish leftwing/liberal movement. This change of alliances might be read as a commentary on the current troubled state of AfroAmerican/Jewish political relations.

such as this that the show transforms the frontier myth, the primary foundational myth of America, from a tale without Jews (but with "vanishing Indians") into a tale in which Jews are coeval with Natives. This re-centering is carried to its logical extreme when Joel, after the fiasco of his relationship with Maggie, heads upstream, into the Alaskan wilds, to become a trapper. Relocated in a Native village, Joel loses his neurotic, obnoxious, and self-absorbed character traits, becomes profoundly spiritual and learns the real meaning of healing, based on holistic medicine, from the surrounding Native population. In a subsequent episode, Joel invites the glamorous Los Angeles doctor whom Maurice has chosen as Joel's successor to a game of golf "up river," confronts him with a golf course consisting of river beds and tundra grass, and teaches him the native way of playing by concentrating on the spirit of the golf ball. Joel then disappears inexplicably into the night, leaving behind the frightened Dr. Capra, who must now, because of Joel's prank, face his initiation into Alaskan manhood: an unprotected night in the Alaskan wilderness. Joel, the comic Jew, has become a Native trickster. At the conclusion of his Bildung, Joel comes to embody the guiding ethic of the show: the intermingling of cultures.[28]

Epilogue

It is only after he has thus been transformed that Joel is able to find his way back to his place of origin. This happens in the final episode in which Joel appears—"The Mythic City." In this epic tale, which closes the circle of Joel's transformation, Joel is shown to have attained the wisdom clearly lacking in his old self. In doing so, the show makes clear that Joel's sojourn in Alaska was less an accident of fate than a necessary part of his evolution.

In "The Mythic City" Joel discovers a map drawn up by a 19th century French explorer, and convinces Maggie to accompany him deep into the Alaskan wilderness to trace the route to "the jeweled city of the north." Submitting completely to the lure of Alaska, he becomes the willing, rather than the reluctant epic hero (Maggie is the skeptic). On the journey, Joel passes three tests: he "slays" (or in this case disarms) a "dragon" in the guise of a samurai whose name translates as dragon (the man is actually a refugee from the Tokyo real estate bust); he frees himself from the spell of a "siren" (actually a wilderness health spa); and he solves a riddle posed by a troll-like guardian of a bridge who is none other than Cicely's feisty gourmet chef (currently involved in some kind of CIA covert operation). With the help of Maggie he finally cracks the map's code and discovers the location of the "jeweled city." Trudging

---

[28] One could argue that Joel, by forcing Dr. Capra to confront the "spirit" of Alaska, and guiding him thereby in a ritual of intiation and transformation, assumes the character of Kanukadee, or Jonah, itself. According to Mircea Eliade, the meaning of being swallowed by a fish has considerable spiritual significance as a death and rebirth as part of a search for spiritual immortality. This has particular significance for shamans and related healers and is sometimes considered a part of rites of initiation. Mircea Eliade, *Myths, Dreams, and Mysteries: The Encounter Between Contemporary Faiths and Archaic Realities* (New York: Harper Torchbooks, 1975) esp. pp. 218-228.

through the snow, they reach the spot, peer through an opening in the woods and discern very faintly at first, then with increasing clarity, Manhattan's glimmering skyline. When Joel starts walking toward it, Maggie decides not to join him. The "Jew-eled" City is Joel's. She belongs in Alaska. The hero has to complete his journey alone.

In the final scene Maggie receives a postcard of the Manhattan skyline. On the back Joel writes, "New York is a state of mind." The New York Joel returns to is no longer the site to act out his crass materialism. Nor is it the site of vice, crime and decay—its typical representation in television and in American culture generally. Instead he sees it through Alaskan eyes, as marvelous and magical, a City on a Hill. In *Northern Exposure* the frontier has done its redemptive work for Joel, New York and for America.

CONTRIBUTORS

Hans Bertens is Professor and Director of American Studies at the University of Utrecht, the Netherlands. He has written extensively on the subjects of postwar fiction, popular literature, mass culture, and postmodern theory. His most recent book is *The Idea of the Postmodern: A History* (London: Routledge, 1995).

Ineke Bockting teaches "Southern Culture" and "Southern Literature" at the Universities of Amsterdam, the Netherlands, and Orléans, France. She has published widely on various aspects of the culture and literature of the American South. Her book *Character and Personality in the Novels of William Faulkner: A Study in Psychostylistics*, recently (1995) appeared with the University Press of America. Her next book will be on suicide in the American South, as "an extreme form of the taboo on (self)-criticism."

Christine Bold is Professor of English at the University of Guelph, Ontario, Canada.

Theo D'haen is Professor of English and American Literature at Leyden University, Leiden, the Netherlands. He has published widely on modern literature in European languages, and specifically on postmodern and postcolonial subjects.

Doeko Bosscher is Professor of Contemporary History at the University of Groningen, the Netherlands. His teaching and research focus on Dutch and American history. He was a Fulbright "Scholar in residence" at Central Michigan University, Mount Pleasant, Michigan, in 1983-84 and taught again at CMU in 1994.

Peter Carafiol, Professor of English and American Literature at Portland State University, Portland, Oregon, USA, has written extensively on issues of historical influence and of American national identity, especially as it has shaped the academic study of American literature and culture. His most recent book, *The American Ideal: Literary History as a Worldly Activity* (Oxford: Oxford University Press, 1991), written with the support of a National Endowment for the Humanities Fellowship, argues that the field of American Literary Scholarship continues to depend on its founding idealist assumptions long after they have lost their force and that the idea of an American national literary coherence should be abandoned. During the past year, with the support of a John Simon Guggenheim Memorial Foundation Fellowship, he has been writing *UnAmerican Literature: Ethnicity, Ideology, and History*, a neo-pragmatist approach to reconceiving literary and cultural studies.

James Deutsch is an Adjunct Professor of American Civilization at George Washington University and a Research Consultant for the Festival of American Folklife at the Smithsonian Institution. His research interests include American popular and folk culture, with special emphasis on motion pictures and contemporary U.S.

history. From 1992 to 1994 he served as Fulbright Lecturer in American Studies at the Universities of Hannover and Leipzig in Germany. He has also worked for the National Park Service, U.S. Forest Service, National Council on the Aging, National Endowment for the Arts, National Endowment for the Humanities, as well as at several libraries and newspapers.

John Dorst is Associate Professor of American Studies at the University of Wyoming. Specialising in Folklore Studies and ethnographic theory, he has published a book entitled *The Written Suburb: An American Site, An Ethnographic Dilemma* (Philadelphia: University of Pennsylvania Press, 1989), a postmodern ethnography of an elite suburb in south-eastern Pennsylvania. He is currently completing a study of visual discourse in the modern American West, focusing on display environments such as museums, living history sites, and national monuments. It is out of this interest that his contribution to the present volume developed.

Cees D. Eysberg studied and now teaches geography at the University of Utrecht, in the Netherlands. His professional interests include economic geography and the regional geography of the USA and Canada. He was a Fulbright Scholar at California Polytechnic University, San Luis Obispo, in 1984-85, and a Research Associate at the University of California, Berkeley, during the Spring Semester of 1987. In 1990 he published *The Californian Wine Economy: Natural Opportunities and Socio-Cultural Constraints*. His article "The Origins of the American Urban System: Historical Accident and Initial Advantage" was recently (1995) selected by Roger Caves for inclusion in the latter's *Exploring Urban America*.

Richard Gray is Professor in the Department of Literature at the University of Essex. He is the author of *The Literature of Memory: Modern Writers of the American South*, *Writing the South: Ideas of an American Region* (which won the Hugh C. Holman Award), *American Poetry of the Twentieth Century*, and *The Life of William Faulkner: A Critical Biography*. He has edited two anthologies of American poetry, a collection of original essays on American fiction, a collection of essays on Robert Penn Warren, and the collected poems of Edgar Allan Poe. He has also written a large number of articles and essays on American literature of the last two centuries. He is Associate Editor of the *Journal of American Studies*, and the first specialist in American Literature to be elected a Fellow of the British Academy.

Lothar Hönnighausen is Professor of English and American Literature and the coordinator of the North America Program at the University of Bonn, Germany. He has published widely on both English and American literature, including a book on the Pre-Raphaelites and various books on William Faulkner, such as *William Faulkner: The Art of Stylization in his Early Graphic and Literary Work* (1987), *Faulkner's Discourse: An International Symposium* (1989, edited), and *Masks and Metaphors* (forthcoming).

André Kaenel was educated in Switzerland and in the United States. He received his Ph.D. in English from the University of Geneva for a study of Herman Melville and the profession of authorship in nineteenth-century America (1992). He has been Professor of American Literature and Civilization at the Université Nancy 2 since 1993. He is currently at work on a book about the discipline of American Studies as a Cold War cultural export from the perspective of post-Cold War Europe. He most recently edited *Anti-Communism and McCarthyism in the United States, 1946-1954* (Paris: Messene, 1995).

Jack Kugelmass is Professor of American Studies at the University of Wisconsin, Madison, Wisconsin. He has a particular interest in mass and popular culture, and has written extensively on ethnic festivals, environmental displays and museums, and media culture.

Anneke Leenhouts is an independent scholar working mainly in the field of Southern Studies. Among her publications are articles on Allen Tate, Walker Percy, the Southern Gentleman, and the United Daughters of the Confederacy. She is a full-time translator for Akzo Nobel Nederland's patent department.

Gene M. Moore is Lecturer in English at the University of Amsterdam. In addition to articles on Conrad, James, and Faulkner, he has published *Proust and Musil: The Novel as Research Instrument* (Garland, 1985), and edited *Conrad's Cities: Essays for Hans van Marle* (Amsterdam/Atlanta: Rodopi, 1992). He is currently editing *Conrad on Film* for Cambridge University Press, and is co-editor of the *Suspense* volume in the Cambridge Edition of Joseph Conrad. He is also co-author of the *Joseph Conrad* volume in the Oxford Author Companion Series to be published by Oxford University Press.

Raymond L. Neinstein is Professor of American Literature at Eötvös Loránd University in Budapest, Hungary.

Duco van Oostrum is Lecturer in American Literature at the University of Sheffield. He is the author of *Male Authors, Female Subjects: The Woman Within/Beyond the Borders of Henry Adams, Henry James, and Others* (Amsterdam/Atlanta: Rodopi, 1995). He has published articles and essays on Wim Wenders, Philip Roth, H.D., and Multatuli.

John Peacock, Professor of Liberal Arts at the Maryland Institute College of Art in Baltimore, Maryland, was Fulbright Lecturer in American Literature at the University of Antwerp when this essay was written (Spring 1994). Other essays on American culture have appeared in *Literature/Film Quarterly*, *New Art Examiner*, *Art and Academe*, *Ethnohistory*, *Canadian Review of American Studies*, *Emerson Society Quarterly*, and are forthcoming in *Post-War Literatures in English* and *Journal of the History of European Ideas*. He has contributed book chapters in *Take Two: Adapting* *the Contemporary American Novel to Film* and *Beyond Cheering and Bashing: New Perspectives on* The Closing of the American Mind. His fiction has appeared in *Gulf Stream Magazine* and his poetry in *Forays* and *Fourteen by Four*.

C. Elizabeth Raymond is Associate Professor of History at the University of Nevada, Reno. A specialist in American Studies, she has published articles on sense of place in the Great Basin and the Middle West. She is the author of *George Wingfield: Owner and Operator of Nevada*, and co-author of *Stopping Time: A Rephotographic Survey of Lake Tahoe*. The essay included in the present volume grows out of a forthcoming study of Midwestern regional perception and image, tentatively titled *Down to Earth*.

Ron Robin is Senior Lecturer in History at the University of Haifa, Israel. His publications include *Signs of Change: Urban Iconographies in San Francisco, 1880-1915* (Garland, 1990), *Enclaves of America: The Rhetoric of American Political Architecture Abroad; 1900-1965* (Princeton: Princeton University Press, 1992), and *The Barbed Wire College: Re-Educating German Prisoners of War in the United States During World War II* (Princeton: Princeton University Press, 1995).

Esther Romeyn is Assistant Professor of American Studies at the University of Minnesota.

Sonia Saldívar-Hull is Assistant Professor of English at the University of California, Los Angeles. She contributed to *Criticism in the Borderlands: Studies in Chicano Literature, Culture, and Ideology* (1991, eds. Héctor Calderón and José David Saldívar), and wrote the entry on "Helena María Viramontes" for the *Dictionary of Literary Biography-Chicano Authors*. She recently published *Feminism on the Border: Contemporary Chicana Writers* (Berkeley: University of California Press, 1995).

Andrea Scheele holds M.A. degrees in English Literature and American Cultural Studies from the University of Amsterdam. The title of her English Literature M.A. thesis—on which the article in the present volume is based—is "The Changed Identity of the American West: A Comparative Study of Owen Wister's *The Virginian* and Thomas McGuane's *Nobody's Angel*." Her American Cultural Studies M.A. thesis is titled: "Sam Shepard's Western Landscapes."